A FATAL
FRIENDSHIP

A FATAL FRIENDSHIP

ALEXANDER HAMILTON AND AARON BURR

ARNOLD A. ROGOW

ꮡ HILL AND WANG

A DIVISION OF FARRAR, STRAUS AND GIROUX

NEW YORK

Hill and Wang
A division of Farrar, Straus and Giroux
19 Union Square West, New York 10003

Distributed in Canada by Douglas & McIntyre Ltd.
Printed in the United States of America
Library of Congress catalog card number: 98-070379
Designed by Jonathan D. Lippincott
First published in 1998 by Hill and Wang
First paperback edition, 1999

For Mary, Haleh, Evan,
and uma centena de beijos for Martha

ACKNOWLEDGMENTS

Many persons have contributed, directly or indirectly, to this book, and I am grateful to them all. I particularly want to acknowledge a debt to Frederick Mosteller, who first suggested, many years ago, when we both were fellows at the Center for Advanced Study in the Behavioral Sciences, that I write a book about the duel between Hamilton and Burr. I hope he is satisfied with the result. I owe much to Arthur Wang, and not only because he is the publisher of this book. His friendship and that of his wife, Mary Ellen, which have been sustaining and encouraging at times when I needed both, have meant much to me in other ways as well.

I also want to express my appreciation to the following individuals who helped with the research: Edith Atkin, Charles Brenner, M.D., Kevin Dempsey, Joan Pyle Dufault, Elgin Eckhart, Pam Fredeen, Susan G. Haas, Coreen P. Hallenbeck, Craig Hanyan, Mary Wilson Leverault, John J. McCusker, Norman MacKenzie, John M. Murrin, Jeanne L. Rogow, Irene Sadko, L. Bond Sandoe, Lord Shore, Dave Swann, James G. Wilson, M.D., and Jennifer R. Wilson. Valerie Fehlbaum and Peggy W. Gowen assisted with translations from the French, and Annette Phillips managed to transfer some chapters from my ancient manual typewriter on which they were written to my obsolete personal computer and printer.

The staffs and facilities of the following organizations were unfailingly cooperative: the New-York Historical Society, the New York Society Library, the New York Public Library, the American Antiquarian Society, the Museum of the City of New York, Butler Library of Columbia University, the New York State Library, Library of the Graduate School and University Center of the City University of New York, the Genealogical and Biographical Society of New York, the Chase Manhattan Bank, and the Bank of New York.

I am exceedingly grateful to the work of the late Harold C. Syrett and his colleagues, the editors of the *The Papers of Alexander Hamilton*, and to Mary-Jo Kline and her associates, the editors of *Political Correspondence and Public Papers of Aaron Burr*. Had it not been for their success in compiling and editing the twenty-seven volumes of Hamilton's correspondence and writings, and the two volumes of Burr's papers, the labor involved in this book would have been far more intensive over a much longer period of time than it was.

All italicized words quoted in the book are italicized in the original; I have not added anywhere an emphasis of my own. With some exceptions, the spelling, punctuation, and grammatical expressions in use two centuries ago have been preserved.

CONTENTS

PREFACE / xi

THE DUEL / 3

one / BASTARDY AND LEGITIMACY / 4

two / THE CANNON'S MOUTH / 26

three / HUSBANDS, WIVES, LOVERS / 54

four / ENDINGS AND BEGINNINGS / 77

five / FROM CINCINNATI TO PHILADELPHIA / 102

six / SEIZING THE DAY / 125

seven / LES LIAISONS DANGEREUSES / 150

eight / FAREWELLS TO ALL THAT / 175

nine / ODD DESTINIES / 201

ten / THIRTEEN WEEKS TO WEEHAWKEN / 228

eleven / A WORLD TOO SMALL? / 251

EPILOGUE / 273

NOTES / 287

SELECTED BIBLIOGRAPHY / 333

INDEX / 339

PREFACE

"**R**eal solemn history," Jane Austen confessed, "I cannot be interested in . . . The quarrels of popes and kings, with wars and pestilence on every page, the men all so good for nothing, and hardly any women at all." *A Fatal Friendship* is not, I trust, that sort of history, and certainly the men, with few exceptions, and the goodly number of women who occupy its pages were not "good for nothing." But no history is without its solemn moments, and while its scale is far from that of "wars and pestilence," the duel in 1804 that cost Alexander Hamilton his life and Aaron Burr his political career was one such moment in the American past.

Like all duels, the "interview," as a duel was sometimes called in those more genteel days, was preceded by a challenge, but it was one that Burr did not have to issue or Hamilton to accept. Burr charged that Hamilton had made remarks derogatory to his honor, but Hamilton declined to admit or deny he had done so, and neither man would or could specify what Hamilton had said. Nor has anyone since been able to venture beyond speculation in identifying the remarks to which Burr took such sharp exception. It nevertheless is clear, as we shall see, that for at least a dozen years prior to the duel Hamilton had been exceptionally hostile although outwardly friendly toward Burr, and that his hatred, which was largely hidden from Burr, was based on more than political rivalry. A reasonable assumption, and one which constitutes the premise of this book, is that the deeper causes of the duel are to be found in the dark recesses of their relationship and in the personal histories that shaped both their characters and that relationship. While no exploration of these complex interactions can claim to be definitive or beyond challenge, the account that follows makes every effort not to stray too far from a believable, plausible, and, I hope, credible truth. An absolute or certifiable truth about a relationship two centuries ago is, after all, impossible to establish.

A further word of caution is necessary. No biographies of Hamilton or Burr, or Thomas Jefferson, who makes an occasional appearance in these pages, can be entirely reliable, and although this book is not a biography, it relies on biographical information and is, therefore, no exception. With the passage of time, which has witnessed the publication of a thousand or more books and articles, most of them dealing with Jefferson and Hamilton (whose bibliography by 1886 already totaled 270 items), what originally was apocryphal or regarded as hearsay often turns into fact, and rumor becomes reality. The process by which these transformations come about begins when misleading or false information is repeated often enough by successive biographers and historians to be accepted as true. But it is not uncommon for the process to be reversed, with unwelcome facts being discarded as rumor or gossip. A few biographers have gone so far in supporting their versions of what transpired on certain occasions as to attribute to their subjects emotions, facial expressions, moods, gestures, and mannerisms that were not recorded by anyone present at the time. Perhaps these authors of "faux novels," as Richard Bernstein has called their books, believe they are not required to recognize boundaries separating biography from the representation of lives featured in movies and on television.

There are related difficulties which in the present case make it especially hazardous, in the apt wording of James Thomas Flexner, "to tamper with myths so passionately believed in." Most Americans as well as a majority of historians regard Jefferson as something of a saint, Hamilton as a martyr, and Burr as an outright villain. If, however, the "tampering" which follows has any credence, all three characterizations are somewhat exaggerated. This is not to deny that Jefferson, in writing most of the Declaration of Independence and insisting upon the addition of a Bill of Rights to the Constitution, achievements of much greater importance for the American political tradition than any accomplishment of his Presidency, insured that he would be remembered forever by those who cherish freedom. Nor can it be doubted that Hamilton, intellectually brilliant, perhaps a genius, contributed more than any other American of his era to the economic stability of the new Republic by restoring confidence at home and abroad in the nation's credit, and by founding the banking system.

Burr, who achieved little and contributed nothing of lasting value to his country, suffers by comparison; no one would argue that he was as gifted as Jefferson or Hamilton. But while the latter two were towering figures in our early history and deserve to be celebrated, there is evidence that neither was a paragon of virtue in private life or of integrity in the public sphere. Burr, on the other hand, while commonly viewed as without virtue or integrity in both domains, was not deficient in redeeming qualities seemingly absent or at least not observed in the behavior of Jefferson and Hamilton. For this reason and others, the questioning of mythologies that sanctify Jefferson, ennoble Hamilton, and demonize Burr appears to be justified.

Mythologies associated with the saints and sinners of the American past have a life of their own insofar as they nourish fantasies that create heroes with whom society can identify cherished images of itself, and antiheroes on whom it can project those weaknesses and failings in itself and its citizenry that it fears most. Such identifications and projections are facilitated when history leaves blank pages that biographers feel challenged to fill in. With respect to Hamilton and Burr, much is still not known or is uncertain, despite the numerous memoirs of their friends and contemporaries. Many letters and documents have been lost, destroyed, altered, or rewritten in part, some having fallen victim to conscious and unconscious prejudices of biographers. The most egregious instances involve family members in Hamilton's case, or, in connection with Burr, close friends. But even the most conscientious biographers are not always able to avoid bias in favor of their subjects. They also are influenced by the prevailing conventional wisdom of the political culture in which they live and work. Accordingly, the saint of one generation of biographers sometimes becomes the sinner of the next, as may be happening today to Jefferson, and the sinner becomes a saint, as was the fate of Hamilton, who was viewed much less favorably in the early nineteenth century than in the years of industrial supremacy and Republican Party ascendency that followed the Civil War. Burr has always been out of favor, and while there have been a few recent efforts to rehabilitate his reputation, for most Amer-

icans his name continues to be another word for deviousness and deceit.

No doubt, some readers will be disappointed to find no saints or
sinners in *A Fatal Friendship*. There are only men and women of greater
or lesser stature whose motivations in public life were not invariably
commendable, and whose behavior at times was severely flawed. While
my book suggests that Hamilton's character structure was more impaired than Burr's, and that as a consequence he was more at fault in
bringing their relationship to a violent end, I do not maintain that Burr
was a wholly innocent victim of Hamilton's machinations, or that he
was incapable of acting as irresponsibly and corruptly as many of his
contemporaries. If I do not place horns on anyone's head, neither do
I endow anyone with a halo.

My concern, in any event, is much less to assess blame for the duel
than to explore the interactions of personality and politics in America
at the turn of the eighteenth century which drove two of its most
prominent citizens to their final, fatal encounter. In pursuing this interest, I have taken as my mentor—and spectral judge—no biographer
or historian but the English political philosopher Thomas Hobbes,
who, in 1629, discerned that in the writings of historians "there be
subtle conjectures at the secret aims and inward cogitations of such as
fall under their pen, which is also none of the least virtues in a history,
where conjecture is thoroughly grounded, not forced to serve the purpose of the writer in adorning his style, or manifesting his subtlety in
conjecturing."

The question whether I have succeeded in being virtuous as opposed
to being only subtle, to borrow Hobbes's terminology, is best left to
my readers.

"My friend Hamilton—whom I shot."
—Aaron Burr

A FATAL
FRIENDSHIP

THE DUEL

Early on the morning of Wednesday, July 11, 1804, as the sun rose in the sky over Long Island, promising a day that would be bright and warm after the haze burned off, two men holding pistols confronted each other on a narrow ledge overlooking the Hudson River at Weehawken, New Jersey. They were about to fight a duel, a not uncommon event in those days, but this was no ordinary duel and these were not ordinary men. Aaron Burr, who by prearrangement arrived first, had been a senator from New York, and was Vice President of the United States in the administration of Thomas Jefferson. Alexander Hamilton, who faced Burr across the clearing, had been the principal author of *The Federalist Papers* and in 1789 was appointed the first Secretary of the Treasury by George Washington.

Following the command "Present!" given by one of the seconds, there were two shots, one of which penetrated Hamilton's lower right side, inflicting a mortal wound. Thirty-six hours later he was dead, and not long after reports of his death reached the public, Burr, indicted for murder in both New York and New Jersey, was a fugitive from justice. Neither man had yet reached the age of fifty, and while Burr was to live another thirty-two years, his political career had also suffered a wound from which it would never recover.

The immediate cause of the duel were remarks hostile to Burr which Hamilton was said to have made the preceding February at a gathering in Albany, New York. But as the following chapters seek to demonstrate, they had begun their travels to Weehawken far from Albany in very different parts of the world, and long before they were to meet for the last time on the dueling ground.

one

BASTARDY AND LEGITIMACY

Alexander Hamilton's beginnings were as inauspicious as Aaron Burr's were promising. The dissimilarity between them could not have been put more succinctly, if somewhat crudely in respect to Hamilton, than by John Adams, who referred to Hamilton as "a bastard brat of a Scotch pedlar,"[1] whereas, in the case of Burr, he had "never known in any country, the prejudice in favor of birth, parentage, and descent more conspicuous."[2] So far as we know, Burr never alluded to Hamilton's illegitimacy, but others, as Adams's remark testifies, were not so kind, Jefferson on one occasion venting his anger at Hamilton by declaring, "It's monstrous that this country should be ruled by a foreign bastard!"[3] For Hamilton, however, who was too shamed by his illegitimacy to reveal it, and who must have been painfully aware of the extreme contrast between their backgrounds, Burr's being born into a family of distinguished clergy and college presidents may have been the first of many reminders that certain differences between them, despite accomplishments on Hamilton's part that far surpassed those of Burr, had been unalterably resolved in Burr's favor.

Hamilton's beginnings were also, in important particulars, obscure, and to this day much about his origin is more a matter of speculation than fact. The date of his birth on the island of Nevis in the British West Indies is reported both as January 11, 1755, and as January 11, 1757, some of his many biographers alleging one date and some the other.[4] There is near-unanimous agreement on the identity of his father, James Hamilton, but still some uncertainty, and significant disagreement regarding the circumstances and events of his childhood and adolescence. More is known about Burr's origins — although, somewhat paradoxically, Burr became less, and Hamilton more, revealing of himself as their life histories unfolded — but Burr's early years, too, do not yield a complete record or one that has gone unchallenged.

Biographers also disagree, in Hamilton's case, on the age and birth order of his brother James, a disagreement that owes a great deal to confused or careless statements by his son and biographer, John Church Hamilton. In J. C. Hamilton's first book about his father, Hamilton is referred to as the youngest of several sons of his mother, Rachel, who died in 1768, but in a later book about his father, Hamilton is described as Rachel's only surviving child. These contradictory assertions have led some biographers to conclude that Hamilton's brother James was a half brother, the issue, before or after Hamilton's birth, of an unrecorded marriage of James Hamilton, Sr., who died in 1799 at the age of eighty-one. An inevitable by-product of these uncertainties is that certain biographers assert that Hamilton was three to five years older than his brother James, while others insist that Hamilton was the younger brother.[5]

Since there is no birth certificate or other reliable documentation establishing Hamilton's birth date as 1757, his own family and many biographers have regarded as authoritative Hamilton's indirect indication that he was born that year. Hamilton told family members that, as he put it in a 1797 letter to a kinsman of his father in Scotland, he was "about sixteen" when he arrived in New York toward the final months of 1772, and "nineteen" when he qualified for the degree of bachelor of arts at the "College of New York"* and in March 1776 became a captain of artillery in the American Army.[6] These statements, if true, support the 1757 date.

But not all evidence points to 1757. In the probate record of his mother's will in February 1768, Hamilton's age is given as thirteen, which, if correct, would indicate that he was born in 1755; his brother James, according to probate, was two years older, or, in other words, born in 1753. Other evidence, admittedly circumstantial, is a published poem of October 17, 1772, attributed to Hamilton by J. C. Hamilton

---

* Until the Revolution, the college was called King's College. It is now known as Columbia University. Hamilton may have qualified for such a degree from King's College, but there is no record that he received it (Harold C. Syrett, ed., *The Papers of Alexander Hamilton*, XXI, 79).

and said to have been written by him "when 18 years old."[7] At that time, Hamilton was less than three months short of his eighteenth birthday. Certain verses of this poem, to which we shall return, could suggest that the writer certainly was no younger than almost eighteen, although given Hamilton's precocity in a variety of areas, the possibility that he was sexually experienced at sixteen or earlier cannot be ruled out.

A further circumstance lending support to the 1755 date is a legal document of 1766 from the island of St. Croix which lists Hamilton as a witness. This document, which was first discovered by the historian George Bancroft, suggests that Hamilton was nine years old when he signed it if, in fact, he was born in 1757; if 1755 is the correct date, he would have been eleven at the time.* In the West Indies in those days, as Henry Cabot Lodge observed, serving as a legal witness at either age was not impossible, but we may reasonably assume that the likelihood of such an appearance increased as one grew closer to adulthood.[8]

Hamilton may well have believed that he was born in 1757, but he may also have had compelling reasons to favor that date, as opposed to the earlier one. For, in addition to the understandable pride he felt in having achieved so much when he was very young — in the letter to his Scots relative he calls attention to his age "sixteen" once and "nineteen" twice — the later date raises fewer questions about his paternity. Certainly, Hamilton was aware of the rumors, at least one of which was believed to be fact by his close friend and associate Timothy Pickering, that his father was not James Hamilton but Thomas Stevens of St. Croix, the father of his boyhood friend Edward (Ned) Stevens, with whom Hamilton remained in touch throughout his life. Pickering, to whom Lodge referred at length, was so impressed by the resemblance between the two that he at first took them for brothers, a conclusion perhaps helped by the fact that the elder Stevens had befriended Hamilton after his mother's death.[9] Some rumors alleging Hamilton's true paternity named Rachel's first and only husband, John Michael Levine, whose name is variously spelled Lavine, Lavien, Low-

---

* Although the evidence is not conclusive, I am persuaded that 1755 is the correct date. References to Hamilton's age at various times will be based on the assumption that he was born in 1755.

ein, and Levin, by whom she was divorced in 1759 but from whom she had separated earlier, while other rumors hinted that his true father was another Hamilton, the Governor of the Islands, William Leslie Hamilton.

The most fascinating as well as the least credible rumor was that Hamilton's biological father was none other than George Washington. Those who were tempted to believe this rumor, one of whom was reported to have been Gertrude Atherton, who devoted a biographical novel to Hamilton, could cite in support of it Washington's presumed presence in Barbados when Rachel was there, and his marked affection for and partiality toward Hamilton.[10] They also argued that Hamilton was too distinguished to have been the son of a father who, failing in everything he attempted, never amounted to much.

The attribution to Washington of Hamilton's paternity is reminiscent of myths alleging that emperors and conquering heroes like the Egyptian Pharaohs, Alexander the Great, and some of the Caesars were descended from the gods. The ancient Egyptians, Greeks, and Romans, if Hamilton had lived among them and was venerated, probably would have had no trouble believing that his father, if not godlike, had qualities far superior to those of ordinary mortals.[11] Unfortunately, Washington was not in Barbados or anywhere else in the West Indies in either 1754 or 1756. He did spend approximately three months in Barbados during the winter of 1751, when he was nineteen years old, and there contracted smallpox. Washington, furthermore, was childless, although his wife, Martha, who had four children by her previous husband, sought to become pregnant; probably he was sterile.[12]

There is no circumstantial or other evidence that James Hamilton was sterile, but was he Hamilton's father? The assumption that he was, although it was widely accepted as fact, is almost entirely based on statements of Hamilton and his family that may or may not reflect the truth. While he and his descendants made much of his descent from the distinguished House of Hamilton based in Ayrshire, Scotland, his immediate family did not reveal that James Hamilton was never married to his mother, Rachel, much less the dates when they began to live together and when they separated. According to Hamilton's son, J. C. Hamilton, who mentions his grandfather James only once, his father was "the offspring of a second marriage," Rachel having divorced her first husband, "a Dane, named Lavine."[13]

Hamilton's grandson Allan McLean Hamilton, writing with Pickering and Lodge in mind, goes to greater length than his uncle to establish his grandfather's descent from the Hamiltons of Ayrshire, who in turn could trace their ancestry to fourteenth-century forebears and the dukes, earls, viscounts, and barons who followed them. In his account, Rachel "when a girl of barely sixteen was forced into marriage with a rich Danish Jew, one John Michael Levine [or Lawein], who treated her cruelly," with whom she had one son, Peter. Leaving him in 1755 or 1756, she subsequently "went to James Hamilton [and] Alexander Hamilton was born a year later." Unlike his uncle, A. M. Hamilton does not claim that James and Rachel were married, giving as the reason they were unmarried that since Levine was granted the divorce on grounds of abandonment, he was able to marry again, whereas Rachel, the defendant, was not. But such was their devotion to each other, writes their great-grandson, that they lived together until Rachel's death in 1768.[14]

While the statements of Hamilton's grandson are more dependable than those of his son, many of them, at best, derive from family legends or reflect what Hamilton wanted them to believe and what perhaps they did believe. Whatever they believed, the facts as opposed to myths are few. The exact date of James Hamilton's arrival in the West Indies from Scotland, a crucial detail in establishing Hamilton's paternity and the year of his birth, is uncertain; as biographer Robert Hendrickson observes, "no one knows exactly where or when Hamilton's mother, Rachel, and his father, James Hamilton, met, or when they began living together, or when they parted. It is little more than tradition that they met . . . about 1750 or a year or two later."[15] A. M. Hamilton, as noted earlier, has Rachel not leaving her husband until 1755 or 1756 to live with James, which, if true, raises the possibility that, whatever the date of his emigration to the islands, James may not have been Hamilton's father, assuming he was born in 1755. The first and only reference to Rachel and James as a couple was occasioned by a baptism on the Dutch island of St. Eustatius in October 1758, where they are referred to as husband and wife.[16]

Hamilton and his family had more reason to favor the 1757 date for his birth than the earlier one of 1755, whereas his brother, if some of his biographers are correct in stating that Hamilton was older, would have had less reason to be concerned about the dates of his father's arrival from Scotland and his own birth. But the probate of Rachel's will, as already noted, refers to her son, James, as two years older than Hamilton, which, if true, and if the elder James was his biological father, lends some credence to the belief held by a few biographers that the elder James Hamilton had, like Rachel, been married before and had fathered a son. In that case, Alexander and his sibling James were half brothers only. Unfortunately, Hamilton's brother or half brother James, who apparently died in 1786, left no letters or other record of his existence, and almost nothing is known about the circumstances of his birth, life, or death.[17]

Hamilton as late as 1802 may have told at least one of his friends, James McHenry, that the marriage of his parents had been dissolved because of a technicality involving Rachel's divorce.[18] Perhaps he told his family as well, but there is no mention of this or of James's and Rachel's separation in his son's or grandson's biography. There also is no mention of a history of marital turmoil and separation on his mother's side and, if certain reports can be trusted, even worse happenings that occurred during Rachel's short life. Rachel herself was probably born in Nevis in 1729, and was eleven or so when her parents, John Fawcett, a physician of Huguenot extraction, and her mother, Mary, Fawcett's second wife, separated. Five years after her marriage to Levine in 1745, by which time she had given birth to her son Peter, Rachel was charged with adultery and "whoring with everyone." As a consequence, she spent an unknown amount of time in jail. For reasons not clear, Levine did not sue for divorce until February 1759, the divorce petition specifying that she was the mother of two illegitimate children, Alexander and James, that she had "twice been guilty of adultery," and that she had abandoned her husband, Peter's father. As if this were not enough, Rachel's connections through her father's first marriage included two bankruptcies and one case of mental illness ending in suicide. What role, if any, these unhappy events played in James Hamilton's desertion of Rachel and her two sons, which probably occurred in 1766 or earlier, is not established, but they could hardly have made a positive contribution to the relationship between James and Rachel.

In addition to emphasizing his Scottish origins, the family made much of Hamilton's closeness to his father and brother, and his affection for his mother. But no one in the family or in Hamilton's circle of friends, with the possible exception of Edward Stevens, ever met James Hamilton, Sr., or could have known what he or Rachel looked like. Nevertheless, A. M. Hamilton and other biographers have had no hesitation in writing that, in Hamilton's grandson's words, "he undoubtedly presented the physical appearance of his Scotch father rather than his French mother."[19] Observations, already mentioned, that Hamilton and Stevens could have been taken for brothers can be neither confirmed nor denied by reference to surviving portraits of Stevens and his father, for there are none.

Evidence that Hamilton had much of a relationship with either his father or his brother is far from convincing. In a letter to his wife, Elizabeth, whom he usually called Betsey, probably written shortly before their marriage in 1780, Hamilton informed her that he had "pressed" his father to come to America "after the peace," and that he would write him again to "present him with his black-eyed daughter, and tell him how much of her attention deserves his affection and will make the blessing of his gray hairs."[20] Despite this urging, which is confirmed in the only surviving letter to Hamilton from his father, dated June 12, 1793, James never left the West Indies to meet his daughter-in-law and his grandchildren, perhaps for reasons, as he wrote his son, of ill health and the "war which has lately broke out between France and England." He refers to another letter to Hamilton of the preceding June, and there may have been others back and forth, but judging by Hamilton's letter to his brother of June 22, 1785, there could not have been many. In that letter, Hamilton asks: "What has become of our dear father? It is an age since I have heard from him or of him, though I have written him several letters."[21] He sent money to his father and brother in 1796 and 1799, according to his grandson, but the amount is in dispute. A. M. Hamilton reported it as several thousand dollars; Hendrickson as "more than a thousand dollars."[22]

On the other hand, when Hamilton was drawing up his will in July 1795, he made some provision for the debts and obligations of himself and certain associates but specifically excluded his father from such consideration, although he knew that James Sr. was "now in indigence." He had "hesitated," he wrote his friend and associate Robert Troup, "whether I would not also secure a preference to the drafts of my father—but these as far as I am concerned being a merely voluntary engagement, I doubted the justice of the measure and I have done nothing. I regret it lest they should return upon him and increase his distress."[23] These remarks, whatever the true state of Hamilton's feelings about his father, reflect, at the very least, a marked ambivalence in his attitude toward the older man.

Hamilton's single surviving letter to his brother is also revealing, indeed so much so that his son James Alexander Hamilton, in his published version, deleted portions of it. In this letter of June 12, 1785, previously referred to, Hamilton agreed to honor his brother's draft upon him of fifty pounds "wherever it shall appear," but he confessed himself unable to do more until some future date, at which time "I promise myself to be able to invite you to a more comfortable settlement in this country." In the meantime, he advised his brother in the sentences that followed, which were omitted in the J. A. Hamilton version: "Allow me only to give you one caution, which is, to avoid if possible, getting into debt. Are you married or single? If the latter, it is my wish, for many reasons, that you may continue in that state." J. A. Hamilton also deleted a concluding paragraph in which Hamilton wrote his brother: "I do not advise your coming to this country at present, for the war has also put things out of order here, and people in your business find a subsistence difficult enough. My object will be, by and by, to get you settled on a farm."[24] Assuming that his brother died in 1786, Hamilton could not have had much opportunity to bring him to America, whether or not he was determined to achieve his "object"; in any event, he apparently never saw his father again after his parents separated, or his brother after leaving the West Indies. When Edward Stevens was planning a visit to St. Croix in May 1796, Hamilton did not suggest that Stevens visit his father or carry messages to him.[25] Hamilton also had no contact with Rachel's son Peter Levine, his half brother, who lived with his father before coming to South Carolina in 1764.

In his 1797 letter to his Scottish relative, Hamilton wrote that when he was "very young," he was thrown "upon the bounty of my mother's relatives" as a result of his father's deteriorated financial situation, a "state of things [that] occasioned a separation between him and me."[26] Despite this perfunctory reference to Rachel, one of two brief mentions of her in his correspondence, Hamilton's family and most of his biographers are confident, in the words of J. C. Hamilton, that "traces of her character remained vividly impressed upon his memory. He recollected her with inexpressible fondness, and often spoke of her as a woman of superior intellect, highly cultivated, of elevated and generous sentiments, and of unusual elegance and manner."[27] J. C. Hamilton's nephew and Hamilton's grandson reaches further back in asserting that Rachel's mother "from all accounts, although a woman of great loveliness and charm, was ambitious and masterful." Whatever the meaning of "from all accounts," it does not appear that Hamilton himself, much less his grandson, ever met Rachel's mother, or, if he did so, did so as an infant. As for Rachel, A. M. Hamilton describes her as "a brilliant and clever girl, who had been given every educational advantage and accomplishment, and has profited by her opportunities."[28] Presumably, this is not a sly, tongue-in-cheek reference to activities alleged by Levine when he sued her for divorce.

Few have surpassed Gertrude Atherton in her affection and admiration for Rachel and her son, but no one has gone so far toward fantasizing the bonds between mother and son as Nicholas Murray Butler, the president of Columbia University from 1902 to 1945. In an address of January 11, 1913, Butler confided: "I like to think of the youthful beginnings of his boyish life, of the admiration of his mother for her brilliant child, who, in infancy, had the maturity of an experienced philosopher; a boy who, at nine, was writing letters worthy of a sage . . . I like to remember that when that dying mother felt the hand of death upon her at the early age of thirty-two, she summoned the little boy to her bedside and said to him: 'My son, never aim at the second best. It is not worthy of you. Your powers are in harmony with the everlasting principles of the universe.' " Butler, making no reference in the address to Hamilton's father or brother, concludes that Hamilton is "the only man whose writings in political science bear comparison with the classic work on politics by the philosopher Aristotle."[29]

A truer portrait of the relationship between Rachel and her son begins to emerge when attention is paid to evidence overlooked by Hamilton's family and most of his biographers that Hamilton's attitude toward his mother was, at best, one of indifference.[30] Nor are the scarcity of letters mentioning her and the lack of any expression of affection on Hamilton's part the only pointers in that direction. In Hamilton's time, a tradition in genteel families was to preserve family names by naming children after the parents and grandparents on both sides, if, of course, a sufficient number of children survived long enough to be christened. Philip and Catherine Van Rensselaer Schuyler, the father and mother of Hamilton's wife, Elizabeth, named children after their parents, as did Angelica, Elizabeth's sister, and her husband, John Barker Church. The Hamiltons named their firstborn son Philip, and after his death in 1801 they gave the name Philip to the eighth and last of their children. Of their two daughters, one was named Angelica, which was the name of both Schuyler's mother and his oldest daughter, and the other Elizabeth. A son was named Alexander after his father, while another son was baptized James Alexander, presumably in honor of his grandfather and perhaps a Scottish Alexander Hamilton. There also was the future biographer, John Church Hamilton, named for the Hamiltons' brother-in-law. Neither daughter was given the name Rachel even as a middle name, and no child bore the name of any of Rachel's relatives upon whose "bounty" he had to some extent depended after her death.

More telling, perhaps, is Hamilton's vote in the spring of 1787 with regard to a bill before New York's Council of Revision. The proposed legislation, to which the Council objected, forbade the guilty party in an adultery-based divorce action to marry again. To deny the right of marriage to such a person, the Council argued, was to condemn that person to a life of celibacy or an immoral existence. The latter had been precisely Rachel's fate thirty or so years before, and the cause of Hamilton's illegitimacy. Nevertheless, Hamilton voted with the majority in the Assembly to disregard the Council's objection to the measure.[31]

Given the scandals of Rachel's divorce and separations, his status as her bastard son, and his father's total withdrawal from his young life, Hamilton had good reason to distance himself emotionally from both parents. Also understandable is his wish and the wishes of his family to conceal much of the truth of his early history. What is less understandable is the tendency of his biographers to repeat and, as in the case of Nicholas Murray Butler, to embroider further the myths and legends that were cultivated by his family into the fabric of a family romance. Presumably, they have done so in the belief that his stature and importance would be severely diminished if certain facts became public knowledge, not realizing that these facts make Hamilton's achievements all the more remarkable.

When he stood at Rachel's graveside in 1768, he may also have felt less grief than his family and many biographers, once again preferring probable myth to probable reality, would have us believe. With his mother dead and his father gone from his life, Hamilton was, in effect, an orphan, and if he—like many orphans, especially those of adolescent age who experience the death of parents as a cruel desertion—had a sense of abandonment, his feelings for Rachel, whatever they were, could not have been totally unaffected. She had not only left him alone; she had left him poor, for almost all her few possessions were turned over to her divorced husband for delivery to their son Peter, Rachel's only legitimate heir.[32]

During the four years that elapsed between Rachel's death and Hamilton's departure for America in 1772, he demonstrated the aptitude, capacity for work despite recurring periods of illness, and driving ambition that were to be even more conspicuous in his later career. Following Rachel's death in 1768, he apparently first went to live with the Stevens family, and was befriended by the Lyttons, Rachel's relations through her father's first marriage, and especially by his cousin Ann Lytton Venton (later Mitchell), who was a daughter of Rachel's half sister Ann. But the Lyttons' own fortunes soon took a downward turn, by which time Hamilton was working for the export-import firm of Beekman and Cruger in St. Croix. For a variety of reasons, including the illness and absence in America of Nicholas Cruger, Hamilton was often left in charge of the business, which dealt extensively in lumber, mules, flour, butter, apples and onions, barrel staves, tea, and other commodities. His letters to the absent Cruger show him to have been a shrewd bargainer who early mastered some of the principles he was to put to use as Secretary of the Treasury. The Crugers were pleased with his work and no doubt gave him every assistance when he left St. Croix for New York.

He had other friends as well who were impressed by his intelligence and ability and who helped him financially. One was his cousin, Ann Lytton Mitchell, whom he remembered in the will he drew up on the eve of the duel, and another was Hugh Knox, a Presbyterian minister and College of New Jersey graduate. While Ann's financial aid cannot be documented, "it seems certain that Ann Mitchell provided [Hamilton] with money from her father's estate and thus enabled him to migrate to North America and to attend college."[33]

The Reverend Hugh Knox may also have contributed money, although in his letters to Hamilton he mentions only his "secret pride in having Advised you to go to America & and in having recommended you to some of my old Friends there." By 1783–84, Knox was already extremely proud of Hamilton's achievements on and off the battlefield, including his "Matrimonial Connection . . . [which] might Enable you to live at your ease." Lauding Hamilton's "Ambition to Excell," Knox encouraged him to write the "History of the American War," and wondered, since he had rarely heard from Hamilton, whether the "History" was the cause of his "long Silence." Was it possible, he asked, "that anything have happened on my part, which Should have So long deprived me of the pleasure of hearing from you?" His letter had the desired effect: nine months later he acknowledged receiving a letter from Hamilton for the first time in almost four years.[34]

Knox also complained that Edward Stevens, who after studying medicine at the University of Edinburgh had established a practice in St. Croix, had not heard from Hamilton. But he could not refrain from adding a private speculation whether Stevens's "torturing so many dogs and other quadrupedes in Edinburgh, in his Experiments on the *Succus gastricus* of the Stomach, may not have a little injured his sensibility, & made him a cooler friend & less cordial companion, I cannot take upon me to Say."[35]

It was to Stevens on November 11, 1769, that Hamilton had written a letter, often only partially quoted, confiding that his "Ambition to Excell," in Knox's words, led him to "contemn the grov'ling and condition of a Clerk or the like, to which my Fortune &c. condemns me and would willingly risk my life tho' not my Character to exalt my Station. Im confident, Ned that my Youth excludes me from any hopes of immediate Preferment nor do I desire it, but I mean to prepare the way for futurity. Im no Philosopher you see and may be justly said to Build Castles in the Air. My Folly makes me ashamd and beg youll Conceal it, yet Neddy we have seen such Schemes successful when the Projector is Constant. I shall conclude saying I wish there was a war."[36]*

---

* Almost exactly two months earlier, in September 1772, the topic of Aaron Burr's commencement address at the College of New Jersey in Princeton was "Building Castles in the Air!" (Milton Lomask, *Aaron Burr*, I, 30).

Hamilton did not mention that, seven months before, he had had poetry published in the *Royal Danish American Gazette* of St. Croix, possibly the first of his many publications. Describing himself as "a youth about seventeen" in an accompanying note of April 6, 1771, Hamilton submitted an untitled poem celebrating the pleasures of carnal love but not without a recommendation of "wedlocks holy band.—" In the poem, the object of his affections is "Coelia," who, despite her willingness to unite with him in bonds of matrimony, is referred to as "an artful little slut." The poem continues:

> *Be fond, she'll kiss*, et cetera—*but*
> *She must have all her will;*
> *For, do but rub her 'gainst the grain*
> *Behold a storm, blow winds and rain,*
> *Go bid the waves be still.*
> *So, stroking velvet paws*
> *How well the jade conceals her claws*
> *And purs; but if at last*
> *You hap to squeeze her somewhat hard,*
> *She spits—her back up—prenez garde;*
> *Good faith she has you fast.*[37]

If Hamilton was, as he said, "about seventeen" at the time, the date of his birth may well have been 1755; when the poem was published, he was three months past his sixteenth birthday. If that was, in fact, his age, he undoubtedly was sexually precocious. Another possibility is that he wished to present himself as older than fourteen, assuming the 1757 birth date, in the belief that his verses would then be more acceptable. Whatever the case, the biographies written by Hamilton family members do not mention the poem, nor do most other biographers. Neither Lodge nor Atherton makes any reference to it, and Mitchell, quoting part of it but unwilling to mention Coelia, the "artful little slut," writes only: "There is more, a bit more carnal."[38] Was Coelia, consciously or unconsciously, modeled after Rachel, and was Hamilton destined to pursue other Coelias during the course of his life? Some writers intrigued by Hamilton's attraction to Maria Reynolds, Eliza Bowen Jumel, and others with reputations as loose women, who entered his life later, have wondered.

By the time he received Knox's letters, in 1783–84, Hamilton had given ample proof of his "Ambition to Excell," as Knox put it. His literary interests had long since shifted from hurricanes and "carnal" poetry to more serious efforts to argue the case for revolution. He had had the war wished for in his letter to Stevens, and was well along on his "way for futurity." He was no longer alone in the world or poor, thanks in large part to his marriage, or without influential friends, one of whom was George Washington. In the remaining twenty years of his life he was to achieve much more, and yet this brilliant record of accomplishment, a record with few equivalents in anyone's history, was never enough. From an early date, probably well before they began their political careers, there was always, for Hamilton, the "apparition" of Aaron Burr.[39]

A year after Hamilton was born to a mother who was living apart but was not yet divorced from her husband, Aaron Burr was born to parents who were very much married and very much in love. His mother, Esther, born in 1732, was the daughter of the Reverend Jonathan Edwards and Sarah Pierpont Edwards, herself the daughter of a minister, who were to bring into the world another ten children. Edwards, the great New England theologian whom some compared with his illustrious Puritan predecessors Increase and Cotton Mather, was a Yale graduate who went on to a ministry in Northampton, Massachusetts, where he brought about the religious revival known as the Great Awakening. But in time his strict Calvinist orthodoxy with its emphasis on predestination became unpopular with his Northampton congregation, and he was dismissed. Moving with his family to Stockbridge, he ministered to an Indian mission and the few white families which had settled there, until 1757, when he became president of the College of New Jersey, now known as Princeton University.

On his father's side Burr's ancestry was less distinguished but no less respectable. His father, Aaron Burr, Sr., one of thirteen children, was the youngest son of Daniel Burr and his third wife, Elizabeth Pinkney Burr, of Fairfield, Connecticut. The Burrs were among the first English colonists to settle in the Connecticut Valley, since which time most of them, including Daniel Burr, had been farmers. Accordingly, Aaron Burr, Sr., who was born in 1716, spent his early years on a farm. Graduating from Yale in 1735, he became a Congregational minister and by 1738 was serving in the pulpit of the First Church of Newark, New Jersey. Originally a believer in a less strict version of Calvinism known as Arminianism, Burr's father came under the spell of the Great Awakening years before he was to meet his future father-in-law, a conversion which no doubt contributed to the welcome he received from Esther, Edwards's oldest unmarried daughter. On June 29, 1752, after a short courtship, they were married.

All reports agree that Esther adored her husband, but it could not have been because he was prepossessing in appearance. A contemporary description presents him as "a little small Man as to body, but of great and well improved mind ... He was an excellent Divine & Preacher, pious & agreeable, facetious & sociable, the eminent Xtian & every way the worthy Man. Like St. Paul his bodily presence was mean & contemptible, but his mental presence charmed all his Acquaintance."[40] These qualities attributed to Burr's father by a fellow minister, Ezra Stiles, help explain his elevation in 1746 to the leadership of the College of New Jersey, then in Elizabethtown (now Elizabeth), New Jersey, following the death of its president, a position he continued to hold when the college moved to Princeton and occupied the newly built Nassau Hall.

In some accounts, the Reverend Burr is credited with characteristics not usually associated with Calvinist clergy: a sense of humor, an interest in music, an openness to new ideas. Perhaps it was these attributes Stiles, later president of Yale University, had in mind when he wrote "facetious & sociable," and they also may have been among the qualities that endeared him to Esther. But whatever they were, they forged strong bonds between them. "Do you think I would change my good Mr. Burr," she wrote a friend in 1755, "for any person, or thing, of all things on the Erth? No sure! Not for a million such worlds as this yt had no Mr. B—r in it." On another occasion, when her husband was absent in Boston, she exclaimed to a friend: "O my dear it seems as if Mr. Burr had been gon a little Age! & it is yet but one Fortnight! I dont know what I shall do with myself the rest of the time. I am out of patience already."[41]

Because we know a good bit about Esther, the qualities that endeared her to him are not difficult to discern. Esther was deeply religious, as befitted a daughter of Jonathan Edwards, and according to contemporaries she was also "beautiful and talented, quick witted and vivacious, strongly inclined to literature, a composer of many manuscripts."[42] Her husband wanted her to study Latin and French as well, but apparently she was too busy as the wife of a minister and college president and the mother of two children to make much progress in either language. She was not too busy, however, to observe the world around her with insight and humor. Her letters and diary abound with reports of marriages, births, including those of her daughter and son, deaths, household hints, and her thoughts about some of the less than sacred mysteries of life. "Pray what do you think every body marrye in, or about winter for" was one entry. "Tis quite merry, isn't it? I realy believe tis for fear of laying cold, & for want of a bed fellow. Well, my advice to such ye same with ye Apostles, Let them marry — & you know the reason given by him, as well as I do — Tis better to Marry than to —" But presumably not better for everyone. "Cousin Billy Vance is going to be Married — did you ever hear the like? Pray what can he do with a Wife? He is more of a Woman than of a man."[43] Her meaning was less evident when she wrote: "Mrs. Sergent is like to have a child, pray what do you think of this? I know you will laugh."[44] Esther made it clear that she did not approve of persons who chose not to marry and gave no thought to burning: "Mr. Burr preached against whoredom & never did people need it more."[45]

By the spring of 1756, Aaron and Esther were the parents of two children, Sarah or Sally, born May 3, 1754, and Aaron Jr., born February 6, 1756. The first characterization we have of the future Vice President came from his mother, in September 1757, when she wrote: "Aaron is a little dirty Noisy Boy very different from Sally almost in every thing. He begins to talk a little, is very Sly and mischievous. He has more sprightliness than Sally & most say he is handsomer, but not so good tempered. He is very resolute & requires a good Governor to bring him to terms." Sally, who was almost four, must have been less of a problem, although she affected "to be thought a Woman" and was expected by her father to "prove a numbhead."[46]

Aaron as a child was often ill, on occasion so ill that his parents were concerned for his life, but, ironically, he outlived them both by almost eighty years. The first tragedy to strike the Burrs was the death from "fever" of his father on September 24, 1757, at the age of forty-two; the "fever" probably was smallpox, but it could have been cholera, yellow fever, typhoid fever, malaria, or one of the other deadly diseases of the time. Six months later, on March 22, 1758, Jonathan Edwards, who had assumed the college presidency left vacant by the death of his son-in-law, died of smallpox or of an infection related to a smallpox inoculation. But death in the family had not yet run its course. Less than a month later, on April 17, Esther, only twenty-seven years old, also died of smallpox, although she, like her father, had been vaccinated. After her death, the two children, now orphans, were to live with their widowed grandmother in Stockbridge, but that was not to be. Stopping in Philadelphia on her way to collect the children in Princeton, Sarah Pierpont Edwards, aged forty-eight, died of dysentery on October 2, 1758. In a little more than a year, Sally, then four, and Aaron, two, had lost their father, mother, grandfather, and grandmother.

Aaron could not have known his parents, and his memories of them, if any, must have been few at best, but he inherited many of their traits and characteristics. Short and of slight build, like his father, Aaron, too, as an adult had a sense of humor, was open to new ideas, and was often "facetious & sociable." As his father had urged his wife to learn Latin and French, Burr later insisted that his wife and daughter read widely, and that his daughter become fluent in French. Nor were his wife and daughter less devoted to him than Esther was to his father.

Perhaps Burr's character resemblance to his mother is more striking. Although he did not share her religiosity, he appears to have inherited her good looks, her wit, her vivacity, her eclectic reading tastes, and, not least important, he may have taken from Esther and put to his own uses her interest, judging by her letters and diaries, in the physical aspects of relationships between men and women. A certain earthiness with sexual overtones was one of Esther's legacies to her son, although, unlike his, her behavior if not always her thoughts conformed to traditional morality. Even so, her remarks about a parishioner or a neighbor show her to have been far from a typical minister's wife, for surely such imprudent comments were not a commonplace with women in her position.

Burr must have had some knowledge of his parents from Esther's surviving brothers and sisters, but he does not mention them in his letters. Perhaps this reserve and his later stoicism in the face of severe loss and adversity owed much to his early experience of parental death and the unhappiness that followed it. Two years after his mother's death, he and his sister, Sally, were the wards of Timothy Edwards, Jonathan Edwards's oldest son and Esther's younger brother. Resident in Elizabethtown, Timothy was a twenty-one-year-old bachelor, but a bachelor not for long. Already the guardian of the two Burr children and several of his siblings, Timothy late in October 1760 married Rhoda Ogden, whose family was well known in the area. Whether because Timothy and Rhoda loved children, or for other, more probable reasons such as ineffective birth-control methods, the two young people eventually became parents of fifteen children of their own.[47]

According to Burr's two earliest biographers, and most of his biographers since, in his adult years he repeatedly told three anecdotes about his life with Uncle Timothy and Aunt Rhoda, and these are the only stories we have from him of that time. Significantly, two of these reminiscences deal with his running away from the Edwards household, the first time when he was four and he was not found for several days, and the second time when he was ten and sought to go to sea as a cabin boy. Both departures were occasioned by controversies with Uncle Timothy, the second of which was resolved when Timothy agreed not to punish the boy if he came down from the ship's mast, where he had taken refuge, and returned home. The third tale was of an incident, when Burr was eight, that could be taken as the first hint that he was to have a lifelong involvement with women of all ages, some of whom would complicate his life. Perched in a cherry tree on the family property, Burr was somehow irritated by the sight of an elderly lady in a silk dress, approaching. He ceased to pelt her with cherries only when she angrily summoned his uncle, who, according to one account, after subjecting him to a lecture and a prayer, "licked [him] like a sack." Also significant as a harbinger of Burr's future is Parton's observation that the "prim behavior and severe morality of this ancient maiden had made her an odious object in the sight."[48]

Because these episodes are not incompatible with Esther's remark that her son, even as a baby, "requires a good Governor to bring him to terms," they have been viewed as evidence that Burr from an early age was something of a rebel against authority who would not conform to accepted standards of conduct. That tendency was certainly present in his life, but another possible interpretation of his youthful misbehavior is that Timothy Edwards, known to have been a stern disciplinarian, may have dealt more harshly with Burr, who was his sister's child and undoubtedly often unruly, than with his own children. Whatever his experience in his uncle's home, Burr as an adult never complained of ill treatment by Uncle Timothy, and in later years maintained a friendly relationship with him. But Burr throughout his long life never complained of any misfortune that befell him, and for the most part tried to remain friends even with those who repeatedly injured him by their efforts to damage his reputation. Nor was Hamilton, until shortly before the duel, an exception.

Knowing little for certain, only in fantasy or imagination can we depict Burr's years in Elizabethtown when he was growing up in the Edwards household. Unlike Hamilton, whose family circumstances required that he go to work at an early age, Burr had a legacy of an unknown value from his father, but apparently it was substantial, since it was enough to pay his school bills in Elizabethtown and at the College of New Jersey. Like most relatively carefree young boys of his age, he probably went hunting and fishing in the nearby woods and swamps, perhaps collected birds' eggs and butterflies, and played at some of the sports popular at the time, such as kite flying, marbles, shuttlecock (badminton), and snap-the-whip. We need to guess less that he became interested in books and at some point began to read widely, for literature of all types was a passion that remained with him until he was a very old man. Certainly, he made friends in Elizabethtown, one of whom, Matthias (Matt) Ogden, a younger brother of Aunt Rhoda, he was close to until Ogden's untimely death in 1791.

When he was old enough to attend school, his uncle sent him to the Presbyterian Academy in Elizabethtown, where, according to another uncle who, only six years older than his nephew, also was enrolled, Burr was "hearty . . . and learns bravely."[49] Pierpont Edwards, who made these remarks, did not say that Burr distinguished himself as a student, and there is no record that he did so. Perhaps he and Uncle Pierpont, described by Parton as "a remarkably free liver" who "likely" influenced his nephew, devoted a good deal of time to noncurricular activities; Parkes's biography of Jonathan Edwards refers to Pierpont as "a clever and erratic Don Juan."[50] Later in life, Burr was to come to his uncle's assistance when a woman with whom he was involved became pregnant. Clearly, the Edwards strain, to judge by Pierpont Edwards, Aaron Burr, and perhaps other descendants of Jonathan

Edwards, contained elements difficult to account for in the prim and straitlaced version of the family history accepted by some biographers and historians.[51]

Although Burr was not an outstanding student, he did well enough in his studies to apply in 1767 to the College of New Jersey, where, named after his father, the college's second president, he could not have been unknown. Eleven years old at the time and still well short of his full adult height of five feet six inches, he probably looked even younger, and perhaps it was then that he was first referred to as Little Burr, a diminutive that was to describe him all his life. Whether because of his youth or because he was not yet fully prepared academically, he was turned away. Returning to Elizabethtown, for two years he studied subjects he would further pursue when he was admitted to the college as a sophomore, not as he had requested a junior, in 1769.

We know something more of his three years at Princeton than we know about his years in Elizabethtown, but not much more. Did he study fourteen hours a day, which left him little time for frivolous pursuits, as claimed by one early biographer, or did he find the prescribed curriculum so undemanding he spent much of his time in "idleness, negligence, and, in some measure, dissipation"?[52] Whatever the truth of the matter, Burr was never placed on probation or expelled, as others were, and he managed to graduate in 1772 somewhere in the middle of his class of twenty-two.

According to Parton, Burr occasionally studied eighteen hours a day, which, if true, must have left him little time for any other activity, including sleep. Nevertheless, he had enough leisure and energy to become active in a literary club known then and now as the Cliosophic Society; its impressive Greek-style building can still be found on Nassau Street in Princeton. He also wrote a number of essays which do not survive but which, Parton again as the source, dealt with such subjects as "Style," "The Passions," and "An Attempt to Search the Origin of Idolatry." In view of his later reputation, "The Passions" is of particular interest. There he stated, as quoted by Parton: "The passions, if properly regulated, are the gentle gales which keep life from stagnating, but if let loose, the tempests which tear everything before them. Do we not frequently behold men, of the most sprightly genius, by giving the reins to their passions, lost to society, and reduced to the lowest ebb of misery and despair." Citing examples in British history,

Burr stressed that in all these cases "the most charming elocution, the finest fancy, the brightest blaze of genius, and the noblest bursts of thought, call for louder vengeance, and damn them to lasting infamy and shame."[53]

More significant for his future than the admonitions of the essays were friendships he made at Princeton. One was with William Paterson, whose career until his death in 1806 included the posts in New Jersey of attorney general and governor, selection as a delegate to the Constitutional Convention in 1787, and appointment to the United States Supreme Court.[54] Another friend of greater eminence in the years ahead was James Madison (1751–1836), the fourth President, to whom Burr was to introduce Dolley Payne Todd, subsequently Mrs. James Madison. Madison, a Virginian who graduated in 1771, was a fellow member of the Cliosophic Society, but he and Burr were not close. In the years that followed, Madison's friendship and political alliance with Jefferson were to prove far more important to him than any connection he had ever had with Burr, or, for that matter, Hamilton, with whom he collaborated in writing *The Federalist*. Perhaps Burr's relationship with Dolley before Madison and Dolley were married, which will be discussed in a later chapter, had some influence not altogether positive on Madison. Other college luminaries in Burr's time were Brockholst Livingston, whose relatives were active in New York and New Jersey politics and who later became an ally of Jefferson, and Henry (Light-Horse Harry) Lee of the distinguished Virginia family, the father of Robert E. Lee; Burr undoubtedly was acquainted with these classmates but probably no more than that.

When Hamilton arrived in New York from St. Croix in 1772, the year of Burr's graduation, neither he nor Burr were aware of each other's existence, but not long after, both were in Elizabethtown.[55] Although there is no evidence they met there or that Hamilton then heard something of Burr from persons who knew him, those possibilities cannot be ruled out, given the small population of the town. Certainly it could not have been very many years before Hamilton became aware that Burr, although orphaned early in life, had enjoyed advantages Hamilton had been denied. Viewing himself as more hardworking and deserving than most of his contemporaries, a view not without validity, Hamilton, when he became acquainted with Burr's history if not yet with Burr himself, could only have been envious of his family background, his comfortable circumstances, and the confidence with which he moved through life. There is no way of knowing when Hamilton first developed this awareness of Burr, but we can be reasonably confident it was not long after they first met, whether in Elizabethtown or later. Whenever it was, it marked the beginning of their long, complex, and ultimately fatal friendship.

THE CANNON'S MOUTH

Hamilton's arrival in New York and Burr's graduation from the College of New Jersey in the fall of 1772 coincided with the first stirrings of patriotic fervor that were to culminate in the American Revolution. In response to a variety of grievances against British rule, the first Committee of Correspondence emerged in Boston from a town meeting in November organized by Sam Adams, then and later a firebrand for independence. By June 1773, other Committees of Correspondence had been formed in Virginia, the members of which included Thomas Jefferson, and not long after in four other future states. The Boston tea party of December 16, 1773, a protest against the East India Company's selling its tea at prices that undercut colonial tea importers, dumped some 342 chests of tea in Boston harbor without, however, affecting either the taste or the color of the water. Other developments increasing the tension between Britain and its American colony were soon to follow.

Hamilton, meanwhile, carrying letters of introduction from Hugh Knox and others, had made his way from New York to Elizabethtown. Presumably, these letters to influential persons in New Jersey served to gain him a place there in the grammar school of Francis Barber. Having had little formal schooling in St. Croix other than instruction in the "Hebrew Decalogue,"[1] Hamilton clearly was not qualified for admission to Knox's alma mater, the College of New Jersey, in nearby Princeton, although he was in some hurry to become enrolled there. While in Elizabethtown preparing for the college, he was a boarder, or more likely a guest, in the home of William Livingston, another prominent member of the large and influential clan of Livingstons which produced governors, senators, congressmen, judges, and mayors in both New Jersey and New York. He may also have lived for a short period in the household of Elias Boudinot, like Livingston a well-to-do lawyer and staunch Presbyterian. Livingston and Boudinot perhaps helped Hamilton with some of the expenses he incurred while he was a student at Barber's Elizabethtown Academy.

Francis Barber, a College of New Jersey graduate, became a close friend of Hamilton and remained one until he died in an accident toward the end of the Revolutionary War. Barber taught young men to read Virgil, Cicero, Horace, Lucian, Xenophon, and the Gospels in Greek and Latin, one result of which was that Hamilton later had easy recourse to Latin proverbs as well as the history and mythology of ancient Greece and Rome. The Elizabethtown Academy also offered instruction in mathematics, geography, elocution, and English literature and composition, all of them subjects that would qualify students for admission to the College of New Jersey, making the academy, in effect, the college's preparatory school.

Hamilton told J. C. Hamilton and his other children that he had done little at Elizabethtown but study. He did not mention that the Livingstons had four daughters older and younger than he, and that he had been particularly taken with one of the older daughters, Catherine, or Kitty, with whom he carried on a flirtation almost until his marriage. Whether more than flirtation was involved is not clear, but some have interpreted a letter from Hamilton to Kitty as implying that he, at least, was willing to carry their relationship further. Writing her on April 12, 1777, he declared: "I challenge you to meet me in whatever path you dare, and if you have no objection, for variety and amusement, we will even sometimes make excursions in the flowery walks, and roseate bowers of Cupid. You know, I am renowned for gallantry, and shall always be able to entertain you with a choice collection of the prettiest things imaginable . . . After knowing exactly your taste, and whether you are of a romantic, or discreet temper, as to love affairs, I will endeavor to regulate myself by it." Gertrude Atherton's reading of this leads her to conclude that Kitty "was the first to reveal to him the fascination of her sex." She does not say what she meant by "reveal" and "fascination."[2]

The attractions of Elizabethtown may or may not have included

Kitty, but even so, they were not enough to deter Hamilton any longer than he thought necessary from seeking admission to the College of New Jersey. No doubt, he was encouraged to do so by Boudinot and Livingston, both of whom were trustees of the college, and he had the enthusiastic support of Knox. He must also have known that John Witherspoon, the sixth president of the college, was making special efforts to recruit students and financial contributions from the West Indies, to which he had a special attachment. With so much in his favor, Hamilton resolved to apply for admission to an advanced class, expecting to enter the college in the fall of 1773.

Perhaps he was not as academically prepared as he thought, or perhaps his interview with Dr. Witherspoon did not go well. But Witherspoon and those he consulted among the faculty and trustees may have heard something of Rachel, Levine, and James Hamilton, and accordingly decided that Hamilton was not someone the college could mold into a God-fearing, upright, and chaste young man who would be a credit to the institution. Nor, they knew, would he bring any significant funds with him to supplement the college's meager resources. Whatever the reasons, Witherspoon within two weeks informed the eager applicant that he and the trustees were unable to make him an exception to the rules governing admission and that therefore his application was rejected. So far as is known, Hamilton was not advised to seek entrance as a beginning or first-year student, or to apply again a year or two later. Hamilton could not have known then, but probably learned later from his collaborator on *The Federalist*, that the rules had been waived for James Madison, who had graduated in 1771 after only two calendar years of study.[3]

A year after Madison had completed his studies, Burr, as mentioned, had also graduated from the College of New Jersey. Spending much of 1773 more or less frolicking in the company of Matt Ogden, Burr divided his time between Princeton and Elizabethtown. Timothy Edwards and his brood had moved to Stockbridge, but Burr still had relatives and friends in Elizabethtown. Since he had already begun to conquer female hearts, one wonders whether Hamilton, even if he never crossed paths with Burr, was privy to gossip and rumors about Burr and his female friends. Although evidence is lacking, the possibility that Kitty and her three sisters had heard stories and shared them with Hamilton cannot be entirely dismissed. Elias Boudinot, who not much later was to recommend Burr and Ogden for military commissions, and still later was to choose Burr to represent him in some legal proceedings, was friendly with Burr at that time, although not as close as he was to Hamilton. Certainly, it is inconceivable that the Livingston, Boudinot, and Edwards families, all prominent in the town, were not acquainted with one another. While we can never know what, if anything, was said about Burr or to whom it was said, we can be reasonably confident that Hamilton and Burr never exchanged reminiscences about Elizabethtown, or discussed the college which had rejected one of them and graduated the other. But Hamilton may have known more than he ever acknowledged of Burr's early history, most of it more fortunate than his own. Almost twenty years later, when he was determined to destroy Burr politically, he repeatedly described him as a "voluptuary." Was this among his first impressions of Burr in Elizabethtown? We can only wonder.

Hamilton's failure to gain admission to the College of New Jersey did not deter him for long. By late fall of 1773 he had been accepted as a student at King's College, matriculating there in the spring of 1774. An Anglican school headed by a president firmly committed to the British cause, King's College, unlike its counterpart in Princeton, agreed to admit Hamilton as a sophomore. Located then in the vicinity of Church, Barclay, and Greenwich streets in New York City, not far from today's World Trade Center, the college, headed by its second president, Dr. Myles Cooper, with a faculty of three, could not compare with the older established and more prestigious College of New Jersey. Hamilton did not record his impressions of King's, but we do know that the college and its curriculum did not concentrate his interests and absorb his energies for more than a few weeks. New York, where he previously had spent little time, was not only a far more interesting place than Elizabethtown or Princeton, with its coffeehouses, taverns, and red-light district not far from the college; it was also a center of political ferment both loyalist and revolutionary. Hamilton had hardly settled in at King's College when he turned his attention to this agitation for and against British rule in North America.

Hamilton, according to J. C. Hamilton, favored the loyalist or "Ministerial" side when he first arrived in the country, and he was never to lose his admiration for British political institutions. A contributing factor of some importance was that he saw in the British system principles

he had embraced even before he came to America, among them the
tenet that government by the few who were rich and well-born, ideally
both, was preferable to government by the many much further down
the social scale. In the growing controversy about British rule in general and such subsidiary issues as the legitimacy of taxation without
representation, the most radical element was made up, in the main, of
farmers, tradesmen, and artisans, who bore the brunt of the taxes and
regulations. Loyalists, or Tories, on the other hand, tended to come
from the upper class of merchants, landowners, and speculators, who
were, for the most part, well off. There were, of course, exceptions on
both sides, and Hamilton, who was born out of wedlock and arrived
poor in America, was one of them at first.

But he did not hesitate very long in moving his allegiance to the
revolutionary cause. Here it is reasonable to assume, given the ambition to which he readily admitted in his letter to Ned Stevens, that he
rightly concluded his best chance to leave behind him "the grov'ling
and condition of a Clerk or the like" and be given the opportunity "to
exalt my station" was in the rebellious colony, not in class-ridden Great
Britain. Perhaps, he also saw ahead the war he had wished for, in
which, after it began at Lexington and Concord in April 1775, he
longed to distinguish himself. His participation in the conflict, however,
did not alter his view of the basic nature of man, especially the common
man, and of society. All his life, he identified with the upper class, and
although he did not mention this identification in his letter to Ned,
there can be no question that his dedication to becoming one of that
class was subsumed in his determination "to exalt my Station." As we
will see, he succeeded in this endeavor all too well; indeed, considering
his unpromising start in life, and even taking into account his impressive achievements before and after the Constitutional Convention of
1787, it was not his least conspicuous success.

His initial essay into revolutionary polemics followed by three
months the first meeting in Philadelphia of the Continental Congress
in September 1774. When he published his *A Full Vindication of the
Measures of the Congress* (short title) in December 1774, he was not yet
twenty years old and was still a student at King's College.[4] Two months
later, in February 1775, not long after the surrender of the British base
at Fort Ticonderoga to Ethan Allen and his Green Mountain Boys,
and the appointment of George Washington as commander of Conti-

nental forces, Hamilton published his second pamphlet, *The Farmer Refuted* (again, short title).[5] Both these writings created a sensation, and later, when it was revealed that he was their author, almost no one believed that they could have been written by someone so young.

A Full Vindication and *The Farmer Refuted* were written in response to pamphlets signed "A. W. Farmer," generally assumed to have been Samuel Seabury, an Episcopal minister in Westchester County, New York. Seabury, who was more than twice Hamilton's age, held that the right to legislate did not derive "from nature, but from the indulgence or grant of the parent state," and that there could be no distinction, as some supporters of colonial rights maintained, between the authority of the King and the authority of Parliament. Two years later, the Declaration of Independence was to reject decisively Seabury's view, listing twenty-seven specific grievances against George III; there is no mention of Parliament in that document.

In *A Full Vindication,* Hamilton defended the proposition that the authority of government rested on "natural justice." A staunch defender of property rights both in his writings and as Secretary of the Treasury, Hamilton did not take exception to the view that a principal purpose of government was to protect property. Believing then and later that property rights were founded on natural law, as was government itself, he did not have to confront that issue. Instead, he emphasized the colonists' right to restrict their trade with Britain if their demands were not met, and he indirectly warned the British that curtailing imports and exports would have the effect of enabling manufacturing to "take root among us," thereby paving "the way still more to the future grandeur and glory of America." He was to make a similar point in his *Report on Manufactures* of November 1791.

The Farmer Refuted is significant less for what it argues against Seabury and the loyalists than as the earliest statement of the philosophy that was to shape Hamilton's political thought and define his political role for the remaining thirty years of his life. Here, again, it is nothing short of remarkable that at such an early age he had worked out the principles upon which he was to base the provisions of the Constitution he advocated at the Constitutional Convention, and the policies he urged or followed as advisor to Washington and Secretary of the Treasury.

These principles, he made clear, owed much to the philosopher David Hume (1711–76). Early in *The Farmer Refuted*, Hamilton approvingly quoted Hume's maxim "that, in contriving any system of government, and fixing the several checks and controls of the constitution, *every man* ought to be supposed a *knave*; and to have no other end in all his actions, but *private interest*. By this interest, we must govern him, and by means of it, *make him co-operate to public good*, notwithstanding his insatiable avarice and ambition. Without this, we shall in vain boast of the advantages of *any constitution*, and shall find in the end, that we have no security for our liberties and possessions, except the *good will* of our rulers, that is, we should have *no security at all*."[6]

But toward the conclusion of *The Farmer Refuted*, Hamilton left Hume far behind when he did not spare the British a gratuitous insult to their officer cadre in the context of arguing the superiority of American forces in the event of war. From an early age he had attached a special value to battlefield valor and distinction, and throughout his life he retained an interest in military rank and achievement. Whether or not, as reported by Jefferson, never one of his admirers, who perhaps "was jealous of Hamilton," he had told the Virginian that he viewed Julius Caesar as "the greatest man that ever lived,"[7] he had the highest regard for the successful armies of history and their officers, among whom, apparently, the British were not always to be counted. "As is always the consequence of a long peace," he observed of their army, "there are many effeminate striplings, among the officers, who are better calculated to marshal the forces of *Venus*, than to conduct the sturdy sons of Mars."[8] No doubt, many in the British officer corps, whom some American women complained of as lacking in amorous zeal, hailed the reference to Venus as a compliment.

In December 1774, when *A Full Vindication* was published, Hamilton began drilling with a military company in a churchyard near King's College, and in August of the following year he had his first experience under fire when he was part of a force attempting to remove cannons from a Battery fort under the guns of a British warship. Within those eight months, the battles of Lexington, Concord, and Bunker Hill, all of them in or near Boston, had been fought. August also marked the beginning of the effort to take Quebec by Generals Richard Montgomery and Benedict Arnold, an effort that was to involve Aaron Burr.

These events, however, did not wholly absorb Hamilton's attention. In November 1775, he gave expression for the first time to his lifelong distrust of the "unthinking populace," or multitude, which, unchecked, was apt "to run into anarchy." He was defending the printer James Rivington, who, though a Tory, or loyalist, had printed his two pamphlets. Rivington's press had been attacked the previous May by a mob of patriots, and the following November by a group of men from Connecticut. Writing to John Jay, a member of the first two Continental Congresses composed of delegates from the colonies, Hamilton advised Jay, with whom he was to have frequent dealings in the years ahead, that "when the passions of men are worked up to an uncommon pitch there is great danger of fatal extremes. The same state of the passions which fits the multitude . . . for opposition to tyranny and oppression, very naturally leads them to a contempt and disregard of all authority . . . When the minds of these are loosened from their attachment to ancient establishments and courses, they seem to grow giddy."[9] But since Rivington's press was "dangerous and pernicious," Tories as well as patriot extremists had to be restrained, and to this end Hamilton recommended that "a few regiments of troops" from anywhere but New England be stationed in troublesome areas. This recommendation, too, is a forecast of the policies Hamilton was to urge on Washington and others when there were outbursts of unrest such as Shays' Rebellion and the Whisky Rebellion.[10]

He was also active in advising Jay on the election of members of the New York Assembly, recommending four men, one of whom was Jay; they were among New York's first delegates to the Continental Congress. Hamilton's pamphleteering, letter writing, and drilling with the militia must have allowed him little time for studies, but somehow he managed to take some instruction in mathematics, natural philosophy, English, Latin, and Greek. Perhaps for a time he also thought of following the examples of Hugh Knox and Ned Stevens in becoming a physician. Unfortunately, we have no records of Hamilton as a student at King's College, from which, as mentioned earlier, he was never graduated.

By the end of March 1776, Hamilton had exchanged his part-time student status for a full-time military career as captain of New York's provincial company of artillery. He was stationed with his battery on Bayard's Hill, at the junction of Canal and Mulberry streets in the section of lower Manhattan which today is part of Little Italy and Chinatown. Thus, his guns were in a good position to defend the area to the south should the expected British attack come from that direction. But when the British fleet of more than one hundred ships arrived in lower New York bay, it disembarked troops not in Manhattan but on Staten Island. In July, not long after the Continental Congress had formally embraced the Declaration of Independence, still more ships and soldiers arrived, among them regiments of Hessians, mercenary soldiers from Hesse in Germany. But when and where, Hamilton must have wondered, will the attack come. Neither Washington nor anyone else on the American side appeared to have the answer. Hamilton, daily drilling his artillery battery, which eventually totaled sixty-eight officers and men, could only bide his time.

Elsewhere in Manhattan, and also in uniform, Burr, too, was waiting, but with a very different recent history and military experience behind him. In the fall of 1773, when Hamilton had been accepted at King's College, Burr enrolled in a divinity school conducted by the Reverend Joseph Bellamy, who had been a pupil and friend of Jonathan Edwards. He may have done so out of deference to his clerical ancestors, for clearly he was no more intended to preach Christian morality than he was to practice it. His tutelage with Bellamy, in any case, was of only a few months' duration. By February 1774, Burr had abandoned religious instruction for the study of law in Litchfield, Connecticut, with his brother-in-law, Tapping Reeve, who in 1771 had married Burr's sister, Sally.

In Litchfield and nearby Fairfield, Burr pursued girls as he had done in Princeton and Elizabethtown; in one of his letters to his sister, he shares with her a tongue-in-cheek observation not out of keeping with some of the sly comments recorded in the diary of his mother, by then dead more than fifteen years. Writing Sally in January 1774, Burr reported to her that at a nearby tavern he had seen "six slay-loads of Bucks & Bells, from Woodberry, and a happier company I believe there never was . . . They were drinking Cherry Rum when I entered the room, and I easily perceived that both Males and Females had enough to keep them in Spirits. The Females looked too immensely good-natured to say *no* to anything. And I doubt not the Effects of this Frolic will be very visable a few Months hence."[11]

Burr was in Litchfield long enough to witness the "Effects," if any, but shortly after Lexington and Concord in April 1775, he was urging Matt Ogden to join him in enlisting in the army then being formed in

Cambridge. A month or so after the American defeat at Bunker Hill, the two set out for Cambridge with letters of introduction to Joseph Reed, one of Washington's aides. But the poorly organized and ill-equipped forces gathering outside Boston had little to do that summer, and Burr, though impatient to see action, could not do otherwise than to idle away his time with the rest of Washington's Army, which, by July, totaled 14,500 men. Finally, in August, he heard that General Benedict Arnold was recruiting volunteers for a march on British-held Quebec. By September 12, he was one of 1,100 men under Arnold's command making their way through Maine, then largely unknown territory, to the St. Lawrence River and Quebec.

The next few months tested Burr physically as he had never been tested before and was not to be tested again. Even before the onset of winter, the six-hundred-mile journey through wilderness country took its toll in exposure and disease, and when food became scarce, the starving men ate any animals they could find, including dogs. By mid-November their number had dwindled to half their original strength, or about six hundred men, and they were still more than a month away from Quebec. At that time, Arnold was joined by General Richard Montgomery, who had taken Montreal, and not long after, Arnold asked Montgomery to appoint Burr, whom he described as a "gentle-man," to his staff. Burr, now a captain and aide-de-camp to Montgom-ery, was with the general in the assault on Quebec on December 31, 1775.

Montgomery, leading his troops and accompanied by Burr and other officers, was not far from a blockhouse, the final obstacle before Que-bec, when a cannon loaded with grapeshot was fired at him and the others point-blank. Montgomery was killed instantly, as were several officers with him, and here, not for the first or last time, there are different stories about the role of Aaron Burr. According to the ex-pedition's chaplain, Samuel Spring, who had known Burr at Princeton, Burr, who was not wounded, attempted to lift Montgomery from the snow where he had fallen and carry his body back to an area where he could be decently buried. Those who doubt that Burr even at-tempted to retrieve the corpse of the fallen general point out that Montgomery was a very large man, "Little" Burr, as he was sometimes referred to, a much smaller one, and the snow very deep. Whatever the truth, it was the British, not the Americans, who found the body and buried it.[12] There can be no disputing, however, that Burr was in the front rank next to Montgomery in the attack on Quebec.

By the summer of 1776, Burr had seen almost a year of active service. Recommended by Arnold, who had been wounded outside Quebec but had witnessed enough to praise Burr's cool courage under fire, he had spent ten days or so on Washington's staff, which, apparently, was time enough for each to develop a lasting, and for Burr costly, dislike for the other. While no one knows what transpired during Burr's brief tenure, speculation has focused on two possibilities, the first that Washington disapproved of one of Burr's illicit amours, the second that he found Burr reading his mail when he was temporarily absent from his room. Whatever the cause of Burr's abrupt departure from his staff, Washington, unlike Hamilton, never disparaged Burr's record as a courageous and able officer.

In late June, Burr was attached to the staff of General Israel Putnam, for whom he developed a fully reciprocated fondness. He and Putnam were in Brooklyn, Hamilton and his artillery battery still on Bayard's Hill, when toward the close of August the pace of the war suddenly accelerated. General William Howe, commander of British forces, reinforced by the ships and transports of his brother, Admiral Richard Howe, swept around the tip of Manhattan and invaded Long Island. Subsequent events, which included an American defeat costing more than 1,500 dead and wounded as against the 400 men lost by the British, found Hamilton and Burr joined together in a retreat more than halfway the entire length of Manhattan to the area known today as Washington Heights. And, again, we have a story celebrating Burr's daring and, for the first time, alleging that he and Hamilton met, with Hamilton cast in a minor role relative to Burr.

Falling back to Brooklyn Heights, on the western edge of Long Island and bordering the East River, Washington, against the advice of some of his generals who wanted to make a stand, evacuated his remaining units across the river. Certain that the British would shortly follow and, moving to the Hudson River, cut off his retreat to the north, he began to lead his troops away from lower Manhattan. But he and his forces did not move fast enough, and on September 15 the British landed at or near what is now 23rd Street and the F.D.R. Drive on New York's Lower East Side. When they formed a line across the island, a substantial number of American soldiers, Hamilton among them, were separated from Washington's main force.

According to a contemporary account, the Americans left behind had just been ordered by General Henry Knox to entrench themselves on Bayard's Hill "when Aaron Burr rode up . . . Major Burr ridiculed the idea of defending the place . . . and . . . urged General Knox to retreat to Harlem Heights; but General Knox said it would be madness to attempt it." Burr then, runs this eyewitness report of two soldiers who were present, addressed himself to the men, and assuring them that he knew a safe route to the north, successfully led the way to the main force in Harlem Heights. But did he and Hamilton meet in the course of the retreat through British lines? There can be little doubt that Hamilton and some part of his battery were among those who rejoined the army in upper Manhattan, but neither Hamilton nor Burr ever mentioned a meeting at that time. Nor did Burr receive any official credit for his feat, news of which earned him the respect of many of the officers and men elsewhere in the army. Perhaps Washington was not inclined to overlook his insubordination to Knox, one of his trusted superior officers.[13]

There are no reports linking Hamilton and Burr in other engagements, but on several occasions they participated in the same military operation, in the course of which they may have encountered each other. Both, for example, were involved in the Battle of Harlem Heights, which ended in another American defeat, and both again retreated with the rest of Washington's Army to White Plains. When the army again withdrew, this time across the Hudson River to New Jersey, Hamilton's battery, according to J. C. Hamilton, fought a rearguard action against a Hessian brigade, and it may have been at this time that he attracted the attention of Washington. Burr, meanwhile, accompanied Putnam, whom he referred to as "my good old General," south through New Jersey into Pennsylvania, where the general and his forces prepared for a British attack on Philadelphia. That attack was halted at Trenton, where Washington surprised and routed a key British position. His crossing of the Raritan River at New Brunswick was covered by Hamilton's artillery, and Hamilton was again with him when he crossed the Delaware on December 25, 1776.

Some military historians hold the view that the war might have ended before that Christmas Day if Howe had been more willing to press his advantage, or Washington less inclined to hesitate whether in advancing or retreating. By nature a cautious man, at that stage less sure of himself than he was to be later, Washington not only gave the

British decisive victories in Long Island, Manhattan, and Westchester—they were to occupy New York City until the end of the war—but managed to lose several thousand soldiers, hundreds of cannon, and tons of supplies. These numbers were significantly increased when General Nathanael Greene was defeated by Cornwallis at Alpine, New Jersey, in November. Consequently, the army Washington led across New Jersey totaled little more than five thousand soldiers, and it was losing men daily due to the expiration of enlistments and to desertions.

Howe's tendency not to push forward when he might have done so against Washington's fleeing forces may have owed something to his sharing the inclination of British officers, as alleged in 1775 by Hamilton, "to marshal the forces of *Venus*." Later, when Howe failed to effect a junction with General John Burgoyne at Albany, the result of which was Burgoyne's eventual surrender in nearby Saratoga, the cause was said to be the wife of his Commissary of Prisoners, a Mrs. Loring. As a bit of contemporary American ribaldry put it:

> *Sir William, he, snug as a flea,*
> *Lay all this time a-snoring,*
> *Nor dreamed of harm as he lay warm*
> *In bed with Mrs. Loring.*[14]

Howe himself claimed that he had never received official orders from London to join Burgoyne, but this was not believed then or later by all of his countrymen. On both sides of the Atlantic there were also doubts, although for different reasons, about Washington's military skill, leading to a British comment that "any other general in the world other than General Howe would have beaten George Washington; and any other general in the world other than George Washington would have beaten General Howe."[15]

Until Burgoyne's surrender in October 1777, this comment might have been thought more unfair to Howe than to Washington. Through most of that year, Washington's Army suffered more defeats than victories, the former culminating in the British occupation of Philadelphia on September 26, which forced Congress to flee, first to Lancaster and then to York. When Washington attempted an encirclement of Howe's encampment at Germantown outside Philadelphia, he was defeated by weather, lack of coordination between the American detachments, and the superior tactics of the British. With the onset of winter and the British in control of the Delaware River from Chesapeake Bay to Philadelphia, Washington had no recourse but to move northward from Germantown and spend the winter at Valley Forge.

Burr may have been in or near Princeton in January 1777, when, according to one story, an American force including Hamilton's battery launched an attack forcing the British back through the town, some of them taking refuge in Nassau Hall. Hamilton, it was said, carefully positioned one of his artillery pieces and sent a cannonball through a portrait of George II which was hanging on a wall. Certainly, one is tempted to believe that Hamilton savored the occasion, which offered him a kind of revenge against the college that had refused him admission, but the only evidence that something like this actually happened was the account of someone thoroughly untrustworthy. Histories of Princeton University do not mention Hamilton or the episode.[16]

Within weeks of the Battle of Princeton, the lives of Hamilton and Burr were again to diverge sharply. If coming to colonial America was Hamilton's most fateful move, geography in a crucial sense being destiny, not far behind it in shaping his future was his appointment to Washington's staff on March 1, 1777. With one interruption, instigated by Hamilton in response to a reprimand from Washington, he was to serve him as scribe, confidant, advisor, and cabinet secretary for more than two decades. Initially appointed as aide-de-camp and promoted to the rank of lieutenant colonel, Hamilton gradually became the most trusted and relied upon of the more than thirty young men in all who were called by Washington his "family," comprising his personal staff during the course of the war. In the four years Hamilton served as aide, he wrote a large number of Washington's letters, directives and orders, reports, and other military papers, carried out missions in many areas of the war, and occasionally was at or near the general's side in military operations. After he left the army, he frequently offered Washington advice on a wide variety of issues facing the new country, and he continued this role when Washington became President in 1789. As the first Secretary of the Treasury, he wrote drafts of speeches and policy statements Washington requested, some of which were issued in the President's name with only minor changes.

Few Americans have related to a President in precisely this way, perhaps because few have viewed themselves, whatever their titles or positions, as exercising in a Presidential system some of the most important functions of a prime minister. In Britain toward the end of the eighteenth century, the evolution of the modern prime minister as *primus inter pares* (first among equals) had begun, and Hamilton was a fervent admirer of the British system of government in almost all its forms. The childless Washington, for his part, twenty-five years older than his closest aide, may have viewed Hamilton not merely as an able officer whose brilliance he had need of as both general and President but as possessing qualities he would have liked in a son. While Washington was never a father figure for Hamilton, or even someone for whom Hamilton had marked respect and affection, Hamilton for Washington may have been less one of his official family than an honorary member of his generic family.

Washington apparently never knew that Hamilton regarded him, if certain accounts can be trusted, with an ambivalence bordering on hostility. Madison reported that "Hamilton often spoke disparagingly of Washington's talents, particularly after the Revolution and at the first part of the Presidency."[17] A few years after the deaths of both Washington and Hamilton, John Adams wrote Benjamin Rush that, at the Battle of Yorktown, Hamilton, seeking a command, "flew into a violent passion and ... declared if he had it not he would expose General Washington's conduct in a pamphlet." According to Rush, General Francisco de Miranda, a Spanish-American veteran of the French and American revolutions who was friendly with Hamilton, had confided to him that Hamilton "spoke with great contempt" of Washington. When Miranda insisted that Washington's fame in Europe was beyond Hamilton's ability to injure, Hamilton allegedly replied, "No, it is not. I have written a history of his battles, campaigns, etc. and I will undeceive them." Still later, Rush informed Adams that a projected biography of Hamilton would show, he had been told by one of Hamilton's friends, "General W. to be a *good* man but General Hamilton to be a *GREAT* man."[18] Adams did not doubt the truth of these accounts, but neither the pamphlet nor the biography was ever published. When J. C. Hamilton's biography of his father appeared, it emphasized the dependence of Washington on Hamilton even after Hamilton resigned as Secretary of the Treasury, insisting, for example, that Hamilton had written Washington's Farewell Address.

Burr, who had no interest in influencing Washington and who rarely took positions on the great issues of the time, never sought a close relationship with him. He essentially moved in the opposite direction when, three months after Hamilton's appointment as aide-de-camp, Burr was provoked to write Washington a letter that could only have increased the estrangement between them dating to Burr's brief service on Washington's staff. Burr earlier had written Ogden that his slow promotion as an officer should not occasion any surprise since he had no expectation of promotion either as a line or as a staff officer. Contented with his position as an aide to Putnam, he assured Ogden, he could not complain of neglect unless "pointed" or, in other words, specifically aimed at him. But when he was made a lieutenant colonel on June 29, he was far from happy with the appointment. "I am . . . constrained to observe," he wrote Washington on July 20, "that the late date of my appointment subjects me to the command of many who were younger in the service, and junior officers in the last campaign . . . I would beg to know whether it was any misconduct in me . . . which entitled the gentlemen lately put over me that preference? Or, if a uniform diligence and attention to duty has marked my conduct since the formation of the army, whether I may not expect to be restored to that rank of which I have been deprived, rather, I flatter myself, by accident than design."[19] So far as is known, Burr's letter, which may have been seen by Hamilton, elicited no reply.

Whatever the cause of Washington's distrust and dislike of Burr, it did not preclude his assignment to a command of the kind Hamilton very much wanted but was never able to attain. Prior to expressing his disgruntlement to the Commander in Chief, Burr had been ordered to report to Colonel William Malcom's "additional" regiment south of Poughkeepsie, New York. For Burr, who, like Hamilton, was never comfortable with authority figures and steered an independent course whenever possible, the assignment was an ideal one. Malcom, a wealthy New Yorker, was unable or unwilling to exercise his command, and he transferred his responsibilities to the newly commissioned lieutenant colonel. Burr moved quickly to increase the regiment's strength to five hundred men and to tighten discipline, which had been lax. During the next few months he led Malcom's Regiment in skirmishes with the British near today's Suffern, New York, west of the Hudson River, forcing them to retreat to New York City. He also repulsed a threatened seizure of the rich farmlands of

Bergen County in New Jersey. Ordered to join Washington's forces in what was to be a failed effort to retake Philadelphia, he and his men spent the winter of 1777–78 at Valley Forge. Again there is the possibility of an encounter with Hamilton, who was also there, but no evidence of a meeting.

While Burr was skirmishing with the British and rebuilding Malcom's Regiment, Hamilton was active on a number of fronts, not all of them military. Soon after joining Washington's family, he began to strike out on his own, writing letters to influential members of Congress commenting on the progress of the war and assessing developments at home and overseas. To Gouverneur Morris, with whom he was in frequent correspondence and who became a close friend and political ally, he wrote on May 19, 1777, that he could "partly agree and disagree . . . respecting the deficiencies of [the new New York State] constitution. That there is a want of vigor in the executive, I believe will be found true. To determine the qualifications proper for the chief executive Magistrate requires the deliberate wisdom of a select assembly, and cannot be safely lodged with the people at large. That instability is inherent in the nature of popular governments."[20] To William Livingston on April 29, 1777, he complained that "a spirit of disaffection shows itself with so much boldness and violence in different parts [of New Jersey], that it is the ardant wish of his Excellency [i.e., Washington], no delay might be used to make examples of some of the most attrocious offenders. If something be not speedily done to strike a terror into the disaffected, the consequences must be very fatal."[21] These two themes, the "want of vigor in the executive" and the need "to strike a terror into the disaffected," were to be emphasized by him again and again in the years ahead as the government faced the formidable challenges of nation-building.

Nor did Hamilton, barely twenty-two years old and a lieutenant colonel, refrain from expressing his opinions of the generals, both British and American, in charge of the war. In one letter, he was critical of the man who was to be his future father-in-law. Following General Philip Schuyler's replacement by General Horatio Gates after the recapture of Fort Ticonderoga by the British in July 1777, a defeat many in Congress attributed to a mistake made by Schuyler, Hamilton on August 7, 1777, wrote Robert R. Livingston that, while had he defended Schuyler's conduct on frequent occasions, "I am at last forced to suppose him inadequate to the Important Command with which he has been Intrusted. There seems to be a want of firmness in all of his actions, and this last instance in my Opinion is too unequivocal to be doubted. The Reason assigned for his last retreat is the panic among the army, which he seems to say is beyond anything that was ever known . . . I never saw anything like a general panic among the Troops. They appeared in the worst of times as resolute & spirited as in the best." It is worth noting that Hamilton's unflattering opinion of Schuyler, whose health was poor at the time, was not shared by Washington and others, who were unwilling to hold him responsible for Ticonderoga and the earlier failure of an expedition he had led against Canada. By 1780, moreover, Hamilton had changed his mind about Schuyler, either because he had come to view him differently or because he was about to marry the general's daughter. In a letter to James Duane in September 1780, he recommended his future father-in-law for appointment as "an excellent President of War."[22]

If Hamilton early in the war was dissatisfied with Washington's generalship, he was not alone. The defeats and retreats culminating in the failure to retake Philadelphia led Congress to recall General Gates from the northern theater of the war, where he had replaced Schuyler, and appoint him president of the new Board of War. Favored by a number of generals to replace Washington, who, it was hoped, would take the hint and resign, Gates was not unfriendly with those associated with the Conway Cabal, an alleged effort to supplant Washington led by Major General Thomas Conway. When Washington was informed of a letter from Conway to Gates urging Gates "to save your country" before it was ruined by "a weak general and bad counselors," he was understandably angry and demanded an explanation from Gates and Conway. Both of them believed that Hamilton had secretly copied the letter, but the real culprit was Colonel James Wilkinson, an aide to Gates, who in the course of a drunken spree revealed its contents to other inebriated officers. Gates initially refused to believe that Hamilton was innocent, but eventually he turned on Wilkinson, who was forced, like Conway, to resign his position. At no point, however, would Washington countenance the suggestion that Hamilton had, in effect, purloined Conway's letter. His loyalty to Hamilton seems never to have wavered, however much, if Adams and others are to be believed, Hamilton's loyalty to him was qualified.

Late in 1777, Burr, too, may have been dealing with insubordination and discontent, but not that of officers eager to take his place. An area near the encampment called the Gulph, through which the British could attack from Philadelphia, was so indifferently guarded by troops as to raise Washington's concern. Burr, according to one account, was sent to enforce discipline and impose rigorous training. Scenting trouble from soldiers who did not welcome the new regime, Burr somehow arranged for their muskets to be emptied of cartridges before he assembled the men for a nighttime inspection. As he passed in front of them, he was accosted by one of the dissidents, who, aiming his unloaded gun, fired at him. Burr, the story recounts, quickly drew his sword and with one slash downward almost severed the man's arm.[23]

Intermittently that winter and spring of 1777–78, both Hamilton and Burr were ill, Hamilton with one of his recurrent "nervous disorders" accompanied by fever, Burr with nausea, diarrhea, and headaches of the migraine type that were to afflict him periodically for many years. Nevertheless, both participated in the Battle of Monmouth in June, and Hamilton testified in the court-martial of General Charles Lee which followed it. Monmouth was preceded by the replacement of General Howe, who, once again in bed with Mrs. Loring or another mistress when he might have routed Washington's weaker army at Valley Forge, missed a further opportunity to win the war. Fearing he would be cut off at Philadelphia by a French fleet coming to support the Americans, Sir Henry Clinton, the new British commander, vacated the city, to march his men through New Jersey to New York City. General Lee was ordered by Washington to attack Clinton's column at Monmouth, but was dilatory in doing so. The result was another defeat, which Washington and Hamilton believed might have been a victory if Lee had stood his ground, instead of a partial defeat allowing the British to reach Sandy Hook and board transports for New York. Lee and his defenders maintained that his actions had avoided a worse disaster with casualties much heavier than the estimated 350 suffered by his forces.

The Lee court-martial found Hamilton and Burr on opposite sides. Hamilton's testimony at the proceedings in New Brunswick was instrumental in convicting Lee of disobedience and misbehavior, in accordance with which he was suspended from the army. Burr, who was not present at any of the twenty-six court-martial sessions, was sympathetic to Lee, less because he took a different view of the Monmouth battle than because he did not regard Washington as an able general and did not like him. According to Parton, Burr saw Washington as someone "who was as fond of adulation as he was known to be sensitive to censure . . . and no officer could stand well with him who did not play the part of his worshiper. He could not bear near his person a man of an independent habit of mind."[24] He may have shared some of these observations with Lee, and while no letter of his to Lee survives, Lee's letter to him the following October expresses gratitude for Burr's interesting himself "so warmly in my favour." Promising to send Burr a transcript of the trial as soon as he could obtain one, Lee confided to Burr that if no "proper reparation" was made to his reputation, he would resign his commission, "retire to Virginia, and learn to hoe tobacco, which I find is the best school to form a consumate *general*. This is a discovery I have lately made."[25] Burr could hardly have missed the bitterly sarcastic reference to Washington, whose tobacco acreage was extensive.

The aftermath of the trial featured one duel and at least two near-duels in which Hamilton was involved. Lee's aide, Major John S. Eustache, in effect, challenged Hamilton to a duel by stating in public that Hamilton had perjured himself at the trial, and calling Hamilton a "son of a bitch." Hamilton, who did not respond, probably encouraged Baron von Steuben, the army's inspector general, who thought himself to have been insulted by Lee, to challenge him, but in the end it was John Laurens, Hamilton's closest friend at the time, who brought Lee to the dueling ground. On December 22, Laurens, with Hamilton as his second, in defense of Washington's honor against real or imagined insults originating with Lee, exchanged shots with the court-martialed general. Lee was slightly wounded but insisted, as did Laurens, on a second round. Lee then made a conciliatory statement, which Laurens accepted, and the duel came to an end.

Steuben, one of the more colorful characters of the war, weaves in and out of Hamilton's life like a human bobbin. Known in the Prussian military service before he came to America as Friedrich Wilhelm Ludolf Gerhard Augustin, Baron von Steuben (1730–94), he wrangled a generalship in Washington's Army by grossly inflating his rank and position as an officer under Frederick the Great. Never higher than a captain in the Prussian military, he is described by a biographer as "a systematic, circumstantial and deliberate liar ... {who} misled his American friends about his life in Germany and his German friends about his life in America."[26] Notwithstanding, he was a successful general under Washington whose military skills were much admired. Twenty-five years older than Hamilton, Steuben never married, but he was something of a ladies' man and shared Hamilton's affection for Angelica Schuyler Church, Hamilton's sister-in-law, and perhaps others. The two were close friends until his death, by which time Hamilton had used his influence in the government to secure for Steuben several land grants and a lifelong pension.

It may be more than coincidence that both Lee's letter to Burr and Burr's letter to Washington requesting "permission to retire from pay and duty until my health will permit" were written in October. Still a lieutenant colonel despite his command of a regiment and service in almost every major engagement of the war since the march to Quebec, Burr may have been urged toward at least temporary retirement by dissatisfaction with his rank and the treatment accorded Lee. His letter to Washington mentioned "excessive heat and occasional fatigues" as the reasons his health was impaired, but he supplied no further details, and clearly Washington was not impressed. In his gracious but cool reply, which may have been drafted by Hamilton, Washington admonished Burr for carrying his "ideas of delicacy too far" in offering to relinquish his pay while recovering his health. "It is not customary and it would be unjust," Washington added, but he did not object to Burr's having a paid furlough.[27] Whatever the true state of Burr's health, he was well enough to leave Elizabethtown, where he had written the letter, and return to Malcom's Regiment within a few weeks of receiving Washington's response.

His official army career, however, was drawing to a close. During its remaining four months, Burr and his Malcom's Regiment, with headquarters at White Plains, defended an area of Westchester County stretching from the Hudson River to Long Island Sound, and not only against British raids and probes from New York City. Bands of guerrillas, deserters, and ordinary marauders from both sides of the war were looting the farms and villages of everything possessing any value, especially livestock and household goods, and Burr was determined to stop them. One of his first efforts was to return to rightful owners, whether patriot or loyalist, what had been stolen by his own men, and severely to punish the thieves. Sentences of up to fifty lashes followed by confinement, according to a soldier who was with the regiment, were not uncommon, with the result that robberies by soldiers under Burr's command came to an end. But his constant patrolling of the outposts, and frequent inspections of the ranks to insure that his orders were obeyed, perhaps took a toll of his health not unlike that he had complained of to Washington in October. This time, Washington accepted his resignation from the army, which was effected in mid-March 1779. Although his military activities did not entirely cease, they were confined to transmitting orders from one senior officer to another, and on one occasion in July aiding Yale students in the defense of New Haven against a British attack.

Burr's earliest biographers, and most of his biographers since, have been agreed that, in Parton's words, he "was an invalid" for eighteen months after leaving the army.[28] They do not identify the nature of his invalidism, and we have few clues to how he occupied himself during his long convalescence, which must have ended before he began to read law the winter of 1780 in Raritan, New Jersey. By that time, he had met his future wife, Theodosia Prevost, with whom he had established a relationship close enough to facilitate correspondence between her and his sister, Sally Reeve, in Litchfield. She and Burr may have been acquainted even before the summer of 1778, when Washington and his family, which no doubt included Hamilton, spent at least four days at Theodosia's home, the Hermitage, in Paramus, Bergen County, New Jersey. Burr may not then have been there, but not long after, he was emotionally involved with Theodosia, who, married to a British officer based in the West Indies, was not yet a widow. When she became one in October 1781, her husband having died on the island of Jamaica, she and especially Burr, who by then were in love, could not have shed many tears. A year earlier, following difficulties with the Bergen County commissioners who were confiscating property owned by British officers, thereby threatening to dispossess her of the Hermitage, she and her five children had moved to Sharon, Connecticut, not far from the Reeves in Litchfield. With the threat removed by her husband's death, and the help of influential friends such as New Jersey's attorney general William Paterson, Theodosia retained ownership of the Hermitage, and there, on July 2, 1782, she and Burr were married.

Hamilton, meanwhile, who had never relinquished his ambition to lead soldiers in combat, was renewing his efforts to obtain a command for the forthcoming campaign against Cornwallis in Virginia. In a letter to Washington on April 17, 1781, he reminded him that he had been in active service since the first days of 1776, beginning "in the line," where, had he remained, he would by now have a higher rank. Asking Washington to put him in command of a light infantry corps, to which appointment "I flatter myself my pretensions . . . are good," he added that he did not expect his appointment to arouse the opposition that had manifested itself in connection with appointing other officers to command positions.[29] Washington did not share this expectation. In a return letter the same day, he confessed himself "not a little embarrassed" by the request. Appointing "an Officer of your Rank" to the command of a corps, he advised Hamilton, "would, I am certain, involve me in a difficulty of a very disagreeable & delicate nature, and might perhaps lead to consequences more serious than it is easy to imagine." Washington was referring to earlier threats of some field officers to resign in protest if he appointed staff instead of field officers to infantry commands. But aware that Hamilton might "impute my refusal of your request with motives other than these," Washington ended his letter: "I beg you to be assured I am only influenced by the reasons which I have mentioned."[30] That undoubtedly was true; in the years that followed, which included his appointing Hamilton Secretary of the Treasury and, later, promoting him to major general, his affection and respect for his former aide never wavered.

His patience in April and May 1781, however, may have been strained by Hamilton's persistence. Despite the entreaties of Betsey, his wife, and her father that he curtail his active military service and, Schuyler urged, pursue a political career, Hamilton in another letter to Washington could not "forbear repeating, that my case is peculiar and dissimilar to all the former; it is distinguished by the circumstances I have before intimated," and this time he was successful.[31] By early July he was training soldiers at Dobbs Ferry, New York, and on July 31 he was given command of four light infantry companies. Although his letters to Betsey thereafter shower her with endearments and voice a passionate longing for her company, Hamilton can barely conceal his eagerness to participate in the coming campaign. Informing Betsey in August that there is "a greater prospect of activity now than there had been hitherto," and that he was about to depart for Virginia, the latter move "a fatal necessity" which would give her pain, he later in his letter of August 22 discounts the prospect on the grounds that "It is ten to one that our views will be disappointed by Cornwallis retiring to South Carolina by land." By "our views" Hamilton clearly meant his own hopes and the hopes of others that Cornwallis would stand and fight in Virginia, thereby affording him for the first time the opportunity to exercise command in combat, rather than escape southward. Having endeavored so long to obtain a line position enabling him to lead troops into action, Hamilton did not welcome a further delay and the possibility that Cornwallis would retreat farther or surrender before he could distinguish himself on the battlefield. Meanwhile, he advised Betsey that, much as he missed her and hoped "it will not be later than November, before we are again restored to each other," she would not be able to visit him or he to visit her.[32]

Hamilton's eagerness to confront the British in Virginia was in sharp contrast to Jefferson's eagerness to avoid an encounter with the enemy. Elected governor of the state in June 1779, Jefferson had the responsibility of organizing its defense against Cornwallis, an effort that involved raising and supplying a militia with a potential strength of 50,000 men. But he was unsuccessful in recruiting sufficient manpower to repulse the British invasion, perhaps partly because he was opposed to arming slaves and promising them their postwar freedom as distinct from employing them in a labor force with no prospect of having their servitude ended when the war was over. As a consequence, "thousands of slaves in Virginia, among them twenty-two of his own slaves, fled to the British side," and while no historian has attributed the collapse of the state's defenses to their desertion, there can be little doubt that it hardly strengthened Virginia's war effort.[33]

Most of Jefferson's biographers have been sparing in their judgment of other aspects of his leadership, or, in the view of some critics, lack of leadership. But even admirers have had difficulty accepting his decision to retire from the governorship on June 2, 1781, less than two weeks after a merger at Petersburg of two British armies with a combined total of seven thousand regulars. That same day, when he was at Monticello although technically still in office, the enemy was seen approaching. Sending his wife and daughters ahead of him to safety, he followed them on horseback "through the woods toward Carter's

Mountain, and made his escape."[34] A modern pronouncement on this behavior is that Jefferson "was cool, and could certainly be described as brave,"[35] but this was not the verdict of many of his contemporaries, including Lafayette, Steuben, "Light-Horse" Harry Lee, Hamilton, and the Virginia legislature; on June 10, the legislature with Patrick Henry in a prominent role voted a resolution of inquiry into Jefferson's governorship. This action no doubt was welcomed by Andrew Jackson, who as a teenager during the Revolutionary War had engaged in skirmishes with the British; when Jackson, the victor and hero of the decisive Battle of New Orleans in the War of 1812, heard that Jefferson at a banquet in 1815 offered a toast to those who had defeated the British, he remarked: "I am glad the old gentleman has plucked up courage enough to at least attend a banquet in honor of a battle."[36]

That Hamilton was "cool" and "brave" at Yorktown, destined to be the last major battle of the Revolutionary War, would never be disputed. On October 14–15, following several days and nights of artillery exchanges, American and French forces under the overall command of Lafayette and Rochambeau began their assault against the entrenched British positions on the York River at a site between Richmond and Norfolk. Hamilton, with Laurens and other officers and men in support, had been assigned to attack one of the fortified redoubts. Ordering his light infantry to fix bayonets and follow him over the parapet behind which the British were entrenched, he and other Americans soon had the British routed at little cost to either side. Four days after the battle, which essentially had been won by the French, who suffered the heaviest losses, Cornwallis, to the surprise of Washington, formally surrendered.[37] Hamilton's opportunity to be in the forefront of battle, in the war he had long ago wished for in his letter to Ned Stevens, had come just in time.

Hamilton might have commanded black soldiers at Yorktown had he earlier been successful in urging that blacks be recruited for military service. In March 1779, he joined Laurens, a native of South Carolina, in urging John Jay and others to support their recommendation to "raise two three or four battalions of negroes" in South Carolina and other Southern states for military service. In arguing their case, Hamilton displayed a lack of conventional prejudices that was highly unusual at that time, but he also put forward a view of "negroes" and others that was consistent with his low opinion of mankind's rank and file. The belief that "negroes . . . are too stupid to make soldiers," he wrote Jay, president of the Continental Congress in March 1779, "is hardly valid considering that their natural faculties are probably as good as ours . . ." What was important, however, is that their "want of cultivation . . . joined to that habit of subordination which they acquire from a life of servitude will make them sooner become soldiers than our White inhabitants. Let officers be men of sense and sentiment and the nearer the soldiers approach to machines, perhaps the better."[38]

The South Carolina legislature and other state assemblies did not agree, and neither did Jefferson, who owned as many as two hundred slaves during his lifetime. Jefferson, who, in Peter Gay's words, managed to "live with, and off" slavery despite the principles with which he is identified,[39] like other slave owners feared that arming slaves would increase the likelihood of slave uprisings. His apprehensions were such that he was opposed to supporting the slave revolt led by Toussaint L'Ouverture against French colonial rule on the island of Santo Domingo mainly on the grounds that it might encourage slaves in the United States to take similar action. Unlike Hamilton and Burr, both of whom owned a few slaves but advocated their emancipation, Jefferson, believing that blacks were inherently unequal to whites and therefore unsuitable for integration, let alone intermarriage, favored their deportation. In his *Notes on the State of Virginia*, his only book, which he wrote in 1785, he held that blacks "secrete less by the kidneys and more by the glands of the skin, which gives them a very strong and disagreeable odor . . . They are at least as brave, and more adventuresome. But this may proceed from a want of forethought, which prevents their seeing a danger till it be present . . . their griefs are transient . . . In memory they are equal to the whites; in reason much inferior, as I think one could scarcely be found capable of tracing and comprehending the investigations of Euclid."[40]

In contrast, Hamilton in his letter to Jay argued that giving slaves "their freedom with their muskets," would secure their "fidelity" and "courage" and would also have "a good influence upon those who remain, by opening a door to their emancipation . . . the dictates of humanity and true policy equally interest me in favour of this unfortunate class of men."[41] Some Hamilton biographers have speculated that Hamilton's attitude toward blacks may have owed something to his having lived in an easy proximity to them when he was growing up in the West Indies. Laurens's views, on the other hand, may have been influenced by his having been educated in London and Geneva.

Certain experiences of Hamilton's West Indies youth may also have played a role in his initial reaction to the discovery in September 1780 that Major General Benedict Arnold (1741–1801), a twice-wounded hero of the war who had been with Ethan Allen at Ticonderoga, General Montgomery at Quebec, and General Gates at Saratoga, had deserted to the British. Initially, it was mistakenly thought that Arnold's wife, Margaret Shippen Arnold, usually called Peggy, who at nineteen was half his age when he married her, was wholly innocent of complicity in her husband's treason, or even ignorant of it. Although Peggy was the daughter of a Philadelphia family known to have had loyalist sympathies before the Revolution, at first she was not regarded with suspicion, and no one was more convinced of Peggy's virtue in the affair than Hamilton. In a letter to his wife, he portrayed her as "an amiable woman frantic with distress for the loss of a husband she tenderly loved . . . she pressed her infant to her bosom and lamented its fate occasioned by the imprudence of its father in a manner that would have pierced insensibility itself . . . Her sufferings were so eloquent that I wished myself her brother, to have a right to become her defender."[42] Unfortunately, his reaction when he discovered that Peggy, at the least, had aided and abetted her husband's desertion to the British is not recorded.

Was Hamilton "taken in by Peggy Arnold" is a question asked but not answered by Broadus Mitchell. "He was only a few years older than she," Mitchell notes, "and ready to ascribe [Betsey's] virtues to a lovely girl in distress. Did his chivalry get the better of his wits?"[43] Perhaps the answer to the first question lies not with chivalry or Betsey Hamilton but with Hamilton's mother, Rachel Levine. She, too, had been deserted, as had, he believed, Peggy Arnold, and when he began his affair with Maria Reynolds ten years later, some part of her appeal, he wrote, was her claim that she had been abandoned by her husband. Still another woman in Hamilton's life, his cousin Anne Lytton Mitchell, of whom he was fond, had not only been deserted by her husband but been betrayed as well. These relationships and involvements of Hamilton suggest that he was vulnerable to women who conjured up associations, conscious or otherwise, with his mother. If her husband

and court records can be trusted, Rachel had been not only attractive and seductive but something more, and Hamilton all his life was susceptible to the charms of women who were attractive, like Peggy Arnold, or attractive, seductive, and willing, like Maria Reynolds and, if contemporary gossip can be believed, others.

Burr, however, was not "taken in" by Peggy Arnold or, as far as we know, by the tearful account of any woman he found attractive or with whom he had an affair. While it is possible that he knew early of Peggy Arnold's role in her husband's treason, neither he nor his future wife, Theodosia Prevost, in whom she may have confided, betrayed her confidence until she had safely departed to join her husband. Burr, like Hamilton, was attracted to women who were pretty and sexually appealing, but we have very little information about their physical appearance and even less about the type of woman who appealed to him. We do know that Esther Burr was no Rachel Levine before or during her brief life as his mother, and the existence of other significant women or possible surrogate mothers in his early years has not been established. His surviving letters to mistresses and other women, who are rarely identified, evidence a certain wariness, as if he did not entirely trust them with intimacies and secrets. Perhaps the only women to whom he ever revealed his innermost self were his wife and daughter. His marriage to Theodosia, a widow ten years older than himself, not beautiful, and already the mother of five children, may suggest that maternal qualities in a wife, whether or not they were part of the appeal of other women, were important to him. In marrying Theodosia, he also was instantly creating, in a sense, the family he never had as a child. And here, too, there is a similarity to Hamilton, who, in marrying into the large, affluent, and influential Schuyler family, was able to enjoy a respectability and security he had never known in the West Indies.

three

HUSBANDS, WIVES, LOVERS

Hamilton and Burr, like soldiers everywhere, found time to court girls while serving in Washington's Army. But biographers have tended to overlook or minimize Hamilton's conquests of the female sex and exaggerate the exploits of Burr. With the single exception of Hamilton's self-admitted affair in 1791–92 with Maria Reynolds, most biographers have had little or nothing to say about the women in his life, among whom the most important was his wife's sister, Angelica Schuyler Church. There is no doubt that this silence owes much to the earliest biographies by his son, J. C. Hamilton, and his grandson, A. M. Hamilton. The former does not refer to the Reynolds affair and barely notes the existence of Angelica Church, his aunt, for whom one of his sisters was named, and the latter treats the relationship between Alexander and Angelica as a mere flirtation. Both omit altogether certain letters or delete sentences and words in correspondence between the two, a practice for which the grandson severely censured his uncle in connection with other letters written by Hamilton.[1]

In contrast, Burr's earliest biographer, his close friend and colleague, Matthew L. Davis, is unsparing in his condemnation of Burr's "dissipation." Although a staunch political ally of Burr, who repeatedly is critical of Jefferson and Hamilton for their treatment of him, Davis frequently describes Burr as "licentious in the extreme, and regardless of consequences in the gratification of his desires. His extravagance was unrestrained when, in his opinion, necessary to the enjoyment of his pleasures." Davis goes so far as to declare it "truly surprising how

any individual could have become so eminent as a soldier, as a statesman, and as a professional man, who devoted so much time to the
other sex as was devoted by Colonel Burr. For more than half a century of his life they seemed to absorb his whole thoughts. His intrigues
were without number. His conduct most licentious. The sacred bonds
of friendship were unhesitatingly violated when they operated as bar-
riers to the indulgence of his passions."[2] Far from being apologetic for
having destroyed Burr's letters to and from women "of no very strict
morality," entrusted to him with other papers, he appears to want
credit for committing "with my own hands . . . to the fire all such correspondence, and not a vestige of it remains."[3]

Biographers and other writers since Davis have not hesitated to
furnish details. Thus Burr at Princeton, where according to Davis he
was engaged during his senior year in the "constant pursuit of pleasure," is said to have seduced one Catherine Bulluck, who, broken-
hearted, died not long after. There was such a person, and Burr may
have had a sexual relationship with her, but her death was the result
of tuberculosis. In other accounts, he is alleged to have taken with him
on the march to Quebec a nineteen-year-old "Indian mistress Jacataqua from Swan Island in the Kennebec River," known to the men
accompanying Burr as "Golden Thighs."[4] Davis was the first to suggest
that in 1776–77 Burr, while serving in New York with Putnam, was
the "American Colonel" who, wrote Margaret Moncrieffe, "subdued
my virgin heart." Moncrieffe, the fourteen-year-old daughter of a British officer, was temporarily living with the Putnams, who, as a consequence of Burr's suspicions that she was a spy, reported her to
Washington. Moncrieffe quickly was transferred to the custody of
General Thomas Mifflin at Kingsbridge, nineteen miles to the north,
in whose care she remained until she joined her father. In 1794, by
which time she had been the mistress of several aristocrats and political figures in London following an unhappy marriage, Moncrieffe,
known as Mrs. Coghlan by 1794, published her *Memoirs*, and it was
this volume that supplied Davis with the grounds for accusing Burr
of having launched Moncrieffe, through his seduction, on her downward course.[5]

Burr may have been her seducer, but as some biographers have
noted, he does not entirely fit Moncrieffe's description of the colonel
to whom "I plighted my virgin heart." At that time Burr was not yet

a colonel, and it was at Mifflin's rather than Putnam's that Moncrieffe met her first lover. But whoever the colonel was, Moncrieffe, far from regarding herself as, in Davis's words, "the victim of seduction" by Burr, presents the relationship as a love affair terminated by obedience to her father and his political principles. Davis, convinced that Moncrieffe was an innocent dupe of Burr, who "in his intercourse with females . . . was an unprincipled flatterer, ever prepared to take advantage of their weakness, their credulity, or their confidence," does not quote her lament that "the barbarous customs of society" prevented her marriage to the man "whom the immutable laws of nature had pointed out for my husband."[6] Moncrieffe's own account of her affair with an "American Colonel" who may or may not have been Burr tends to support the contention of a recent biographer that Davis's report and that of others "is a very good example of the propensity of chroniclers to link Burr's name with women, particularly notorious ones."[7] But even respectable women were not exempt from Burr's embraces, if certain rumors can be believed, such as one that circulated long after Moncrieffe to the effect that Burr was the father of Martin Van Buren (1782–1862), eighth President of the United States.[8] Here, adulterous betrayal of Theodosia Prevost Burr as well as immorality was alleged, Van Buren having been born December 5, 1782, by which time Burr and Theodosia had been married five months.

Hamilton, meanwhile, at the encampment in Morristown in 1779–80 was not giving his entire attention to his duties as Washington's aide-de-camp, or to the threatened mutiny of entire regiments of soldiers whose rations had been cut and who had not been paid for months. Amid the hardships of a winter so cold that the British were able to slide their heavy cannon five miles across the thick ice of the Hudson River from lower Manhattan to Staten Island, he found the time and energy for several courtships. One of the women, about whom he was teased by fellow officers, was Cornelia Lott, who lived nearby; Cornelia probably was the subject of a poem about Hamilton written by a friend at the camp, some lines of which ran

> *(You'd think him Ovid's self or Jove)*
> *Now feels the inexorable dart*
> *And yields Cornelia all his heart.*

There also was Polly—last name unknown—and there were others as well, equally unknown, if various accounts of life in Washington's family can be believed.[9]

These accounts have led at least one biographer to conclude that "in youth and maturity Hamilton loved the ladies and they him; there was scarce a one he could not charm, and none who could not deceive him. They were susceptible to him because of his attentiveness and flirtatious pleasantries, his polished manners, his gracefulness as a dancer, his wit, and his good looks. He was, in the phrase of his time, a very pretty fellow. His male friends called him 'little Hammy' or the 'little lion' . . . Women doubtless called him little things more intimate."[10] Except for the reference to deception, the same statement with minor changes could be made about "Little Burr."

Despite the sternness and stiffness of Washington's headquarters, which "was always the last place for mirth," another aide of the general wrote, Hamilton and his friends in their free time made merry with the local females. That Martha Washington, who had a lighter side than her husband, named her tomcat "Hamilton" may testify to his off-base activities. Steuben, who had similar proclivities, may have been an accomplice. Apparently, he was apt to recommend a boardinghouse to the young men of the family if he could assure them "vous trouvez une jeune veuve charmante," or some young lady "with a beautiful waist, a reason the more for you to hurry your departure."[11]

But as early as April 1779 Hamilton's dalliances did not preclude thoughts about marriage and the type of woman he would require as his wife. In a long letter to Laurens requesting his friend to find him a wife, he detailed his specifications, leaving almost nothing to Laurens's imagination or guesswork. "Take her description," Hamilton began, in his letter of April 1779:[12] "She must be young, handsome (I lay most stress upon a good shape) sensible (a little learning will do), well bred (but she must have an aversion to the word *ton*) chaste and tender (I am an enthusiast in my notions of fidelity and fondness) of some good nature, a great deal of generosity (she must neither love money nor scolding, for I dislike equally a termagant and an economist) . . . As to religion a moderate stock will satisfy me. She must believe in God and hate a saint. But as to fortune, the larger stock of that the better. You know my temper and circumstances and will therefore pay special attention to this article in the treaty. Though I run no risk of going to Purgatory for my avarice; yet as money is an essential ingredient to happiness in this world — as I have not much of my own and as I am very little calculated to get more either by my address or industry; it must needs be, that my wife, if I get one, bring at least a sufficiency to administer to her own extravagancies."[13] Hamilton's admirers, beginning with his first biographers, have had great difficulty with the latter part of this letter. A note in pencil on the first page, "presumably written by J. C. Hamilton," reads: "I must not publish the whole of this." And in addition to omitting the sentences quoted, he may also have crossed out some words, which, as a consequence, cannot be read.[14] The letter does not appear in A. M. Hamilton's *Intimate Life*, and biographers since have tended to deny that Hamilton meant what he wrote and later married for money. "What we know," maintains one of them, "gives the lie to these insinuations of motive. Hamilton's letters to Betsey . . . show a tenderness, confidence, and deepening regard . . . Alexander Hamilton, by all the signs, fell in love and remained in love with his Betsey."[15] Another biographer argues in Hamilton's favor: "It is not easy to identify any Founding Father or Framer of the Constitution who married young who married a woman who failed to bring him a respectable stock of fortune of her own: Martha Custis Washington, Martha Wayles Jefferson, and Sarah Livingston Jay are ready examples."[16] Still another biographer strikes a compromise between the view that Hamilton married Betsey because her father was wealthy and the opposing view that he married her for love: "Doubtless he would never have considered a lowborn woman for a wife, but otherwise the suggestion [he married for money] is nonsense. His devotion to her was passionate and constant . . . however, he remained susceptible to female wiles."[17]

Whatever the strength of the differing motives for marriage attributed to him, Hamilton's susceptibility "to female wiles" was manifest during his courtship of Betsey as well as after his marriage. While it is not known exactly when Hamilton met his future wife, his acquaintance with her began some time before he wrote her sister, Margarita Schuyler (Peggy), praising her charms. "She is most unmercifully handsome," he wrote Peggy in February 1780, and he went on to celebrate Betsey's "good nature, affability and vivacity . . . In short she is so strange a creature that she possesses all the beauties virtues and graces of her sex without any . . . amiable defects."[18] His attentions to

Betsey, however, did not preclude "his being attentive to C[ornelia] Lott, Jany 1780," in the words of his friend Colonel Webb.[19] His description of Betsey in a letter to Laurens also struck a more subdued note than his celebration of her in his letter to Peggy. "She is a good hearted girl," he wrote Laurens on June 20, 1780, by which time he had become engaged, "who I am sure will never play the termagant; though not a genius she has good sense enough to be agreeable, and though not a beauty, she has fine black eyes — is rather handsome and has every other requisite of the exterior to make a lover happy."[20] There is no record of a letter from Laurens in response, but he may have been one of those friends who when they heard of the engagement "went into raptures. 'You will get all that family's [Schuyler's] interest,' exclaimed [French] Colonel Fleury. '. . . You will get a very easy Situation & happiness is not to be found without a Large Estate.' "[21]

In marrying Betsey, the second daughter of Philip Schuyler, on December 14, 1780, Hamilton was marrying into a family that possessed more than a "Large Estate." The Schuylers were one of the oldest established and most respected families in New York State, as well as one of the wealthiest. Betsey's father, born in 1733, was a major general in the Revolutionary War whose ancestors had emigrated from Holland in the seventeenth century to become prominent landowners in the Albany and Saratoga areas. Inheriting property from his father, mother, and uncle, who was murdered on his own estate at Saratoga, Schuyler added to it through his own efforts. He was comfortably situated even without the addition of his wife's extensive holdings. The original manor of Van Rensselaerwyck owned by Catherine Van Rensselaer Schuyler's forebears was twenty-four miles square, and although her inheritance of land from her father was much less than that, it nevertheless was substantial.

Betsey's mother, born in 1734, according to contemporaries was a "lady of great beauty, shape and gentility" who was devoted to her husband, as he was to her. She also was a capable wife, mother of fifteen children, eight of whom survived infancy, and manager of the extensive Schuyler household of servants, slaves, and hired hands. These qualities may have been passed along to her daughter Betsey, who, unlike her sister Angelica, was educated at home and had few interests other than her husband and family. If, in fact, Catherine was a "great beauty," this attribute may have been inherited by her daughter Angelica, who probably was the most attractive as well as most spirited of her five daughters. Delicate as a young girl, Catherine became corpulent later in life, but was no less capable of bearing children. Her last child, named for her, was born February 20, 1781, when she was forty-seven years old, by which time her daughter Angelica was the mother of children of her own.[22]

Perhaps Catherine's corpulence and her husband's chronic gout were the results of an opulent lifestyle at their Albany mansion, known as the Pastures, and their estate in Saratoga. They were renowned for setting a fine table and for their generous hospitality, benefits enjoyed by numbers of American, French, and other officers fighting with Washington, including Lafayette and Steuben and even captive British generals. General John Burgoyne, known as Gentleman Johnny, under house arrest after his surrender, was entertained by them, although he had burned down their house and barns earlier in the war. Presumably, they did not welcome his mistress, who, like General Howe's Mrs. Loring, may have distracted him at crucial moments, thereby contributing to his defeat at Saratoga.

By 1777, or about the time Hamilton may have first set eyes on Betsey, Schuyler's property in Saratoga alone was worth, according to Burgoyne, who had destroyed it, some £10,000, a considerable sum in those days.*[23] He also owned thousands of acres in the Mohawk Valley, Hudson River Valley, and areas north of Saratoga, farms, a flour mill and the first flax mill built in America, choice timberland, and one schooner and three sloops used for transporting his produce, wood, and other products to markets south of Albany. As early as the French and Indian War (1756–63), Schuyler had made money supplying the British Army on Lake George and at Oswego, and by April 1776 he was purchasing large quantities of supplies for the American Army, and from his own stocks selling flour, lumber, and other supplies to the quartermaster general. From 1776 to 1779 "he certainly

---

* It is difficult to estimate the values in today's money of pounds and dollars in late-eighteenth-century America. One effort to do so by John J. McCusker calculates the value of the New York pound of 1796 as roughly equal to $30.00 in 1997, and the New York dollar of 1796 as roughly equal to $12.00 in 1997. Based on these figures, which, Professor McCusker warns, are crude rather than exact estimates, Schuyler's Saratoga property was worth about $300,000. But this figure and all other 1997 equivalents of 1796 money should be thought of as suggestive only. In the pages that follow, 1997 rounded-out equivalents of 1796 money will appear in parentheses.

had a good deal to say about supplies for the Northern Department."
In 1781, he furnished flour to the main army on Robert Morris's "urgent plea," Morris "later complaining that the five percent commission charged was double what he was accustomed to pay."[24] Earlier, when as an officer Schuyler was involved in supplying British forces prior to the Revolutionary War, he was charged and acquitted of benefiting personally from such transactions, and of not being able to account for large sums of money entrusted to him.

By the time Hamilton was Secretary of the Treasury, Schuyler held some $60,000 ($720,000) worth of securities to be funded,[25] a holding that may have been responsible, according to Senator William Maclay, for his hair standing "on end as if Indians had fired at him" when there was opposition to Hamilton's plan to fund the national debt.[26] Clearly, Schuyler, while not the wealthiest man of his time, was among the most affluent.

That Hamilton benefited from this affluence, despite the lack of documentary evidence and despite assertions to the contrary by his son and grandson, there can be little doubt. While A. M. Hamilton does not deny that the Hamiltons often were the beneficiaries of the bounty produced by the Schuyler farms and other properties, he insists, as do many of Hamilton's later biographers, that his grandfather was too proud to accept financial aid from his father-in-law. But in the early period of his marriage and during the more than four years that he was Secretary of the Treasury, he clearly could not have earned enough to support a growing family in the comfortable manner he and Betsey affected. Not long after November 1783, when he opened his law practice in New York City and his income was still modest, he was the father of two children, and by the time he joined Washington's cabinet in 1789, there were two more, with a fifth to follow in 1792.

His earnings had increased by then, but it is unlikely that without the aid of the Schuylers he could have afforded the large investments he made in western land and several commercial enterprises. It is even more uncertain that he could have accepted the Treasury appointment without that help. Vice President John Adams complained that his own salary of $5,000 was not sufficient, and Hamilton as a cabinet secretary was paid only $3,500 ($42,000). Occasionally having to borrow small sums of money from his aides and assistants, in August 1792, by which time his efforts to keep his affair with Maria Reynolds from becoming public knowledge had cost him more than $1,000, he nevertheless was able to provide $600, with the promise of a further $400, to pay the headmaster of a boys' school in Philadelphia. Assuming that at least Hamilton's oldest son, Philip, attended the school, Schuyler must have contributed to his being able to pledge thirty percent of his income toward the education of the Hamiltons' oldest son, his namesake. How Hamilton was able to part with another thirty percent as payment to Maria Reynolds's husband remains a mystery.

Patrician to the core, the Schuylers had little use for those who were not, like themselves, well-born. Catherine's father was distressed when an innkeeper had been made a colonel, and both Schuylers attached great importance to the social rank of those chosen to be civil and military leaders. If, as reported, "Elizabeth's father was a gouty old aristocrat, noted for his proud and imperious bearing, his strong conviction that New Englanders were socially not much better than Yahoos, and his fondness for family trees,"[27] what led him not merely to accept Hamilton as his son-in-law but to accord him a warmer welcome into the family than that given his other sons-in-law?

There can be no certain answer to this question, but one factor weighing heavily with Schuyler may have been Hamilton's serving as aide-de-camp to Washington. An unconditional admirer of the future President under whom he had served, Schuyler could only have been impressed by Hamilton's role in Washington's family, which, by the time of his engagement to Betsey in 1780, had spanned three years. If, as some biographers maintain, Hamilton did not inform him of the circumstances of his birth but chose instead to emphasize his father's ancestral Scottish background, Schuyler could have had no compelling reason to view his prospective son-in-law other than in a favorable light.[28] On the contrary, setting great store by "family connections," his ignorance of which had prejudiced him against another son-in-law, the husband of his daughter Angelica, and the lack of which contributed to his adverse judgments of political figures from humble backgrounds, Schuyler would have heartily approved of Hamilton's descent from a Scots family whose roots extended back to the Middle Ages. He may have known of Hamilton's relatively modest circumstances, which had been confided to Betsey, but more than rich enough for them both, and confident that Hamilton in his future career as a lawyer would be able to support a wife and children, Schuyler, as he put it in a letter to Hamilton, could not have been "more happy at the connection you have made with my family. Until the child of a parent has made a judicious choice his heart is in continual anxiety; but this anxiety was removed the moment I discovered on whom she had placed her affections."[29] By January 25, 1781, the date of the letter, at which time Hamilton and Betsey had been married a month, Schuyler must also have known that his son-in-law's views on a great variety of issues were similar to his own, and this, too, was very much in Hamilton's favor.

The belief that Hamilton may have informed Schuyler of his illegitimacy derives from Schuyler's writing, "I am pleased with every Instance of delicacy in those that are so dear to me, and I think I read your soul on the occasion you mention."[30] His reference to an "Instance of delicacy" could have related to Hamilton's "disclosure, suitable under the circumstances, that he was an illegitimate son," according to Mitchell's guess.[31] But given Hamilton's pride in his Scottish ancestry and the importance Schuyler attached to "family connections," it may not have been based on Hamilton's admission of illegitimacy but, rather, on his having revealed that his parents had separated or divorced when he was still a child.

If Hamilton did not withhold the truth about his birth, he may have indirectly reminded his father-in-law that, despite a reputation for piety and probity, Schuyler himself was in no position to reject Hamilton on that account. When the Schuylers were married on September 17, 1755, Catherine was four months pregnant with her daughter Angelica, who was born on February 22, 1756, presumably a normal full-term baby, since there is no mention of her being born prematurely. This marriage, in fact, was somewhat hasty, taking place three days after the license was issued, instead of the customary three weeks after the banns were published, and requiring Schuyler, a captain at the time, to leave his post, thereby missing the Battle of Lake George.[32] Had he not done so and been killed, Angelica, too, would have been illegitimate. Perhaps, finally, in January 1781, he also was grateful that Alexander and Betsey, unlike some of his other children, had been married in the proper way. By that date, one of his five daughters had eloped and three more were to arrange their own marriages, much to his and Catherine's displeasure.

Schuyler's regard and affection for Hamilton, like Washington's, may not have been fully reciprocated. Because "the bulk of their correspondence with each other, found in a trunk at Albany, had . . . been burned by the son of a Schuyler executor in one of those monstrous acts of private prerogative,"[33] knowledge of their relationship is largely based on their relatively few surviving letters and the memoirs of their contemporaries. Hamilton's letters, like those he wrote to Washington, are respectful, but they are not warm or reflective of a close personal relationship, as distinct from one founded on shared political and financial interests. Perhaps one of his letters to someone other than Schuyler reveals something of his attitude toward his father-in-law. Writing to Jeremiah Wadsworth, a business partner of Angelica's husband, on April 7, 1785, Hamilton dealt at length with financial matters he was handling for his brother-in-law, before adding in a final paragraph, almost as an afterthought, "By our advices from Albany I have great reason to apprehend General Schuyler is no more. This I consider as a great loss to his family, friends and the public."[34] His unemotional, almost unfeeling report of Schuyler's presumed death and the lack of any mention of his own personal loss may tell us something about the extent of his fondness for his father-in-law.

Not least among the blessings and benefits Betsey brought to her husband was her sister Angelica, who had eloped on June 23, 1777, to marry John Barker Church, then known as John Barker Carter.[35] Hamilton met the Churches not long after they were married, and for the remainder of his life he was to have a close personal and business relationship with Church, and at times apparently an intimate one with Angelica. His love for his sister-in-law, like the letter he wrote to Laurens about his requirements for a wife, has posed awkward questions for many of his biographers, most of whom have assumed that their feelings for each other never led to a sexual relationship. But the evidence that they had an affair, while circumstantial, is persuasive. Hamilton's son and grandson, as noted earlier, maintained a silence about such evidence, but others, including another sister of Betsey and friends of Hamilton, did not.

Given the gossip that circulated widely, Betsey must have known of the relationship between her husband and her sister, and if so, it is fortunate for them both that she was docile and long-suffering. A story she could hardly have avoided hearing concerned a dinner in Philadelphia attended by her husband (there without her, apparently), An-

Alexander Hamilton, 1804. Portrait by John Trumbull

Aaron Burr, 1802. Portrait by John Vanderlyn

Elizabeth Schuyler
Hamilton, 1787.
Portrait by Ralph Earle
*Museum of the City of New
York*

Philip Schuyler,
1792. Portrait by
John Trumbull
*© Collection of the New-
York Historical Society*

Theodosia Burr Alston, 1802. Portrait by John Vanderlyn, oil on canvas
© *Collection of the New-York Historical Society*

Angelica Schuyler Church in 1785. The child she is holding is her daughter, Elizabeth. Painted by John Trumbull
Owned by the Belvidere Trust

gelica, Peggy, and others, at which Angelica dropped her shoe bow. Picking it up, Peggy put it in Hamilton's buttonhole, "saying, 'There brother I have made you a Knight.' Angelica asked, 'But of what order he can't be a Knight of the garter in this country.' Miss Schuyler replied: 'True sister but *he would be if you would let him.'*" Harrison Otis, later a Massachusetts senator, the source of the anecdote, also reported a conversation he had had with Christopher G. Champlin, congressman from Rhode Island. Champlin, disliking Hamilton's casting "some liquorish {i.e. lustful} looks at his cara sposa," complained that Hamilton "appears to him very trifling in his conversations with ladies."[36]

Born August 9, 1757, Betsey was more than two years younger than her husband, and from the start of her marriage lived in the shadow cast by him and Angelica. Unfortunately, little is known about Betsey apart from information provided by the two Hamilton biographers in her family and some recollections of her published by friends. She wrote few letters, and apparently none to Hamilton survive, assuming she wrote to him on occasions, not infrequent, when he was absent from home. Judging by the only existing portrait of her, she was no beauty or even striking in appearance, as Hamilton claimed; her best feature in the portrait is her eyes, which are large, dark, and luminous.[37] According to her grandson, Betsey, unlike Angelica, who had attended "the best school at the time" in New Rochelle, "had but few educational advantages" and was lacking "the superficial grace and accomplishments of many of her more sprightly and dashing friends," among whom he could have included, but did not, her older sister. He adds that "she was gentle and retiring, but full of gayety and courage, fond of domestic affairs, and probably her mother's chief assistant in the management of the house and slaves."[38] She seems to have accepted without complaint her husband's liaisons with women both high and low. Although she was often ill during the years of her marriage, partly the result of having to cope with eight pregnancies and several miscarriages, she was Hamilton's widow twice as long as she was his wife, living more than fifty years after his death. She died on November 9, 1854, aged ninety-seven. Many of those years were devoted to enhancing her husband's reputation and his place in history, in the course of which she made certain her son's biography of his father "will make even Scotland, so fertile in genius and virtue, proud to enumerate him among her descendants."[39] She undoubtedly was behind the purchase and destruction of Hamilton's pamphlet detailing his affair with Maria Reynolds, now one of the rarest of late-eighteenth-century Americana.

But she was no Matthew Davis, at least where her sister's and her husband's letters to each other were concerned, and as a consequence the correspondence between Hamilton and Angelica remains eloquent testimony to their feelings. There is no way of knowing, however, if her husband's letters to other women, and the more intimate correspondence between brother-in-law and sister-in-law, were destroyed. Many of the letters that have survived are incomplete, and others have been edited, with words crossed out or substituted by an unknown hand. Nor have the relevant letters of Schuyler been spared; from those that survive, one can infer disapproval, but no more than infer. Much about these relationships will never be known, thanks to Hamilton's widow, children, and grandchildren, carefully edited family memoirs, the fading of historical memory, and the tendency in biography to apply heavy makeup to heroes.

While sexual attraction between a husband and his wife's sister is hardly unknown, as witness the Deceased Wife's Sister Act, a British statute for many years prohibiting marriage between a man who had lost his wife and the wife's sister,[40] there can be few collections of letters comparable to those between Alexander Hamilton and Angelica Schuyler Church. There also were few contemporaries of Hamilton, whether men or women, who were not charmed by beautiful, witty, gay Angelica. These included John Jay, James McHenry, Chancellor Kent, who declared her "one of his great favorites," and not least Thomas Jefferson, who saw a good deal of her when they were both in Paris after the signing of the treaty that ended the Revolutionary War. In a letter to her of July 27, 1788, when she was back in London, Jefferson wrote: "I esteem you infinitely" with "the *suave odeur* of . . . warm emotions . . . if you install me your physician, I will prescribe to you . . . a month in Paris." The "esteem" must have been mutual despite the growing animosity between Jefferson and her brother-in-law; she sent Jefferson her copy of *The Federalist*, which had been given to her by Betsey.[41]

Her husband, on the other hand, had few if any admirers. Born in 1748 in Lowestoft, England, Church had emigrated to America by 1776 and in July of that year was appointed Commissioner of Accounts for the Northern Department the army. In September he met Schuyler and not long after laid siege to Angelica's hand in marriage. Facing disapproval by her father, who never liked Church but occasionally made use of his business acumen, Church and Angelica ran off to the Van Rensselaers, where, on June 23, 1777, they were married. "The *ceremony*," the portrait painter John Trumbull wrote his wife on June 30, "passed at the Manor without the knowledge of *Parents* . . . [they] have not yet been to her Father's house nor seen her *Mother* They remain at *Grand Papa's* [Catherine's father, John Van Rensselaer's] over the River."[42] The Schuylers, Catherine especially, were furious, and for a time spurned the pleadings of the Van Rensselaers to make peace with the couple; Schuyler was reported to have "scarcely spoke a dozen words . . . Mrs. S was in a most violent Passion and said all that Rage & Resentment could inspire."[43] Eventually they accepted the marriage, but they were never fully reconciled to their eldest daughter's wanton ways, such as dressing herself in the latest London fashion, a style that included exposing more bosom than was considered proper in those days, and looking "like Washwomen with their sleeves above their elbows."[44]

The Schuylers had good reason to accord Church a cool reception. Arriving in this country as John Barker Carter, a name by which he was known until late in 1783, more than six years after his marriage, Church later was believed to have changed his name and left England because he had killed someone in a duel. That legend is still maintained by those of Hamilton's biographers who do not accept another story to the effect that he was fleeing England because of an unhappy love affair. The presumed truth is that he was a bankrupt who was escaping from debt incurred by speculation and gambling.[45] Once in America, he proceeded to make a fortune in a variety of undertakings: procuring supplies for the American and French forces; speculating in land, securities, and currency; investing in banks and shipping companies, the former including the Bank of New York in 1784 (Hamilton, who served on the board, arranged for Church and Wadsworth to have seats and to own shares); and other ventures, not excluding "a flutter in rum."[46] Regarded by Hamilton's friends as, in McHenry's words, "a mere man of business,"[47] Church appears to have had no other interest but gambling. He was known to play cards three or four times a week, on one occasion in Philadelphia losing $1,500 ($18,000).[48]

Although Hamilton had earlier declared, "I hate money making men," Hamilton was involved as partner or agent in many of these activities, with the exception of gambling.[49] Since Church as an alien could not own land, Hamilton purchased land for him, taking title in his own name. He also bought and sold securities in Church's behalf, handled his business affairs when he was abroad, bought or leased residences in New York for Church and his family, and borrowed money from him; when Hamilton made out a will in 1795, he owed Church £5,000 ($150,000). In his later will of 1804, still owing him money, Hamilton named Church one of his executors. But although they were close business associates, Church was not always happy with Hamilton's handling of his financial affairs. He wrote Wadsworth in May 1797, "I will thank you as soon as you can to send me our Account Current, for our Friend Hamilton not being very accurate in his Accounts is not clear that he had not made some Mistakes respecting the Monies you have Paid him on my Account." Certainly, one of Hamilton's mistakes was lending $10,000 ($120,000) of Church's money, apparently without his consent, to Robert Morris, most of which Morris was unable to repay. In his 1795 will, Hamilton acknowledged: "As this money was thus disposed of without being warrented by the spirit of Mr. Church's instructions, I consider myself as responsible for it."[50]

Their relationship may have gone further. According to one report, "after allusions to Hamilton's extra-marital activities, Church wrote Hamilton: 'As for the widow I suppose by what you say she will be out of the way and nothing can be feared on her account.' "[51] In a letter from London describing a visit to the Churches, Gouverneur Morris, hinting that Church himself was not the most faithful of husbands, wrote that they had employed a "young enough and handsome enough" French governess to whom, he suspected, Church "was trying to give . . . a lesson."[52] He did not identify the nature of the "lesson," but the implication seems clear.

Church, a worldly man, must have known, and accepted, his wife's infatuation with Hamilton. Assuming that he did so, we can only speculate that a principal reason was his valuing his relationship with Hamilton as far more important to him than Angelica's reputation. In the England Church knew when, as a wealthy man, he returned to live like a gentleman and win a seat in the House of Commons, husbands frequently had mistresses and at least some wives lovers, the respective spouses tending to accept the situation as a fact of life. A friend of the Prince of Wales, the future George IV, the Whig leader Charles James Fox, like himself a dedicated gambler, and Talleyrand, the former Bishop of Autun, all of whom disregarded conventions whether marital or otherwise, Church, like Sir William Hamilton, the husband of Lord Nelson's celebrated mistress, Emma, may have been less possessive of his wife than of his property and status, especially a wife whose lover was no ordinary man. But whatever Church's reasons for tolerating the relationship, they must have included an awareness of the many benefits he received from his association with Hamilton.

While it is not known exactly when Hamilton first met Angelica, apparently it was sometime after her marriage and before his own. Some biographers suggest that had he met her earlier, she, not Betsey, might have become his wife. Whatever the date of their meeting, he had a special affection for Catherine, Angelica's daughter, usually thought to have been born in 1780. In a letter to Angelica sixteen years later, Hamilton requested that his love "in particular" be given to "Caty," who "I am told . . . justifies all my anticipations of her. I take credit to myself for having discerned her worth in embryo when no one else had yet found it out."[53] The letter indicates that Hamilton was at least acquainted with Angelica in 1779 or 1780, depending on which is accepted as Catherine's birth year.[54]

The affair may have begun before 1787, when Hamilton, whose surviving letters are more discreet than Angelica's, read significant meaning into a slip of the pen in one of her letters that unintentionally revealed something of her feeling for him. In a letter to Hamilton from London of October 2, 1787, which started with an apology for not answering his previous "Letter not found," a frequent notation by the editors of Hamilton's *Papers*, Angelica wrote: "Indeed my dear, Sir if my path was strewed with as many roses, as you have filled your letter with compliments, I should not now lament my absence from America."[55] In the version of the letter published by Hamilton's grandson, the comma is moved from "dear," to "Sir," making the phrase read "Indeed my dear Sir, . . . "[56] Hamilton himself, far from certain the comma after "dear" was a simple mistake, wondered if the slip had a special meaning. In a paragraph dealing with it, he began, "You ladies despise the pedantry of punctuation. There was a most critical *comma* in your last letter. It is my interest that it should have been designed, but I presume it was accidental. Unriddle this if you can. The proof that you do it lightly may be given by the omission or repetition of the same mistake in your next." As a further indication that he hoped for a "repetition," he insisted that the "eloquence" for which she had praised him in one of her earlier letters was "but a feeble image of what I should wish to convey . . . I seldom write to a lady without fancying the relation of lover and mistress. It has a very inspiring effect . . . Betsey sends her love. I do not choose to say *joins in mine*. Tis old fashioned." And finally, "Adieu ma chère, soeur."[57] Clearly, Hamilton's placement of his comma, preceded by his "fancying" a lover-mistress relationship, was no slip. Nor was it any accident that this letter, unlike others, was sent separately from one to Church, and it also did not include, as some letters did, a note from Betsey. Unfortunately, we have no letter indicating whether Angelica responded as he wished her to do, with still another misplaced comma; her next recorded letter to Hamilton was almost two years later and after her visit in 1789.

Her subsequent letters, in any case, leave no doubt she wanted something more than a friendly, familial relationship with her brother-in-law. On January 30, 1789, she wrote Betsey ecstatically that she would be coming alone to New York, and asked her sister to find her "very handsome lodgings as near you as you can." She would need accommodations "for myself and four servants . . . [and] a coach with horses and a sober coachman . . . immediately on my arrival. My love to Hamilton he shall have a holiday when I come."[58] Between May, when she arrived, and November, when she returned to London, Hamilton's cash book records cash advances from himself and Betsey, and payments for her lodging, horses, and other expenses, totaling more than £1,700 ($56,000), most of which was reimbursed by Church. An unexplained entry, which at least one biographer regards as evidence that Hamilton and Angelica spent some weeks together,[59] reads: "Paid Mrs. Cuyler for your lodgings from May 10 to October 7. 21 weeks She deducts three weeks for time they were occupied by Mrs. Morris."[60] Her whereabouts those three weeks and for the month between October 7 and her departure in November is not known. Perhaps she was in Albany visiting the Schuylers or seeing other friends elsewhere, but the possibility that she was with Hamilton cannot be eliminated. On May 28 he wrote

Betsey from an unknown location that he was "miserable" because he could not immediately return to her in New York, as he was detained by "this miserable business." What this "business" was, and how long he was detained, is not established.[61]

But his father-in-law at about the same time appears to have been uneasy about a certain relationship in the family, writing Hamilton on May 20 that he was pleased by Hamilton's "anxiety that the Harmony of the family should be compleat . . . since the receipt of yours and Angelica's letter announcing she is to come by land, I have written Philip and Sally {his son and daughter-in-law} to accompany their Sister home. Mrs. Schuyler before she left was persuaded that it could answer no one valuable purpose to continue unreconciled I encouraged the sentiment. And trust in a perfect reconciliation on her part."[62] Schuyler may have been referring to a reconciliation with Philip's wife, Sarah Rutsen Schuyler, with regard to whom earlier in the letter he expressed the hope that "a message from me . . . will afford her comfort & confidence in my friendly intentions towards her." If Schuyler was alluding to a need for reconciliation with Sarah, still another mystery is why Sarah required assurance of her father-in-law's friendly intentions.

Whatever transpired between Hamilton and Angelica during her six months' visit, it added to the strength of feeling they had for each other. While still at sea on the return voyage to England, she wrote Hamilton in a letter of November 5–7: "Me voilà mon très cher bien à mer {i.e., amer} et le pauvre coeur bien effligé de vous avoir quitté {Here am I my dearest very bitter and with a heavy heart to have left you}. I have almost vowed not to stay three weeks in England." Asking him to assure Betsey that she will return to take care of her, she instructs him: "Remember this also yourself my dearest Brother, may god bless and protect you, prays your ever affectionate Angelica ever ever yours . . ." She concludes: "adieu mine plus cher" (literally, "farewell, dearest face," but perhaps the French should be translated as "farewell my dearest one").[63]

On November 8, a day or two after her departure, Hamilton confided to her in a letter that he, Steuben, and his son Philip, without Betsey but "with her consent," had walked to the Battery to watch her ship depart "in full sail, swiftly bearing our loved friend from our embraces. Imagine what we felt. We gazed, we sighed, we *wept*. Some of us," he added, Betsey especially, "are and must continue inconsolable for your absence." And, again, there is a mysterious reference to yet another reconciliation involving Angelica's father. "I have no doubt," Hamilton assured her, "the arguments I have used with him will go far towards reconciling his mind to the unexpected step you took. I hope the enclosed letters may not be such as to give you pain."[64] Was the "unexpected step" her coming to the United States in May? Her return to her family in London could hardly have been "unexpected," but we have no clue as to what Hamilton was referring to that required him to negotiate a reconciliation between Angelica and her father.

Still another letter of November 7, a lengthy one from Steuben to Angelica, is mysterious in that it seems to conflict in certain respects with Hamilton's letter the following day. Steuben, to judge by his effusive declarations of love written in awkward French, was hardly less an admirer of Angelica than was Hamilton. Beginning "If your husband is often jealous, be very careful not to let him see this letter. But if he is as jealous as Othello, it would cause me to conceal the tender feelings with which you have inspired me. Yes, Madame, I seriously love you . . . if Church were an Italian, this opening would be sufficient to close the gap between the use of a dagger and . . . all these destructive means in the hands of a jealous person; since he is a good Englishman, give him a good beefsteak, a bottle of port, tire him during the day, call him 'my dear husband.' "

In the following pages, Steuben makes it clear that he was not with Hamilton at the Battery seeing her off. "But you are cruel," he continues, "you have left me without a farewell kiss. Here the Minister {Hamilton} flees with his sister-in-law—leaving me as the guardian of his lamenting wife; oh, what a situation I am in at this moment—I fear for you—I fear for Hamilton. His crying wife is distressed . . . I throw myself into an armchair—and I fall asleep. All is calm, Hamilton returns. She has left, he says. I awake. She has left, he is saying. The deceitful one—and without giving me a farewell kiss! . . . In a bad humor I take my hat and go to the Batteries. Hamilton accompanies me . . . Indeed there is the man who is taking away my charming friend. Did I say . . . Hamilton. Ah, Ah, yes, my lovable sister-in-law."[65]

Steuben's letter makes it clear that Hamilton, and Hamilton alone, was with Angelica when she boarded the ship taking her to England,

and that he may have been with her for some time before it sailed. Nor does the letter with its "I fear for you — I fear for Hamilton" establish that Betsey's distress was wholly the result of Angelica's departure, as indicated in Hamilton's letter, and not, at least in part, occasioned by the affair between her husband and her sister during the preceding six months.

Two months later, there was another letter from Hamilton and another slip. Writing Angelica on January 7, 1790, he incorrectly dated the letter 1789. One does not have to be a Freudian to suspect that the slip may have owed something to Hamilton's wish that the year 1789 with its lengthy visit from Angelica could be relived.[66] In her reply that February, she either did not notice or chose not to mention his mistake, instead writing: "I sometimes think you have now forgot me and that having seen me is like a dream you can scarcely believe . . . this idea . . . does not enliven my spirits."[67] Perhaps she was not entirely wrong about Hamilton, at the time the newly appointed Secretary of the Treasury, who was to become increasingly busy with budgets and reports, not to mention personal and political business, including his 1791–92 affair with Maria Reynolds. In January 1793, Angelica requested Betsey to "bid [Hamilton] write to me for he is too silent . . . pray, pray, pray, a letter by the next packet," signing herself "A sturdy Beggar."[68]

By March–April 1793, when more than three years had passed since their last meeting, Hamilton may have been having second thoughts about their relationship. In a pseudonymous article on America's foreign policy with regard to the expected war between Great Britain and France, he invoked images of a husband, wife, and mistress. "To speak figuratively," he began, a United States citizen "will regard his own country as a wife, to whom he is bound to be exclusively faithful and affectionate, and he will watch with a jealous attention every propensity of his heart to wander towards a foreign country, which he will regard as a mistress that may pervert his fidelity, and mar his happiness. Tis to be regretted, that there are persons among us, who appear to have a passion for a foreign mistress; as violent as it is irregular — and who, in the paroxysms of their love seem, perhaps without being themselves sensible of it, too ready to Sacrifice the real welfare of the political family to their partiality for the object of their tenderness."[69]

Hamilton was writing with Jefferson, whom he frequently accused of partiality to France, clearly in mind, but did such phrases as "mistress that may pervert his fidelity, and mar his happiness" unintentionally reveal some misgivings about his "partiality" for Angelica? Such questions cannot be given unequivocal answers, but Angelica by this time may have discerned diminishing passion in his feelings for her. After 1793 there are fewer letters to her from Hamilton, and more letters from her to Betsey.

But on her part there was no slackening of love. On July 4, 1793, she was urging Betsey to "embrace my dear Hamilton for me à la Francaise, and a month later she was referring to him as "petit Fripon {i.e., little rascal or rogue}."[70] Another term for him was "my Aimiable," which she used frequently in letters to Betsey. Hardly making a secret of her feelings for him, she wrote Betsey on July 30, 1794: "by my *Aimiable* you know that I mean your Husband, for I love him very much and if you were as generous as the old Romans, you would lend him to me for a little while."[71] In December, expecting to leave England "in about twelve months" and resume life in America, Angelica asked her sister whether there "is a hope of your going to New York to fix for life. My inclinations lead me to prefer New York, my affections for where you reside, but not altogether for my love to you, Eliza, my dear Hamilton has his share in this determination." In the version of this letter published by Hamilton's grandson, there is, once again, a deletion, the elimination of the "not" in "not altogether for my love to you."[72]

Following Hamilton's resignation as Secretary of the Treasury on January 31, 1795, three weeks after his fortieth birthday, Angelica wrote congratulating her sister "on his resignation & on your return to New York where I hope to pass with you the remainder of my days, that is if you will be so obliging as to permit my *Brother* to give me his society."[73] A year later, her departure for New York delayed, she scolded Hamilton, her "dear and naughty Brother," for not having sent her details of the house the Churches were to occupy.[74] A June 1796 letter from Hamilton to her, chiding Church "for his tardiness" in arranging the family's passage, ended "Yrs. as much as you desire,"[75] and not long after, he wrote her again that her return to the United States was one of his and Betsey's "dearest objects." In a playful as well as an affectionate mood, he teased her that Rufus King, who had just been appointed Minister Plenipotentiary to Great Britain, would "do nothing but after a previous consultation with you. What do you say to this Madame? Will it have no charm for your . . . ? But I had forgotten. You have none." Adding that King was accompanied by his "better self," who had "not the proverb in her favour *The nearer the bone* &c" but was nevertheless "sweet enough," he asked: "How do you manage to charm all that see you?"[76] He no doubt received a satisfying answer to that question when the Churches finally did arrive in New York in May 1797.

Almost eight years had passed since they last had seen each other, but if Hamilton's passion for his sister-in-law had cooled during that time, it did not stay chilled for long. His close friend Robert Troup, who was unable to persuade him to terminate the affair, wrote bitterly to King in May 1799: "Though not yet in the field of Mars he maintains an unequalled reputation for *gallantry* — such at least is the opinion entertained of him by the ladies. When I have more leisure, I will give you the history of Baron [Ciominie] & Mrs. Church as published by our Gallant General."[77] Two years later, Troup's disapproval of both Churches was even stronger. He wrote King on May 22, 1801: "There is as little respectibility attached to {Church} as to any man amongst us; and unfortunately the whole family are enveloped in such a cloud that they may enjoy nothing of esteem." Expressing sympathy for Catherine Church, "an aimiable girl" who because of her family "had little prospect of marrying in a suitable manner," Troup continued: "I believe I wrote you some time ago that I had ventured, at every risk, to communicate with a certain friend of ours on a certain subject. I fear not withstanding that things continue on the same course. You can hardly (word illegible) are the consequences of the general belief."[78]

Whether Burr, who fought a duel with Church on September 1, 1799, shared this "general belief" is not known, but he and his daughter, Theodosia, knew, or knew of, members of the Church family. In a letter to Theodosia on August 8, 1803, he informed her that Catherine Church Cruger, the "aimiable girl" whose marriage prospects were not viewed favorably by Troup, "has a son," and on March 28, 1804, he had news of two other Church children. "Ph. [Philip] Church and Miss Stewart, of Philadelphia, it is said," he reported correctly, "are to be married . . . Bunner and {Elizabeth} Church said to be mutually in love; on his part avowed, on hers not denied."[79] They, too, were eventually married.

Where Troup and others were disapproving of Hamilton's behavior,

John Adams was condemnatory. Adams never forgave Hamilton, even after his death, for, among other things, "the profligacy of his life — his fornications, adulteries, and his incests."[80] When he wrote these words, in September 1807, Hamilton had been dead three years. Angelica died in New York on March 13, 1814, and was buried, as was Hamilton, in Trinity Church. John Barker Church, back in London, his fortune much reduced, died on April 27, 1818. In death as in life, Alexander and Angelica remained close.

four

ENDINGS AND BEGINNINGS

On January 8, 1780, Hamilton wrote Laurens from Washington's headquarters at Morristown that although he was grateful to his friend for recommending him to Congress for appointment as American Minister at Versailles, he did not expect to be approved. "I am a stranger to this country," he confided. "I have no property here, no connections. If I have talents and integrity (as you say I have) these are justly deemed very spurious titles in these enlightened days." After he had enclosed the letter and signed it, he had a further confession to make: "In short Laurens I am disgusted with every thing in this world but yourself and *very* few more honest fellows and I have no other wish than as soon as possible to make a brilliant exit. 'Tis a weakness, but I feel I am not fit for this terrestrial country."[1]

At the time, Hamilton was courting Betsey, by whom, he wrote her sister Peggy a month later, he had been changed "into the veriest inamorato you perhaps ever saw."[2] Not long after, he was engaged to be married, an event that was to do more than marginally remedy his lack of property and connections. While his letter to Laurens was not the first to give evidence of a melancholic tendency, and it was not to be the last, the tone of the letter, taking into account his promising situation on the eve of his twenty-fifth birthday, is difficult to understand. What, then, might have been responsible for it?

The only clue Hamilton himself provided is in the preface to these remarks, which begins: "I have strongly solicited leave to go to the Southward. It could not be refused but arguments have been used to dissuade me from it, which however little weight they may have had in my judgement gave law to my feelings. I am chagrined and unhappy but I submit."[3] Hamilton had had to submit to Washington's rejection of his requests for a transfer to a field command, but this time, for reasons unknown, his request may have had special urgency. His dark mood may have been due in part to his expectation, borne out, that he would not receive the appointment to Versailles, and he also was disappointed in the reception accorded his proposals for reform of the government. There may have been other depressing developments, perhaps of a personal nature, in his life, but if there were, they were not, apparently, confided to Laurens.

His reference to "brilliant exit" in his letter to Laurens may have referred to a battlefield death similar to that which was to end Laurens's life at the age of twenty-eight on September 27, 1782, in an unnecessary skirmish with a British patrol. By then Hamilton's closest friend, Laurens in his short life had left Charleston, South Carolina, to study law in London, married there and conceived a child he was never to see, volunteered for the army and participated in major battles, been wounded in action, served as a diplomat in France, and joined Washington's family, where, in all probability, he met Hamilton. In the years that followed their meeting, he probably reciprocated in his letters those effusive expressions of affection Hamilton could address to men as well as women. "Cold in my professions, warm in [my] friendships," Hamilton began his letter specifying his requirements for a wife. "I wish, my Dear Laurens, it m(ight) be in my power, by action rather than words, (to) convince you that I love you. I shall only tell you that 'till you bade us Adieu, I hardly knew the value you had taught my heart to set upon you . . . You sh(ould) not have taken advantage of my sensibility to ste(al) into my affections without my consent. But as you have done it and as we are generally indulgent to those we love, I shall not scruple to pardon the fraud you have committed."[4] Even in an age, unlike the present one, when a man could address another in terms of endearment without running the risk of being thought sexually deviant, Hamilton was exceptional. As his grandson observed, "There was something almost feminine in Hamilton's gentleness and concern for the comfort and happiness of other people,"[5] and perhaps this quality was an important component.

But Hamilton's "gentleness" in his relationships with men, especially men who were close to his own age, was largely confined to those individuals who, like Laurens, were not rivals, or whom, like the British spy Major John André, he could admire without feeling threatened. When André, an aide to Sir Henry Clinton, the British commander in New York, was captured in September 1780 and sentenced to death, Hamilton in the course of several visits in less than a week developed an attachment to the condemned man that went beyond ordinary sympathy.[6] Four years older than Hamilton, André had been engaged in a mission related to Benedict Arnold's plans to seize West Point. Unwisely choosing to wear civilian clothes instead of a uniform, André had made himself ineligible for treatment as a prisoner of war. It is not certain that Hamilton wrote a letter to Clinton suggesting that André be traded, in effect, for Arnold,[7] but there is no question that he tried to persuade Washington to change the manner of execution from hanging to death by firing squad, in accordance with André's wishes. So strong was his attachment to André that in a letter to Betsey of October 1, 1780, he expressed the wish that he was "possessed of André's accomplishments for your sake, for I would wish to charm you in every sense."[8]

These accomplishments had included, he wrote Laurens on October 11, nine days after André was hanged, "an excellent understanding well improved by education and travel . . . a peculiar elegance of mind and manners, and the advantage of a pleasing person . . . a pretty taste for the fine arts . . . some proficiency in poe(try) music and painting. His knowledge appeared without ostentation, and embellished by a diffidence . . . His sentiments were elevated and inspired esteem, they had a softness that conciliated affection."[9] Had Hamilton admired André less, he might have accepted more easily Washington's decision to deny him the more honorable death he requested, and not observed to Betsey on October 2, the day André was hanged, that "some people are only sensible to motives of policy, and sometimes from a narrow disposition mistake it."[10] Betsey did not have to ask whom he had in mind.

Unlike Hamilton, Burr, who apparently took little or no notice of the André affair, was reserved in expressing, at least in writing, his admiration or affection for male friends. More secure and self-confident than Hamilton, he was less demonstrative and more apt to invoke loyalty where Hamilton spoke of love. Nevertheless, he was as capable of eloquence on those occasions when he wished to acknowledge a relationship that had special meaning for him. In June of 1776, when he was unhappy that he had not heard for some time from Matt Ogden and felt somewhat abandoned, he wrote his friend: "Should fortune ever frown upon you Matt.; should those you now call friends forsake you; should the clouds gather force on every side, and threaten to burst upon you; think then upon the man who never betrayed you . . . and if my heart, my life, or my fortune can assist you, it is yours."[11] It is not difficult to discern in these sentences that Burr was seeking, as well as giving, reassurance, but almost all his other letters suggest that his need for it was less than that of Hamilton. Perhaps his attachment to friends was also less. Hamilton, deeply moved by Laurens's untimely death, lamented the "loss of a friend I truly and most tenderly loved, and one of a very small number."[12] Burr left no record of his response to the death from yellow fever of Ogden, also untimely, at age thirty-seven in 1791.

Washington's "narrow disposition" toward the mode of André's death that Hamilton favored may have played a role in his resigning as his aide on February 10, 1781. By that time, bored with his staff duties, Hamilton may have been searching for reasons to resign. Perhaps he found them in Washington's "ill-humor"[13] and in other characteristics of the general that he disliked, and as a result he lost the ability to control his temper and "[be at all] times supple — {and} often dissemble."[14] His marriage two months earlier and the advantages it brought may have encouraged a belief that Washington, who was left at the time with only one other aide, needed him more than he needed Washington. Most biographers, however, including his grandson, have attributed his resignation to his "short-lived anger" and the impulsiveness of "his extreme youth" rather than to the imperiousness with which he charged Washington.[15]

The anger is all too apparent in Hamilton's subsequent letter to McHenry, in which he refers to Washington as "The Great Man" whose "Proposals of accomodation" intended to effect a reconciliation he rejected. "I pledge my honor to you," he continued, in his letter of February 18, two days after his resignation, "that he will find me inflexible . . . Without a shadow of reason and on the slightest ground, he charged me in the most affrontive manner with treating him with disrespect. I answered very decisively — 'Sir I am not conscious of it but since you thought it necessary to tell me so, we part.' " Hamilton closed his letter: "May the time come when [characters may] be known in their true light."[16]

The immediate cause of his resignation, according to Hamilton—Washington never wrote about the incident—was Washington's reaction to Hamilton's slight delay in attending a meeting with him on staff business at his headquarters in New Windsor, New York. En route to the general's room on the second floor, Hamilton had encountered Lafayette, with whom he conversed briefly. That pause of "about half a minute" so angered Washington that he accused Hamilton of keeping him "waiting at the head of the stairs these ten minutes." Following Hamilton's rejoinder, which concluded "we part," Washington responded, " 'very well Sir, if it be your choice' or something to this effect."[17]

The lines quoted above are taken from Hamilton's letter to his father-in-law written the same day as his letter to McHenry. Conscious that Schuyler would be unhappy with his decision to withdraw from Washington's family, Hamilton in this letter strikes a rather different note. Eager to justify himself, he assigns a context to his resignation that was absent in his letter to McHenry, one that dispels any suspicion that anger and impulsiveness on his part may have influenced his behavior. Lafayette, he began, would testify "how impatient" he was to join "The General" after an absence that "did not last two minutes." Seemingly unaware that he had contradicted his earlier statement that he had absented himself "about half a minute," and disregarding Washington's assertion that Hamilton had kept him waiting "ten minutes," he tried to assure Schuyler that he had not been rash either in resigning or in rejecting Washington's offer of an accommodation, and that these actions had not been motivated by resentment. Governed by "maxims I had long formed for the government of my own conduct," he wrote Schuyler, he had "always disliked the office of an Aide de Camp . . . as having in it a kind of personal dependence." Schuyler, knowing the place he held in Washington's confidence, would find it all "the more extraordinary . . . to learn that for three years past I have felt no friendship for him and have professed none. The truth is our own dispositions are the opposites of each other." Characterizing Washington as "a man to whom all the world is offering incense," a view of him with which Burr, as reported by Parton, would not have disagreed, Hamilton referred to this statement as the "key" with which Schuyler "will easily unlock the present mystery," and added, compounding the mystery: "At the end of the war I may say many things to you concerning which I shall impose upon myself 'till then an inviolable silence." What these "things" were, and whether or not he confided them to Schuyler, is not known.[18]

Despite Hamilton's assurance that he would continue to support "The General," whose "popularity {was} essential to the safety of America," Schuyler, "surprized and afflicted," urged his son-in-law to "sacrifice" his "laudable" maxims in favor of a reconciliation. "It is evident my Dear Sir," he wrote, "that the General conceived himself the Agressor, and that he quickly repented of the Insult . . . It falls to the lott of few men to pass thro life without one of those unguar[d]ed moments which wound the feelings of a friend; let us then impute them to the frailty of human nature, and with Sternes recording angel, drop a tear, and bloc It out of the page of life."[19] Hamilton was not moved, but he delayed his formal resignation from the family until April 30, presumably because of the absence or illness of Washington's other aides.

By that time, the Articles of Confederation had been ratified and the first government departments created. On these developments and in regard to financial policies to be pursued, his special interest, Hamilton had decided opinions, and he somehow found the time while serving on Washington's staff and preparing for Yorktown to express them in lengthy letters and articles. In 1779 or 1780, writing from Morristown to a person whose identity is uncertain but who was probably either Robert Morris or Philip Schuyler, Hamilton put forward views which he had held for some time and was to affirm often in the years ahead. Concerned about the depreciation of money and what could be done to establish a stable monetary system, he emphasized "the only plan that can preserve the currency is one that will make it the *immediate* interest of the monied men to cooperate with government in its support." He attached equal and related importance to the creation of an "American bank" to be called "The Bank of the United States," supported by a foreign loan and a stock subscription, with the government entitled to "share one half of the whole stock and profits of the Bank."[20]

On April 30, 1781, two months after Robert Morris had been made Superintendent of Finances, Hamilton wrote to him and again stressed the importance of a national bank. Displaying a familiarity with banking systems in Great Britain, France, and Holland, and making reference to banks in "Genoa, Venice, and Hamburg," he extolled the "tendency of a national bank . . . to increase public and private credit . . . Industry is increased, commodities are multiplied, agriculture and manufactures flourish . . . Great Britain is indebted {to banks} for the immense efforts she has been able to make in so many illustrious and successful wars." Elsewhere in his letter, discussing revenues and the substantial contribution made to them by taxes, Hamilton cited Massachusetts as a state "where taxation has been carried furthest {and where} Taxes were so heavy last year, that I am informed there were real marks of distress among some classes of the people."[21]

By July 12, when the first of six papers he wrote was published in a series called "The Continentalist," a national bank, the Bank of North America, was in place. Signing himself "A.B.," Hamilton occasionally resorted to capital letters when he wished to draw particular attention to a weakness of the existing governmental system or a threat to it.[22] In his articles that appeared beginning in July 1781 and ending on July 4, 1782, he repeatedly emphasized the evils of "A WANT OF POWER IN CONGRESS" and the consequences that followed when, as in Greece and other countries of the past and present, there was "JEALOUSY OF POWER" wielded by rulers. If the federal government "is too weak at first," he warned, "it will continually grow weaker . . . till it comes to a dissolution" or a combination of its enemies brings it "to a more SPEEDY AND VIOLENT END." Stressing that a weak central government would not be strong enough either to govern effectively or to safeguard the liberties of the people, he nevertheless recommended, six years before it became the most celebrated doctrine of the Constitution, a "distribution of the sovereign power, as to make it morally impossible for one part to gain an ascendancy over the others, or for the whole to be united in a scheme of usurpation."

Identifying "THE EVILS TO BE APPREHENDED" at a time when "Cornwallis [was] still formidable in Virginia," which included a depreciated currency, a deteriorating public credit, and an inadequate and poorly supplied army, he warned that nothing less was at stake than the possible loss of the war, following which the "affairs of America MAY CEASE TO BE OF PRIMARY IMPORTANCE." If this dire event was not to happen, the government must immediately be given "THE POWER OF REGULATING TRADE" and levying both a tax on land and a "moderate capitation tax" on every male inhabitant above fifteen years of age but excluding soldiers, seamen, day laborers, "cottagers and paupers." He also strongly urged that the states cede to the central government the right to tax imports, an act requiring, under the Articles of Confederation, the unanimous consent of all thirteen states. Although he and the others who favored the impost almost succeeded in gaining this consent, they were unable to persuade Rhode Island to join the other twelve states in approval, and in the end Virginia, which had originally agreed, reversed its vote. Not until Article I, section 8, and the rest of the Constitution was ratified did Congress have the power to tax imports.[23]

By July 4, 1782, when the last "Continentalist" article was published, Hamilton had almost completed his law study in Albany, and Burr had qualified for the New York bar. In late 1783, both men were establishing law practices and living in New York City, where, as a consequence of the departure of or disqualification of loyalist attorneys, lawyers were in short supply. In a matter of months, each had a respectable number of clients, Hamilton benefiting from legal business coming to him from relatives and family connections, including the Van Rensselaers and Church. But Hamilton characteristically gave some time to political affairs. The flood of litigation, much of it concerned with the validity of deeds, mortgages, contracts, and wills drawn up before or during the British occupation of the city, enabled both men to employ assistants to help with the mundane paperwork and simultaneously acquire sufficient training to qualify as lawyers.

New York City at this time was smaller than Philadelphia, whose population was approximately 41,520. But with the war over and the British gone, New York grew rapidly through the 1780s and 1790s. The city also was expanding in all directions. Despite frequent fires during and after the British occupation, some of which Angelica and others suspected had been set by disgruntled blacks, houses and other buildings west of Broadway (on old maps Broad Way and, before that, the Bloomingdale Road) reached north to Reade Street, almost a mile from Battery Park, in the area known today as TriBeCa, and on the east as far north as Broome Street on the Lower East Side. Houston Street, not quite two miles from the Battery, was the northern boundary by 1796, and both South Street, running parallel and close to the East River, and West Street, alongside the Hudson River, each seventy

feet wide, had been laid out and graded. A bridge over an outlet of
Collect Pond, once called Fresh Water Pond, near Canal Street, a
major source of New York's water in the early years, facilitated the
extension of Broadway northward.

The rapidly growing number of prospering merchants, lawyers,
speculators of all sorts, and other "monied" men tended to build their
homes and open offices on Wall Street, where the Hamiltons and the
Burrs lived for a time, Greenwich Street, Broadway, and the Battery.[24]
In November 1783, Hamilton and his family occupied a house at 57
Wall Street, next door to which, at 56, he had his office. Not far away,
also on Wall Street, were the Burrs, but they moved more frequently
than the Hamiltons; within a ten-year period they lived in houses on
Little Queen (now Cedar) Street, Maiden Lane, Broadway, and Partition (now Fulton) Street, in addition to Wall Street. By 1795, Burr
also had a country house, known as Richmond Hill, in the area of
Charlton and Varick streets, almost two miles from Battery Park and
not far north of the entrance to today's Holland Tunnel, in lower Manhattan. From its veranda he could shoot waterfowl making their way
to or from nearby ponds or the Hudson River, visible from his house.
When Hamilton later built a country house in Harlem, almost nine
miles from the Battery, which he called the Grange, taking for it the
name of his father's ancestral estate in Scotland, he, too, could hunt
on his land stretching to the Hudson River.

Richmond Hill and the Grange, the latter especially, were relatively
isolated. As late as 1800, only the lower end, or approximately two
miles, of Manhattan's total length of eleven and a half miles qualified
as more than sparsely settled. Dense woods above what is now Union
Square were home to a variety of animals and birds, including deer,
beaver, grouse, wild turkey, and small mammals of practically every
description. The Hudson and the East River teemed with salmon,
trout, shad, and almost all types of shellfish and crustaceans. As far
north as Albany, shad were so abundant that soldiers and workmen
being provided meals protested their daily diet of shad.

In 1782 and the years immediately after, Richmond Hill and the
Grange, not to mention the hunting and fishing opportunities they
afforded, were no more than dreams, if that. From May to the end of
October 1782, Hamilton at the urging of Robert Morris served as the
official receiver or commissioner of New York taxes, which were to

be collected for deposit in the Confederation treasury. The states combined were expected to raise a total of eight million dollars in specie, of which New York's share, Morris informed Hamilton, was "three hundred and seventy three thousand, five hundred and ninety eight dollars." As salary he was to be paid "one fourth pr Cent on the monies you receive" or, Hamilton calculated, not more than one hundred pounds ($3,000) during the war since he was certain that no more than forty thousand pounds would be collected and hardly more than double that after the war ended. Initially declining Morris's offer as not providing "sufficient inducement," Hamilton wrote from Albany that he would continue with his law studies.

Morris was not so easily dissuaded. In response to Hamilton's letter, Morris assured him that his salary would be based on the total amount assessed and not on the amount collected, and would therefore be approximately $934 ($11,208). And, he added, "the business might probably be effected without more attention than you can spare from your Studies." On this basis Hamilton undertook "the business," but there is no record that he was, in fact, paid the full amount he was due. He was able to collect only two percent of the state's quota, or about $6,250. Paltry as this contribution was, it was still better than that of six states, including Virginia, which paid nothing.[25]

As might be expected, Hamilton's failure to collect more than a fraction of what he himself had anticipated did nothing to weaken his conviction that the decentralized existing Confederation with its emphasis on states' rights could not survive for long. On June 17, he was wondering out loud in a letter to Morris "whether the services I can render in the present state of things will be equivalent for the compensation. The whole system (if it may be so called) of taxation in this state is radically vicious, burthensome to the people and unproductive to government."[26] While he did not resign as Continental receiver of New York taxes until October 30, by July he was addressing himself to other concerns, among which the most important was the need to amend the Articles of Confederation. On July 22 he was appointed one of four New York delegates to the Continental Congress, and took his seat November 25. By that time he not only had completed his law studies and served as tax collector for five months but also had written a manual for lawyers titled *Practical Proceedings in the Supreme Court of the State of New York*. He had also "been employed," he wrote Lafayette playfully in October or November, "for the last ten months in rocking the cradle" of baby Philip, his firstborn child, in addition to "studying the art of *fleecing* my neighbors."[27] He was not to demonstrate this "art," however, until much later, and he was never to display an aptitude for "fleecing" his clients similar to that of which Burr and other successful lawyers were accused.

In Congress and out of it, Hamilton stressed again and again the urgent need to increase the powers of the central government, restore public credit, and strengthen the financial system. Measures to effect these ends, he advised Washington early in 1783, were most critical in view of the rising discontent in the army among soldiers who had not been paid, and the resulting threat of mutiny. Not all historians agree that Hamilton favored using the army to force Congress to fund the debt and pay off all creditors, but he certainly "toyed with this notion" and perhaps did more than toy with it in his letter to Washington of February 13. "The claims of the army," he advised, "urged with moderation, but with firmness, may operate . . . to produce . . . the measures which the exigencies of affairs demand." Foremost among these "measures" was "the establishment of general funds, which alone can do justice to the creditors of the United States (of whom the army forms the most meritorious class) . . . and supply the future wants of government." To that end, he proposed that Washington should intervene "to bring order, perhaps even good, out of confusion."[28]

Hamilton may have anticipated Washington's disinclination personally to lead the army in what Washington believed might "be productive of Civil commotion and end in blood." Recommending to Washington that he "take direction" of the army's efforts to pressure Congress, Hamilton urged that this be done "by the intervention of confidential and prudent persons" rather than by Washington directly. Such intervention would enable Washington to "preserve the confidence of the army without losing that of the people. This will enable you in case of extremity to guide the torrent." Events took a more serious turn in March; two anonymous letters urged officers either to leave the army or to march on Congress, and Washington believed both letters had originated "in, or near Camp." For a time Washington himself was alarmed, but there was no "torrent," despite a mutiny by some units of General Anthony Wayne's troops in Lancaster, Pennsylvania, and the resulting move of Congress from Philadelphia to

Princeton. By December, unrest within the army had quieted sufficiently for Washington to take leave of his officers at Fraunces Tavern
in New York City. Hamilton, whom he had recently promoted to full
brevet colonel, a rank carrying with it no command, was present.[29]

Meanwhile, Burr, who did not attend the farewell, had taken a house
at 3 Wall Street, practically next door to City Hall. By that time, he
had been married more than a year to Theodosia, who in June 1783
had given birth to their daughter, Theodosia (henceforth identified as
Theo, to distinguish her from her mother), whose name, apparently,
had been chosen by Burr rather than by his wife, who had wished to
call her Sally after Burr's sister. Following their marriage, Theodosia's
two sons and three daughters were also part of the household, but
subsequently no mention is made of her three daughters and it is presumed that they died early. There may have been two stillborn children
and one other child born to the Burrs who was named Sally, but if so,
she did not survive long. By all accounts, Burr was a devoted father
to the two boys, sixteen-year-old Augustine James Frederick, usually
called Frederick, and fourteen-year-old John Bartow, commonly referred to as Bartow. In later years Burr and his daughter Theo were
closer to Bartow than to his brother.

Unlike Betsey Hamilton, whose interests were almost entirely domestic, Theodosia, to judge by her letters, read widely and had a number of interests outside the home.[30] But she apparently could not read
enough to satisfy her more widely read husband. With her and later
with their daughter, Theo, Burr frequently cast himself as a demanding
schoolmaster, and his letters to her sometimes were more reading lists
than personal communications. One letter of December 4, 1791, recommended no fewer than seven authors: Gibbon, Lemprière, Macbeau,
Plutarch, Beloe's *Herodotus*, Paley, and Plautus. Gibbon, presumably
the *Decline and Fall of the Roman Empire* (1776–88), was a special favorite
of his. He also gave her detailed instructions about how to read: "To
render any reading really amusing or in any degree instructive, you
should never pass a word you do not understand, or the name of a
person or place of which you have not some knowledge. You will say
that attention to such matters is too great an interruption. If so, do but
note them down on paper, and devote an hour particularly to them
when you have finished a chapter or come to a proper pause."[31]

Perhaps she did not need these instructions, however, since she was,

years before marrying Burr, already familiar with the writings of Voltaire, Rousseau, and Chesterfield, among others, regularly read newspapers, and had decided opinions about some of the personages who
commanded attention. For Catherine the Great she had nothing but
praise. "I wish I had wit and importance enough to write her a con-
gratulatory letter," she wrote her husband in Philadelphia on July 21,
1791. "The ladies should deify her, and consecrate a temple to her
praise . . . How enviable that she alone should be the avenger of her
sex's wrongs for so many ages past."[32]

She had much less admiration for Rousseau and Chesterfield. "If
Rousseau's ghost can reach this quarter of the globe," she admonished
Burr, "he will certainly haunt you." She probably was thinking more
of Chesterfield than of Rousseau when she added: "*Les foiblesses de
l'humanité*, is an easy apology; or rather, a license to practice intem-
perance, and is particularly agreeable and flattering to such practitioners, as it brings the most virtuous on a level with the vicious."[33] But
she was not wholly critical of Chesterfield, whose name, even then,
was associated with immorality. "The indulgence you applaud in Chesterfield," she wrote in a 1781 letter, "is the only part of his writings I
think reprehensible. Such lessons from so able a pen are dangerous to
a young mind, and ought never to be read till the judgment and heart
are established in virtue."[34]

She was referring to Chesterfield's *Letters to His Son and Others*, first
published in England in 1774 and in America five years later. She
could not have imagined that her gentle scolding of Burr for approving
Chesterfield's "indulgence" would contribute to the widespread belief
later that, as Parton put it, "Chesterfield himself was not a more con-
summate Chesterfieldian than Aaron Burr. The intrepidity, the self-
possession, the consideration for others, the pursuit of knowledge,
which Chesterfield commends, were all illustrated in the character of
the young American, who also availed himself of the *license* which that
perfect man of the world allowed himself, and recommended to his
son."[35] But was Burr a clone of Chesterfield and was Chesterfield an
example and exponent of "*license*"?

No one can dispute that there were similarities between Philip Dormer Stanhope, Fourth Earl of Chesterfield (1694–1773), and Burr, and
even more similarity in their reputations, but there were also important
differences. Burr, like Chesterfield, believed that proper manners and

behavior in public, or what Chesterfield spoke of as breeding, as opposed to vulgar display and indecorum, helped define the gentleman.
Burr, too, could be contemptuous of certain conventional values, and
be a sardonic and often cynical observer of the human scene, in the
privacy of his letters. Both believed that flattery would carry one further than frankness, and that a modest and even self-effacing pose was
always more effective than a display of arrogance or superiority. In a
different vein, there is clearly a Burr-like quality in the theme and even
the language of Chesterfield's reflection "I should have thought that
Lord — — —, at his age, and with his parts and address, need not have
been reduced to keeping an opera whore, in such a place as Paris,
where so many women of fashion generously serve as volunteers."[36]

Hamilton's biographers appear to have found no reference to Chesterfield in his correspondence, and although widely read, Hamilton
may not have been familiar with the *Letters*. Probably for that reason,
some similarities between his views and those of Chesterfield have not
been noticed, but a resemblance is by no means entirely absent. Hamilton's opinion of mankind was no better than Chesterfield's, and although he was less discreet, he was no less given to secrecy and
concealment. Nor would Chesterfield have disagreed with him about
the value of "delicacy," a word Chesterfield himself used in identifying
one of several desirable qualities in an individual; and he would not
have dissented from Hamilton's urging Laurens in the letter quoted
earlier to be at all "times supple — {and} often dissemble." But perhaps
the essential point to be made is that in Britain and France and increasingly in America in the latter half of the eighteenth century men
who were educated, rich or moderately affluent, sophisticated and upper class tended to view the world much the same way.

There was an important difference between Chesterfield and Hamilton on the one hand and Burr on the other. Chesterfield had little
respect for women apart from their sexual services. Writing his son in
1748: "Women . . . are only children of a larger growth, they have an
entertaining tattle and sometimes wit; but for solid, reasoning good-
sense, I never in my life knew one that had it . . . A man of sense only
trifles with them, plays with them, humours and flatters them, as he
does with a sprightly, forward child; but he neither consults them
about, nor trusts them with, serious matters; though he makes them
believe that he does both." Hamilton was less extreme, but when Cath-

erine Livingston asked him to become her "political correspondent," he did not take her altogether seriously. While he declared himself "perfectly willing to harmonize with your inclination," and added that he would refrain from "making the cynical inquiry, whether it proceed from sympathy in the concerns of the public, or merely from female curiosity," he quickly proceeded to flirt with her. He included a brief discussion of the war, but most of the letter and the subsequent one a month later dealt with his "motto" of "ALL FOR LOVE."[37] Hamilton may have discussed politics with Betsey, as he did with Angelica, but there is no evidence he consulted her or that Betsey shared many of his interests.

Burr, in sharp contrast to Chesterfield and to a lesser extent Hamilton, was that rarity in his day or in any day since, a man whose views about the role of women did not fall far short of those associated today with feminism. Apparently, he was the first American to praise and recommend to everyone Mary Wollstonecraft's *Vindication of the Rights of Woman*, published in 1792. On February 16, 1793, he wrote Theodosia from Philadelphia that he had heard the *Vindication* spoken of with "coldness," but as he read "with avidity and prepossession every thing written by a lady," he rushed to acquire it and spent almost an entire night reading it. "Be assured," he told his wife, "that your sex has in *her* an able advocate. It is, in my opinion, a work of genius." Only "ignorance or prejudice," he believed, kept the work from receiving the favorable attention it deserved.[38]

Vindication confirmed Burr's overall opinion of women, which was, as he wrote Theodosia a day before he praised the book, that "female intellectual powers" rarely were able to manifest themselves because of "errors of education, of prejudice, and of habit." Holding that men were "much more to blame than women" for this situation, he proceeded to observe: "Boys and girls are generally educated much the same way till they are eight or nine years of age, and it is admitted that girls make at least equal progress with the boys; generally, indeed, they make better. Why, then, has it never been thought worth the attempt to discover, by fair experiment, the particular age at which the male superiority becomes so evident?" Clearly, he did not believe there was such an age, in accordance with which his daughter Theo would be denied the opportunity to develop her "intellectual powers." Denouncing the "cursed effects of fashionable education! of which both

sexes are the advocates, and yours eminently the victims," Burr ended
his letter: "If I could foresee that Theo would become a *mere* fashionable woman, with all the attendent frivolity and vacuity of mind,
adorned with whatever grace and allurement, I would ernestly pray
God to take her forthwith hence."[39]

To avoid the necessity of such a dire prayer, Burr closely managed
his daughter's education even into the years of her marriage. She was
not only to read widely, like her mother and himself, but to study the
sciences, philosophy, languages, especially Greek, Latin, and French,
geography, and to keep a journal. Above all, she was to learn new
words daily, to improve her writing and style of expressing herself,
and to be careful of her diction, manners, and deportment. A stickler
for correct usage of English, Burr was forever criticizing Theo's grammar and punctuation, and could appear cold and unfeeling when the
occasion clearly called for more than pedantry. Thus, when his daughter wrote to him in Philadelphia, not long before Theodosia's death,
that "Ma begs you will omit the thoughts of leaving Congress to join
her in New York," he could not refrain from scolding her for writing
"omit" instead of *"abandon, relinquish, renounce,* or *abjure* the thoughts,
&c."* His letter of January 14, 1794, four months before Theodosia's
death, was entirely concerned with his daughter's use and misuse of
words.[40]

While Burr sometimes went to extremes in developing Theo's intellectual gifts, his general view of female capabilities was much closer to
the modern position than the views of Hamilton and Jefferson, both
of whom took some interest in their daughters' educations. Hamilton's
Angelica, his second oldest child, received instruction in French (perhaps because her aunt of the same name insisted upon it), and she
could play the harp and pianoforte as well as accompany her father in
song, but her other interests, like those of her mother, apparently were
of a domestic nature. Jefferson's daughters were better educated, but
only up to a point. Proud of his role as founder of the University of
Virginia, he nevertheless did not believe in "systematized schooling for
women," or in women participating in "the public meetings with men."
He felt strongly that women should confine themselves to domestic
affairs, stay at home as much as possible, give up dancing after marriage, and leave political affairs entirely to men. It need hardly be
added that he was opposed as well to other forms of female equality;

unlike Burr, as one of Jefferson's biographers noted, "he would liberate the human mind as long as it was male."[41]

The deaths of their wives left both men widowers with young children, and Burr remained unmarried for four decades. His years with Theodosia, not quite twelve in all, were relatively happy, to judge by their letters, but they were not without problems. She was ill much of the time and in more or less constant pain toward the end of her life. Burr consulted numerous physicians, including Benjamin Rush, but they could prescribe little more than ineffective diets and inadequate painkillers such as hemlock, which was recommended by Rush, and laudanum, an opium derivative, for Theodosia's stomach cancer. Undoubtedly, Burr was not the most faithful of husbands, but Theodosia, like Hamilton's Betsey, was an adoring wife, frequently addressing him as "my Aaron" or "my dearest Aaron" and signing herself *Toujours la votre.*" Her husband was, as usual, less effusive, but he occasionally ended his letters "Affectionately," although almost always signing them "A. Burr." She could be difficult, however, and often complained of his absences from home. On one occasion, in July 1791, when, in her view, he was unnecessarily away, she wrote him: "I don't understand why your lordship can't pay your obeisance at home in this four week vacation. I think I am entitled to a reason."[42]

She probably never received one from Burr, who apparently was in Albany. And he could be harsh, even cruel with her. A letter from her two weeks previous to the one quoted above provoked a response that began "your letter of the 15th of June . . . is truly one of the most stupid I had ever the honor to receive from you . . . If your pride is wounded by a Confession (as you term it) of the nature of that contained in this last letter, I should recommend to you to supress not only your Confessions but your letters."[43] In another letter he labeled as "bad taste" her "allusions to departed angels," and in other letters he was critical of her relatives, apart from her children, or expressed doubt that she was paying enough attention to Theo's study habits. Perhaps he sometimes believed that in her letters she was describing the supposed benefits of her medicines more often than she was taking them in the dosages prescribed, and he may have doubted that she was devoting to her health the care that it required if she ever was to make a full recovery.

Burr's two letters written shortly after her death on May 18, 1794, suggest that he was uncomfortable that he had not been with her when she died. Writing to his uncle Pierpont Edwards on May 24, he assured Edwards that letters he received a day or two prior to her death had indicated "she was easier & apparently better . . . for some weeks before. Indeed so sudden & unexpected was her death that no immediate danger was apprehended until the Morning" she died.[44] He struck a similar note in his letter to Timothy Edwards: "Though her situation had long been considered as helpless, yet no apprehension was entertained of any immediate danger until a few hours before her death." His daughter, he added, "though much afflicted and distressed, bears the stroke with more reason and firmness than could have been expected from her years."[45] Theo herself, who presumably was at her mother's bedside when she died, left no record of her feelings.

With Theodosia's death, the connection that already existed between Burr and Theo gradually developed into a relationship closer than almost any other known to us between a father and a daughter outside the pages of fiction. That relationship began, in a sense, as early as May 1785, when Theodosia wrote her husband: "Your dear little daughter"—she was not quite two—"seeks you twenty times a day calls you to your meals, and will not suffer your chair to be filled by any of the family."[46] But of the hundreds of surviving letters that passed between them, fewer than a score written by Burr before Theodosia's death, and none of Theo's written before 1802, were deemed worthy of preservation, or, alternatively, of public notice by Davis, who was the first to reproduce the correspondence.[47] Hence, the earliest letters known are from Theo to her stepbrother Bartow in the autumn of 1794, when she had joined her father in Philadelphia. In those letters, as in later ones to her father, Theo emerges from childhood to become a person in her own right, and also the most important woman in Burr's life. Since it would be premature to deal with those years and the unique mutual involvement between father and daughter that lasted until Theo's accidental death in early January 1813, the relationship between the two will be reserved for a later chapter. But it may be observed here that Burr in his long life probably never loved any woman, with the possible exception of his wife, as much as he loved his daughter, and probably she never loved any man, not excluding her husband, as much as she loved her father.

But in April 1784, when Burr was elected to his first political office,

Theo was less than a year old, and no one could have imagined such a relationship or that his career and her life would end as they did. Burr himself was only twenty-eight when he took his seat in the New York State Assembly, the lower house of the legislature, but he hardly permitted the office, which, it is worth noting, he had not sought, to divert him from his increasingly lucrative law practice. He was absent most of the time during the Assembly's first session, perhaps because its proceedings did not interest him much. He was present and active more during the second session, which began in January 1785, particularly in connection with two bills, one to abolish slavery in New York, the other to allow mechanics, as the word was understood in the 1780s (that is, artisans, or craftsmen, skilled workers, and small businessmen), to incorporate, a step that would afford them better protection of their earnings.

As originally introduced, the anti-slavery bill would have gradually granted freedom to those born in New York "of Negro, mulatto, Indian, and mustee (that is, mixed white and quadroon) blood."[48] Burr favored amending this measure to require the immediate freedom of all slaves of whatever color, legislation also favored by Hamilton. Both the measure and the amendment were rejected in favor of a bill prohibiting Negro voting or election to office, and fining both parties in a white–Negro marriage £100 each. When the senate insisted on fewer restrictions in the proposed legislation, the state's Council of Revision, the approval of which was required, rejected the measure, and the whole issue was dropped.

On the bill to incorporate the mechanics, Burr alone among New York City's nine assemblymen cast a negative vote. Why he did so, thereby running the risk of alienating potentially useful allies, is unknown. His opposition to the mechanics bill exposed him to the charge that he was hostile to the less affluent elements of society and partial to those who commanded wealth and influence. Thus he may have unwittingly set the stage for the doubts and suspicions of subsequent years that he was firmly attached to any political grouping, Republican or Federalist, and the belief instead that he was opportunistic and unprincipled.

From April 1785, when the Assembly adjourned, until the spring election of 1788, when he again was nominated for the Assembly but lost, he devoted himself to private affairs, mainly practicing law and, not unrelated to it, making money. But neither then nor later was his income from law and speculative enterprises, mainly in land, sufficient to pay for a lavish lifestyle that denied nothing to his family and friends, or to Burr himself. Like Hamilton and Jefferson, Burr liked to live well, and like them he was always in debt. But while all three lived beyond their means, Burr more than the others seemed often to be borrowing money from relatives, friends, and clients, and not always paying them back. His enemies and some hostile biographers have accused him of worse: susceptibility to bribery, stealing from his widowed and orphaned clients, and cheating his relatives until some of them faced bankruptcy and forfeiture of their property. No doubt, some of these charges were true, but true or not, they were and are widely believed, and are responsible, at least in part, for the opinion, as expressed by John Quincy Adams shortly after Burr's death, that his life, "take it altogether, was such as in any country of sound morals his friends would be desirous of burying in profound oblivion."[49]

Once again, however, a comparison of the treatment accorded Burr, on the one hand, and Hamilton and Jefferson, on the other, is instructive. Hamilton's enabling his relatives and friends to engage in what today is called insider trading in securities is more or less dismissed by one of his biographers with the statement that "the finance minister of purest integrity, at that period of American history, could not have escaped such charges."[50] Jefferson's reluctance to pay debts, to a large extent incurred by his borrowing money to indulge "himself like a prince," is seemingly justified by a sympathetic biographer as proceeding from confidence "that such was his right as an aristocrat of the spirit and valued servant to the state."[51] Certainly, Burr was no saint, but it is by no means clear that his ethics and behavior were significantly worse than those of some of his contemporaries whose reputations have suffered much less.

Even less clear are the reasons why he left no record of his views on most of the great issues of his day. Where Hamilton was outspoken in urging Congress to adopt this or that policy, and, in his pseudonymous articles, the public to follow suit, Burr was silent or, assuming he had definite opinions, kept them to himself or within the small circle of relatives and close friends. Though it is unlikely that letters and documents recording his views were destroyed by Matthew Davis, or somehow lost, that possibility cannot be ruled out. In any event, we do not know what he thought of the Pennsylvania mutiny of June 1783 that so agitated Hamilton, and we have no indication of his attitude toward the treaty of peace that formally ended the war in January 1784.[52] Events leading up to the Constitutional Convention of 1787, such as the Annapolis Convention and Shays' Rebellion of 1786–87, both of which significantly influenced most of the men who met in Philadelphia to amend the Articles of Confederation, apparently did not elicit any reaction from Burr. The Constitutional Convention itself and the unique system of government it created, about which almost all prominent and many not so prominent Americans of the time had an opinion, brought no response, or at least none that has survived on paper. Burr was to be quoted on the subject of the Constitution by Hamilton and others, but there is nothing in his own writing to indicate his position.

Rarely do we have to imagine where Hamilton stood on these and other issues. But his writings and services in the public interest, which not only far exceeded those of Burr but surpassed those of any contemporary, did not preclude his steady rise to eminence in the legal profession. His stress on the urgency of restoring credit by fully funding the federal and state debt was reflected in the suits he brought, which "were mostly for debt, he appearing oftenest for the plaintiff."[53] A related emphasis on property rights in general, the sanctity of contracts, and the supremacy of federal laws and treaties, found expression in his defending British and loyalist property holders against the efforts of patriot claimants, operating under state laws, to confiscate their holdings or to be reimbursed for damage incurred during the British occupation of New York City. Signing himself "Phocion,"[54] he was sharply critical of the state legislature for refusing to restore to British and loyalist owners property that had been confiscated, arguing that the refusal was a violation of the peace treaty.

It was in connection with this refusal, incorporated in a New York statute known as the Trespass Act, that Hamilton argued a case amply demonstrating his proficiencies as a lawyer but one that, like Burr's vote against the mechanics, was to be interpreted to his disadvantage in subsequent years. In *Rutgers v. Waddington*, heard by a seven-man Mayor's Court in the summer of 1784, Hamilton was the chief counsel for the British merchants Joshua Waddington and Evelyn Pierrepont, who had been sued for £8,000 ($240,000) in connection with damages they allegedly had caused to a commercial building occupied by them for five years. The plaintiff, Mrs. Elizabeth Rutgers, enjoyed the advantages of being a patriot, a widow, a New Yorker, and, seemingly, of having the Trespass Act altogether in her favor. Hamilton perhaps would not have undertaken the unpromising case had he felt less strongly about the underlying issue. The fundamental question raised by the proceedings was whether the State of New York could countermand and, in effect, nullify a treaty of the Confederation acting through Congress. If the court held for Rutgers in defiance of the treaty provision prohibiting future injury to those who had supported the British, Hamilton argued, according to his notes, that each state within the Confederation, and each county within a state, could go its own way without regard to the laws of the United States. Since treaties were part of that law, and required conformity to the international-law principle that the treaties of a country were binding upon its inhabitants, those provisions of the Trespass Act invoked by Rutgers could only be null and void.[55]

The decision of the Mayor's Court, largely favorable to Hamilton and his clients, did not settle the matter. The ruling was vehemently protested in the state legislature, the originator of the Trespass Act, and elsewhere, and was later used, together with statements he had made at the Constitutional Convention, to support the charge that Hamilton was an Anglophile. The Republicans, including Jefferson, were never to believe otherwise, but he and they lived to see the argument Hamilton had advanced in *Rutgers* become the keystone of the Constitution of the United States. The so-called Supremacy Clause in Article VI of the Constitution reads in part: "the laws of the United States . . . and all Treaties made, or which shall be made, under the Authority of the United States, shall be the supreme Law of the land; and the Judges in every State shall be bound thereby, any Thing in the Constitution or Laws of any State to the Contrary notwithstanding."

Burr's role as an attorney, meanwhile, was almost wholly confined to cases which had no bearing on constitutional issues. His appearances in court, sometimes with Hamilton, more often without him, occasionally against him, made a different impression than Hamilton's, if certain contemporary observers are to be believed. One such observer was Chancellor Kent, a close friend and dedicated admirer of Hamilton who disliked Burr, but when it came to the law he was capable of rendering an impartial judgment that did not spare Hamilton when he believed him to be in the wrong. Presumably, therefore, he was being objective if somewhat hyperbolic rather than simply biased when he declared that Hamilton in court "generally spoke with great earnestness and energy, and with Considerable, and sometimes vehement, gesture. His language was clear, nervous, and classical. He went to the foundation and reason of every doctrine which he examined."[56] Kent was not the only admirer of Hamilton's forensic ability; Burr, according to Davis, "accorded the palm of eloquence to General Hamilton, whom he frequently characterized as a man of strong and fertile imagination, of rhetorical and even poetical genius, and a powerful declaimer."[57]

Of Burr as an attorney, Kent observed that he was "acute, quick, terse, polished, sententious, and sometimes sarcastic . . . He seemed to disdain illustration and expansion, and confined himself with stringency to the point in debate."[58] Another observer who was also a lawyer remarked that Hamilton and Burr "were equal in reasoning powers and scholarship, but that Burr would say as much in half an hour as Hamilton in two."[59] Certainly, succinctness was one of Burr's characteristics, as illustrated in the statement he was alleged to have made that "the law is whatever is boldly asserted and plausibly maintained." As a biographer has noted, the remark has some of the quality of "judicial realism" associated more than one hundred years later with Associate Justice of the Supreme Court Oliver Wendell Holmes, Jr.[60]

Burr's legal fees, the total of which may have exceeded $10,000 ($120,000) annually, were regarded by some as exorbitant, especially in comparison with Hamilton's, but this opinion is largely based on what is known or surmised of their fees in the case of *Le Guen v. Gouverneur & Kemble* and one or two other cases. In the Le Guen litigation, Hamilton was paid $1,500 and Burr $2,900 of the $119,915 Le Guen was awarded, which, by today's standards, would not appear to be excessive. But that was not the only financial transaction between the three. Both Burr and Hamilton borrowed money from Le Guen, and although the exact amounts are unknown, their debts were never entirely repaid. When Hamilton died, he still owed Le Guen $3,000 ($36,000); as late as 1826, Le Guen's widow was trying to collect from Burr the unpaid balance of the money due her husband.[61]

The Le Guen case, one of Hamilton's and Burr's most important cases, had its ugly and, by modern standards, unethical, side. In what Hamilton's staunch friend Robert Troup called the "manner of his treating the witnesses & persecuting poor Gouverneur," Hamilton reminded his listeners that Gouverneur was Jewish by comparing him with Shylock. This tactic was deplored not only by Troup but by Kent, who also disapproved of the verdict, and, not surprisingly, by Gouverneur, who wrote Hamilton complaining of his efforts "to move the feelings of the jury" by comparing him "to the odious character of 'Shylock in the Play.'" Hardly less surprising was the assurance of Gouverneur, who died on February 28, 1800, four days after the final verdict of the Court of Errors, that despite being "extremely hurt . . . I am not without regard for you."[62]

There is no reason to believe that Hamilton, like many other Federalists, was anti-Semitic, but at times he did manifest ambivalence toward Jews, on one occasion identifying a "Mr. Ephraim Hart" in a letter to Betsey as "of the tribe of Benjamin or Judah," a wholly unnecessary characterization of Hart, who was delivering a letter from him in Albany.[63] But nothing in Hamilton's correspondence and papers suggests that he shared widespread Federalist beliefs that Jews invariably were Republicans, and as such were to be counted among "the filth of society," the description given to a Republican convention, a member of which was singled out as "a Jew, a Republican, and poor," by the rabidly Federalist Philadelphia *Gazette of the United States*, whose editor received financial support from Hamilton. There also is no evidence that Hamilton, or for that matter Burr, lent his efforts to abolishing laws which, by requiring political candidates to declare that they were Christians or, in some instances, Protestants, had the effect of denying Jews the right to hold elective public office. Such restrictions were eliminated early in Virginia, Pennsylvania, and New York, but the right of Jews to hold civil office in Maryland was not established until 1826, and in New Hampshire not until 1877.[64]

Assuming that Hamilton's courtroom performance in the Le Guen case did not reflect attitudes toward Jews common to many other Federalists, his "animosity and cruelty," in Troup's words, may have related to his early years in St. Croix. Following his mother's death, Hamilton had been cheated, he believed, of his pitiable inheritance by Rachel's former husband, John Michael Levine, his mother's few pos-

ENDINGS AND BEGINNINGS 101

sessions thereby going to Rachel and Levine's son, Peter. Le Guen, like Hamilton, had come to New York a stranger. He had entrusted a cargo of cotton and indigo to Gouverneur and Kemble, who were unable to dispose of it in New York and sold it to "three Spanish Jews" for resale in Europe. They, too, failed to find a market for the cargo, which, apparently, was inferior in quality to competing products. Reneging on their promise to pay Gouverneur and Kemble £48,966 ($1,468,980), they exposed the two, who had gained nothing, to a suit by Le Guen for the amount due. On the face of it, and in keeping, according to Kent and others, with conventional and customary commercial principles, Le Guen had no grounds for his suit and therefore was hardly entitled to an award two and one half times the sum contracted for by Gomez, Lopez, and Rivera, the "three Spanish Jews." One can do no more than speculate that Hamilton's exceptional "passion" and "heated" argument, as Troup termed the latter, which occupied two full days of the trial, may have owed something to his identification with a client who was a foreigner in America and who, Hamilton was able to convince the jury, had been cheated, Gouverneur somehow reminding him of Levine.

The verdict perhaps would have been against Le Guen if half the jurors in the two trials, the first of which awarded only a nominal amount, had not been Hamilton's clients in other cases. We do not hear that any of Burr's clients was a jury member, but that possibility cannot be entirely eliminated. Since no one challenged the verdict on the grounds of conflict of interest on the part of half the jurors, we can only imagine that ethical standards were somewhat different in the early days of the Republic. We can also believe, as the Le Guen case and Hamilton's services to John Barker Church testify, that adherence to such standards in and out of court does not serve to sharply differentiate Hamilton's ethics from those of Burr.

five

FROM CINCINNATI TO PHILADELPHIA

In the decade between 1785 and 1795, the years of Hamilton's greatest achievements, the United States went from a weak federation of thirteen states to a strong union of fifteen states which now included Vermont and Kentucky. During those ten years, the population increased from under three million to almost five million, with Americans in 1795 living in a country that stretched from the Canadian border in the north to Spanish Florida in the south. The Articles of Confederation had given way to the Constitution, the party system was almost in place, and George Washington was in the final years of his second term as President. Hamilton was involved in almost all these political developments, Burr in almost none. But in 1795 Hamilton resigned as Secretary of the Treasury, although he continued to wield influence, and Burr was still in the Senate, with two years left to serve. The future of both was promising, perhaps including even the Presidency, but both had already given evidence of the instability that was to contribute to their later undoing, Hamilton by becoming politically reckless and also vulnerable to scandal and blackmail, Burr by involving himself in a number of questionable political and financial schemes. As a consequence of these and other self-destructive acts, ten years after 1795 there was nothing left of the promise and, for Hamilton, nothing left of the future.

The decade began well for both men, if less well for the country. Legal business was booming, especially for Burr, who could give it more attention than Hamilton; he, as usual, was taking an active part in political affairs and pursuing one or two other interests. And there were welcome additions to both families. Angelica Hamilton, named for her aunt, arrived in September 1784, and two years later, in May 1786, Alexander became the third child and second son. In June 1785, Theo Burr celebrated her second birthday, and by that time, or not long after, she may have been followed by at least one sister who did not survive. But whether they related to law, politics, or procreation, almost all these activities of Hamilton and Burr during this period were carried on in New York City, until 1790 the temporary capital of the United States.

A concern of Hamilton not immediately shared by Burr was the establishment of a loose association of officers who had served in Washington's Army, subsequently known as the Society of the Cincinnati. Taking its name from Lucius Cincinnatus, the legendary fifth-century B.C. Roman patriot, part-time soldier, and sometime dictator who went from his farm to the battlefield and back again, the society was organized for fraternal purposes, which included providing some assistance to destitute former officers and their families. Another of its functions may have been to keep a watchful eye on developments threatening liberty and national unity. Any officer, American or foreign, who had served three years, or to the end of the war, was eligible for membership, and membership was to be hereditary. Certain individuals would also be eligible to become honorary members. The first meeting of the Cincinnati at New Windsor, Washington's former headquarters, in May 1783, was chaired by Steuben, but the first president could be none other than Washington.

Washington presided over the Cincinnati until his death in 1799, following which his place was taken by Hamilton, but he did so with misgivings. A hereditary military order with its connotations of military elitism was viewed with suspicion by some and with outright hostility by others. The critics included Jefferson, Adams, and John Jay, none of whom, it should be noted, were Revolutionary War veterans. Washington himself did not share their views, but he was sufficiently sensitive to the criticism that the society, in effect, would establish a hereditary aristocracy to urge at the first general meeting in Philadelphia in 1784 that the hereditary aspect of membership be abolished and the provision for honorary membership be reconsidered. His recommendations were accepted on that occasion, but subsequently several state branches of the Cincinnati, including the New York chapter, refused their assent, and since their approval was essential if the changes were to be adopted by the society itself, both hereditary and honorary membership remained in force. Hamilton, who was chairman of the New York chapter's committee considering the recommended changes, apparently lent his support to the proposed revisions, but he probably did so with little or no enthusiasm. In 1791, when he was vice president of the New York Cincinnati, his brother-in-law Stephen Van Rensselaer became an honorary member, and in 1799 he was followed by John Barker Church.[1]

While the society survived the deaths of the original members and their immediate male descendants, it did so in much attenuated form. But even in its best days it never exercised the influence of the American Legion, founded in Paris at the close of World War I.[2] Washington's and Hamilton's successors as the society's presidents never enjoyed the prestige of its first two leaders, and in at least one case a president did not possess even a symbolic representation of office until he had served a number of years. The Diamond Eagle, a decoration that was presented to Washington as first president of the Cincinnati by French naval officers, went to Hamilton following Washington's death in 1799. For reasons unknown, it was not entrusted to Hamilton's successor, Charles Cotesworth Pinckney, until August 7, 1811, at which time it was given to him by Hamilton's widow, Betsey.

Another minor mystery concerns Burr's failure to join the New York Society until some twenty years after it was founded. On July 1, 1803, the membership committee of the New York chapter unanimously approved his application for membership, and on July 4, the "Anniversary Meeting" of the New York Cincinnati unanimously endorsed the committee's action. Apparently, Hamilton was either absent when the vote was taken or was one of those favoring Burr's membership; whichever the case, it is all the more striking that the *American Citizen*, a New York newspaper almost always critical of Burr, should have published a comment on July 8 making use of the exact language Hamilton had employed almost thirty years earlier with reference to British officers in *The Farmer Refuted* of 1775. Stating flatly that Burr had seen "very little service" during the war, a point Hamilton had made when he was urging Federalists not to support Burr in the 1800–1 Presidential election, the newspaper added that following his retirement from the army Burr had lived in Paramus, "preferring the field of Venus to that of Mars."[3] The *American Citizen* did not need to identify as "Venus" Theodosia Prevost of Paramus, Burr's deceased wife. Burr's reaction to the belittling of his military career is not recorded.

Burr's reasons for delaying twenty years in applying for Cincinnati membership are not known. One can only speculate, in the absence of facts, that he had applied earlier and had been rejected, but he may also have decided not to seek membership until Washington was dead, perhaps anticipating that Washington would be as opposed to his application as he had been antagonistic to Burr's being appointed to other positions for which he had been recommended by Madison, Monroe, Adams, and others. Burr may have particularly remembered Washington's disinclination to support his promotion by Adams to brigadier general. Those tending to view Burr as always motivated by political considerations may suspect that his late interest in the Cincinnati, who in the main were Federalists, was related to the coming New York gubernatorial election, where, to win, he would need Federalist support. By July 1803, Burr knew that he would not be renominated by Republicans for a second term as Vice President. Clearly, his political prospects in the immediate future lay in New York, and there his success in any contest for office would depend on whether he received bipartisan support. Perhaps this was his motivation in joining the Cincinnati in 1803, perhaps not. We can only guess at his reasons both to delay his membership application for two decades and then, only months before he began his campaign for the New York governorship, to submit it.

But if Burr was not much interested in the Cincinnati in 1783 and, apparently, for twenty years thereafter, Hamilton, an active member, was much less involved in the society's activities than he was engaged in an effort to promote major revisions of the Articles of Confederation. His anonymous articles and private letters had long urged such changes, especially with regard to the powers of Congress, and in July 1782 he formally urged the New York State legislature to pass a resolution calling for a convention to amend the Articles. From November of that year until July 1783, when he was a New York delegate to Congress, he employed all his courtroom skills as a lawyer to persuade his fellow delegates to strengthen Confederation finances, but with little result. He was no more fortunate in protesting efforts of the states to disregard provisions of the Treaty of Peace designed to insure that American debts to British citizens were not set aside on legal grounds and prohibiting future confiscations of loyalist property. He also lent his support to a treaty provision which held that Congress should recommend to the states that British or loyalist property already confiscated be returned to the original owners. The resolution giving effect to his views was committed, that is, not brought up for consideration. Hamilton cast the only vote against commitment. It is highly probable that the rejection of his resolution played a role in his leaving Congress not long after, for Hamilton was never one to take defeat lightly.

Though absorbed in efforts to reform the system of government, he did not abandon his law practice, but at times it was distinctly secondary to his political interests. Neither did he neglect private business affairs, especially those of importance to his brother-in-law John Barker Church. Church, it appears, was largely responsible for Hamilton's lending his efforts to the organization of the Bank of New York in March 1784.[4] According to a history of the bank, Hamilton wrote its constitution, and although he may never have owned more than one share of the stock, he was a director of the bank until 1788 and had a major influence on its policies in the years that followed.

Hamilton's early involvement in establishing a bank in New York, which, unlike Philadelphia, had none in 1784, may have been at the behest of Church. A month before the bank was organized, Church, then in Paris, wrote Hamilton that in June or July he was bringing to New York a substantial portion of his wealth for investment in America. Seeking a "preponderance" in a commercial bank that would give him and his business partner, Jeremiah Wadsworth, effective control, but which Church hoped could be kept secret to avoid any challenge to his "preponderance," Church requested Hamilton to purchase for him 250 shares of new stock being issued by the Bank of North America in Philadelphia. Such stock could be sold, he further advised Hamilton, "if we want funds for a Bank that we may establish in New York."[5]

The "Bank" would have little chance to succeed if a rival bank catering to mainly upstate landed interests were to obtain an exclusive charter from the state legislature. When Hamilton learned that Chancellor Livingston and his associates had petitioned the legislature to charter the Bank of the State of New York, most of the capital of which was to be in land, he viewed the petition not only as a threat to the bank envisaged by Church and himself but as an effort to benefit landowners at the expense of the commercial and business class. Moving quickly when a group of New York City merchants floated a proposal "for a money bank," he joined them, viewing their effort as the opportunity for that "preponderance" of control Church and Wadsworth were seeking.

But first there was the problem of the votes to be allocated to each shareholder. The initial plan provided that holders of up to four shares would have one vote for each share, four votes for five shares, five votes for six shares, six votes for eight shares, and seven votes, the maximum, for ten shares or more. Manifestly, this voting limitation would have deprived Church and Wadsworth of effective control, leading Hamilton, as he wrote Church, "after meeting of some of the most influential characters [to] engage them so far to depart from this ground as to allow a vote of every five shares above ten."[6] By this device, Church and Wadsworth were able to accumulate a large number of shares and votes, one result of which was that Wadsworth was chosen president of the bank in 1785.

In certain respects, Hamilton's connection with the bank, and through him Church's and Wadsworth's, became even closer when he was appointed Secretary of the Treasury in 1789. At that time and after, the bank served as a depository for government funds, and it also made loans to the government, both of these services earning it interest which some regarded as overly generous. By buying and selling government securities, it was able to influence their market value, thereby often, although not always, benefiting the private holders of these securities, who included Church, Schuyler, and friends of Hamilton. While Hamilton's biographers have stressed that the bank's "ties with the federal government were inevitable with or without the Hamilton relationship," some of them have added, in the words of one, "all this does not deny that the Secretary gave the Bank preferential treatment."[7] Another has observed that "the Treasury's relations with the Bank of New York were eminently satisfactory: it served as the agent of the United States government in that city and Hamilton had been able to turn some profitable government business its way."[8] The bank, in its turn, "continuously gave him {legal} business."[9]

In 1792, Hamilton, still Secretary of the Treasury, persuaded the bank to finance a business venture of his own contriving for which he had great hopes. His hopes, in fact, were such that he gave the bank a "virtual guarantee" of the $5,000 ($60,000) loan which could "be construed as a perversion of his official powers."[10] As he envisaged this endeavor, it would be called the Society for Establishing Useful Manufactures, and would be principally located in the area that today is the vicinity of Paterson, New Jersey. Seven hundred acres at the Great Falls of the Passaic River were to be devoted to a cotton factory and other manufacturing enterprises, all of which would have access through the river and a series of canals to major waterways. For a variety of reasons, the society was not a success, and by 1796 it was functioning only in skeletal form.

Some may see a certain irony in Hamilton's failing in a business venture at a time when he was succeeding in organizing the nation's finances, but that is only one of many ironies in his life. Still another, far more significant irony arises from the contrast between his success in making the case for major changes in the Articles of Confederation and, later, the ratification of the Constitution, and his failure in the Convention to have a decisive influence in shaping the Constitution itself. One could cite additional instances of irony embedded in Hamilton's contradictory behavior, such as his preferring Jefferson in 1800–1 to Adams or Burr, Jefferson being the man he had earlier characterized as "the epicurean" pretending to be a stoic, "the concealed voluptuary" who affected "Quaker simplicity," and "Caesar *coyly* refusing the proffered diadem . . . but grasping the substance of imperial domination."[11]

But there were no ironies or contradictions in his determination to play an important role in the Annapolis Convention which convened on September 11, 1786, ostensibly to deal with problems of trade and commerce in the Confederation. By then it was clear to all but a few prominent Americans that the entire system of government would collapse if, as Madison put it, "the present anarchy of our commerce" was not remedied. In addition to printing with little restraint paper money which quickly lost value, states could and did levy heavier duties on each other's exports coming to their markets than on those of Great Britain and other countries. Some of them, moving in an opposite direction, prohibited the export of American products in British ships, whereas others imposed protective tariffs in an effort to promote their own manufactures. States lacking good harbors for ships carrying their goods were taxed by their more fortunately situated neighbors through which their commerce passed. New Jersey, one such state in that early period, Madison in a letter to Jefferson likened "to a cask tapped at both ends {by Philadelphia and New York}; and North Carolina, between Virginia and South Carolina, to a patient bleeding at both arms."[12]

The Confederation as a whole was hardly losing less blood in the form of accrued interest on the foreign and domestic debt, the former largely held by the French and the Dutch. In 1790 Hamilton in his first report as Secretary of the Treasury estimated the total foreign debt to be $10,070,307, with arrears of interest up to December 1789 an additional $1,640,071, for a total of $11,710,378 ($140,245,536). The domestic United States debt exclusive of state debts was judged to be $27,383,918, which, with accrued interest adding $13,030,168, made for a total of $40,414,086 ($484,969,032). Hamilton estimated the states' debts as $25,000,000, of which $21,500,000 was later funded, making a grand total of foreign, domestic, and state debt (taking the lower figure above as the more realistic) of $73,624,464 ($883,493,568). In modern terms, this estimated total debt in 1790–91 would not appear to be large, but for a new nation struggling to find its way a per capita debt of $18, or in today's terms $216, was a heavy burden. *

These financial difficulties were exacerbated by a banking crisis in 1784, and a mid-year American depression in 1786. Imports from Great Britain fell by a third, and although exports declined less, farmers, merchants, and others dependent on British trade were adversely affected. One consequence of such developments was a money shortage that greatly increased demands in some states for debt relief in the form of a moratorium on debts, and an increase in the supply of paper money. The conflict between debtors and creditors was particularly strong in Massachusetts, where, late in 1786, it culminated in numer-

---

* In 1790, daily wages in Philadelphia averaged $.50 ($6.00) for laborers and $1.01 ($12.12) for "artisans"; by 1800, laborers were averaging $1.00 ($12.00) and "artisans" $1.64 ($19.68) in daily wages. "Domestics" in 1800 were earning $1.00 ($12.00) per week. (Donald R. Adams, "Wage Rates in the Early National Period: Philadelphia, 1785–1830," *Journal of Economic History* XXVII: 3, September 1968.) In 1803, the Rufus Kings were able to hire "an accomplished French cook" for $20 per month. In 1791, the weekly wage of the highest ranking bookkeeper at the Bank of New York was $15 ($180), which was three times that of the bank's "porter," the lowest-paid employee. (Parmet, *200 Years of Looking Ahead*, 21.)

ous demonstrations, the most serious of which was Shays' Rebellion.

It was against this background that Virginia on January 21, 1786, invited the other twelve states to attend a commercial convention in Annapolis, Maryland. But of the nine states which agreed to be represented, only five sent delegates who arrived in time. Four of the six delegates chosen by the New York legislature did not appear, with the result that Hamilton and his friend Egbert Benson were the entire New York delegation when the convention opened on September 11.[13] With a total attendance of twelve delegates representing fewer than half the states, the convention had no choice but to adjourn *sine die* on September 14.

A major reason the Annapolis Convention did not arouse more interest was the suspicion that its principal supporters, notably Hamilton, Robert Morris, and Madison, secretly intended not to amend the Articles of Confederation but to create a new system of government in which the states would have a minor role. In this suspicion they were not far wrong with respect to Hamilton. In accordance with his precept that leaders of men should strive to shape events rather than to be shaped by them, Hamilton took steps to insure that the Annapolis meeting would deserve credit for at least one positive achievement. On September 15, he drafted a report to the legislatures of the five states represented urging a further meeting in May 1787 to deal with the "delicate and critical" situation of the country. Declining "an enumeration of those national circumstances {calling for} more enlarged powers {and attached to it} an useless intrusion of facts and observations," Hamilton, aware of the renewed controversies such an "enumeration" would generate, chose merely to summarize the problems that had brought him and the others to Annapolis as "serious . . . calling for the exertion of the united virtue and wisdom of all the members of the Confederacy." Accordingly, the report, adopted unanimously the following day, called on the states to send commissioners "to meet at Philadelphia on the second Monday in May next . . . to devise such further provisions as shall appear to them necessary to render the constitution of the Federal Government adequate to the exigencies of the Union."[14] With this declaration, the first step was taken toward convening the Constitutional Convention in 1787, termed by some historians the "Second American Revolution," and it also marked the beginning of Hamilton's rise to national prominence.

Perhaps this resolution of the Annapolis Convention would have been less welcome had it not coincided with growing unrest in Massachusetts and elsewhere. Even so, Congress was in no hurry to approve it. The resolution did not receive an endorsement (if a somewhat cautious one) until February 21, 1787, by which time four of the five states represented at Annapolis had named delegates to the convention in Philadelphia. New York, however, had still to take action.

From Hamilton's point of view, Shays' Rebellion, a protest against the taxes, high interest rates, and foreclosures that were impoverishing Massachusetts farmers, was a gift from heaven. Designating the uprising a rebellion, a somewhat exaggerated term first applied to it by an unknown observer, Hamilton and other supporters of law and order cited it again and again as evidence that the Confederation was about to give way to anarchy. Those who held this opinion urged Congress to take strong action, and in October 1786 Congress did so by authorizing General Henry Knox to raise an army of almost 1,400 men for service in Connecticut and Massachusetts, the most affected areas. But with the collapse in November of the insurrection in eastern Massachusetts, these soldiers were not required. Although the so-called rebellion was not finally over until February 1787, long before that date it was clear that the principal effect of the uprising would not be to benefit the debt-ridden farmers who had launched it but to promote attitudes favoring a thorough revision of the Articles of Confederation.

Certainly, this was not Daniel Shays's intention. Shays (1747–1825), an impoverished farmer in western Massachusetts, had risen from the ranks to become a captain in the Revolutionary War and fight at Bunker Hill, Ticonderoga, Saratoga, and Stony Point. The events that insured that his name would be remembered began in July 1786 when the Massachusetts legislature adjourned without addressing grievances brought to it by the state's farmers. Protests, some of them involving armed men, in Worcester, Northampton, Great Barrington, Springfield, and other towns, followed. The demonstration in Springfield, the site of a federal arsenal, was regarded as the most serious. Counting on reinforcements (which never arrived), Shays in January 1787 attempted to seize the arsenal, but he was routed by artillery, losing four of his men. His efforts elsewhere to defeat the state militia were equally unsuccessful, and in February, Shays, to avoid capture, fled to Vermont. Eventually, the Massachusetts legislature extended a pardon to all but a few of Shays's men, but it was not until June 13, 1788, that Shays himself was pardoned.[15]

A week later, New Hampshire, the ninth state required for its approval, ratified the Constitution, and the Constitution was formally adopted. But despite Hamilton's efforts in Philadelphia and New York, the Constitution was not the document he had wished it to be, and New York was not one of the nine states. For a time it was even uncertain that New York would send a delegation to Philadelphia, Governor Clinton and his allies being opposed to major changes in the existing form of government they rightly suspected would be enacted at Philadelphia. But skillful maneuvering in the Assembly, to which Hamilton had been elected, and in the Senate, where Schuyler was influential, resulted in the selection of a three-man delegation to attend the Constitutional Convention. In accordance with the unit rule for voting in Philadelphia, two of the three would determine the state's vote on any issue, and two members of the New York contingent, unhappily for Hamilton, were Clinton men almost certain not to support revisions of more than a minimal nature. His own vote and persuasive powers, he knew, would have no effect on the votes and views of his fellow New York delegates, but as he told himself and a few close friends, perhaps he could affect those of delegates from other states. Certainly he intended to try, as is manifest in his drawing up his own plan for the organization of the new government and presenting it to the Convention.

Robert Yates and John Lansing, the two Clintonites, were opposed not only to Hamilton's proposals but to the Virginia and New Jersey plans, the former favored by the more populous states, since it would give them greater representation in a one-chamber legislature based on population, and the latter by the states with a smaller number of citizens, since it proposed that each state regardless of size be represented equally. In the end, the compromises that were voted, but by narrow margins, were a bicameral legislature, the upper house or Senate to have two members for each state, the lower body or House of Representatives to have a membership based on population, which would include in the total number to be represented three-fifths of the slaves.

Yates (1758–1801), who had earlier opposed giving the federal government the right to collect impost duties, was later to come out against the state's ratifying the Constitution. Yet in 1789, supported by Hamilton and Burr, he ran against Clinton for governor, and in 1795, Clinton having declined nomination, he again sought the governorship, this time in a contest with John Jay. Consistently unlucky in politics, he lost both elections.

John Lansing (1754–1829?) was somewhat more fortunate in his political career. Six times elected to the state assembly, he was a member of Congress in 1784 and 1785, and later chief justice of the state's supreme court. In 1804 New York Republicans nominated him for governor, and with Hamilton urging Federalists to support him in the absence of a Federalist candidate, perhaps he would have won. But when Burr was nominated, he withdrew, thereby arousing the suspicions of Hamilton and others that he had done so in collusion with Burr. Lansing himself gave as the reason Clinton's demand that he, if elected with his support, would carry on certain Clinton policies. Whatever the truth of the matter, his refusal to run was not the last occasion for bafflement with which Lansing's biographers would be confronted. In December 1829, on his way to post a letter in New York City, Lansing disappeared and was not seen again. Many of his contemporaries believed he was murdered, but that has never been proven, or the possible murderer identified.

In 1787, his credentials and those of Yates as Clinton stalwarts could not be questioned. In no hurry to reach Philadelphia, Lansing did not arrive there until June 2, almost three weeks after the Convention was scheduled to begin and one week after it held its first session, on May 25. Nor did he or Yates, who made notes of the proceedings, stay until the end, September 17. Both left on July 5, never to return, because, they wrote Clinton, they had not been authorized by the state legislature to undertake the "subversion" of the existing constitution (i.e., the Articles of Confederation) and replace it with "a system of consolidated government." The "leading feature" of amendments to the Articles, they insisted in the letter, "ought to be the preservation of the individual states in their uncontrolled constitutional rights {in accordance with which} a mode might have been devised of granting to the Confederacy, the moneys arising from a general system of revenue, the power of regulating commerce and enforcing the observance of foreign treaties, and other necessary matters of less moment." Finally, they concluded in their letter, the country was too large and its population too diverse to be administered by a general government, without sacrifice of the liberties of its citizens.[16] This opinion in various renderings would be expressed again and again by Anti-Federalists during the ratification debates in the months ahead.

The departure from Philadelphia of Yates and Lansing left Hamilton the sole remaining New York delegate, and in that capacity he signed the Constitution on September 17. But he had been in Philadelphia intermittently after June 29, and despite claims that he "may almost be called the author of the Constitution,"[17] he was a far less important figure in the deliberations than Madison, who became the "Diarist" of the Convention, and James Wilson of Pennsylvania, both of whom had more of a claim than any of the other fifty-three delegates to be regarded as architects of the Constitution. It was no easy task to excel in this "assembly of demi-gods," as Jefferson described the Convention in writing to Adams.[18] The Virginia delegation was clearly the most distinguished, with, in addition to Washington and Madison, Edmund Randolph, the state's governor, who introduced the Virginia Plan of Government, and George Mason, author of the Virginia Bill of Rights; although neither signed the document, and Mason remained opposed to it, Randolph, who disliked the final draft, later supported ratification.

New Jersey was represented by, among others, William Paterson, with whom Burr had studied law and who had come to Theodosia's aid, the sponsor of the New Jersey Plan of Government, and Governor William Livingston, with whose daughter, Kitty, Hamilton had flirted eight years earlier. Robert Morris, the financier who was Hamilton's friend, and Gouverneur Morris, another of his friends, were, with eighty-one-year-old Benjamin Franklin, Convention members from Pennsylvania.[19] Joining them in Philadelphia's State House were South Carolina's Charles Cotesworth Pinckney, who as a Federalist was to run unsuccessfully against Burr for the Vice Presidency in 1800, and fail again in seeking the Presidency in 1804 and 1808; Rufus King, then of Massachusetts, who was to become Hamilton's close friend and in 1789 one of New York's first senators; and Elbridge Gerry, also of Massachusetts, who is mainly remembered in connection with the practice which took the name of gerrymander during his tenure as governor.* Neither he nor fifteen others signed the Constitution, to

---

* Gerrymander refers to the drawing of election districts to maximize the voting strength of a particular party. Contrary to popular belief, Gerry did not originate the practice.

which there was opposition even before the Convention met. Sam Adams of Massachusetts, the Revolutionary firebrand, and Virginia's Patrick Henry, whose cry "Give me liberty or give me death!" made him immortal, did not attend, Henry giving as his reason "I smelt a rat." Ambassadors Jefferson and Adams, in Paris and London, respectively, could not attend.

Hamilton undoubtedly had been waiting for the Virginia and New Jersey plans to be introduced — they were on May 29 and June 15 — before offering his own plan on June 18. His speech on that occasion, his only major address at the Convention, is far more reflective of his political philosophy than most of his other writings, including his essays in *The Federalist*, designed for public consumption. In his address to which was attached his own plan of government, he was free to outline, since the proceedings were secret, not only his core beliefs, which had both inspired and given direction to his political behavior, but also a skeletal form of the constitution which, he was convinced, was the necessary foundation of a stable political order in the United States. While his Plan of Union received, as he expected, little notice from the other delegates, it reminds us of how remote his thinking was from the main currents of American political thought in his time. Indeed, so clear is his own perception of the differences between his views and those of his fellow delegates, that one wonders what his motives were in presenting his plan.

Madison's and Yates's notes offer versions of what was said by Hamilton and other delegates that do not precisely agree, but they are not far apart in reporting Hamilton's introductory remarks in his speech of June 18.[20] Both have Hamilton beginning his five-hour-long speech by confiding that "his delicate situation with respect to his own state, to whose sentiments, as expressed by his colleagues, he could by no means accede," had hitherto caused him to be relatively silent, but the situation was too serious for him to refrain from speaking out. "I have well considered the subject," he continued, "and am convinced that no amendment of the Confederation can answer the purpose of a good government, so long as the state sovereignties do, in any shape, exist." The phrase "in any shape" must have aroused any delegates who were dozing, and perhaps when Hamilton reached that point in his speech, none were. From this preamble he proceeded to voice his objections to the Virginia and New Jersey plans, especially the latter.

Both plans, in his view, left the states with too much sovereignty and the central government with too little power.

Had he stopped after making a few more remarks about the necessity of shifting authority from the states to the central government, his subsequent plan for a new constitution might have received more consideration, although it would never, given the ideological composition of the Convention, have been approved. But he did not stop, and what he then went on to say was to be used against him by his political opponents in every election to the end of his life.

Since what he said has shadings and nuances in Yates's version of his speech that differ from those in Madison's account, relevant portions of both are given here to facilitate comparison:

Madison's notes
June 18, 1787

Hamilton. . . . This progress of the public mind led him to anticipate the time, when others as well as himself would join in the praise bestowed by Mr. Neckar on the British Constitution, namely, that it is the only Govt. in the world "which unites public strength with individual security."—In every community where industry is encouraged, there will be a division of it into the few & the many. Hence separate interests will arise. There will be debtors & Creditors &c. Give all power to the many, they will oppress the few. Give all power to the few they will oppress the many. Both therefore ought to have power, that each may defend itself agst. the other. To the want of this check we owe our paper money—instalment laws &c. To the proper adjustment of it the British owe the excellence of their Constitution. Their house of Lords is a most noble institution. Having nothing to hope for by a change, and a sufficient interest by means of their property, in being faith-

Yates's *Secret Debates*
June 18, 1787

Hamilton. . . . I believe the British government forms the best model the world ever produced, and such has been its progress in the minds of the many, that this truth gradually gains ground. This government has for its object public strength and individual security. It is said with us to be unattainable. If it was once formed it would maintain itself. All communities divide themselves into the few and the many. The first are the rich and well born, the other the mass of the people. The voice of the people has been said to be the voice of God; and, however generally this maxim has been quoted and believed, it is not true in fact. The people are turbulent and changing; they seldom judge or determine right. Give, therefore, to the first class a distinct, permanent share in the government. They will check the unsteadiness of the second, and, as they cannot receive any advantage by a change, they therefore will ever maintain good government. Can a democratic assembly, who an-

ful to the National interest, they form a permanent barrier agst. every pernicious innovation, whether attempted on the part of the Crown or of the Commons. [Max Farrand, ed., *The Records of the Federal Convention of 1787*, I, 288–89.]

nually revolve in the mass of the people, be supposed steadily to pursue the public good? Nothing but a permanent body can check the imprudence of democracy. Their turbulent and uncontrolling disposition requires checks. . . . It is admitted, that you cannot have a good executive upon a democratic plan. See the excellency of the British executive. He is placed above temptation. He can have no distinct interests from the public welfare. Nothing short of such an executive can be efficient. [Robert Yates, *Secret Proceedings and Debates of the Convention Assembled at Philadelphia in the Year 1787 for the Purpose of Forming the Constitution of the United States of America* (shortened title), second ed., 144–45.]

Hamiltonians have been as disturbed, and as apologetic, about this speech as about Hamilton's letter to Laurens outlining his requirements for a wife, which included "the larger stock of [fortune] the better," and some have gone so far, as they did earlier, to question whether he meant what he said. But even his friend and fellow delegate, Gouverneur Morris, did not doubt that Hamilton believed "a Republican Government to be radically defective (to) the British Constitution which I [i.e., Morris] consider as an Aristocracy in fact, though a monarchy in name."[21] James Fenimore Cooper (1785–1851), the novelist, later declared: "I have no doubt that Hamilton was, at heart, a monarchist."[22] If Cooper did not know Hamilton, which is possible, he may have heard this opinion expressed by his father, William Cooper, who was Hamilton's friend and client. Nor was Cooper alone in his view. Adams, Jefferson, and probably the majority of Anti-Federalists were inclined to agree.

But if he was not a monarchist, there can be no doubt that he favored a form of government with features similar to those of the monarchical system that had developed in Great Britain, but without its hereditary feature. Although he later denied it, writing in 1803 that "I never proposed either a president, or senator, for life,"[23] he endorsed the concept of the "supreme judicial authority," serving "during good behavior"; that is, for life, unless impeached. His own notes for his speech stress that the power of the aristocracy "should be permanent . . . so circumstanced that they can have no interest in a change . . . There ought to be a principle in government capable of resisting the popular current . . . there must be a permanent *will*."[24] In his remarks to the Convention as reported by Madison, and in his plan of government, he uses the word "permanent" once in connection with a reference to the British House of Lords, and in Yates's *Secret Proceedings* twice with regard to the place in government of "the rich and well born."[25] The only popularly elected body was to be the "Assembly," whose members were to serve three years, whereas the "supreme executive authority" and the senators were to be selected by "electors chosen for that purpose by the people." The person exercising supreme authority was to have, in addition to other executive powers, "a negative on all laws about to be passed — and the execution of all laws passed." Some of these provisions, substantially modified to make them more acceptable, became part of the Constitution, but Hamilton's emphasis on the need for permanence in government is found in the Constitution only in Article III, which stipulates that Supreme Court Justices and judges of the inferior courts of the United States shall serve for life.

Perhaps because his plan was coldly received and his influence overall was at a low ebb,[26] Hamilton left Philadelphia on June 29 for New York, one result of which, after the permanent departure of Yates and Lansing, was that at times there was no representative from New York at the Convention. Although it is not known for certain how many days after June 29 he was present in Philadelphia, there is evidence that he was there only a few times during July and August. He was at the Convention in September for the signing.

Well before that date, he had expressed his opposition to the Virginia Plan, which, in a comparison with the Articles of Confederation, he called "pork still, with a little change of the sauce."[27] He was even more critical of the New Jersey Plan with its emphasis on the sovereignty and the equal status of the smaller states. He voted against measures that directly or indirectly preserved the existing role of the states as such, and he did not support efforts to weaken executive authority by, for example, giving Congress the power to overrule a Presidential veto by a two-thirds vote. Hamilton had not favored any restriction of the veto power, but if there was to be one, he wanted a veto to be overruled by nothing less than a three-fourths vote, a provision which, in the end, was rejected by six states, as against four in favor of the measure, with one state divided. In Virginia, one of the four preferring a three-quarters vote to two-thirds, the delegation was split three to two, with Washington and Madison among the three in favor of three-quarters. The Maryland vote for two-thirds did not include delegate James McHenry, Hamilton's friend from the time they both had been members of Washington's family, who was later to serve as Hamilton's occasional physician and full-time spy within the Adams Administration.

The final session of the Convention marked the beginning of the long, intense, and sometimes acrimonious discussion of its accomplishments, with the focus often on the backgrounds and motivations of the men who met in Philadelphia in the hot summer of 1787. Today no one can doubt that the Constitution, which has been amended only twenty-six times in more than two centuries, was a remarkable achievement. But that fact does not address the question whether the delegates truly were selfless "demi-Gods," as Jefferson termed them, or "plain, honest men," in the words of Robert Morris, interested only in creating the best possible system of government for the country as it was in 1787.[28] Or were they, as some have argued, mainly well-to-do persons whose principal intention was to frame a Constitution that would protect their property and privileged position? There has not even been agreement on the role of individual delegates, particularly Hamilton, in creating the document. Thus, Hamilton's contribution has been viewed both as relatively minor, an opinion supported by comparing the Constitution with his plan of government,[29] and as greater than that of anyone else in Philadelphia, inasmuch as the Constitution "owes more to Hamilton for what it is, as we see it plain after almost 200 years, than it does to any other man, of his own time or since."[30] This, however, was not Hamilton's own evaluation of his contribution, to judge by his closing statement to the Convention that, while he favored approval of the Constitution, "no man's ideas were more remote from the plan than his own was known to be."[31] But he probably would have agreed with one of his biographers that he "did more than others to produce the Convention and to persuade the states to accept the Constitution."[32]

The most influential interpretation of the Constitution as written in 1787, at least until recently, has been that associated with Charles A. Beard, professor of history at Columbia University from 1904 to 1917. Beard's *An Economic Interpretation of the Constitution of the United States*, published in 1913, created a furor by arguing: "The overwhelming majority of members {of the Convention}, at least five-sixths, were immediately, directly, and personally interested in the outcome of their labors at Philadelphia, and were to a greater or lesser extent economic beneficiaries from the adoption of the Constitution."[33] Beard's sharp and seemingly well-documented rebuttal of the conventional wisdom of the time, the accepted truth of which was that the Founders were free of any wish to confer financial benefits on themselves, led to demands by some Columbia trustees and alumni that he resign. But they did not prevail, or prevent Beard's book from persuading a generation of American historians to pay more attention to economic influences before, during, and after the American Revolution, and to undertake a reappraisal of the Founding Fathers, including Hamilton.

Beard's *Interpretation* and works inspired by it have, in general, excluded Hamilton personally from membership in the Philadelphia "five-sixths" but not from making his relatives, especially Schuyler and Church, and some of his friends richer as a consequence of policies and practices he later followed as Secretary of the Treasury. Of Beard's thesis with regard to the other Convention delegates, the prevailing view of a later generation of historians is that he overstated his case by exaggerating the property holdings of those who assembled in Philadelphia, and minimizing the extent to which most Americans at that time owned some property and were middle-class. He also has been charged with emphasizing a class division — the enfranchised affluent generally being for adoption of the Constitution, and the less affluent, often without the vote, generally against it — that in reality did not exist. Perhaps the most extreme criticism of Beard and those sympathetic to his approach dismisses his *Interpretation* not merely as a flawed portrait of the Founders but as based on a " 'noble dream,' not history."[34]

This is not the place for a lengthy discussion of Beard's thesis or the dissenting views, but it may be appropriate to mention that many of his critics have missed his essential point and the context in which he was placing the economic interests represented at the Convention. Beard's basic argument was that most of the Founders were not "disinterested" men, because, taking account of the political realities upon which all stable governments must be founded, they could not be other than interested men. "As a group of doctrinaires," Beard wrote, by which term he meant idealists with lofty visions, "they would have failed miserably; but as practical men they were able to build the new government upon the only foundations which could be stable: fundamental economic interests."[35] Hamilton would not have disagreed with this statement, which serves to remind us, at least indirectly, that Beard was no vulgar Marxist making the case for an upper-class conspiracy in 1787. He was a historian, rarely found in universities eighty years ago, who wished to draw attention to the role of economic factors in American history. If he went to extremes in that direction with reference to the framing of the Constitution, he nevertheless made a vital as well as a unique contribution to American historiography. But whatever the final judgment on the motivations of the Founding Fathers, there can be little question that Hamilton will be remembered less for what he did at the Constitutional Convention in 1787 than for what he did in the months following to promote ratification of the Constitution. Despite his private opinion, according to Jefferson, that the Constitution was "a shilly-shally thing, of mere milk and water, which could not last, and was only good as a step to something better,"[36] and still later description of it in 1802 as a "frail and worthless fabric,"[37] he gave it his full support on his return from Philadelphia.

Of that support, there can be no doubt, as there is in the case of Burr. Neither the Convention nor the Constitution is discussed in Burr's papers and letters, and no biographer has been able to state with any certainty Burr's view of the Constitution and its adoption. Matthew Davis, his friend and first biographer, has him taking "a neutral stand," and Parton, whose biography contains no reference in the index to the Constitution, does not record that Burr in 1787 took any position on the outcome in Philadelphia.[38] But toward the end of his life, according to Parton, Burr, in referring to "the new system," of which he had "a low opinion, used language like this: 'When the Constitution was first formed,' said he, 'I predicted it would not last fifty years. I was mistaken. It will evidently last longer than that. But

I was mistaken only in point of *time*. The crash will *come*, but not quite
as soon as I thought.' "[39] Hamilton described Burr both as "equivocal"
in his attitude toward the Constitution and as labeling it in 1800 as "a
miserable paper machine." These words of Burr, as quoted by Hamilton, are not unlike those used by Hamilton himself in 1802, but Burr,
Hamilton also reported, added: "General, you are now at the head of
the Army . . . You have it in your powers to demolish it, and give us
a proper one, and you owe it to your friends and the country to do
it."[40]

Hamilton, of course, was concerned to demonstrate that Burr as late
as 1800 was no supporter of the Constitution or the political system it
had created. But had Burr made clear during the Convention his attitude toward it, and in later years testified to the benefits it had
brought the country, his enemies would have had a much more difficult
time establishing that he at any time had been ambivalent. It is not
even known that he read, much less had an opinion of, *The Federalist*,
regarded by some political scientists as America's greatest contribution
to political theory.[41]

The Federalist was a series of eighty-five articles written by Hamilton,
Madison, and Jay, almost all of them published in New York City
newspapers, designed to promote ratification of the Constitution by
New York. Without the approval of New York, the pivotal state in
terms of its geographical position and its importance as a center of
trade and commerce, it was apparent to the three authors, two of them
New Yorkers, that the Constitution was destined to fail. Addressed
"To the People of the State of New York," the first number of *The
Federalist* was published on October 27, 1787, and the last, one of the
final seven in a bound volume, on May 28, 1788. All of them were
signed "Publius," and although they were written in some haste over
a period of seven months, there is no evidence in their approximately
175,000 words that their composition was either hurried or harried.[42]

The intention of the papers, most of which were written by Hamilton
and Madison, was to anticipate the objections to the Constitution that
would be expressed by its Anti-Federalist opponents in the state conventions that were meeting to vote on ratification, some of which had
already appeared in print. To that end, it would not have been politic
for Hamilton to reveal anywhere in *The Federalist* the significant differences between the Constitution and his own plan of government,

and he did not do so. Aware that Jefferson, among others, although inclined to be friendly to the Constitution, did not like the provision enabling a President to serve more than one term of office, fearing it might lead to a permanent President or some form of monarchy, Hamilton could hardly have admitted that he had favored precisely that. The closest he came to indicating his displeasure with the outcome in Philadelphia was in *Federalist 85*, the concluding paper, in which he wrote: "I shall not dissemble, that I feel an intire confidence in the arguments, which recommend the proposed system to your adoption; and that I am unable to discern any real force in those by which it has been opposed. I am persuaded, that it is the best which our political situation, habits and opinions will admit, and superior to any the revolution has produced."

But "dissemble" he did to some extent by not expressing his conviction that the proposed "consolidated government," as it was often termed by Anti-Federalists, was not consolidated enough. In not making such a statement, however, Hamilton was only following his own earlier advice to Laurens of the need in politics to "[be at all] times supple — {and} often dissemble."[43]

In one of his most important contributions to *The Federalist*, Hamilton used all his intellectual and verbal skills to disarm critics who feared the judiciary would emerge as the most powerful branch of government. Yates, perhaps the most formidable and certainly the most far-seeing of these critics, had written articles signed "Brutus" arguing that the power of judicial review "will enable {the courts} to mold the government, into almost any shape they please . . . The supreme court then have a right, independent of the legislature, to give a construction of the constitution and every part of it, and there is no power provided in this system to correct their construction or do it away. If, therefore, the legislature pass any laws, inconsistent with the sense the judges put upon the constitution, they will declare it void and therefore in this respect their power is superior to that of the legislature."[44]

What Yates feared was altogether in keeping with the spirit of Hamilton's plan of government, but he would hardly have been wise to say so. Instead, in *Federalist 78*, Hamilton's reply to Yates and other Anti-Federalists equally apprehensive made a Rousseau-like distinction between the will of the legislature as reflected in its enactments and the will of the people as incorporated in the Constitution.[45] The conclusion that "the intention of the people {ought to be preferred to} the intention of their agents" does not "by any means suppose a superiority of the judicial to the legislative power. It only supposes that the power of the people is superior to both; and that where the will of the legislature declared in its statues, stands in opposition to that of the people declared in the constitution, the judges ought to be governed by the latter, rather than the former." Yates, of course, was prophetic in his assessment of the role of the judiciary and, in particular, the Supreme Court as it evolved under Chief Justice John Marshall and after. But it is worth noting that although judicial review is accepted without question today, it was extremely unpopular until well into the nineteenth century. Prior to the Civil War, only two acts of Congress were declared unconstitutional by the Supreme Court.

Occupied as he was in writing more than half of *The Federalist*, Hamilton still had time for other efforts in behalf of the Constitution, one of the most curious of which was a New York broadside of April 12, 1788. Addressed to "Friends and Countrymen," the broadside, which was probably inspired and may have been written by Hamilton, was an appeal for votes to elect Federalists to the state's ratifying convention, and it carried an assurance "that the SCOTSMEN of this City, with very few Exceptions, are friendly to the new plan of Government." Not all the fifty-five New Yorkers, among them Hamilton and fifteen residents of Albany who signed the broadside, were of Scottish origin, but it may have been the first printed election document in America issuing from, or directed to, a particular ethnic population or one based on country of origin.[46]

six

SEIZING THE DAY

The influence of *The Federalist* in the state ratifying conventions is difficult to assess. By May 28, 1788, when the last paper was published, eight states had supported ratification, but not the two most important, Virginia and New York. On June 26, by which time New Hampshire had qualified as the crucial ninth state required for the adoption of the Constitution, Virginia became the tenth state to vote for ratification, but it was another month before New York gave its approval. The votes in these states were also among the closest, the Virginia delegation dividing 89 to 79, that of New York 30 to 27.

Hamilton, who undoubtedly was disappointed at the closeness of the New York vote, did not agree with lamentations expressed at the Poughkeepsie convention over the absence from the Constitution of protections accorded rights and liberties. Whatever the effect of *The Federalist* in New York and Virginia, states that were home to all three of its authors, the vote in both owed much to accompanying resolutions recommending the speedy addition to the Constitution of a bill of rights. Neither Hamilton nor Madison believed there was need for such amendments, but Madison in response to Jefferson's urging supported what became the first ten amendments to the Constitution, the Bill of Rights, which were approved by Congress on September 25, 1789, and ratified on December 15, 1791.

Burr, who was drawing closer to the Clinton camp in New York politics in 1788, may or may not have been sympathetic to those who were demanding a bill of rights. Whatever his views at that time, not until July 29, 1788, when he knew the Constitution had been ratified by ten states, did he commit to paper his approval of it, but even at that late date it was a somewhat qualified approval. In a letter that dealt mainly with legal matters, Burr concluded: "I congratulate you on the adoption of the Constitution. I think it is a fortunate event and the only one which could have preserved peace; after the adoption by ten States, I think it became both politic and necessary that we should adopt it — It is highly probable that New York will be for some time the seat of the federal Government."[1] Burr here seems to be distancing himself from the whole issue of ratification with his "I congratulate you," which appears to imply that his correspondent, not he, had been in favor of the Constitution, and while he refers to its adoption as "a fortunate event" which has preserved peace, he nowhere makes a case for it in terms other than expediency.

Six days before he wrote this letter, New York City, which as a business and financial center had much to gain from the adoption of the Constitution, celebrated its ratification with a parade that began at ten in the morning and went on for hours. The parade, with sections honoring the ten states that had ratified the Constitution, was dominated by the frigate *Hamilton*, the "chief feature of the parade, but . . . only one of numerous displays proclaiming Hamilton's leadership in securing the new national government." Floats representing sailmakers, coopers, block- and pump-makers, tailors, brewers, furriers, hatters, shipwrights, printers, farmers, and others paid tribute to New York's sole signer of the Constitution, who, in effigy, was shown with "the new constitution in his right hand, and the (Articles of) Confederation in his left. Fame with a trumpet and laurels to crown him . . ."[2] One of those present and taking a prominent role was Nicholas Cruger, Hamilton's employer in St. Croix. One wonders whether Aaron Burr was present, and if so, what he made of New York's celebration of the man he thought of as a friend.

The cause of ratification had benefited greatly from common knowledge that, if the Constitution was approved, Washington would serve as the first President, but there was less agreement on the choice of Vice President. John Adams was strongly favored in New England and had support elsewhere, but not everyone was enthusiastic. Hamilton preferred Adams to Clinton, who was a possible choice, but neither then nor later did he ever regard Adams as anything more than an alternative to someone worse. In October 1788, six months before

Washington was inaugurated, Hamilton in a letter to Theodore Sedgwick expressed an early reservation about Adams that was to emerge in one form or another at every election up to and including the Presidential election of 1800, by which date Hamilton had come to view Adams with strong disfavor. His "only hesitation" regarding Adams, he wrote Sedgwick, who, like Adams, was from Massachusetts, "has arisen within a day or two; from a particular Gentleman that he is unfriendly in his sentiments to General Washington." Sedgwick in reply wrote Hamilton that while Adams "was formerly infinitely more democratical than at present" and had lacked the "unlimited confidence in the commander in chief as was then the disposition of congress," he was "a man of inconquerable intrepidity & of incorruptible integrity." Making it clear that Adams was not one of his "particular friends," Sedgwick added that he nevertheless held Adams in the "highest esteem."[3] Hamilton's response to this letter, if there was one, is not recorded, but Sedgwick may have succeeded more in lowering Hamilton's confidence in himself than in raising it with regard to Adams.

By early 1789, Adams was on Hamilton's mind much less than George Clinton, Governor of New York since 1777. Clinton, popularly regarded as the Anti-Federalist candidate, was running for a fifth term, but this time, with Federalists in the ascendancy, his victory was far from assured. It became even less certain when in February 1789 Robert Yates, by then a moderate Anti-Federalist, was selected as the opposition candidate by a mainly Federalist group of New Yorkers but one that included, in addition to Hamilton and Troup, Aaron Burr. Yates lost by the narrow margin of 429 votes, but the election is remembered less for that reason than for its marking the first and also the last time that Hamilton and Burr made common political cause. How closely they worked together is unknown.

Also unknown are Clinton's reasons for appointing Burr attorney general in September 1789. Perhaps he saw in Burr a possible future candidate against Schuyler, whose Senate term would end in 1791, and assumed that the appointment would promote that possibility. If, in fact, those were his expectations, he was not disappointed with respect to the Senate contest and its outcome, but he may have been less happy with some aspects of Burr's attorney generalship.

In that position Burr was empowered to make recommendations respecting changes in the state's civil and criminal laws, and also to serve as an ex-officio member of the state's Land Office Commission. In a little-noticed report of March 2, 1791, he made it clear that he did not endorse certain aspects of the criminal code which provided that "many kinds of forgery" were punishable by death. Noting that the British had made all varieties of forgery a capital offense, Burr maintained that "there are gradations in this crime, in regard both of the guilt of the offender, and of the injury and danger to the community." Following an analysis of the different types of forgery and their differing consequences, Burr held that "gradations in crime require corresponding gradations in punishments." He also observed that stealing horses, a "simple larceny" which in England until 1832 was punishable by death, was "so prevalent the punishment does not appear to have had, in any considerable degree, the effect either of deterring or reforming." Burr's recommended changes, which in general would have given a more humane direction to the state's criminal code, were not adopted.[4]

Not long after he submitted these recommendations, the Land Office Commission was given authority "to sell and dispose of any of the waste and unappropriated lands in this State, in such parcels, on such terms, and in such manner as they shall judge most conducive to the interest of this State."[5] The apparent intention of the enabling law was to promote settlement of wilderness areas in the north and west of the state, deemed to be uninhabited in keeping with the customary disregard, then and later, of Indian rights — Native Americans being, for all intents and purposes, non-persons. During the months that followed, the Commission sold 3,365,200 acres at a price of eight cents each to Alexander Macomb, a New York City speculator and friend of Hamilton with whom he was associated in other land ventures, one of which may have been a later sale to Church of an unknown number of Macomb's acres.[6] When newspapers reported that Macomb had purchased an area larger than Connecticut for what amounted to a pittance, rumors began to circulate that Clinton, Burr, and other commissions had profited from the sale. Nothing was ever proven in the course of the subsequent investigation, but Burr was never entirely exonerated in the public mind, although Commission records showed that he had not been present when the decision favoring Macomb had been made. Suspicions that he was not an innocent party flared again when he later bought 200,000 of Macomb's acres. Whatever the background of that transaction, he clearly was not an innocent party when he voted with other Commission members to establish a road system west of the Hudson River that benefited the interests of, among others, some of his relatives and friends.

To his credit, however, is the lack of any evidence that as attorney general he allowed his private legal affairs to intrude on the duties of his office. State regulations at that time permitted him to maintain his law practice while serving as New York's highest-ranking law-enforcement official, and almost certainly he had opportunities to bend the law in favor of his clients. Not even the most hostile biographers have been able to demonstrate that he did so.

Two weeks before Burr became attorney general, Hamilton had been appointed Secretary of the Treasury, the highest and most important office he was ever to hold. Recommended to Washington by Robert Morris and perhaps others, Hamilton now was in a position to pursue policies he had favored even before the Revolutionary War was concluded and the Constitution adopted. As early as September 1782, in an "Address to the Public Creditors in the State of New York," probably written by Hamilton but attributed at the time to Schuyler, he stressed that "a good opinion of public faith" was a requisite to "confidence in public securities," and that both required "a disposition to do justice to . . . creditors." The "Address" did not provide details, but there was no doubt that by "justice" he meant full payment to creditors of both national and state debts.[7]

Moving quickly to give effect to these views, Hamilton incorporated them in his first "Report on the Public Credit," submitted to Congress on January 14, 1790. While it is not known that he discussed his proposals with Angelica, whom he had seen off to England two months before, he may have done so, inasmuch as she was interested enough in his economic program to have sent him Adam Smith's *The Wealth of Nations*. But whether or not he discussed his plans with Angelica, he unfortunately discussed them with others who did not hesitate to transform themselves into "inside traders." Even before he became Secretary of the Treasury, speculators or their agents, some of whom may have had advance knowledge or at least heard rumors of his appointment, were beginning to buy up much depreciated federal and state indentures and other forms of debt paper at a fraction of their par value. Traveling by boat, carriage, and horseback to all parts of the country, Americans in search of these bargain-basement securities were joined by foreign speculators, and abroad, bankers in England and Holland were eagerly acquiring debt instruments and underwriting loans to the Treasury.

One of the most active participants in this debt market was William Constable, a friend and client of Hamilton who had helped launch the Bank of New York. As early as March 1789, one month before Washington's inauguration but several months after the new governmental system was no longer in doubt, Constable, writing to a friend, expressed his "firm conviction that the public Debt affords the greatest object of speculation . . . Funded Debt is now secure & in demand." To another correspondent the following November, Constable, predicting that the debt would recover its par value if it were funded at 6 percent, wrote that *"those in the secret"* should be careful to check the rise in value in order to insure "that a considerable portion of it may be got possession of by these and their friends . . . [we should endeavor to] keep the price down to 10/7 which will afford a profit of 100 per Cent in less than 3 years."[8]

One of *"those in the secret"* was, of course, Constable himself. A frequent guest at Hamilton's table, Constable, following one of these dinners, confided to Robert Morris: "I dined with Hamilton on Saturday. He is Strong in the faith of maintaining public Credit . . . I tried him on the subject of Indents — 'they must no doubt be funded tho it cannot be done immediately' was his remark, 'they must all be put upon a footing,' meaning these as well as the funded Debt. In short I am more & more of opinion that they are the best object at present."[9]

Another speculator even more *"in the secret"* was William Duer, a friend of Schuyler and Church who was a close associate of Hamilton in the Bank of New York, the Society for Useful Manufactures, and other enterprises. Betsey's cousin through marriage, Duer became Assistant Secretary of the Treasury within days of Hamilton's appointment. His principal interest, however, was not public finance but the buying and selling of securities on his own account, and investing in land. At first he was successful enough to amass a fortune, which enabled him to live "in the style of a nobleman," but he plunged heavily on the assumption that prices would continue to rise. When they began to fall in the spring of 1792, by which time Duer owed more than $200,000 ($2,400,000), he and other speculators were forced to sell at a loss, thereby further depressing the market, which led to the panic of 1792. As if this were not enough misfortune, on March 12, 1792, Duer, who had left the Treasury, was accused of having departed with a shortage in his accounts of $238,000 ($2,856,000). One day later, he was arrested and sent to prison, where, except for a short period of freedom obtained through Hamilton's intercession, he remained until his death in May 1799.

Despite this record, Hamilton, who made at least one other effort to secure Duer's release from prison, never relinquished his friendship for Duer. Why he continued the relationship is, as Mitchell comments, not easily "explainable. The secretary could not have been ignorant of Duer's speculation in the funds before he was named [assistant secretary] . . . and after he was in an official position that should have ended such indulgence." According to Julian Boyd, Hamilton continued to lend money to Duer, who "had long since hinted that he . . . might reveal much from a jail cell," during the years he was in prison. There is no way of knowing whether Boyd intended by this remark to convey the impression that blackmail was involved.[10]

Others "*in the secret*" no doubt included Schuyler and Church, who were large holders of securities, and several relatives and close friends of Hamilton. While there are no detailed records of financial transactions between Hamilton and his father-in-law, letters and other documents establish that before, during, and after he was Secretary of the Treasury, Hamilton was trading in securities, making investments, and buying and selling land and other property in behalf of Church. Some of Hamilton's friends did not approve of his business and other involvements with Church, but there is no evidence the relationship was ever the object of adverse comment in official government circles.

Constable, Schuyler, Church, and other debt holders could hardly have been happy when Hamilton's funding measures related to indebtedness of the states initially were rejected in the House of Representatives. The widespread speculation at the expense of those who had been forced to sell their bonds and indentures for a fraction of their original value touched a sensitive nerve, especially in the Southern states, and rekindled controversies that ratification of the Constitution was supposed to have put to rest. Jefferson, who had been appointed Secretary of State on September 26, 1789, and Madison, in

Congress—both believed that only the original holders of debt certificates should be paid their full value—led the fight against Federal
assumption of state debts, and for a time in April and May the issue
appeared to be in doubt. The most vehement of funding opponents
raised the specter of countless war veterans, widows, and orphans being forced into poverty because of having to pay the interest required
to reward speculators; others resorted to xenophobic and anti-Semitic
comments about bloodsucking foreign bankers, "Jew Brokers," and "a
host of uncircumcised Jews," the latter apparently a reference to brokers and bankers in general.[11] Still others cited the many examples of
persons in outlying areas of the country who, unaware of the funding
plan and probably of Hamilton as well, were still selling their debt
paper for a fraction of what it was eventually worth.

Despite these objections, the funding measure in its entirety probably would have been passed in some form, supported as it was by the
country's "monied men" and because of the need to reestablish public
credit. But a case can be made that final passage in the House of
Representatives of the funding bill on July 26, 1790, was made possible by Hamilton's agreeing to have the national capital on the Potomac rather than at Philadelphia, in return for Jefferson's and
Madison's using their influence to secure Southern votes for assumption. The story, which has been told many times, is that the bargain
was struck at a dinner party hosted by Jefferson and attended by
Hamilton and Madison a month or so earlier. According to Jefferson's
first version of that evening's conversation, Madison initially offered
to acquiesce in the House's reconsideration of the funding bill, which
had been rejected four times, but he indicated that he would not vote
either way. Hamilton or Madison then suggested moving the capital
to the Potomac, a step that would "soothe" the Southern states' feelings
about the "bitter pill" of assumption.

A quarter of a century later, Jefferson recalled the evening somewhat differently, on this occasion giving himself a less passive role and
claiming that the agreement encompassed making a site on the Potomac the permanent capital. As early as 1792, however, he had convinced himself, and tried to convince Washington, that, as he phrased
it in his letter to the President, he had been "duped" by Hamilton "and
made a tool for forwarding his schemes, not then sufficiently understood by me."[12] Jefferson's lack of understanding is difficult to credit

if only because neither Madison nor anyone else close to him ever indicated that their understanding was similarly impaired. He was not, after all, "a simple-minded rustic," in Bowers's words, "and his correspondence previous to the bargain shows that he had given serious consideration to Assumption. He had been in daily contact with Madison who led the fight against it."[13]

But whether Jefferson understood the assumption plan or not, it was approved, following which Hamilton turned his attention to a bill chartering the national bank, for which he had more or less been campaigning since the early 1780s. Washington, uncertain whether Congress had the power to establish a national bank, solicited written opinions from his cabinet. As may be expected, Jefferson, no friend of banks, was of the opinion that such a bank would be in violation of the Tenth Amendment, the adoption of which was still some months away, declaring: "The powers not delegated to the United States by the Constitution, nor prohibited by it to the States, are reserved to the States respectively, or to the people." Hamilton's view, which prevailed, was that the power to charter a bank was implied in the power granted to Congress under Article I, section 8, to raise taxes and regulate trade. Arguing that the government under the Constitution enjoyed "*implied* powers as well as *express* powers, and that the *former* are as effectually delegated as the *latter*," he concluded: "If the *end* be clearly comprehended within any of the specified powers, and if the measure have an obvious relation to that *end*, and is not forbidden by any particular provision of the Constitution, it may safely be deemed to come within the compass of the national authority." In 1819, fifteen years after Hamilton's death, his reasoning was followed closely by Chief Justice Marshall of the Supreme Court when, in *McCulloch v. Maryland*, he held for the Court that the doctrine of "implied powers" was subsumed in the Constitution.

Hamilton was less successful with the excise tax on distilled spirits that he recommended in his Second Report on the Public Credit in March 1791. The distilling of whiskey from grain by farmers and others in backwoods areas was not only a source of income but a convenient way of shipping that grain to markets which would otherwise be difficult to reach over nonexistent or bad roads; for these reasons the tax was bitterly resented. The unrest in parts of the South and in western Pennsylvania, the sections of the country most affected, was at first largely confined to peaceful demonstrations and protests, but then, in the summer of 1794, the Whisky Rebellion broke out in western Pennsylvania. Washington, prodded by Hamilton, who regarded the protesters as incipient revolutionaries, called out the militias of four states. Initially totaling 15,000 men, they were under the command of General Henry Lee, who in September, accompanied by Hamilton, proceeded to quell the rebellion and arrest its leaders. Judging by his letters to Angelica and others, Hamilton, who as Secretary of the Treasury was not required to join Lee on the march west, was happy to be away from Philadelphia and back in uniform. But perhaps he was not unaware that his personal response to the rebellion was somewhat exaggerated and might even make him look ridiculous in the eyes of some. Writing Angelica from Bedford, Pennsylvania, which he carefully noted in late October, was "205 miles westward of Philadelphia," he self-mockingly informed her that "I am . . . on my way to attack and subdue the wicked insurgents of the West . . . You must not take my being here for proof that I continue a quixot [i.e., a Don Quixote]."[14]

In his overwrought reaction to the upstart whisky farmers of western Pennsylvania, whom he characterized in a pseudonymous paper signed "Tully" as "Catalines" bent on treason,[15] one can detect Hamilton's indifference to the problems and needs of those who made their living on the land, as opposed to his solicitous regard for the welfare of the "monied men" who would finance and direct the industrial expansion of the United States in the years ahead. Nowhere is this more evident than in his Report on Manufactures of December 1791. As early as 1774, he had predicted that one consequence of a British boycott would be the establishment of "manufactures . . . [which] will pave the way still more to the future grandeur and glory of America,"[16] and now as Secretary of the Treasury he was in a position to recommend further steps to bring about that "grandeur and glory." Rejecting the argument that "agriculture is the most beneficial and productive object of human industry," the viewpoint of Jefferson, whom he did not name, and others who favored a mainly agrarian America, Hamilton insisted that agriculture was neither the most productive nor the most beneficial form of enterprise, although it had its uses, among them that of being "most conducive to the multiplication of the human species." Its "real interests," however, "will be advanced rather than injured, by the due encouragement of manufactures" by government, which, in addition to conferring other benefits, would promote "Additional employment to classes of the community not ordinarily engaged in the business."

It was in connection with this statement more than any other that Hamilton, in elaborating upon it, earned the reputation for coldness and cruel indifference that has followed him ever since. For one of the "classes" benefiting from "Additional employment" was composed of "women and children [who would be] rendered more useful, and the latter more early useful, by manufacturing establishments, than they would otherwise be. Of the number of persons employed in certain manufactories of Great Britain, it is computed that four-sevenths nearly are women and children; of whom the greater proportion are children, and many of them of a tender age." This was too much for Tench Cox, Hamilton's friend and for a time an assistant to him in the Treasury Department. Cox, who later joined the Anti-Federalists, wrote that under "the manufacturing system . . . you must . . . have a large proportion of the people converted into mere machines, ignorant, debauched, and brutal, that the surplus value of their labor of 12 or 14 hours a day, may go into the pockets and supply the luxuries of rich, commercial and manufacturing capitalists. I detest the system, and am grieved to see that so sensible a man as Mr. Hamilton can urge, in his report on American manufactures, their furnishing employment to *children*, as an argument for their being established in America."[17] As Vernon L. Parrington much later observed of Hamilton, "Something hard, almost brutal lurks in his thought—a note of intellectual arrogance, of cynical contempt."[18] Perhaps even those who accord Hamilton full honors for his unique achievements will not feel obliged to disagree with this judgment.

On these issues of public credit, the establishment of a national bank, the importance of manufacturers, and other matters that were occupying Hamilton's attention and that of Congress, we have only hints from Burr of his own position. His only surviving letter offering any comment was one to Sedgwick, and in that document his attitude is far from categorical. The "Bank," he wrote Sedgwick, who was serving in Congress on February 3, 1791, when the bill conferring a charter had not yet been passed, "is thought by our Speculators and Brokers, and indeed by many others, to be the most interesting object which can engage their time—to me the promised advantages appear prob-

lematic." In his letter Burr then referred to David Hume's essays on
"Money, on Interest, and on . . . Trade," which he had "not leisure to
turn to . . . nor even to read with proper attention the proposed establishment & am therefore wholly incompetent to give an opinion of its
merit . . . you . . . may Discern benefits not obvious to me and adapt
remedies to some Inconveniences . . . It certainly Deserves deliberate
Consideration — a Charter granted cannot be revoked."[19] Whatever his
attitude toward the future Bank of the United States, he apparently
did not purchase its stock, as did Church, Schuyler, and others. Over-
subscribed when it was issued in early July 1791, the stock in Philadelphia increased in price from $45 ($540) on July 13 to $185 ($1,920)
on August 27.

By that summer Burr had been in the Senate for almost six months,
his election in January owing indirectly but in no small part to Hamilton and his father-in-law. Two years earlier, in the first election to
choose New York's two senators, the state legislature had initially nominated Schuyler and, with Schuyler's approval, James Duane, Mayor
of New York City, who was related to the powerful Livingston family
by marriage. On the grounds that Duane's successor as mayor would
probably be "some very unfit character," whom he did not identify but
who may have been Burr, Hamilton successfully urged Schuyler, who
had drawn the short two-year term in the Senate, and other Federalists
to drop Duane and support Rufus King. King could hardly be regarded as a New Yorker, having moved to New York City from Massachusetts only the year before, but that, as it developed, was the least
of his and, more to the point, Hamilton's and Schuyler's problems. In
backing King for the Senate, to which he was elected, Hamilton alienated the Livingstons, thereby committing "one of the major blunders
of his career."[20] As if this were not enough insult to the Livingstons,
they were further injured when Jay, another friend and ally of Hamilton, was appointed Chief Justice of the Supreme Court in place of
Chancellor Livingston, who had wanted the post. Angry not only at
Hamilton but also at Schuyler, who was viewed by many Federalists
and Anti-Federalists alike as "the supple jack" of his son-in-law,[21] the
Livingstons abandoned them both and forged an alliance with Clinton,
thereby assuring Schuyler's defeat by Burr in 1791.

Burr, still attorney general in 1791 when he was elected to the Senate, apparently did not actively campaign against Schuyler. For reasons

having to do with the changing balance of political forces in New York, he did not have to make more than a minimal effort in appealing to voters. With the first election as governor of George Clinton in 1777, power had begun to shift from the landed aristocracy and the lords of the manor, among whom Schuyler was prominent, to "middling men" who had risen from modest beginnings to positions of eminence and, in many instances, wealth. Clinton was one of these men, whose "plain manners, blunt speech, and easy accessibility of a commoner" appealed to those of similar origin, and as such he was in sharp contrast to the imperious and often arrogant Schuyler, who made no pretense of liking, much less mixing with, common people. Born into an aristocratic and wealthy family, Schuyler never doubted that only people like himself were fit for office, and certainly not George Clinton, of whom he complained, following his defeat by Clinton in 1777, that the governor-elect's "family and connections do not entitle him to so distinguished an eminence." Boasting that no matter whom the voters chose for the state legislature, he "will command them all," Schuyler made certain of his "misfortune to be very generally disliked," a political friend of his commented in February 1793, "& I am afraid will ever remain so; I have long predicted that no party can flourish under his direction."[22] The future was to show he might also have predicted that no party under his son-in-law's direction was likely to flourish.

Burr probably had Hamilton in mind when he wrote Sedgwick shortly after his election: "I have reason to believe that my election will be unpleasing to several Persons now in Philada."[23] But he probably did not know the full extent of Hamilton's displeasure. Disturbed as he was by Schuyler's defeat, for which, he knew, some were holding him responsible, and aware that Burr's support among Federalists and Anti-Federalists was increasing, Hamilton's attitude toward the new senator was hardly improved by his being told by a friend that Burr "is avowedly your enemy, & stands pledged to his party, for a reign of indictive declamation against your measures." Duer, not yet in prison and not to be outdone, warned Hamilton that Burr in the Senate would oppose chartering a national bank and other legislation regarded by Hamilton as essential. But it remained for Robert Troup, who often functioned as Hamilton's Cassandra, to sound the loudest alarm: "We are going headlong into the bitterest opposition to the Gen'l Government. I pity you most sincerely, for I know you have not a wish but . . . is combined with the solid honor & interests of America. *Delenda est Carthago* [Carthage must be destroyed] is the maxim applied to your administration."[24]

This was not the way Chancellor Kent, customarily evenhanded, viewed Burr's election to the Senate, but he could hardly be heard over the chorus of voices forecasting gloom and doom. On January 16, 1791, informing a friend who favored Burr that he would "vote differently from what you would wish," Kent added that "things look auspicious for Mr. Burr. I shall not be grieved either way." Nor was he "grieved" when he wrote the same friend on January 27: "I congratulate you [on Burr's election] because I know it is agreeable to your wishes. I was of the minority. The objection of Schuyler's being related to the Secretary had weight with me, and I should have preferred another man equally attached to the administration of the government, if we could have found him . . . In this instance the objection was with me borne down by opposite objections of a more powerful nature. I saw the administration of Hamilton, which I conceive essential to the prosperity of the nation, violently opposed . . . To send a character, then, who has always been regarded as unfriendly to the government and its administration . . . and who himself possessed talents that might be exerted in a powerful degree, was with me to contradict the most obvious dictates of good policy . . . I therefore voted from the conviction of my judgment."[25] Unlike Hamilton's other friends, Kent chose to emphasize policy differences in preference to personalizing the election as a conflict between Hamilton and his enemies represented by Burr. Unfortunately, Kent's calm assessment did not succeed in cooling the fevered response of Hamilton and other Federalists to the election.

Their temperatures also may have owed something to an extended trip beginning in late May, allegedly devoted to botanical interests, that Jefferson and Madison made to New York City, Albany, Connecticut, Vermont, and Long Island. Jefferson later denied that he had seen Burr at that time, but it was widely believed that he had, and in addition to Burr, Clinton and Chancellor Livingston. Once again Troup sounded the alarm with another *Delenda est Carthago* letter, but probably Hamilton did not require much convincing to conclude that his enemies north and south were uniting against him. Jefferson, to be sure, was an amateur botanist, and a crop pest known as the "Hessian fly," allegedly brought to America by Hessian mercenaries during the Revolutionary War, was of interest to him as a planter and part-time natural scientist. Still, it is unlikely he would have absented himself from the State Department for more than a month merely to learn more about an insect, and for only that purpose taking Madison with him, not known to have fully shared this interest. According to Hamilton's son and biographer J. C. Hamilton, his father never doubted that Jefferson was hunting not the "Hessian fly" but allies from New York and New England in the coming Presidential election, among them Burr.

By 1796, the year that was to witness both the New York gubernatorial contest and the third Presidential election, Burr had joined Jefferson, in Hamilton's estimation, as a major threat to himself and to the Federalist cause. In New York, when Yates decided not to run against Clinton a second time, thereby disappointing Hamilton and Schuyler, some Federalists turned to Burr. Either because he was bored with his relatively minor role in the Senate, where he had barely served one year, or for reasons that remain unknown, Burr was receptive for a time to their overtures. At least two of those who approached him, seemingly unaware that Hamilton was fast becoming his enemy, tried to persuade Hamilton that Burr was hostile neither to the government nor to its Secretary of the Treasury; that, on the contrary, he was a supporter of both. Evaluating the situation that might follow Burr's defeating Clinton without any assistance from Hamilton, Isaac Ledyard wrote him on February 1: "If B. finally succeeds & you have not the merit of it, it will be an event extremely disagreeable to me." Ledyard reported to Hamilton that in an interview with Burr, Burr had expressed "a sincere regard for the safety and well being of the [Union]," and "an entire confidence in the wisdom & integrity of your designs, & a real personal friendship, & which he does not seem to suppose you doubt of, or that you ever will unless it may arise from meddling Interveners."[26]

The following day, another letter favoring Burr was sent to Hamilton which struck a different note. Urging the expediency of giving "him the Federal interest," James Watson, a director of the Bank of New York, cautioned Hamilton: "If that Interest is denied him, & he succeeds; will it not make him an enemy if he is not one now, or increase his enmity if he now has any? If he is refused this support,

& fails; will he not return to the senate of the United States, imbittered against the government & its ablest advocates? . . . If this aid is given him, & he fails, will it not serve to moderate his conduct, or rather to bind him by the ties of interest & gratitude to his supporters?" Watson then made a point that might have been taken up, but was not, by those at that time and since who have censured Burr for his lack of ideological conviction and party commitment. "I shall only add," he concluded his letter, "that the cautious distance observed by this gentleman, towards all parties, however exceptional in a politician may be a real merit in a Governor."[27]

Far from convinced, Hamilton prevailed on Jay to become the Federalist candidate for governor, with Stephen Van Rensselaer as his running mate. Burr consequently withdrew his name from consideration and did so, Ledyard hastened to assure Hamilton, without any ill will. Burr was aware, Ledyard wrote Hamilton on February 17, that as an "advocate" for Jay he could hardly contribute to the "advancement" of Burr, who, he added, "has reasons to be unwilling to offend even me by offending you on whose account principally he knows I have been his friend . . . I shall therefore presume to act as a bond of union between you until I have the honor to hear further from you."[28]

If Ledyard and Watson persuaded Hamilton to entertain second thoughts about Burr, which is as improbable as their causing him to adopt a more favorable view of Jefferson, any such tendency in Hamilton could hardly have survived Burr's role in the bitterly disputed vote count that gave the election, for the sixth time, to George Clinton, sometimes referred to as the "Old Incumbent," then a mere (by modern standards) fifty-three years of age. A month or so after polling began on April 24, a committee of twelve canvassers, six from the Assembly and six from the Senate, met to count ballots. As some had anticipated, the canvassers, most of whom were Clintonians, voted seven to four to disallow on technical grounds the ballots from Otsego, Clinton, and Tioga counties, most of them marked for Jay, according to the minority canvassers—the effect of which was to decide the election in Clinton's favor. The decision not to count the ballots was based on the alleged violation of the law requiring ballots in each county to be delivered to the sheriff for transmission by him to the secretary of state and, eventually, the canvassers.

In Otsego, a county dominated by Federalists under William Cooper's leadership, the ballots had been handled by a man whose commission as sheriff had expired two months before the election. In Tioga and Clinton counties, the sheriffs had entrusted ballots to men who were not sheriffs or even deputy sheriffs. Although it is not known for certain that, had these ballots been counted, Jay would have won the election, the ballots having been burned shortly after the canvassers disallowed them, Federalists believed that Jay would have won easily with a majority of at least five hundred votes in Otsego alone. Perhaps, had Clinton been elected by a substantial margin instead of 108 votes, the controversy would have ended when the canvassers made their decision. The dispute also might have terminated had the canvassers revealed that Cooper in Otsego "was such a Jay partisan that he had threatened to ruin tenants and debtors if they did not vote as told."[29] Whatever might have been, the canvassers' decision in early June set off a controversy that continued through the summer.

Not long after it began, Burr against his wishes was drawn into it. He and Rufus King, New York's other senator, were asked by the canvassers for their opinion, which, had it been unanimous, would have carried weight. But they could agree only on the admissibility of the Clinton County votes, the least important. When they knew they were irreconcilably divided with respect to the other two counties, Burr urged King to join him in declining to offer any opinion. King, perhaps because he, Hamilton, and Schuyler realized that a refusal to take a position would defuse the controversy and with it the opportunity to challenge Clinton and weaken Burr's Federalist support, insisted on submitting a written opinion. Burr had no option but to follow suit, which he did on June 8.

Although no one, not even biographers friendly to Burr, has maintained that he distinguished himself in his brief upholding the decision of the canvassers, no partisan of Hamilton has suggested that King, who admittedly had the better case, as a Federalist and ally of Hamilton, could have arrived at any other conclusion. Burr's opinion, based wholly on technicalities, did not question the validity of the ballots as such, only the manner in which they had been collected and forwarded to the canvassers. This argument was easily discounted by King, who insisted that while the Otsego sheriff "when he received and delivered the notes to his deputy was not *dejure*, he was *defacto* sheriff of Otsego."[30] Although King's legalistic analysis of the controversy was hardly incendiary, Hamilton was concerned that it would fuel agitation that might end in violence. "I believe you are right," he wrote King on June 28, "but I am not without apprehension that a ferment may be raised which may not be allayed when you wish it . . . Some folks are talking of Conventions and the Bayonet. But the case will justify neither a resort to first principles or to violence. Some amendments of your election law and possibly the impeachment of some of the Canvassers who have given proofs of *premeditated* partiality will be very well . . . beware of extremes!"[31] When he wrote these cautionary words, Hamilton may well have had one eye on his letter paper and the other on the "extremes," already in progress, of the backwoods distillers in western Pennsylvania. Perhaps he was thinking of them still when he wrote King almost a month later: "I do not feel it right or expedient to attempt to reverse the decision by any means not known to the Constitution or Laws. The precedent may suit us to day; But tomorrow we may rue its abuse . . . Mens minds are too much unsettled every where at the present juncture. Let us endeavour to settle them & not to set them more afloat."[32]

Burr himself was occupied in defending his decision in favor of the canvassers up to and including a meeting of the legislature in November to finally settle the matter, which it did in favor of the canvassers. He solicited opinions from those he supposed would give him support, but not all of them fulfilled his expectations. Those who did included Attorney General Edmund Randolph and Burr's uncle Pierpont Edwards, but not Theodore Sedgwick, of whom Burr had been confident, or John Trumbull, one of the so-called Connecticut Wits, among others. With his reputation at stake, and in September an interest in the Vice Presidential nomination at risk, Burr defended himself as best he could from charges he had acted in collusion with the Clintonians, but Randolph, Edwards, and the others who came to his assistance were not sufficient to clear his name. As a consequence, any hope he had of becoming a candidate for the Vice Presidency ended well before Clinton, who let it be known that he was interested in the position, was nominated on October 16. When the electoral college met in December, it voted unanimously for Washington, as had been expected. With seventy-seven second-ballot votes, Adams would continue as Vice President, but Clinton's fifty votes, which included all of New York's and almost all of Virginia's and North Carolina's, could be seen as evidence that party lines were becoming stronger even before the expiration of Washington's Presidency. Perhaps had Burr not stood aside, he would have received more than the one vote he was given by South Carolina. Whether as his reward for having done so, or in an effort to reduce his political visibility, Clinton in early October nominated him to be an associate justice of the New York supreme court. Whatever the governor's motivation, Burr declined the appointment.

Hamilton, far from appeased by the successive defeats accorded Burr's aspirations to become New York's governor and the nation's Vice President, began writing in September the series of letters vilifying Burr that were to continue at intervals for twelve years. A remarkable feature of these letters is that almost none refer to Burr's role in the Senate, which had little resemblance to the "Delenda est Carthago" behavior Troup and other friends of Hamilton had predicted. In the three Congresses of 1791–97 in which he served, Burr usually voted with the Republican minority, on the losing side, but there were no longer any issues to be decided comparable to those of the first Congress, which had addressed Hamilton's funding and assumption measures. The committees of which he was a member, almost sixty in all, mainly dealt with internal government affairs such as organization and frontier defense, the judiciary, government salaries and pensions, relations with the Indians, and kindred matters. Only three of Burr's committees were concerned with the European wars and American foreign policy.

Both King and Burr, in accordance with instructions from the New York legislature, endeavored to open the Senate's closed doors to the public, but not until 1795 were visitors admitted on a regular basis instead of occasionally, and summaries of debates published. Burr was no more successful in defending the right of Albert Gallatin, the future Secretary of the Treasury, to continue to hold his Senate seat in 1794; Geneva-born Gallatin, the Federalists argued, should not have been seated in the first place, since, when he took his seat in December 1793, he had not been a United States citizen for nine years, as required by the Constitution. Burr was not even successful in May 1794 with a motion that Congress take account of the yellow-fever epidemics in Philadelphia, usually in the summer, by moving its next session to Boston. The epidemic of August 1793 had killed thousands of people and made perilously sick many thousands more, including

Alexander and Betsey Hamilton. Nevertheless, Burr's motion was tabled, but it is not known that any members of Congress died in the subsequent yellow-fever outbreak of August 1794.

In still another effort in 1794 which ended in defeat, Burr opposed the appointment of Jay, who was being sent to England to negotiate a treaty that would resolve certain issues and promote trade relations between the two countries. Hamilton had sought the position, his reasons for doing so no doubt including the presence there of Angelica, but despite the urging of King, Robert Morris, Jay, and other Federalist friends, Washington made it clear that he did not favor the appointment, because Hamilton did not enjoy everyone's confidence. Burr undoubtedly had nothing to do with Washington's decision, but the same cannot be said of Jefferson, Madison, and Monroe, who were vehemently opposed to sending Hamilton to England; they were all consulted by the President. Hamilton, aware that he would not be appointed, withdrew his name from consideration. Angelica, who was prepared to welcome the Hamiltons to London with "tears of joy and affection," would have to remain dry-eyed for several years to come.[33]

The vote along party lines confirming Jay's appointment, and later approving the treaty bearing his name, perhaps would have been reversed if Burr and the other twenty-nine senators had known of Hamilton's discussions with the British secret agent, George Beckwith. Termed by Julian Boyd "a part of the pattern of Hamilton's sustained effort to guide the conduct of American foreign policy that began in the autumn of 1789 and culminated in the Treaty of 1794,"[34] Hamilton made a point of keeping Beckwith informed about American policies as they related to Britain and the individuals who supported and opposed them. Beckwith on his part reported regularly to Lord Dorchester, the Canadian Governor General, and through him, or on occasion directly, to the British government in London. Hamilton made no secret of the policies he favored, whether or not they were endorsed by Washington or Secretary of State Jefferson, much less approved for transmission to London. Beckwith also met with Schuyler, and in London with John Barker Church, the latter sometimes serving Hamilton as a conduit to Charles James Fox, a personal friend of Church, and others.

The effect of these meetings between "Number 7," Hamilton's code designation, "Number 2," Schuyler's, and Beckwith was to relieve British anxieties regarding the role America would play in their war with France. Assured by Hamilton that, in Beckwith's words, there was no American military or other threat to British interests in North America and the West Indies, the British were less inclined than they might otherwise have been to softening the terms of the treaty being negotiated by Jay in London. There was no need to do so, Beckwith having been told by Hamilton: "I have always preferred a connexion with you, to that of any other country, *we think in English*, and have a similarity of prejudices and predilections." When Beckwith asked him whether the "different communications you have been pleased to make to me" originated with "that source, which . . . is alone competent to make them," Hamilton did not hesitate to inform him that while he was "not authorized to say to you in so many words that such is the language of the President of the United States . . . my honor and character stand implicated in the fulfillment of these assurances."[35]

None of this, of course, was known to Burr in 1795, and if he had his suspicions, as did others, that the treaty might well have been called the "Hamilton treaty," he left no record of them.[36] He may have sought an appointment with Washington "to converse with him on the subject of the treaty," but there is no evidence that the meeting took place or that he ever received a reply to his letter requesting the meeting.[37] He was no more successful with resolutions he introduced or supported lifting the requirement that the Senate debate the treaty in secrecy, and with proposed amendments cancelling or altering some treaty provisions. When, finally, a resolution was passed conditionally ratifying the treaty and demanding "further friendly negotiations" concerning an article disapproved of by all thirty senators, its sponsor was not Burr but King.

Burr's defeats in the Senate and in New York politics were accompanied by personal disappointments, which some of his biographers believe reflect Hamilton's influence with Washington. In late 1792, Burr may have been interested in learning more or writing a book about the diplomatic side of the Revolutionary War, and to that end obtained from Jefferson, the Secretary of State, permission to spend some early hours in the morning before the Senate met, exploring State Department archives. Whatever progress he made was abruptly terminated when he received a note from Jefferson dated January 20,

1793, reading: "Th. Jefferson presents his respectful compliments to Colo. Burr and is sorry to inform him it has been concluded to be improper to communicate the correspondence of *existing ministers*. He hopes this will, with Colo. Burr, be his sufficient apology." Assuming that by *existing ministers* Jefferson was referring to current American representatives abroad, such as Gouverneur Morris, Hamilton's close friend, and not to those of the Revolutionary War period, Jefferson may have believed that Burr's interest in the archives was not as innocent as some biographers have claimed.[38] Certainly Hamilton, if he was informed of Burr's poring over the files, might well have gone to the President with suspicions of his motives and urged Washington to intervene. Long since convinced that Burr was habitually engaged in "intrigues" of all sorts, Washington would not have required much persuasion.

Washington's role, if not Hamilton's, is clearer in the rejection of Burr as the successor to Gouverneur Morris, whose recall as United States Minister was demanded by the French in March 1794. Burr, who wanted the post, initially was favored by Madison and Monroe, but not, apparently, by other Republicans and certainly not by Washington and Hamilton. According to Davis, Washington several times refused to appoint Burr on the grounds "that he had it a rule of life never to recommend or nominate any person to a high and responsible situation in whose integrity he had not confidence; that, wanting confidence in Colonel Burr, he could not nominate him."[39] Another version is that Washington "wou[ld] not appoint Colo. Burr lest it wo[ul]d seem as if he sought persons from [New York] only," presumably a reference to Morris, who had moved to New York City from Philadelphia, and to Jay and to Chancellor Livingston, who earlier had refused the position. A third version is that, behind the scenes, Republican support for Burr was weak because of his Federalist support, and because, in Sedgwick's words, "they knew {Monroe who was appointed May 27, 1794} would & the other {Burr} would not condescend to Act as their tool. They doubtless respect Burr's talents, but they dread his independence of *them*. They know, in short, he is not one of them, and of course they will never support but always effect to support him."[40]

The perception that Burr was "not one of them" was a succinct summary of the reasons why Burr was never completely trusted by

Republicans or Federalists, and although distrust is not responsible for Jefferson's dislike and Hamilton's hatred of Burr, the view of him as independent of either party and in thrall to no one was important in depriving him of allies when they were most needed in confronting his enemies.

But had he had allies, his relationship with Hamilton almost certainly would not have taken a different course. The more Burr failed in his political objectives, the more Hamilton saw him as a threat to himself, the Federalist Party, and the country; the more he succeeded, which was infrequent, the more Hamiton hated and feared him. Burr's defeats in the 1790s were seen as temporary at best, and at worse as leading to new, perhaps invincible Burr alliances. Probably nothing would have ended Hamilton's obsession short of Burr's exile or death.

In one of his early letters excoriating Burr, Hamilton referred to him as "embarrassed, as I understand, in his circumstances, with an extravagant family."[41] Financially "embarrassed" Burr certainly was much of the time, but it was not because of "an extravagant family." Burr's family then consisted of his wife, Theodosia, who was dying of cancer; his daughter, Theo, nine years old; one or both stepsons; and perhaps Nathalie Delage, a young Parisian refugee from the French Revolution. There were, in addition, servants, tutors, carriages, fine clothes, choice wines, and still other amenities to which persons of substantial means were accustomed. Since Hamilton, by that time the father of five children, also lived well, he may have had in mind as evidence of Burr's extravagance his acquiring Richmond Hill in 1791 or 1792 from Trinity Church, and sparing no expense in furnishing it. Built by a senior British officer fifteen years before the Revolution, the house had subsequently been occupied by Washington, and during that period Burr may have visited it. In 1789 and 1790, Richmond Hill was the residence of Vice President John Adams and his wife, Abigail, who thereafter remembered it as one of the most beautiful houses they had ever known. Abigail never forgot the "fields beautifully variegated with grass and grain," the stately oaks and cedars in great abundance, the "lovely variety of birds" serenading them "morning and evening," while "in front of the house the noble Hudson rolls his majestic waves."[42]

Burr may have been no less impressed by the property's acreage, which could be divided into 360 lots, not including the house and gardens. Although he sold some of the "Lotts" when financial stringencies forced him to consider parting with all or most of Richmond Hill, the income from them did not enable him to protect the property from the claims of his numerous creditors. In 1797 he was forced to part with some of the furnishings of the house and, not long after, was compelled to mortgage the property itself. Still later, after his treason trial in 1807, what was left of the land was bought for a pittance by John Jacob Astor and resold by him at an enormous profit.

In the few years remaining to her before her death in May 1794, Theodosia was too ill to make much use of Richmond Hill, and Burr probably was too busy in New York and Philadelphia to spend more than short periods there. But on these occasions he loved playing host to visitors of all sorts, and entertaining them lavishly. Hamilton sometimes was a dinner guest, and if certain reports can be believed, he occasionally was accompanied by his daughter, Angelica, who went riding with Theo.[43] Other visitors included struggling young Englishmen with literary ambitions who sought Burr's aid in getting published, and there were those who came to dinner and stayed on, among them French men and women fleeing the guillotine. Andrew Jackson never forgot a wine he had enjoyed at the Burr table in 1797, which he termed the best he had ever drunk, and perhaps he also was impressed, as were many visitors, by the warm reception they received from Theo, who served as her father's hostess after Theodosia's death. Unfortunately, there was no guest book for visitors to sign, and hence no record of the number of persons who enjoyed Burr's hospitality, but it probably was in the hundreds.

Did Hamilton envy Burr his Richmond Hill estate? Hamilton had no country house of his own until 1801, and was able to enjoy the Grange barely three years. While the Hamiltons often visited the Schuylers in Albany, where Betsey may have spent as much as a third of her married life, Hamilton himself could join her there for only a month or so each year, on average, and the trip to Albany, whether by stagecoach or by packet boat, was an uncomfortable journey from Manhattan that required at least several days by the land route and a week or more if travel was by water. Burr and his guests could reach Richmond Hill in an hour or two, and when he chose to, he could commute from his Wall Street office or Partition (Fulton) Street home. Hamilton was familiar with the charms and advantages of Burr's country estate, and he probably knew or could guess that Richmond Hill was contributing substantially to Burr's financially "embarrassed" condition. His reference to Burr's "extravagant family" could be interpreted to mean that he both envied and resented the lavish expenditure that had made Richmond Hill possible.

seven

LES LIAISONS DANGEREUSES

In his letters, Hamilton frequently described Burr as "profligate" and "a voluptuary in the extreme," and during meetings with friends he probably alluded to behavior by Burr which he regarded as reprehensible or, in his own word, "extreme." But when John Adams portrayed a leading political figure as suffering from "a superabundance of secretions" which "he could not find whores enough to draw off," he was referring not to Aaron Burr but to Alexander Hamilton.[1]

While Adams did not supply details, he undoubtedly had in mind Hamilton's "amorous connection," in Hamilton's own words, with Maria Reynolds—a married woman of Philadelphia who may or may not have also been a fallen woman—which began in 1791 and continued into 1792. By the time or shortly after the words quoted had appeared in a pamphlet written by Hamilton in 1797, the affair had involved Hamilton in a near-duel with James Monroe, with Aaron Burr as a peacemaking intermediary between the two and attorney for Maria Reynolds in her divorce suit. It also left Thomas Jefferson and other Republicans believing that Hamilton was guilty of much more than adultery, and Federalists, including many of Hamilton's friends, convinced that the scandal he had insisted on bringing to public attention would forever cast a dark shadow upon his reputation. What passed into history as the Reynolds affair also left behind it a tangle of contradictory facts, statements, and interpretations that has become more rather than less raveled over the years.

According to Hamilton's account of his relations with Maria Reynolds and her husband, James, the affair began sometime during the

summer of 1791.[2] Maria had come to the Hamiltons' house in Philadelphia one day, Betsey and the children being elsewhere in the city
or with the Schuylers in Albany, to ask for money, her husband having
left her destitute after running off with another woman.[3] In his first
draft of the account, Hamilton referred to Maria as a "Beauty in distress," but he did not employ this expression in the printed pamphlet,
and there is no reliable description of Maria's physical charms. Perhaps
because he did not have sufficient funds on hand, or wished to see her
again in a more discreet setting, he arranged to meet her that evening
at her rooming house, and did so, giving her thirty dollars ($360). The
transaction, which took place in Maria's bedroom on the second floor,
was followed by "Some conversation . . . from which it was quickly
apparent that other than pecuniary consolation would be acceptable."[4]

Apparently, there were numerous occasions during the following
months when "other than pecuniary consolation" was offered and accepted, sometimes at the Hamilton home when the family was not in
residence, at other times in Maria's second-floor bedroom. Maria
clearly was a welcome diversion from Hamilton's labors in preparing
his Report on Manufactures, which was presented to Congress in November, and from the events culminating in Duer's arrest a few months
later. Perhaps the "consolation" would have continued indefinitely, or
at least until Angelica's return from England, had not Maria's husband,
James Reynolds, written Hamilton a series of letters beginning in December 1791, expressing indignation over his wife's infidelity, and demanding as compensation $1,000 ($12,000). Hamilton, fearful of
exposure, paid Reynolds $600 on December 22, $400 on January 3,
1792, and by August a further $750, for a total of $1,750 ($21,000),
an amount which represented half his annual salary. As late as that
month, and more than a year after the first "consolation," Hamilton
was still seeing Maria, presumably with her husband's consent.

Unfortunately for all concerned, Reynolds and an associate, Jacob
Clingman, had engaged in speculation and a variety of frauds at the
expense of the government which led to their being sent to jail. While
there, Reynolds told Clingman he had personal knowledge of "several
very improper transactions" of Hamilton when he was Secretary of the
Treasury. Clingman subsequently conveyed this information to Frederick A. C. Muhlenberg, a congressman from Pennsylvania for whom
he had once worked as a clerk, who in turn shared it with Monroe,

then a senator from Virginia, and Representative Abraham B. Venable, also a Virginian. On the evening of December 12, 1792, Monroe and Muhlenberg met with Maria, who corroborated her husband's story, and three days later Monroe, Muhlenberg, and Venable told Hamilton that, as he put it, "information had been given them of an improper pecuniary connection between Mr. Reynolds and myself; that they thought it their duty to pursue it and had become possessed of some documents of a suspicious complexion." When they met again that evening, Hamilton told them, as he wrote in his pamphlet, that his "real crime is an amorous connection with his wife [i.e., Maria], for a considerable time with his privity and connivance, if not originally brought on by a combination between the husband and wife with the design to extort money from me." To support this assertion, he showed them letters and receipts for money from both Maria and her husband, all of which were included among the documents published in the pamphlet.

Hamilton was left that day believing that his three visitors were convinced he had not violated public trust or engaged in any speculative transaction with Reynolds, and that his only misconduct was his affair with Reynolds's wife. He also had the impression that there had been agreement not to publicize either the charges that had been made against him or his admission of adultery. In short, he regarded the incident as closed, and for almost five years, during which nothing more was heard of it, he had reason to believe he would not again have to confront it.

But copies of the incriminating documents were made, and some of them had been passed along to individuals who had no reason to keep them secret. Monroe's own copy he apparently entrusted to Jefferson, who knew of the Reynolds affair as early as December 1792, and another copy was in the possession of John Beckley, Republican clerk of the House of Representatives and no friend of Hamilton. Probably it was Beckley who transmitted a copy to James T. Callender, a hack journalist whose specialty was character assassination of a particularly vicious kind. Callender later put in print the story of Jefferson's allegedly fathering several children of Sally ("Dusky Sally") Hemings, one of the house slaves at Monticello, but at that time Callender still was on good terms with Jefferson, who had befriended him after his arrival in America from Scotland.[5]

When in the summer of 1797 Callender published the documents in his *History of the United States for the Year 1796*, Hamilton concluded that he had been betrayed by Monroe, basing this belief on the statement in Monroe's notes following the December 1792 meeting: "We left him under the impression our suspicions were removed." The angry exchanges between them that ensued, some of them witnessed by Church, led Monroe to believe that Hamilton had challenged him to a duel, in which case he wanted Burr to represent him. But in the end there was no duel, owing at least in part to Burr's influence with Monroe. "I have again read over the correspondence," he wrote Monroe on August 15, "& wish it all burnt; which I hope and believe will be the result. If you and Mulenburgh really believe, as I do, and think you must, that H. is innocent of the charge of any concern in speculation with Reynolds, it is my opinion that it will be an act of magnanimity & Justice to say so in a joint certificate."[6] Although Monroe was never entirely convinced by Hamilton's story, he drafted such a certificate, but there is no evidence it was sent to Hamilton.

Hamilton's anger was not confined to Monroe. Suspecting Jefferson of being an accomplice, he threatened him, according to Jefferson's secretary, with exposure of his affair some years before with Betsey Walker, the wife of a close friend. Jefferson for his part maintained, as did other Republicans, that Hamilton's confession of an adulterous relationship with Maria Reynolds seemed "rather to have strengthened than weakened the suspicions that he was in truth guilty of the speculations."[7] But both those who believed Hamilton innocent of the charge and those who were convinced of his guilt were bewildered by what Madison termed "the ingenious folly of its author" in publishing the pamphlet. Even some of Hamilton's closest friends, such as Robert Troup, bemoaned the recklessness and instability to which they attributed his confession that while he had not betrayed his trust as a public official he had betrayed his wife and family.

Burr four years earlier had represented Maria Reynolds in her suit for divorce on grounds of her husband's adultery, and this has led some historians to suggest that he, too, had an affair with her. Hendrickson has gone so far as to accuse Burr of conspiring with Maria and her husband to involve Hamilton in a "badger game," or sexual entrapment, that would discredit him.[8] Hamilton himself, in introducing his pamphlet, referred not to any "badger game" but to a widespread plot to undermine "all the props of public security and private happiness . . . [and] to threaten the political and moral world with a complete overthrow." Behind this effort was "jacobinism," which he termed a greater threat to society than "the three great scourges of mankind, WAR, PESTILENCE, and FAMINE."[9] The "Jacobins" of America were, of course, certain Republicans, the chief of whom was Jefferson, and he may have had Burr in mind as well as Monroe.

If Hamilton knew or suspected that Burr had had an affair with Maria at any time, he left no written record of this belief, and although the possibility cannot be wholly ruled out, taking into account Burr's proclivities, there is no evidence that he and Maria had such a relationship, or that he engaged in any conspiracy with her and her husband. Burr's letter to Monroe holding Hamilton innocent of financial wrongdoing was written after Maria had obtained her divorce, in connection with which she and Burr probably discussed the relationship between Hamilton and her husband. So far as is known, Maria never ceased to insist that Hamilton and her husband had been involved in joint speculations with Treasury funds, and if she communicated this conviction to Burr, he must have chosen not to believe her, or not to forward the information to Monroe. But whatever was responsible for his urging Monroe to agree with him that Hamilton was innocent of having collaborated with Reynolds, his doing so reminds us that while Burr had many faults, he was not a malevolent man.

Most historians and biographers have tended to accept Hamilton's version, not Maria's or her husband's, of what transpired between the three of them in 1791–92. In recent years, however, Julian Boyd, the Jefferson scholar quoted earlier in connection with Hamilton's efforts to control foreign policy, has attempted to demonstrate that Hamilton forged the letters from Maria and James Reynolds, did not include in his pamphlet at least two documents that weakened his case, and misrepresented Monroe's role. Basing his argument on a comparison of the letters published by Hamilton with those known to have been written by Maria and her husband, Boyd concluded that the spelling and grammatical construction of the pamphlet letters do not accord with those of the letters known to have been written by the two. "Mrs. Reynolds' charge that the letters were forged," he wrote in 1972, "cannot be supported by objective truth . . . {But they} exhibit in their texts, in their substantive incongruities, and in their conflict with verifiable evidence overwhelming proofs of their own insufficiency. They are the palpably contrived documents of a brilliant and daring man who, writing under much stress in the two or three days available to him in 1792 {i.e., days preceding the meeting of December 15}, tried to imitate what he conceived to be the style of less literate persons. The result was inexpert to the point of naivete, but its character is beyond doubt. The purported letters of James and Maria Reynolds . . . cannot be accepted as genuine."[10]

As may be imagined, Boyd's view is not accepted by every historian and biographer of Hamilton, and it may or may not influence what they ultimately decide about the Reynolds affair. Against Boyd and in Hamilton's favor is Reynolds's malodorous reputation as a swindler, which makes it difficult to believe that Hamilton would have joined him in any venture, speculative or otherwise. Maria's efforts to obtain her husband's release from jail, and her subsequent marriage to Clingman, will suggest to some that she lent herself to the plot against Hamilton. But there is evidence that, whatever her relationship to Hamilton, she was from a respectable family and related by marriage to a Livingston. She still could have been a loose woman, as most Hamilton biographers assume, but that is nowhere confirmed, and there is some reason to believe that she lived not in a rooming house, where no questions were asked of male visitors late at night, but in a comfortable town house situated in a respectable neighborhood. Her loyalty to her husband could be interpreted to mean that she was neither deserted by him nor destitute, as Hamilton alleged, however many other grievances she had against him. Clearly the facts, statements, and interpretations that constitute the Reynolds affair do not wholly support Hamilton or Maria and her husband, and the truth or truths of what transpired between them probably will never be known without some trace of doubt. The original letters and documents no longer exist, presumably having been destroyed by Betsey, to whom they were delivered after her husband's death, and there was no further testimony from Reynolds, his wife, or Clingman following publication of the pamphlet.[11]

Hamilton's pamphlet may have been "folly," in Madison's view, but with his record as Secretary of the Treasury and his political future at stake, he perhaps had no practical alternative. Certainly he was aware that accusations of financial wrongdoing imposed "a more serious stain," as he put it, on his name and reputation than an admission of marital infidelity, then as now a much more forgivable offense committed by those holding public office. Charges of such, if not comparable confessions, were commonplace at that time, being leveled at, among others, Washington and Jefferson, not to mention Burr, as well as a host of lesser figures. The political careers of none of them, it appears, were much affected, not even that of Gouverneur Morris, who in Paris shared a mistress with Talleyrand in what amounted to a *ménage a trois*.

Theft or misuse of public funds was a very different matter, and almost from the time Hamilton took office in Washington's Administration, he was suspected by some of initiating and pursuing policies that benefited himself, his relatives, and friends. A few of his enemies even believed that he was transferring money from the Treasury to his own pocket, a charge that, on at least one occasion, almost resulted in a duel between Hamilton and his accuser. But the more frequent claim of his critics was that he had aided the "monied men" by paying more for government securities in the open market than the going price, thereby inflating the value of the bonds held by banks and private investors, and by borrowing money and paying interest on these loans to the government when tax revenues and other Treasury income were held on deposit in banks and therefore available for spending purposes. The more serious charges in 1792–93 were incorporated in a series of impeachment resolutions in Congress, known as the Giles Resolutions, which, while introduced by William Branch Giles of Virginia, were and are generally regarded as having been inspired and perhaps even written by Jefferson with the assistance of Madison. After lengthy debate and Hamilton's submission of detailed reports on his handling of Treasury responsibilities, the resolutions were defeated, but rumors and suspicions, as the Reynolds affair demonstrates, lingered long after Hamilton had ceased to hold office.

His reputation for integrity was not helped by his close association with Church and other speculators who were known to heavily invest in government bonds and other securities. Throughout his tenure as Treasury secretary, Hamilton continued to supervise the investments of his brother-in-law, often employing for that purpose William Seton, cashier of the Bank of New York. In his frequent reports to Hamilton, Seton kept him informed of his purchases and sales on Church's account of "US Bank Stock" and other securities in accordance with Hamilton's instructions or expressed opinion. These detailed communications refer to letters of instruction from Hamilton, usually noted by the editors of his *Papers* as "not found."[12]

Few believed that Hamilton himself was, as John F. Mercer of Maryland was said to have alleged in October 1792, "a Stock Jobber or Dealer in Certificates on your own Account," but Mercer, who denied making the charge, remained convinced Hamilton "had unjustifiably sacrificed the other Interests of the United States to a particular and by no means a meritorious Class . . . who from their immediate situation on the spot — their connections and information (however acquired) of the intended purchases of Stock on Public Account, could make a certain profit." Citing instances when Hamilton had paid more than current prices for such "Stock," Mercer concluded that he had done so not for personal financial reward but in order to attach "to your administration a Monied Interest as an Engine of Government."[13] To that charge Hamilton could hardly plead innocent.

Never doubting that Mercer and the others were voicing Jefferson's thoughts if not his exact words, Hamilton by 1792 was making a determined effort to force Jefferson from the cabinet, while Jefferson, for his part, was no less dedicated to destroying Washington's confidence in his Secretary of the Treasury. In a lengthy reply to a letter from the President expressing concern that in his cabinet there was not "more charity in deciding on the opinions, & actions of one another," Jefferson accused Hamilton of harboring monarchist sentiments and of "the shuffling of millions backwards and forwards from paper into money, and money into paper, from Europe to America, and America to Europe, the dealing out of Treasury secrets among his friends in what time and measure he pleases, and who never slips an occasion of making friends with this means."[14]

Hamilton's response to a similar letter from Washington held Jefferson responsible for efforts to "subvert" both the government and himself "from the first moment of his coming to the City of New York."[15] But his letter was short and forbearing in comparison with other letters and several newspaper articles, the latter of which appeared pseudonymously, excoriating Jefferson and intermittently Madison for a variety of hostile acts and intentions, including, above all, attempts to bring about his "overthrow." In an 8,000-word letter of May 26, 1792, to a Virginian, Edward Carrington, one of the longest letters he ever wrote, Hamilton insisted that Jefferson "did not in the first instance cordially acquiesce in the new constitution for the U States, [and] had many doubts and reserves," in France after the Revolution "drank deeply of the French Philosophy, in Religion, in Science, in politics," at every moment "aims with ardent desire at the Presidential Chair," and was, in sum, "a man of profound ambition & violent passions."[16] Madison, whom Hamilton never forgave for deserting to Jefferson, fared better in the letter to Carrington, but he was accused of acting "from a spirit of rivalship" in becoming "personally unfriendly to me." His character, too, was tainted, and while Hamilton had once believed in his "candour and simplicity and Fairness" when they had been engaged in writing *The Federalist*, he now was convinced that Madison's character "is *one of a peculiarly artificial and complicated kind.*"[17]

Both Jefferson and Madison, he continued, "*have a womanish attachment to France and a womanish resentment against Great Britain.*"[18] Whatever he meant by "womanish," he persisted in thinking that Jefferson, in particular, had been deeply influenced by the French Revolution, in response to which he had become an American "Jacobin." Hamilton's view of Jefferson's commitment to democratic values is not far from that which history associates with his name, but there is much evidence that Jefferson's embrace of the common man was, at best, a timid one. Certainly it would have been "strange," as Richard Hofstadter observed, if Jefferson, an aristocrat by temperament and preference, had become "one of those bitter rebels who live by tearing up established orders and forcing social struggles to the issue."[19] When he wrote this, Hofstadter may well have had in mind Jefferson's attachment to his Monticello mansion with its thousands of acres, his scores of slaves, his hundreds of bottles of choice vintage wines, and, perhaps even more revealing, his request to a friend en route to London in 1771 to "search the Herald's office for the arms of my family . . . It is possible there may be none. If so, I would wish with your assistance to become a purchaser, having Sterne's word for it that a coat of arms may be purchased as cheap as any other coat."[20]

Jefferson had more faith than Hamilton in human nature and man's ability to govern himself, but he also believed "the bulk of mankind are schoolboys through life." Hamilton would not have disagreed with this statement, and he probably would not have taken strong exception to Jefferson's confessing "I do not believe with the Rochefoucaults and Montaignes, that fourteen out of fifteen men are rogues . . . But I have always found that rogues would be uppermost."[21] As "ambitious as Cromwell," in Adams's words, "a politician to his fingertips," to quote Page Smith, Jefferson as President led Andrew Jackson to conclude that Jefferson was "the best Republican [Democrat] in theory and the worst in practice he had ever seen."[22] Had Hamilton lived to the end of Jefferson's second term in 1809, he might have been inclined to agree. As early as Jefferson's first inaugural address in 1801, Hamilton had already revised his earlier opinion to the extent of regarding the speech "as virtually a retraction of past misapprehensions, and a pledge to the community, that the new president will not lend himself to dangerous innovations, but in essential points will tread in the steps of his predecessors."[23]

By the end of December 1793, Jefferson, worn down by the seemingly endless political turmoil and ceaseless attacks upon himself, had resigned from Washington's cabinet, and a little more than a year later, on January 31, 1795, Hamilton, too, returned to private life. By that time he had become friendly with Charles Maurice de Tallyrand-Périgord (1754–1838), by even the most tolerant standards one of the foremost of Jefferson's (and Rochefoucault's and Montaigne's) rogues. Having fled France in 1794, where he feared for his life, Talleyrand spent two years in the United States. There, because of his reputation for corruption and scandalous behavior, many doors were closed to him, but not those of Hamilton and Burr. Hamilton in particular, perhaps influenced by Angelica, who seems to have liked Talleyrand, saw a good deal of the Frenchman.

Apparently, they impressed each other, Talleyrand ranking Hamilton the greatest of the three great men of the time, the other two being Napoleon and Charles James Fox, Hamilton praising Talleyrand as "the greatest of modern statesmen, because he had so well known when it was necessary both to suffer wrong to be done and to do it." Unfortunately, we do not know when Hamilton expressed this opinion, but it is unlikely to have been after 1797, when, with war threatening between France and the United States, Talleyrand, by then the French Foreign Minister, attempted to extort $250,000 from the American peace mission to France in what became known as the XYZ Affair.[24]

While Talleyrand did not like the three members of the mission or most other Americans, he made an exception of Hamilton, who, he said, "avait deviné l'Europe."[25] He prefaced this remark with the statement "that he had never, on the whole, known one equal to Hamilton," presumably meaning that Hamilton, who had never seen Europe, possessed, like himself, an understanding of its political culture which required that its leaders accept the necessity of suffering "wrong to be done and to do it." For Burr, on the other hand, whose Richmond Hill guest he occasionally was, he later had little use, perhaps because he had always made it a point to be the first off a sinking ship, and Burr by then no longer possessed any power or influence. Sometime during the years after the duel, declaring him to be "the most unprincipled man he had almost ever known," Talleyrand told his listeners that as Vice President between 1801 and 1805 Burr had advocated "separating the States under the influence and with the aid of France," and that later still he had tried to interest Napoleon in his scheme to dismember the Union.[26]

Hamilton and the Federalists, including Schuyler, whose sympathies lay with Britain and who feared the spread of French revolutionary doctrines more than they feared war, were opposed to the American mission to Paris and other initiatives of Adams, by then President, designed to achieve a peaceful solution.[27] Hamilton may also have been influenced by a vision of himself as, if not "the Man on Horseback,"[28] the commanding general of an army that would vanquish the French and go on to conquer New Orleans, Mexico, and, with British assistance, all of Spanish America.[29] Perhaps he had entertained this latter dream for several years, during which he had discussed the possibility of such an expedition with a Venezuelan exile, Francisco de Miranda, an adventurer and self-styled liberator whose declared purpose in life was the liberation of his country and most of Latin America from Spanish rule. In the course of his relationship with Miranda, dating back to 1784 and apparently ending in 1789, Hamilton may have encouraged Miranda to believe that Washington and other American generals were sympathetic to such an effort, but in the end nothing came of it, and Hamilton minimized the significance of his dealings with the Latin American.[30] In 1806, Miranda may have sought aid from Burr, but there is no evidence he had more than one meeting with Burr, which, however, was enough for someone signing himself "A

Friend" to warn Jefferson that Miranda's actions formed a link in "Burr's Manouevres."[31]

If, in fact, Hamilton was indifferent toward Miranda by late 1798, he was far from uninterested in the selection by Adams of army Commander in Chief. Washington, retired to Mount Vernon, was the obvious choice, and in June 1798 he was nominated. In view of his age — he was sixty-six and was to die less than two years later — and his known desire to enjoy an uninterrupted retirement, the appointment of ranking officers to serve under him or in his place in the event of a war involved decisions of the highest importance. Even before June, Hamilton, who coveted the position of second-in-command and was determined to have it, brought every pressure to bear on his supporters in Adams's cabinet and in Congress, on Adams, and on Washington himself. Adams, whose dislike of Hamilton by that time was almost equal to Hamilton's dislike of him, was determined not to make the appointment if he could possibly avoid doing so. Sending a list of senior officers, one of whom was Burr, to Washington, Adams requested his opinion regarding the choice of Inspector General, Adjutant General, and Quartermaster General.

Washington had decided that the three men most qualified to be his second-in-command were Knox, Pinckney, and Hamilton, but he knew the selection of one of them to be his lieutenant would not be easy. While both Knox and Pinckney were senior to Hamilton in rank and service, it was no secret that Hamilton, as Pickering wrote Washington, "who will gladly be *your second* . . . will not . . . be second to any other military commander in the United States."[32] Washington did not disagree with Pickering that Hamilton's services should be secured at "almost any price," but he could not be certain that Knox or Pinckney would consent to serve under his former aide-de-camp. When eventually Hamilton at his insistence was appointed Inspector General with the rank of major general, in which capacity he would function as his second-in-command, Washington's doubts regarding Knox, although not Pinckney, proved to be correct. In a letter to McHenry, the Secretary of War, who, while serving in Adams's cabinet, was totally devoted to Hamilton, Knox made it clear he would not accept an appointment inferior to Hamilton's. Writing McHenry on August 5, 1798, Knox reminded him: "It is to be presumed you are not uninformed of the military precedence I sustained in the late war . . . General Hamilton was a Captain in the year 1776 in the Corps of Artillery which I commanded, and the latter part of the same year, I had the rank of Brigadier General. In 1777 he . . . [held] the incidental rank of Lt Colonel, which was his highest grade. I was established a Major General from November 1781."[33] Knox might have mentioned, but did not, that he was a veteran of the Monmouth and Yorktown battles, among others, and had been Secretary of War from 1785 to 1794.

Lest Washington should have any second thoughts, Hamilton assured both him and McHenry that, as he put it to McHenry, he had "esteem and friendship" for Knox, but nevertheless would have "a very great difficulty in waving a station, to which I am well convinced I have been called no less by the public voice of the Country than by the acts of the Commander in Chief and of the President and Senate." Striking a similar note in his letter of August 20 to Washington, Hamilton began by stating that Knox's attitude "though not very unexpected is very painful to me . . . I have a warm personal regard for him." But, he continued, "it is a fact that a number of the most influential men in our affairs would think that in waving the preference given to me I acted a weak part in a personal view and an unwarrantable one in a public view. And General Knox is much mistaken if he does not believe that this sentiment would emphatically prevail in that Region, to which he supposes his character most interesting, I mean New England."[34]

When he wrote this, he could not have been thinking of Adams, who was born in Massachusetts and whose roots were deeply planted in New England soil. Although Adams spared no effort to avoid making Hamilton the senior major general in the army, he was threatened with Washington's resignation if he did not, and on July 25, 1798, he believed he had no choice but to appoint Hamilton Inspector General with the rank of major general, carrying with it precedence over Pinckney and other general officers. If Adams accurately represents the situation in which he found himself with respect to Hamilton's appointment and the rejection of Burr's, few episodes in Hamilton's life are as revealing "of his ambition and quest for military fame," in the words of the editors of his *Papers*,[35] both of which he expressed in his 1769 letter to Ned Stevens, or testify better to his success in depriving Burr of the position for which he had been recommended. "I proposed to General Washington," Adams recalled in a letter he wrote to a friend in 1815, "and through him to the triumvirate [Hamilton, Pinckney, and Knox], to nominate Colonel Burr for a brigadier-general. Washington's answer to me was, 'By all that I have known and heard, Colonel Burr is a brave and able officer, but the question is, whether he has not equal talents at intrigue.' How shall I describe to you my sensations and recollections at that moment? He had compelled me to promote over the heads of Lincoln, Gates, Clinton, Knox, and others, and even over Pinckney, one of . . . the most restless, impatient, artful, indefatigable and unprincipled intriguers in the United States, if not in the world, to be second in command under himself, and now dreaded an intriguer in a poor brigadier! He did, however, propose it to the triumvirate, at least to Hamilton. But I was not permitted to nominate Burr." Had he been able to do so, Adams continued, "what would have been the consequences? Shall I say, that Hamilton would have been now alive, and Hamilton and Burr now the head of our affairs? What then? If I had nominated Burr without the consent of the triumvirate, a negative in the Senate was certain. Burr to this day knows nothing of this."[36]

In the end, Hamilton's elevation to major general and Burr's being denied promotion to brigadier general did not much matter. There was no war with France other than an undeclared naval war, and while Hamilton's favorite portrait of himself was in his uniform as major general, the two stars of his rank in plain view, he had no opportunity to wear it on a battlefield. Burr, who was regarded by the Federalists as partial to France, to the surprise of Troup was eager to take part in the expected conflict, and probably to his own surprise was recommended by Hamilton in February 1799, as was mentioned earlier, to take charge of fortifying the port of New York in preparation for a possible attack. Hamilton may have urged this appointment on Jay, by then Governor of New York, in response to a twinge of conscience — which would not be his last with reference to Burr — brought on by the role he had played in Washington's recent treatment of him, but Hamilton's telling Jay that "Burr will be very equal" to the appointment was not unqualified. Burr would accept, he added, "if an *adequate compensation* be annexed."[37] Perhaps in retaliation for Knox's refusing to serve under him, Hamilton made only a limited effort to find him a place in the high command. In a letter to McHenry, he suggested that "General Knox if he can be drawn to the seat of Governt may be rendered extensively useful especially in whatever relates to the Artillery branch."[38]

Adams never forgave Hamilton for manipulating Washington into insisting that he be appointed second ranking general in the army, but by 1798 he had other grievances against Hamilton that pained and angered him more. Washington having declined reelection, the approach of the 1796 Presidential election, the nation's third, found not only Adams as Vice President a clear contender but also Federalist Thomas Pinckney of South Carolina, who was favored by Hamilton, and, representing the Republicans, Jefferson and Burr, the latter enjoying some Federalist support. Hamilton left no doubt in the minds of friends that of all these candidates Jefferson, whose chances of becoming President were far better than Burr's, inspired the most trepidation. It is "far less important," he wrote an unknown correspondent on November 8, 1796, "who of many men that may be named shall be the person, than that it shall not be Jefferson. We have every thing to fear if this man comes in . . . the exclusion of Mr. Jefferson is far more important than any difference between Mr. Adams and Mr. Pinckney."[39]

He apparently did not regard Burr as a serious contender. Although he knew Burr was interested in running with Jefferson as Vice Presidential candidate, he was certain that the President-elect would be Adams, Jefferson, or Pinckney. To insure that Pinckney would win the highest or second highest number of electoral votes, Hamilton urged Federalists throughout the country to cast ballots for Adams and Pinckney rather than, as he put it, "throwing away . . . votes in New England lest *Pinckney* should outrun *Adams*." While there were "machinations to cheat us into Mr Burr," he wrote Jeremiah Wadsworth on December 1, 1796, "I have no apprehensions of its success. My chief fear is that the attachment of our Eastern friends to Mr. Adams may prevent their voting for Pinckney likewise, & that some irregularity or accident may deprive us of Adams & let in Jefferson."[40]

"Some irregularity or accident" engineered by Hamilton was precisely what Adams and his allies believed would "let in" Pinckney. Slow to realize that Hamilton was maneuvering to have Pinckney elected President and himself Vice President for a second time, Adams at first did not suspect that Hamilton was working secretly to undermine support for him even in Boston. Hamilton may have done so, at least in part, because he knew that his influence with Adams if Adams was elected President would be much less than his influence had been with Washington. He may also have calculated, as Adams came to suspect, that Adams's defeat would clear the way for himself as the Federalist candidate in 1800. Whatever his motivations, he failed to secure Pinckney's election, but he came close. Of the 276 electoral votes cast by the sixteen states, Adams received 71, Jefferson 68, making him the Vice President, Pinckney 59, and Burr 30. The remaining votes were distributed among nine other candidates, only one of whom received as many as 15.

Even before the results were final, Adams and his wife, Abigail, could hardly find words to describe what they both regarded as Hamilton's treachery. The New Yorker, Adams wrote Abigail, was "a proud-spirited, conceited, aspiring mortal, always pretending to morality, with . . . debauched morals . . . As great a hypocrite as any in the U.S., his intrigues in the election I despise." Abigail went further, condemning Hamilton for being as "ambitious as Julius Caesar, a subtle intriguer . . . His thirst for fame is insatiable." In another letter she confided to her husband: "Beware of that spare Cassius, has always occurred to me when I have seen that cock sparrow. Oh, I have read his heart in his wicked eyes many a time. The very devil is in them. They are lasciviousness itself, or I have no skill in physiognomy."[41]

But ahead there were worse "intrigues" of Hamilton, in the opinion of both Adamses, although, once again, Adams was not aware of them until late in his Presidency. As his Secretaries of State, War, and the Treasury, Adams retained Pickering, McHenry, and Walcott, who had served under Washington, the three of them friends of Hamilton, whom they regarded as their mentor. From Adams's inauguration in 1797 to 1800, they not only provided Hamilton with reports of cabinet meetings and Adams's views on a variety of subjects but regularly turned to him for guidance on policies to be followed in their own departments and in the Administration. Acting, in effect, as the secret prime minister of a government in whose leader he had little confidence, Hamilton did not hesitate to issue instructions to Pickering, McHenry, and Wolcott that he intended them to follow whether or not their resulting actions were in accord with Adams's wishes. Thus, on one occasion in March 1797, Hamilton urged McHenry, the most pliant of the three: "When the Senate meets . . . send a Commission extraordinary to France. Let it consist of *Jefferson* or *Madison Pinckney* & a third very safe man . . . When Congress meet, get them to lay an Embargo with liberty to the executive to grant licenses to depart to Vessels *armed* or sailing with *Convoys* . . . Increase the Revenue vigorously . . . Form a provisional army of 25000 men." Ending his letter: "I am really my friend anxious that this should be your plan," Hamilton added: "I write you this letter on your fidelity. No *mortal* must see it or know its contents."[42]

For Adams, McHenry's role in the appointment of Hamilton as ranking major general may have served as an additional provocation, but he did not take action until, in May 1800, he suspected that McHenry was working with Hamilton against his reelection. Calling him in for an angry confrontation, he forced him to resign. Pickering, who, Adams discovered, had long been implementing Hamilton's foreign policy, which conflicted with that of the Administration, refused to resign on request, and as a result was abruptly dismissed on May 10. Wolcott, however, remained in office until 1801.

In a letter to King of December 16, 1796, Hamilton observed of the election result that the "event will not a little mortify Burr," and while Burr did not reveal in public any mortification, Hamilton probably was right. Although Burr had sought support in more than half the states for Jefferson and himself, he received no votes from Georgia, South Carolina, all of New England, and, perhaps most galling to him, none from New York. North Carolina, where he had been led to believe he would receive the same number of votes as Jefferson, gave him six as against Jefferson's eleven. When he later complained, according to Gallatin, that in the 1796 election he had been "ill used" by Virginia and North Carolina, and that the Virginians had "deceived him" and were "not to be trusted," he probably knew or suspected that, in the words of a modern historian, "only great pressures from the party leadership," that is, Jefferson and Madison, could have persuaded leading Virginia Republicans to "sacrifice Burr."[43]

By 1796, Burr was familiar with Republican tendencies to "sacrifice" him in favor of another candidate. The previous year, when Governor Clinton announced that he would not seek a seventh term as New York governor, he caused many to think his death was imminent (they were wrong about this: he died in 1812), and Burr became a candidate once more. There were rumors, believed by Hamilton, Schuyler, and other Federalists, that Clinton would exert influence in behalf of Burr in return for his support in 1797 when Clinton would seek the Senate seat he was vacating. Burr had some backing from Federalists, but it was far less than they gave Jay and Van Rensselaer, who became the party nominees for governor and lieutenant governor. Burr's candidacy, in any case, ended almost as soon as it began, when Republicans early in 1796 endorsed Robert Yates and William Floyd. Whatever his feelings about his second failure to become New York's governor, Burr, as usual, kept them to himself. Nor, as usual, did he harbor hard feelings, making clear, as Clinton did, his support for the Yates ticket. But with his Senate term coming to an end and his political future uncertain, he must have regretted the decision of the New York Republicans, although it probably would have made no difference in the outcome if he had been nominated. Despite the unpopularity of the treaty which he had brought back from London, Jay was elected governor and in 1798 was rewarded by New York voters with a second term of office.

Quite possibly, Burr would have won or done a good deal better in the 1795 and 1796 elections had women been able to cast ballots, for he was popular with women high and low of all ages and conditions. One of his conquests not long after he took his seat in the Senate may have been Dolley Payne Todd, more familiar to us as Dolley Madison (1768–1849). He probably met Dolley shortly before or after he became a resident in her widowed mother's boardinghouse in Philadelphia, temporary home to legislators who were bachelors or who, like Burr, did not have their families living with them. Within months of their meeting, Dolley, too, was a widow, with one son aged two and the likelihood that she would lose what she was left to a brother of her husband. She turned to Burr for assistance, and according to one of her biographers, Alice Curtis Desmond, received and reciprocated something more than that. Perhaps she still hoped, even while being courted by James Madison, who was regarded as neither handsome nor charming, that Burr would propose to her, but he did not. Whether he refrained because he did not become a widower himself until Theodosia's death on May 28, or whether he did not care for Dolley as much, if her biographer can be believed, as she cared for him, is not known, but what is certain is that it was he who introduced twenty-six-year-old Dolley to forty-three-year-old Madison, whom she married a few months later. Some indication of her feeling for Burr may be found in her will, dated May 13, 1794, not long before her marriage, which reads in part: "And Aaron Burr to be the sole guardian of my son and as the education of my son is to him and to me the most interesting of all earthly concerns and far more important to his happiness and eminence in Life than the increase of his estate, I direct that no expense be spared to give him every advantage and improvement of which his Talents may be susceptible."[44] She may have been influenced to make Burr the boy's guardian by her observations of Theo, who was eleven years old at the time, and the education she was receiving under her father's supervision.

Had Burr married Dolley, whose engaging manner captivated almost everyone and made her the most appealing of our early First Ladies, he would have had in her a valuable asset in his efforts to win higher office. Perhaps she also would have made it possible for him to lead a life less vulnerable to the gossip and rumors that followed him everywhere, but it is unlikely that Burr was capable of ever being faithful to one woman for long. He was equally unable to avoid accusations that he exploited public office for private gain. Here he was less fortunate than Hamilton, who was mainly suspected of pursuing policies as Secretary of the Treasury that benefited his relatives and friends, not himself, and while some Republicans even after his death continued to believe he personally had profited, nothing was proven then, nor has evidence come to light since. But it remains true, as stated earlier, that Burr's behavior in the public and private spheres of his life has always been judged more harshly than Hamilton's.

In 1797, for example, both Hamilton and Burr became involved in the affairs of the Holland Land Co., a Dutch enterprise heavily invested in New York State land acquired from Robert Morris and others. Because aliens were prohibited from ownership of such land, title was required to be in the name of United States citizens, a requirement which, as indicated earlier, necessitated Hamilton's holding title to land owned by his brother-in-law, John Barker Church. In 1796, however, a New York statute was passed enabling agents of the Holland Land Co. to hold land in its behalf for seven years, after which, if the Dutch investors had not become citizens or sold their land to Americans, the company would lose possession. A further enactment of February 1797, shepherded through the legislature by Schuyler, extended the seven years to twenty, or to 1816, but this was hardly a reflection of Schuyler's attachment to his Dutch roots. In return for his efforts, the Holland Land Co. through its American agent, Theophile Cazenove, contributed $250,000 ($3,000,000) to a business venture headed by Schuyler, the Western Inland Lock Navigation Co. Hamilton's role in this transaction is unknown, but he may already have been giving legal advice to Dutch interests, or at least counseling his father-in-law.

By 1798, the Holland Land Co. became aware of ambiguities in the legislation governing land ownership by aliens, and, "understandably concerned by the blackmail required to obtain this concession,"[45] turned to Hamilton for clarification. Whether because he failed to convince Cazenove that the legislation offered adequate protection to his Dutch employers or because of other reasons, Cazenove consulted additional lawyers, one of them being Burr. By that time, Burr had been succeeded in the Senate by Schuyler, who, because of recurrent illness, served only a short time, during which he strongly urged his son-in-law and others to mount a campaign that would lead to Burr's defeat in his expected run for the New York Assembly. Their efforts failed, and within weeks of his election to the Assembly in April 1797 Burr had begun to participate in discussions that, a year later, resulted in new legislation related to alien ownership of land. The Burr-supported statute, which passed in late March 1798, provided that all aliens except those of countries at war with the United States could buy and hold land in New York, subject to only two restrictions: they could not lease their lands, and the law unless extended would expire in three years.

For their legal services, Hamilton, Burr, and two other lawyers apparently shared a fee of $400 ($4,800), payment of which no one could object to, but on April 16, two weeks after the alien law had been given final approval by the Council of Revision, Burr received the first installment of a $5,500 ($66,000) loan from the Holland Land Co. As may be imagined, Hamilton and other enemies of Burr, alleging that he had been bribed—although he had long favored the right of aliens to own land—were outraged.[46] Critics of Burr since, while less irate, have tended to take this loan as further evidence of Burr's lack of integrity and relentless pursuit of self-interest, almost as if the Alien Act had not been passed by both houses of the New York legislature and approved by the Council of Revision, but enacted into law by Burr alone.[47] They also have excluded from the balance sheet the $250,000 ($3,000,000) contribution to Schuyler's Western Inland Lock Navigation Co., and Hamilton's inducing, according to his son, James A. Hamilton, "the Holland Land Company to give Mrs. Robert Morris, the widow of the eminent financier of the Revolution, an annuity which supported her comfortably. He also obtained for his friend, Col. Troup, the agency of that Company in the western part of New York, by which he became quite independent if not wealthy."[48]

There is some merit in the observation that Burr's activities in connection with Cazenove and the Holland Land Co., "while open to criticism as being improper for a legislator, differed little from the maneuverings of Schuyler and his famous son-in-law."[49] Perhaps less defensible are other ventures Burr undertook to rescue himself from chronic "embarrassment," in the wording of contemporaries, due to speculating not always wisely in land and a propensity for living beyond his means. As we have seen, he borrowed from everyone, including relatives, friends, and clients who had money to lend, and also from persons whose financial situation was too precarious for them to forgo reimbursement or allow Burr more time for repayment. One of these unfortunate individuals was John Lamb, a war veteran who had been a friend of Burr since they were together at Quebec. In 1796 Burr borrowed some $23,000 ($270,000) from Lamb, then collector of customs for the Port of New York, to finance purchases of land, neither of them knowing then that the assistant collector at the Port had embezzled an amount of money estimated to be $250,000 ($1,800,000) before "retiring" to England. When the loss was discovered, Lamb as the responsible official was required to make good and, in order to do so, mortgaged his property.

Burr made an effort to pay off his debt to Lamb, even leasing Richmond Hill and selling some of its contents, but the $3,500 ($42,000) he raised fell short of the total Lamb needed to rid himself of the mortgages, and as a consequence he lost his holdings. More than sixty years old, in poor health, depressed and embittered, he died not long after. While Burr repeatedly assured him that he was doing everything possible to assist him short of selling his own land at a loss, its value having depreciated, Lamb felt that he had not done enough. He also accused Burr of favoring other creditors ahead of him, and he apparently believed in 1797 that Burr, against his wishes and behind his back, was negotiating the transfer of his property to the federal government as security for the amount stolen. Defending himself against Lamb's charges that in discussing the possibility of such a transfer with Richard Harison, the United States district attorney for New York, he had acted from "improper Motives," Burr in a letter to Lamb of May 4, 1797, protested that Lamb's "insinuations" were "injurious to me — I am as little influenced by Considerations of Interest as you can be, and it is with astonishment I perceive that you can have harboured such ungenerous and groundless suspicions." Admitting that he "made a proposition without your knowledge" to Harison, he added that "it was during an accidental Conversation with Mr. H. . . . mere Conversation, it pledged you Nothing — it committed you in no way."[50] Because no letters from Lamb to Burr survive, what Lamb meant by "improper Motives" and "insinuations" is not known.

In still another of Burr's speculations in land which ultimately involved Hamilton as attorney for the creditor, Burr and William Stephens Smith, Adams's son-in-law, arranged in 1794 to purchase 200,000 acres of land, originally owned by Alexander Macomb, from John Julius Angerstein, an English merchant. Angerstein had purchased the property in upstate New York on the assumption that the law prohibiting alien ownership would be waived in his favor, and when it was not, he decided to sell. In due course, Smith withdrew from the venture and Burr, forced to find another partner, joined forces with James Greenleaf, who not only bought, sold, and traded large parcels of land but was, in the words of one historian, "the most important land speculator that the United States had produced."[51]

After their agreeing to pay £24,000 for Angerstein's land, or £12,000 ($360,000) each, Burr discovered that Greenleaf had mortgaged his share of the land for £12,000 and, instead of sending it to Angerstein in London, used it to settle his own debts. Since the purchasing agreement had provided as a penalty that in the event of non-payment for his land, Angerstein would be entitled to keep his land and still collect the £24,000, Burr could only try desperately to raise the necessary money. His borrowing from Lamb and others, which, as noted earlier, only added to Lamb's financial difficulties, did not produce sufficient funds to satisfy Angerstein, and increasingly suspicious that Burr and Greenleaf were selling portions of his land without consulting him, he hired Hamilton in March 1797 to represent him in legal proceedings against the two partners. The suits and countersuits continued for years as Burr, who was the principal defendant in the trials and hearings, tried to prove that he was innocent of any intent to defraud Angerstein or not pay him for his land.

He did not entirely succeed, according to Hamilton, who reported in a letter of January 1801 that Burr "is without a doubt insolvent for a large *deficit*. All his visible property is deeply mortgaged, and he is known to own other large debts, for which there is no specific security. Of the number of these there is a judgement in favor of Mr. Angerstein for a sum which with interest amounts to about $80,000 [$960,000]."[52] In late 1802, however, the case of *Aaron Burr v. John Julius Angerstein* in New York's Court of Chancery was dismissed when Hamilton on behalf of Angerstein agreed to accept the $25,000 Burr was able to raise through loans and mortgages provided by the Manhattan Company bank, a creation of Burr's brought about by his adroit handling in the New York Assembly of legislation establishing a company to supply clean water to New York City. Today the company, which will be discussed in the following chapter, is known as the Chase Manhattan Bank, and although it invests in real estate and helps finance other business ventures, supplying water to New York is no longer one of them.

Always willing to believe the worst of Burr, Hamilton by 1800 may have accepted as true the rumors that he was involved with others in a scheme to purchase, in the words of Robert Liston, the British Ambassador to the United States, "extensive territory in Upper Canada . . . {and} to see an independent Republick, established in Canada in the room of the present Colonial and Monarchical Government."[53] Liston and others in the British Foreign Office suspected that the underlying motive of the scheme was to recover Canada for France, and to serve that ultimate end, Americans "of high-flying democratick sentiments" were acquiring land in upper and lower Canada. Among those Americans, who included some Indian tribes, were, in addition to Burr, Ethan Allen and his brothers, who had previously tried unsuccessfully to gain British support for an independent Vermont, and the Mohawk chief Joseph Brant, a friend of Burr who, having moved to Canada, was also unhappy with British rule. But if there was such a scheme that was based on more than fantasies entertained by French Canadians, American Francophiles, disgruntled Vermonters, and the French government, nothing came of it. While Burr borrowed to finance Canadian land purchases, and apparently had a sum of money on deposit in Paris, there is no evidence that he colluded with the French to detach all or part of Canada from Britain. But Hamilton, in whom Liston or other representatives of the Crown probably confided their apprehensions, may have thought otherwise, since he mentioned in at least two letters that Burr's desperate finances could lead him to engage in *"bargain* and *sale* with some foreign power."[54]

If he really believed that this was possible, Hamilton's recommending to Governor Jay Burr's appointment in February 1799 as "Superintendent" of fortification at the port of New York is all the more difficult to explain. Simple logic would seem to indicate that an individual who was possibly for sale to a foreign power, presumably France, was hardly a fit person to be in charge of preparing the port of New York for a possible war with France. Inconsistency, of course, is the hobgoblin of large minds like Hamilton's as consistency is the hobgoblin of small ones, but there may be another explanation for the seeming contradiction in Hamilton's attitude toward Burr at this time. Perhaps he did not really believe that Burr would sell himself to France but deemed it politically useful on the eve of the 1800 Presidential election to raise that possibility. Or perhaps he did not really believe, by February 1799, that there would be a war with France, or that New York in the event of war would come under attack. As noted, his recommendation of Burr may have owed something to discomfort with his role in Burr's recently being passed over for promotion to brigadier general.

But it may be significant that in February 1799 Hamilton was assisting Burr in obtaining a charter from the New York legislature for the Manhattan Company, an endeavor in which his brother-in-law, John Barker Church, was interested to the extent afterwards of becoming a member of the company's first board of directors. Within days of his letter recommending Burr to Jay, Hamilton had been appointed by Burr one of three Federalists on a committee seeking the necessary approval of the company from New York City's Common Council. Hamilton later was to turn against the company and find in its operations new reason to accuse Burr of duplicity and dishonesty, not that he required new reasons to oppose Burr's continuing efforts to attain political office. For a brief time in 1799, however, and for whatever reasons, Hamilton's ill will toward Burr appears to have abated, but, as is often the case with other ills of the mind and body, the diminution of symptoms turned out to be false indication that the disease had run its course.

eight

FAREWELLS TO ALL THAT

U ntil well into this century, the authorship of *The Federalist* was disputed by historians; Washington's Farewell Address, also "one of the great documents of American history," is still a matter of controversy.[1] The *Federalist* dispute had originated in the rival claims of Madison and Hamilton to have written certain numbers, whereas the later disagreement has centered on Hamilton's role in assisting Washington with successive drafts, the earliest of which was supplied by Madison, of his Farewell Address in 1796, when he declined to be nominated for a third term of office. John Jay, the third author of *The Federalist*, whose contribution was a modest one, was also involved, but peripherally. Recalling in 1811 that he had discussed the Farewell Address with Hamilton, Jay, modest once more, asserted only that while some amendments emerged from the discussion, "none were of any consequence."[2]

Not surprisingly, biographers of Hamilton have not taken issue with Jay's statement, but they have been far from accepting claims of even partial authorship put forward in behalf of Madison. Acknowledging that Madison in 1792 wrote a farewell speech for Washington when he was contemplating retirement at the conclusion of his first term, they nevertheless insist that he used little or nothing of Madison's draft four years later when, as Schachner put it, "the times had changed." Taking into account "the troubled foreign situation, the vast European war and the delicate situation of the United States as a neutral," he continues, Washington wished "to add to the original simple phrases some notes of warning, some outline of future policy, by which his country might steer its course in the days to come."³ Turning to Hamilton, who in the past had committed many of his thoughts to paper, Washington sent him Madison's draft of 1792 with his own additions and revisions, and asked Hamilton to return it "with such amendments & corrections" as he thought necessary, even "if you should think it best to throw the *whole* into a different form."⁴ Hamilton as requested made a number of changes in the Madison draft and also submitted a draft of his own, the first eight and the last six paragraphs of which were based on the 1792 Madison draft Washington had revised.⁵ It was this draft as further modified by Washington that became the Farewell Address, first published on September 19, 1796.

In light of this history, a reasonable conclusion would appear to be that all three men involved in the writing of the Farewell Address deserve credit—Washington for supplying or at least endorsing its substantive content; Hamilton and to a lesser extent Madison for giving it coherence, form, and fluency. Also arguable, since Madison's contribution to the final draft was a small one, is the view that "the *ideas* were Washington's; the *phrasing* mainly that of Hamilton."⁶ These judgments were challenged as early as 1825 by Hamilton's widow and other family members, and more recently some of Madison's biographers, among whom Irving Brant has been prominent, have contested claims that Madison's role in drafting the Address was both limited and insignificant. Emphasizing the importance of Madison's draft of 1792 in response to a request from Washington for an appropriate speech on the occasion of his leaving office, Brant maintained in 1950 that in "recasting the address, Hamilton used nearly all of Madison's draft, most of it paraphrased . . . The first ten paragraphs of the Farewell Address—about one fifth of the whole—are Madison's . . . A comparison of the Washington, Madison, and Hamilton contributions leaves no doubt that practically every important idea came from the President. Not so the wording. Madison forged the link between Washington and the people, and gave the address its inspirational tone. Hamilton added force and amplitude—also partisan politics—to the advice about public affairs."⁷ While admitting that Madison's draft contained no reference to what Washington termed "the insidious wiles of foreign influence" and the need "to steer clear of permanent alliances with any portion of the foreign world," Brant nevertheless insisted that Washington's "advice against foreign entanglements stemmed from Madison's 1783 resolutions in the Continental Congress."

Madison himself did not take credit for this or any other theme in the Farewell Address; indeed, he disapproved of the "alliances" warning, which he interpreted as originating with the Federalists and being aimed at revolutionary France. Writing a letter in code to Monroe on September 29, 1796, less than two weeks after the Address was published, Madison complained that "every channel has been latterly opened that could convey to {Washington's} mind a rancor against {France} and suspicion of all who are thought to sympathize with its revolution and who support the policy of extending our commerce and in general of standing well with it."[8] Madison did not mention Hamilton, but he could have had little doubt that Hamilton for some time had commanded one of those "channels" which had influenced not only Washington's Farewell Address but policies the President had followed during the eight years of his Administration.

Madison was still living when Betsey Hamilton in behalf of her dead husband laid claim to a role for him in the preparation of the Address that went far beyond mere influence. Apparently, she had been unhappy for some time that in 1810 Nathaniel Pendleton, Hamilton's second at the duel and an executor of his will, had entrusted Hamilton's papers relating to the Address to Rufus King, Hamilton's longtime friend and confidant. He had done so, according to King, "to prevent their falling into the hands of the General's family," who would use the papers to demonstrate that Hamilton, not Washington, "was the author and writer of the farewell address."[9] Presumably, Pendleton and King, both of whom had been devoted to Hamilton, were motivated by a desire to preserve the memory of Washington as a truly national leader, above the fiercely partisan Federalist politics of which Hamilton had been the exemplar, and to prevent any additional allegations by either Hamilton's friends or his enemies that, in Adams's words decribing the Federalists' view of the first President, Washington "was the painted wooden head of the ship and Hamilton the pilot and steersman," or, in short, that Hamilton had been the de facto President from 1789 to 1796.[10] In 1810, when Madison was President and it was almost certain that Republicans would continue to hold that office for some time, Pendleton and King must have recognized that the claim that Hamilton and not Washington was the author of the Farewell Address could only serve to deepen Republican suspicions that in the early period of the Republic Washington for the most part had been President in name only.

Betsey Hamilton, determined to regain possession of the papers from King, who refused to give them up, filed a suit against him in 1825 which was withdrawn a year later when the papers were delivered to her son, James A. Hamilton. But whatever her intentions, the successive drafts of the Farewell Address that had passed back and forth between Washington and Hamilton, and the correspondence related to it, do not establish that Hamilton wrote the address.[11] While there can be no doubt that he contributed much to the final version, there is little question that Washington made significant changes in the various drafts by deleting observations and expressions inserted by Hamilton that he regarded as too provocative, and by adding paragraphs expressing his own thoughts about the future course of the country. The only evidence, if evidence it is, that Hamilton was the sole author of the Farewell Address is the testimony of Betsey herself in 1840, at a time when her husband's services to the country during its first years were either being minimized or, in her opinion, misunderstood and distorted. In her reminiscence of Hamilton's involvement in drafting the Address, Betsey recalled that "the idea" of a farewell address to be delivered by Washington had originated with her husband, and that Washington, "well pleased" with it, had asked Hamilton to "prepare an address for him" based on a list of "subjects on which he would wish to remark."

Betsey further recollected that "the whole or nearly all the 'Address' was read to me by him as he wrote it . . . The original was forwarded to Genl. Washington, who approved of it with the exception of one paragraph, of, I think, about four or five lines, which if I mistake not was on the subject of public schools, which was stricken out. It was afterwards delivered to Mr. Hamilton who made the desired Alteration, and was afterwards delivered by General Washington, and published in that form, and has ever since been known as 'General Washington's farewell address.' Shortly after the publication of the address, my husband and myself were walking in Broadway, when an old soldier accosted him, with a request of him to purchase General Washington's Farewell address, which he did, and turning to me said, 'The Man does not know he has asked me to purchase my own work.' "[12]

In fairness to Betsey Hamilton, it should be mentioned that she probably was not aware that in 1792 Washington had discussed his "idea" of a farewell speech with Madison, who proceeded to draft one;

that Washington himself had written the first version of his 1796 fare-well speech, which, with modifications and revisions, was transformed into the Farewell Address; and, finally, that in connection with the *Federalist* papers her husband had also claimed authorship which right-fully belonged to someone else.

Given his interest in the 1796 Vice Presidential nomination as the Republican candidate, Burr must have enthusiastically welcomed Washington's farewell, but not his Farewell Address, with its condem-nation of what Washington termed "the baneful effects of the spirit of Party" and the "alternate domination of one faction over another . . . which, in different ages and countries has perpetrated the most horrid enormities [and] is itself a frightful despotism." While Burr's letters make no reference to the Address, there is indirect evidence that he, like Madison, strongly disapproved of Washington's warning against foreign influence which the retiring President and Hamilton mainly associated with France. Fearful that the doctrines of the French Rev-olution would somehow make their way to the United States, and convinced that Jacobins or French sympathizers were already influ-ential in Republican circles or as journalists, the Federalists in the summer of 1798 had sufficient votes in Congress and in most of the Northeastern states to enact a series of legislative measures known as the Alien and Sedition Acts. The first three of these laws, aimed at aliens, extended the period of required residence for citizenship from five to fourteen years, authorized the deportation of aliens regarded as a threat to law and order or as inclined to "treasonable or secret" behavior, and empowered the President in time of war—which many believed was imminent with France—to arrest, imprison, or banish aliens suspected of being under enemy control.

As if these early manifestations of patriotic zeal were not enough, the Sedition Act went even further toward repression by providing for fines and imprisonment of persons who combined with others to op-pose the execution of laws, or to prevent federal officers from per-forming their duties, or to promote "any insurrection, riot, unlawful assembly, or combination." A final section of the Sedition Act, and by far the most extreme, sanctioned a fine of up to $2,000 and impris-onment up to two years for persons convicted of publishing "any false, scandalous and malicious writing or writings against the government of the United States . . . Congress . . . the President . . . with intent to defame the said government . . . or to bring them, or either of them, into contempt or disrepute."[13] The Alien Acts were in effect only until 1802, and the Sedition Act only until March 1801, when Jefferson became President, but by then seventy individuals, according to some estimates, had been fined and jailed under the Sedition Act. Although President Adams, who had been reluctant to sign the measures, did not deport any aliens, there is evidence that a number of foreign residents uncertain of a continuing welcome in their adopted country left voluntarily, and still others were deterred from emigrating to the United States.

At the high point of the Francophobic hysteria, several states, including New York, debated a constitutional amendment declaring, in the language of the Massachusetts Amendment Resolutions sent for approval to the other states, that no person was eligible to be President or a member of Congress who, if not a natural-born citizen, was not resident in the United States at the time of the Declaration of Independence in 1776. By January 1799, the Massachusetts Resolutions had been approved by the Connecticut and Vermont legislatures, by lower houses of the Rhode Island and New Hampshire legislatures, and by the New York State Senate. On January 8, the resolutions came before the New York Assembly, to which Burr had been elected in 1797, and a newspaper account of the debate over their approval provides the first and only extended report of a speech delivered by Burr in connection with a significant public issue. On this occasion, at least, Burr would leave no doubt of his position. He would not maintain his usual silence or seeming neutrality with regard to an important policy controversy.

The report in the Republican *Albany Register* of January 8, 1799, quoted Burr as taking sharp issue with the distrust of aliens manifested in the proposed constitutional amendment. Noting that the "people are already sufficiently distrustful of strangers," he argued that not only was there no evidence of any alien "intrigue against our government," but that aliens were serving honorably in command of key military positions; "even the commander of the navy of America," he added, "is a foreigner." Incidents of conspiracy or treason, he reminded his fellow assemblymen, were "effected, not by foreigners, but by natives, was [Benedict] Arnold a foreigner, is not [William] Blount an American?" In later remarks, described as "a speech of considerable length,"

Burr's further enumeration of foreigners rendering distinguished service included three Supreme Court Justices, two Revolutionary War generals, and "a long train of worthies" he did not identify but "whose names should sufficiently prove the futility of excluding such men from any important station in the power of our country to bestow." Burr and other opponents of the proposed amendment must have been persuasive; the vote on concurring with the Senate, which had approved the measure, was 40 in favor, 62 against. One month later, the defeat of the proposed amendment to the Constitution was assured when, seven states having refused to ratify it, it failed to secure the necessary two-thirds majority of all the states, then sixteen in number, required for Congress to call a convention to consider its adoption.[14]

Most of the states opposed to the Massachusetts Resolutions supported in varying degrees the spirit though not the letter of the Kentucky and Virginia Resolutions of 1798 affirming, in the words of the Kentucky Resolutions drafted by Jefferson, that the government was created by a "compact" of the states in which *each party had an equal right to judge for itself, as well of infractions as of the mode and measure of redress.*" Lest there be any doubt what these words meant, the Virginia Resolutions, drafted by Madison, declared the Alien and Sedition Acts "unconstitutional," and called on the other states to coordinate with Virginia in taking "necessary and proper measures . . . in maintaining unimpaired the authorities, rights, and liberties reserved to the states respectively, or to the people."[15] Burr, in agreement with these sentiments, was unable to muster sufficient votes in the New York Assembly to endorse the resolutions, and the efforts of others in states dominated by Republicans were no more successful beyond evoking expressions of sympathetic interest. Nevertheless, the Kentucky and Virginia resolutions established a precedent for future attempts by states to nullify acts of the federal government, the most fateful of which occurred during the years leading up to the Civil War.

Hamilton's role, unlike Burr's, in the Alien and Sedition Acts controversy was one of subdued support for the measures, and of outraged opposition to what he regarded as the Jacobin-inspired "compact" theory and its nullification derivative. When the legislation was being debated in Congress, he wrote Pickering: "Let us not be cruel or violent,"[16] advice some of his biographers have interpreted as indicating that he did not favor severe enforcement of the statutes. Often overlooked in their discussion of his attitude, however, is his prefatory remark that in his opinion "the mass [of aliens] ought to be obliged to leave the Country [but] the provisions in our Treaties in favour of Merchants ought to be observed & there ought to be *guarded* exceptions of characters whose situations would expose them too much if sent away & whose demeanour among us has been unexceptional. There are a few such."[17]

Miller is one of the few Hamilton biographers to observe that while the Alien and Sedition laws "were not the result of Hamilton's initiative . . . it could never be said of Hamilton that he was guilty of under-estimating the menace of 'Jacobinism' at home or of extending charity to the Republicans . . . As for Jefferson, Hamilton left no doubt that he suspected the Virginian of treachery against the independence of his country: 'To be the proconsul of a despotic Directory over the United States, degraded to the condition of a province,' he exclaimed, 'can alone be the criminal, the ignoble aim of so seditious, so prostitute, a character.' By thus whipping up hysteria, Hamilton contributed toward the creation of the poisonous atmosphere of party rancor and fear in which the Alien and Sedition Acts were conceived."[18]

Convinced that the Virginia Resolutions, in particular, sanctioned non-compliance with the Alien and Sedition Acts and threatened the dissolution of the Union by armed force, Hamilton warned the Virginians and other Jacobins that the army would be called out, if necessary, to deal with such massive civil disobedience. The dangers, in his view, of French subversion, an attempted invasion by France, and talk of insurrection in Virginia and elsewhere, demonstrated the need for a standing army of up to 50,000 men, permanent army and navy academies to train cadres of professional officers, a navy of respectable size, and, finally, an effective secret service to spy on enemy agents and report their activities to the President. As it became clear that there was not to be a war with France, the case for a military establishment was less apparent to many outside Hamilton's circle, a clear majority of the citizenry. But it was still necessary, Hamilton believed, to remain vigilant with regard to demonstrations and protests potentially even more destructive than Shays' Rebellion of 1786–87 and the Whisky Rebellion of 1794. Hamilton's allegations that disruptive tendencies could be seen at work in the country were, if not proven, at least somewhat supported by an angry Pennsylvania gathering in early 1799 of several hundred men, this time protesting a direct federal tax on property rather than on whisky. John Fries, the organizer, was sentenced to death on a charge of treason but was pardoned by Adams.

Hamilton, who earlier had ordered a militia detachment and two companies of artillery into action against Fries, did not approve of the pardon, and he liked even less Burr's efforts in the New York Assembly to organize opposition to the Alien and Sedition Acts and the Massachusetts resolutions. He privately may have favored another Burr initiative in the Assembly which has received little attention from Burr's biographers. While they have speculated at length about the extent, if any, of his religious beliefs, and biographers of Hamilton have repeatedly posed the question, in the phrasing of Douglass Adair, "Was Hamilton a Christian Statesman?" neither the Burrites nor the Hamiltonians have explored the possibility that Hamilton's attitude toward religion may have had much in common with that of Burr.

Burr's initiative in a session of the Assembly on February 6, 1799, related to a motion "to dispense with the attendance of the Rev. Mr. O'Brien as one of the chaplains to this House." Presumably encouraged by a vote on the measure of fifty-nine in favor and thirty-three against, Burr introduced an amendment to the approved resolution: "That this House will dispense with the further attendance of the Rev. Mr. O'Brien, the Rev. Mr. Ellison, the Rev. Mr. Johnson, the Rev. Mr. Bassett, the Rev. Mr. Miller, the Rev. Mr. Nott, the Rev. Mr. Braun and the Rev. Mr. Jefferson as chaplains to this House." The Assembly journal does not specify that the eight clergymen, each of whom probably represented a different denomination, comprised the total number of chaplains, but we can surmise that they did. On this second vote, the negative side was more successful, with forty-nine assemblymen voting against Burr's amendment.[19]

Unfortunately, the *Albany Register* did not report Burr's remarks, assuming that he spoke in support of his motion, but however he put the case, his motion seemingly abolishing Assembly chaplains is consistent with his lifelong history of distancing himself from religious observance of any kind. It also is remarkably similar in spirit to a comment Hamilton allegedly made toward the end of the Constitutional Convention. At that crucial time, when the fate of the Constitution was not yet decided, Benjamin Franklin is said to have proposed that henceforth sessions open with a prayer asking divine assistance.

Hamilton then, according to the anecdote, "made a little humorous speech in opposition . . . certain they were competent to transact the business which had been entrusted to their care without 'the necessity of calling in foreign aid!' Accordingly, the convention decided to do without the services of a chaplain."[20]

Spurious the anecdote may be, considering that it was first recounted in 1825, but it does not run counter to what is known of Hamilton's attitude toward religion during the greater part of his life. Although his family after his death insisted that he had lived and died a practicing Christian, he is known to have made only a few references to his religious convictions prior to the duel, and, like Burr, to have attended church services infrequently other than on occasions of marriages, baptisms, and funerals. Both were skeptical of the claims made by those who adhered to a literal interpretation of scriptures or who maintained that one Christian dogma was superior in revealed truth to another.

Hamilton apparently repented of these views when he was preparing for the duel, and abandoned them altogether when he was near death. As Hamilton lay dying, Wolcott, who visited him, confided to his wife that Hamilton "in his late years expressed his conviction of the truths of the Christian Religion, and had desired to receive the Sacrament."[21] But his previous indifference to religion was not immediately forgiven by the two clergymen from whom he requested a final benediction. Episcopal Bishop Benjamin Moore initially refused to administer the sacrament, as did the Reverend John Mason of the Dutch Reformed Church, a minister Hamilton had known for thirty years, who was asked to give Hamilton Communion. Bishop Moore relented after Hamilton agreed to forgive Burr and, if he lived, renounce dueling. Not long after the Bishop offered a last prayer at Hamilton's bedside, he officiated at his funeral in Trinity Church.

Burr, by contrast, died as he had lived, an agnostic. Visited by another Dutch Reformed minister as he was dying, who asked whether he believed God in his mercy would pardon him for his sins, Burr, who did not request or receive the sacrament, would say only: "On that subject I am coy."[22] Burr's questioner was hoping for a more positive response, as had other clergymen over the years, some of whom had known Burr's parents and grandparents, when they felt impelled to question his religious beliefs. "It is reported, and is believed

by a number," one wrote him, "that you do not believe in divine rev-
elation, and discard Christianity as not worthy of credit." These words
in an 1802 letter to Burr from the Reverend Samuel Hopkins, a Congregational minister who had been a close friend of Jonathan Edwards
and had been acquainted with Burr's mother, were followed by Hopkins's observing that Burr's "pious and worthy ancestors" would be
"inexpressibly" grieved "were they now in this world, to know that
one of their posterity, for whom they had made so many prayers who
was educated in a Christian land, and is possessed of such great and
distinguished natural powers of mind, was an infidel." There is no
record of any response to this letter from Burr, then Vice President,
perhaps because Hopkins died before Burr was able to compose a
reply, or, alternatively, because he was not pleased to read that "all
infidelity, whether it be called Deism, theism or Skepticism renounced
the true God, {and} has its foundation in a very depraved and corrupt
heart, and will land in endless misery."[23]

Had the isms condemned by the Reverend Hopkins included he-
donism, and the "misery" of mounting debt and overdue bills that
sometimes is one of its consequences, he might have struck a more
responsive chord in Burr. Habitually living beyond his means, and
almost always in financial difficulty, in 1797–98 he was particularly
"distressed for money," as he wrote John Nicholson, a sometime partner in speculations, on March 18, 1798. But distressed as he was, he
often was more sparing of his debtors than his creditors were of him.
In one letter he wrote Nicholson, who owed him money, that he had
too much "sympathy" for Nicholson's "misfortunes . . . to add a particle
to their weight."[24]

Continually on the alert for opportunities to rid himself of debt and
live a life free of money worries, Burr in 1799 saw a chance to accom-
plish both by interesting himself in a proposal to establish a company
to supply New York City with safe drinking water. Until that time,
the city, like many others, depended for fresh water on wells and
streams, much of which were unsafe and were believed by some to be
responsible for the repeated yellow-fever epidemics of the 1790s. With
a population of 56,000 that was growing rapidly, the city also needed
new sources of water if it was not to import it at considerable expense
from other localities. In March 1799, as mentioned, legislation chartering a municipal water company in New York, to be known as the

Manhattan Company, was introduced in the Assembly and approved within days by both the Assembly and the Senate. By then Burr had organized a city committee of six—three Republicans, one of whom was Burr himself, and three Federalists, one of whom was Hamilton—to speed approval of the Manhattan Company by the Common Council of the city and by the legislature as a stock-issuing private company rather than as a city-owned enterprise.

Apparently, neither Hamilton nor the other members of the committee knew that from the beginning Burr had intended to add a provision to the company charter, as the legislation was nearing final passage, that read: "*be it further enacted*, That it shall and may be lawful for the said company to employ all such surplus capital as may belong or accrue to the said company in the purchase of public or other stock, or in any other monied transactions or operations . . . for the sole benefit of the said company." In short, the Manhattan Company was designed to be both a water company, which it was for forty years, until 1840, and a bank, which it is still, known worldwide today as the Chase Manhattan Bank.[25]

Hamilton initially welcomed the establishment of the Manhattan Company and was instrumental in gaining approval for it from the Common Council. Largely due to his efforts, his brother-in-law John Barker Church became one of the company's first directors, and among those investing in it were his close friend Robert Troup and, in 1800, another Hamilton brother-in-law, Stephen Van Rensselaer. Only after the Manhattan Company bank opened for business in September 1799 did Hamilton gradually become convinced that, as he described it in January 1801, the company was "a perfect monster in its principles, and a very convenient instrument of *profit & influence*."[26]

Certainly, he had good reason to dislike it. A success from the start, the bank competed with Hamilton's Bank of New York and the local branch of the Bank of the United States, and it did so with distinct advantages. Its charter permitted it to have a larger paid-up capital than that of the Bank of New York, and its more favored status included the right to own property of all sorts, including real estate, to contract debts and issue notes of a type forbidden to the other two banks, to give its directors and stockholders an unusual degree of decision-making freedom, and to retain its charter in perpetuity, unlike the Bank of New York, whose charter was due to expire in twenty years.[27]

While the view of some historians and biographers is that Burr never intended the Manhattan Company to supply much water to New York,[28] there is evidence that its performance in that respect was a creditable one during its early years. Abandoning its original plan of piping water from the Bronx River, presumably because of fear that the wooden pipes in which it was carried would freeze and burst in winter, the company turned to the Collect Pond and nearby springs and wells situated slightly north of City Hall's present location. There was also to be a reservoir kept filled by well water pumped from below by horses. By the end of its first year of operation, the company was supplying water to more than four hundred homes and shops, and a number of fountains, through six miles of wooden pipe. Eventually, the system covered twenty-five miles of water main reaching into more than two thousand houses.

But there were many complaints that the supply of water was inadequate, partly because of low water pressure, which made access to it difficult, and, a more important reason, because the company directors were not investing sufficient funds in upkeep and expansion of the supply and its distribution. The situation was made worse by frequent fires, which were difficult to extinguish because water was not available in quantity. The Manhattan Company's water service continued for some years, however, even surviving a disastrous fire in 1818 that destroyed many buildings, and a severe cholera epidemic in 1832 that took a number of lives. Finally, in 1842, the city assigned to itself the function of supplying water, thereby allowing the Manhattan Company to concentrate on what it did best, namely, banking.

While Burr benefited financially from the creation of the Manhattan Company bank, his shares of bank stock dramatically increasing in value, as did the shares of Church, Troup, and other Federalists and Republicans, and on the signature of friends borrowed from it heavily, he paid a political price for sponsoring it that more than offset these gains. Whatever else he intended, at the outset he and many of his fellow Republicans saw the bank as offering party members economic influence similar to the economic benefits enjoyed by Federalists at the Bank of New York and the city branch of the Bank of the United States. This was reason enough for Hamilton to condemn Burr for his "Trick," as he called it, in attaching the charter proposal, without attracting notice, to the Manhattan Company legislation immediately prior to passage. Burr's Republican enemies, for their part, could accuse Burr of presiding over the birth of an institution they viewed, following Jefferson's lead, as favoring "stock-jobbers," the "monied" interest, and speculators in general over the farmers whom Jefferson had termed "the chosen people of God" in his *Notes on Virginia*. Those who also believed that Burr might have done more in the Assembly to promote approval of the Kentucky and Virginia resolutions now had new grounds for believing that his Republicanism was heavily tainted by Federalist leanings. The consequence was that Burr, once again, faced mounting distrust from both sides, accompanied by renewed charges in each camp that "he is not one of us." Seeking another Assembly term in April 1799, Burr was defeated when enough Republicans joined enough Federalists to bring down not only him but the other Assembly Republicans from New York. Of Manhattan's seven wards, only one supported the Republican Assembly ticket. But Burr and his Republican allies, as the federal and state elections of 1800 were to demonstrate, were not vanquished for long.

These ups and downs of Burr's political fortunes were closely monitored by his daughter, Theo, who referred to her father's allies in New York politics as the "Tenth Legion."[29] Seventeen years old on her birthday in June 1800, she was involved even more closely in his personal life, including his affairs with women. His letters to her, reporting his numerous liaisons, made use of such code designations as "Celeste," "C.," "Madame G.," "La R.," "Le Planche," "La G.," and "Clara," for his female friends, one of whom he mentioned repeatedly in his letters to Theo over a period of two years. Apparently, they both had known "Celeste," a young, wealthy, and very proper young lady of Philadelphia and her "père," as Burr referred to him, for some time before June of 1803, when he was "meditating" whether to take "the fatal step" of proposing marriage. Calling himself "Reubon" in his letters to Theo recounting "the Story of the Loves of Reubon and Celeste," he reported that "Celeste," who had previously declared her intention never to marry, once again requested that he not renew his suit, but when he was making his departure she asked him to return. All of which only served to convince Theo that her father, experienced with women as he was, still had much to learn about the complexities of the language to which they resorted in the company of courting men. "As to Celeste," twenty-year-old Theo wrote her forty-seven-year-old father on June 14, "she meant, from the beginning, to say that awful word—*yes*; but not choosing to say it immediately, she told you that *you* had furnished her with arguments against matrimony, which in French means, Please, sir, persuade me out of them again. But you took it as a plump refusal, and walked off. She called you back. What more could she do? I would have seen you to Japan before I should have done so much."[30] The courtship dance of "Reubon" and "Celeste" was to continue intermittently until shortly after the duel, when one or the other brought it to a final end.

While not all of Burr's female friends, as his relationship with "Celeste" demonstrates, were his mistresses or responded positively to his advances, his habit of confiding some of his experiences with them to his daughter has had few defenders even among his admiring biographers. One of those not so admiring has been particularly critical of his letter to Theo relating to his papers on the eve of the duel, going so far in censure of Burr as to label him an "unnatural parent" for instructing Theo "to read, in the event of his death in the duel with Hamilton, the confidential letters which came to him in the course of his love intrigues and affairs of gallantry. It imports a moral obliquity that, happily for society, is found in few human beings."[31]

Whether one agrees or disagrees that Burr was an "unnatural parent," no one can doubt that Theo was the woman he loved most in his life, that she was also his most trusted friend and confidante, and that the relationship between them was much closer than that customary between a father and a daughter. On Burr's side, the closeness was evident in the thousand or more letters, sometimes as many as eight in one month, he wrote to her in the course of her relatively short life, and while he rarely expressed his feelings in an effusive manner, he did not hesitate to write Theo from Albany on January 4, 1799, when she was fifteen years old: "The happiness of my life depends on your exertions; for what else, for whom else do I live?"[32] Ten years later, when Burr was effectively an exile in Europe with no money or future prospects of any sort, Theo wrote him: "You appear to me so superior, so elevated above all other men; I contemplate you with such a strange mixture of humility, admiration, reverence, love, and pride, that very little superstition would be necessary to make me worship you as a superior being; such enthusiasm does your character excite in me. When I afterward revert to myself, how insignificant do my best qualities appear . . . I had rather not live than not be the daughter of such a man."[33] When she wrote these words on August 1, 1809, Theo was not the lonely motherless adolescent of fifteen she had been when her father wrote to her "for whom else do I live?" but a twenty-six-year-old woman who had been married more than eight years and had been a mother for seven of them.

She was also a woman whose shaping by her father almost evokes the image of the sculptor molding a figure in clay or working it in marble. Burr made his influence felt not only in every area of intellectual interest and aesthetic taste but in such matters as her health, posture, need for exercise, carriage and deportment, diet and table manners, conduct when persons deserving respect were present, and performance as a hostess when his friends or political associates were coming to dinner. Urging her in January 1799 to develop an "open, serene, intelligent countenance" that was "not wrought into smiles or simpers," he advised her to "avoid, forever avoid, a smile or sneer of contempt; never even mimic them. A frown of sullenness or discontent is but one degree less hateful."[34] Complimenting her for the impression she made when she visited Indian Chief Brant on a trip north in October 1801, he informed her she had made "two, perhaps more conquests . . . King Brandt and the stage-driver . . . Brandt has written me two letters on the subject. It would have been quite in style if he had scalped your husband and made you Queen of the Mohawks."[35] He insisted she take harp lessons, learn to dance and to sit a horse, and apply herself to languages, especially French. A number of his letters express concern about a slave or servant who was injured, and who, as a result, deserved her attention: "Poor Tom," he wrote her in March 1794, when she was not quite eleven years old, referring to a slave: "I hope you take good care of him. If he is confined by his leg, &c., he must pay the greater attention to his reading and writing."[36]

Tom was not the only one whose reading required more attention. Burr was forever criticizing Theo's spelling, punctuation, and grammar, telling her how to make her letters more informative, interesting, and, when he could not make out what she had written, more legible. When she was only eight years of age, Burr complimented her for improving "much in your writing,"[37] and a year later he informed her that he was searching for books that were not fairy tales but appropriate reading for *an intelligent, well-informed girl of nine years old.*"[38] He recommended certain historians—"the ancient and modern history of

Millet . . . is concise, perspicuous, and well selected"; and dismissed others — "Rollin is full of tedious details and superstitious nonsense."[39] When he made these comments to Theo, she was fifteen years old.

Calling her attention to a novel of "Miss Burney or D'Arblay," the name of which he could not immediately recall, he asked Theo to note the heroine's "account of little details on her debut in London, and particularly of a ball where she met Lord Somebody and did twenty ridiculous things." He did not do so because he was urging her to read novels, but because "I want a description of a ball from you. Be pleased to read those first letters of the novel referred to, and take them for a model."[40] When he had no model to serve as an example, he improvised one of his own. A journal keeper himself, he insisted in a letter that Theo, ten years old or perhaps even younger, begin a daily journal to which he expected her to devote ten or, better, twenty minutes each day, and send to him "every Monday morning." To insure that Theo understood what he had in mind, he sent her a "Sample of the Manner of your Journal for one Day."[41]

Burr's efforts to transform his daughter into a woman whose interests were not confined to home, husband, and children, and who, it seems fair to say, was intended to become something like a female version of himself, did not end with Theo's marriage. "In your reading," he wrote her in December 1801, when he was Vice President and she had been living in South Carolina almost a year, "I wish you would learn to read newspapers; not to become a partisan in politics, God forbid; but they contain the occurences of the day, and furnish the standing topics of conversation . . . With the aid of a gazeteer and atlas, you must find every place that is spoken of. Pray, madam, do you know of what consist the 'Republic of the Seven Islands?' Do you know the present boundaries of the French republic? Neither, in all probability. Then hunt them."[42]

He frequently ended his letters with "your affectionate papa," "ma chère amie," or, more playfully, "Adieu, my dear little negligent baggage" (he had not had a letter from her), and "get to bed, you hussy." And Theo sometimes closed her letters: "I kiss you with all my heart." That this display of feeling was highly unusual at the turn of the eighteenth century is attested to by the letters of Jefferson and other contemporaries of Burr to their daughters, which lack such expressions. (No letters of Hamilton to his daughter Angelica have been found.)

Jefferson, like Burr, could be demanding of his daughters, Martha (known as Patsy) especially, in terms of the education he wished them to have which he regarded as suitable for women, but with them there was not the "easy camaradie," to quote Brodie's phrase, that existed between Burr and Theo. It is difficult to imagine him writing Theo, as Jefferson wrote Patsy, who, like Theo, was motherless, when she was eleven years old: "at all times let your clothes be clean, whole, and properly put on . . . Some ladies think they may under the privileges of the dishabille be loose and negligent of their dress in the morning. But be you from the moment you rise till you go to bed as cleanly and properly dressed as at the hours of dinner or tea. A lady who has been seen as a sloven or slut in the morning will never efface the impression she then made . . . Nothing is so disgusting to our sex as a want of cleanliness and delicacy in yours."[43]

The relationship between Burr and Theo has been thought by a few observers not merely to have been close but to have possessed some of the affective qualities commonly associated with marital love. "There has hardly ever been in the world," one of them proclaimed in 1906, "a more famous pair of lovers than Burr and his gifted, noble daughter."[44] Another historian, who probably did not intend to make a similar point, however indirectly, nevertheless did so by devoting more pages to Theo than to her mother in a book whose topic was the wives of Lincoln, Madison, Burr, Benedict Arnold, Jefferson Davis, James G. Blaine, and other well-known Americans.[45] No historian or biographer, however, whatever his or her belief about the relationship between Burr and Theo, has expressed a view similar to that of acclaimed novelist Gore Vidal. In his novel *Burr*, which will be referred to again in a later chapter, there is explicit mention of a sexual connection between Burr and his daughter.[46]

Perhaps it is permissible to speculate, but no more than speculate, that Burr, a sexually active widower thirty-eight years old in 1794, who never again attached himself to any woman for long, was, like many such fathers in a similar situation, sometimes very physical with his daughter. If, as rumored, Hamilton's daughter, Angelica, and Theo knew each other, Angelica may have reported to her father incidents she observed of Burr's being physically playful or mockingly flirtatious with Theo that Hamilton interpreted as evidence of Burr's depravity and immorality. Hamilton, who, like Burr, was inclined to eroticize relationships with women, and who for some years carried on a love affair with his sister-in-law, may not have required much proof that Burr's conduct with Theo had incestuous overtones.

Certainly, he was convinced that, as he frequently put it, Burr "is indefatigable in courting the *young* and the *profligate*."[47] Burr's ability to charm men and women of all ages had a pronounced seductive quality, and Hamilton may have believed, as did others, that Burr's "veritable passion for adopting and rearing children" was not wholly innocent of "profligate" intent.[48] As Parton observed, Burr's "life-long habit of adopting and educating children . . . tended to increase his reputation for criminal gallantry."[49] While Henry Cabot Lodge did not endorse this view of Burr, he nevertheless was led sarcastically to observe that Burr possessed "what women and young men call 'fascination.' "[50] Hamilton, in short, may have attached a seductive sexual component to Burr's "fascination," but without intending to imply that there was an incestuous relationship between Burr and his daughter.

Theo, too, could charm and fascinate, and in the confines of her family be playful, flirtatious, and a tease, and not only in relation to her father. Writing her half brother John Bartow Prevost, in April 1797, when he was in Paris, she confided: "I hope Madame Tallien is well for by all accounts you are at present one of her gallants, which although it may be a great honor is not a very rare one."[51] At eleven years of age, she wrote what probably was her first bit of poetry, and sent these "few verses on female fashions" to Bartow:

> *Shepherd I have lost my waist*
> *Have you seen my body*
> *Sacrificed to modern taste*
> *I have become a dotty toddy.*
>
> *Never will you see me more*
> *Till common sense returning*
> *My body to my legs restored*
> *To gladness turn my morning.*
>
> *For fashion's sake I have forsook*
> *What sages call the belly,*
> *And fashion has not left a nook*
> *For: cheese, cakes, or jelly.*

Lest he think her verses wholly original, she added: "Taken from, Shepherd I have lost my love."[52]

The poetry was preceded by a request that Bartow write a love letter for Alexis, a slave or servant in the Burr household, who was in love with "a mulate girl" living in Virginia but who could not, apparently, write a letter himself. Bartow did so, satisfying not only Alexis and, we may hope, his lady friend, but Theo as well who praised his love letter as "warm, languishing & passionate. I suppose it is nearly a copy of what you have made use of in times of distress or at least affected distress."[53]

Much as Burr missed her company when she married into a wealthy South Carolina family in February 1801, he welcomed the match and even more the birth of her son, Aaron Burr Alston, on May 29, 1802. Theo's husband, Joseph Alston, was the son of a millionaire rice planter, William Alston, whose land in the low country along the Waccamaw River was tended by hundreds of slaves. Theo did not much like him or her husband's other relatives, complaining on one occasion to her father: "We travel in company with the two Alstons {Joseph's father and brother}. Pray teach me how to write two *A's* without producing something like an *Ass*."[54] Theo had been in no hurry to become an Alston, but Joseph made repeated proposals of marriage, one of which, in December 1800, she finally accepted.

Apparently, he had Burr's support from the beginning, and from the beginning there were suspicions in certain quarters that, to please her father, she had married for money. "It is understood here," Troup wrote Rufus King on May 27, 1801, "that the marriage was an affair of Burr, and not of his daughter, and that the money in question was the predominating motive."[55] Some Republicans friendly to Burr also had questions. Maria Nicholson, whose father was prominent in the "Tenth Legion," informed Gallatin's wife that a report of Alston's behavior "does not speak well of him; it says that he is rich, but he is a great dasher, dissipated, ill-tempered, vain and silly . . . Can it be that the father has sacrificed a daughter so lovely to affluence and influential connections?"[56] Suspicions that Burr had done so became more widespread when it was rumored, and with reason, that he had borrowed large sums from his son-in-law.

Almost without exception, Burr's biographers have declared him innocent of connivance and cupidity in arranging his daughter's marriage, which, they have also assumed, was a happy one. Perhaps it was for a time, despite Theo's not liking the climate and the treatment of slaves as well as her husband's relatives in South Carolina. But a letter of Theo's written on August 27, 1800, which hitherto has been overlooked, could be interpreted to suggest that Alston was not the only object of her affections five months before she accepted his proposal. Writing William Eustis from Providence, Rhode Island, one of the New England cities where she and her father were exploring political sentiment on the eve of the 1800 Presidential election, Theo confessed to him: "Your visit appears to me like a dream, and every night I wish to dream it over again, for according to modern superstitions after three times it would be verified; It is, however, I believe, better for me, that you should be absent, for in one day your pretty flatteries almost turned my head; it is only since your departure that I have recollected the folly of putting faith in anything uttered by a gentleman, even by Dr. Eustis in these matters. But great as the danger is and conscious as I am of it, in the true spirit of my sex, it is one which I sincerely wish to risk whenever you choose. Goodbye, we shall leave Providence tomorrow. TB."[57]

Perhaps these lines from seventeen-year-old Theo should be regarded as, at most, evidence of the passing infatuation of a young girl for a much older man who was her father's closest friend and with whom she could share her uncertainties above love and marriage. William Eustis (1753–1825), three years older than Burr, who himself was to marry a much younger woman when he was fifty-seven years old, in 1810, was a Harvard graduate and a Boston surgeon who in 1800 was elected to Congress as an Anti-Federalist and reelected in 1802. He and Burr, in addition to discussing politics, often exchanged impressions of women in whom one or the other was interested or, in at least three recorded instances, both. Burr's frequent references to Theo in his letters to Eustis, the earliest known in a letter of December 16, 1796, suggest that Eustis and Theo had been friends for some years and that Burr could not have been unaware that his daughter had a special feeling for Eustis. In a letter to Eustis introducing Alston, written almost three weeks before Theo's letter fondly remembering their visit, Burr wrote Eustis that he would shortly be coming to Providence together with Theo, "who sais that you will be so very glad to see [her] that she must accompany me." He then requested in his letter of August 10 that Eustis pay "particular attention" to Alston, who would shortly call upon him. "I beg you to analyze and anatomize him Soul & heart & body," Burr continued, "so that you may answer me all questions which I may put to you on that head when we shall meet in Providence."[58]

Unfortunately, we do not know the results of Dr. Eustis's "anatomization" of Theo's would-be fiancé, but however favorable it was, it apparently had little effect on Theo. This supposition is supported by another letter of Theo's to her sister-in-law, Frances Prevost, written in Providence on August 26, one day before she wrote to Eustis. By that time she had seen something of Alston and, apparently not much taken with him, wrote Frances, who anticipated the betrothal: "Mr. A. is with us but your prophecy is not likely to be verified notwithstanding your usual accuracy on all subjects."[59] As late as November 9, less than three months before she was married and only a day before the election in which Jefferson and her father were the Republican candidates for President and Vice President, Burr wrote Eustis that Theo "is with me and is more solicitous about your election than any other thing." Presumably, he did not mean she was more concerned about Eustis than about his own fate at the polls.[60] What Eustis made of all this, and the extent to which he reciprocated Theo's affections, is unknown; his few surviving letters to Burr make no mention of her, and there are no extant letters from him to Theo.

Burr's attachment to children who were not his own, and to young adults, was manifest in his having himself appointed guardian of several, who lived with him for varying periods of time. Some of those he befriended were young men of limited means, who, aspiring to careers as writers or artists, became temporary members of Burr's household. One of them, the painter John Vanderlyn, was partly supported by Burr when he continued his studies in France. Vanderlyn subsequently painted portraits of Burr and Theo. A number of others, such as William Peter Van Ness, later to be his second in the duel, became his political protégés.

Of all the young people in Burr's life, none was as important to him, apart from Theo, as a French refugee girl, thirteen years old in 1795, whom Burr regarded as his adopted daughter. Fleeing the Revolution in France, Nathalie Marie Louise Stephanie Beatrice Delage de Volude and her governess, Madame Senat, made their way to New York, where Madame Senat opened a school for adolescent females in which they were taught French and were introduced to European culture and manners. Theo attended the school, which was not far from her home on Partition (now Fulton) Street, and by 1795 Natalie, as she called herself, was living with the Burrs.

Burr clearly was taken with her, and probably Natalie, whose mother remained in Spain and whose father died in the Caribbean not long after she arrived in New York, was delighted with the welcome she received in the Burr household. But Burr on occasion may have carried the welcome too far, and apparently did so, in her eyes, when he wrote Eustis in November 1795: "At my side, in my library in the country, at the table at which I sit this dark stormy night, sits reading, but more than half the time laughing & talking, the loveliest creature that I know of her age (now in her 14th) . . . it is impossible to write where she is." Below this passage, Natalie added, in French: "I do not wish to sign a thing that is not true Natalie." Burr then contributed "witness her hand — she has read only what is on this [second] page," which was followed by Natalie's writing on a third page, again in French: "Mr. Burr misled me — pay no attention to all I wrote except this Natalie."[61]

Theo never saw this letter praising Natalie, who was a year older, as "the loveliest creature that I know of her age," or her father's much later one referring to Natalie as a "precious article," which no doubt was just as well.[62] While they seem to have been fond of each other and apparently continued their sisterly relationship for some years after each of them was married, they also competed for Burr's favor and as a consequnce there were occasional frictions. Perhaps Madame Senat sometimes was involved, as Burr appeared to imply when he wrote Theo on February 11, 1799: "What the deuce can have got into Madame S. and N, I am utterly at a loss to conjecture, and beg you not to give the remotest hint, but meet them as usual." Elsewhere in his correspondence there are indications that he was well acquainted with Madame Senat, but nothing is known about her or her role in Burr's life.

His love for his daughter did not preclude his comparing her unfavorably with Natalie, and at times he could be cruel or at least insensitive in his praise of Natalie at Theo's expense. "Observe how Natalie replies to the smallest civility which is offered to her," he wrote Theo on September 17, 1795, in a letter criticizing Theo's manners. Within a space of five days, he informed Theo that Natalie's "letters are full of good sense, of acute observation, of levity, of gravity, and affection," whereas "your last letter," he wrote his daughter less than a week later, "is pleasant and cheerful. Careless, incorrect, slovenly, illegible. I dare not show a sentence of it even to Eustis."[63] In another two weeks he had received "three letters from Natalie," he wrote Theo, "All full of interest and amusement. Her remarks are equal to those of Lady Mary W. Montague for their truth and spirit," Mrs. Montagu being famous for her "Turkish Letters" written from Constantinople.[64]

On June 24, 1804, when the exchange of messages with Hamilton culminating in the duel was already under way, he made no mention of it in writing Theo that he and some friends on her birthday "laughed an hour, and danced an hour, and drank [your] health at Richmond Hill. We had your picture in the dining-room; but as it is a profile, and would not look at us, we hung it up, and placed Natalie's at table, which laughs and talks with us." Urging them both to transform "ancient mythology" into children's stories, he concluded his letter: "I'll bet that [Natalie] makes the best tale." Whether he won his bet is unknown, as is Theo's reaction to this and similar taunts, but perhaps something of her feeling about her father's praise of Natalie can be detected in Theo's description of Natalie's physical appearance, which, she probably wanted him to believe, was inferior to, or at least no better than, her own in December 1803, when she had not fully recovered from the birth of her son. Natalie, she wrote him, while "still pretty . . . has grown thinner, much thinner; but her complexion is still good, although more languid. The loss of her hair is, however, an alteration much for the worse." In short, her father's "loveliest creature" now was less lovely, but Theo was forced to concede that Natalie had not lost her ability to charm or to benefit from comparisons. "The people of Charleston," she added in her letter, "have paid Natalie every possible attention; indeed, much more than I ever received."[65]

Natalie also enjoyed the advantage of a much longer life, and a happier one. Married in March 1802 to Thomas Sumter, Jr., of South Carolina, the son of General Thomas Sumter, a Revolutionary War hero known as the "Gamecock," Natalie eventually had seven children and lived to celebrate their marriages and the birth of grandchildren.

By the time she died in 1841 at the age of fifty-nine, she had made a number of visits to Paris, one lasting several years, and spent nine years in Rio de Janeiro, where her husband served as Minister Plenipotentiary to the Court of Portugal. Until the Sumters left for Rio in 1810, where they arrived after a voyage of eighty-five days, Natalie and Theo continued to see each other in South Carolina, but it is not clear whether she maintained contact with Burr during the years that followed the duel. Since her husband and his father were friends and allies of Madison, by whom, as President, her husband was appointed to the post in Brazil, Natalie may not have thought it prudent to continue the relationship, especially after Burr's trial for treason in 1807.

By that time Theo, who never regained her health after childbirth, and her worried father were consulting a number of doctors with regard to her physical complaints; Theo was also visiting spas where miraculous cures were said to occur, but to no avail. Her letters to Burr reporting various symptoms of illness, about which she was vague, hint that her problems may have related to a prolapsed uterus or other morbid condition of the reproductive tract, which is consistent with her not having a second child. Little Aaron, too, was often ill, and she and her father agreed that the malarial, swampy lowland area in which the Alstons lived much of the time was not healthy for the boy. There were also problems with her in-laws, who more than reciprocated her dislike of them by urging her husband, without success, to separate from her. All these difficulties combined to make Theo feel very much alone in South Carolina, and on October 31, 1808, to write her father, who was in Europe: "Oh, my guardian angel, why were you obliged to abandon me just when enfeebled nature doubly required your care? Alas, alas! how often have I deplored the want of your counsel and tenderness! How often, when my tongue and hands trembled with disease, have I besought Heaven either to reunite us, or let me die at once."[66] Severely depressed as she often was, she had premonitions of her own death and, what troubled her even more, fears that her little boy would not long survive.

"For personal reasons," she wrote her father in London on May 16, 1812, "I am very desirous of having some unrestrained conversation with you," words which may have indicated to him that her marital problems were growing worse.[67] Her letter crossed with one of Burr's, who was anticipating his return to the United States from his four-year exile abroad. No less possessive of his grandson than he had been of her, he made it clear that when he was settled in New York he intended to supervise ten-year-old Aaron Burr Alston's education much as he had supervised hers. Instructing Theo to "send me the boy *and his tutor*" soon after his return from abroad, he also insisted: "They both must live with me. The college in New-York has excellent teachers in every branch, good mathematical instruments, philosophical apparatus, and library . . . I shall superintend his studies and his pursuits of every kind (for which I shall have abundant leisure, proposing to abstract myself from all political concerns), awaken his genius, and keep every faculty on the stretch."[68]

Perhaps it was well that Burr had almost two months in which to savor the prospect of having his daughter's only child share his home with him. Bereft of funds as he was in Europe, Burr was constantly buying little gifts for Theo and her son, whom he affectionately referred to in his letters as "gampy" or "gamp" (occasionally reserving the latter term for himself as well), "little *chose*," "bang," and "the brat." Less than two months after he wrote Theo of his plans for the boy, Aaron Burr Alston, whose "little soul," she wrote him in her letter of May 12, "warms at the sound of your name," was dead of a fever, cause unknown.[69]

In Burr's life, death rarely made a solo appearance, and once again, as in 1757–58, when he lost both parents in less than a year, it was not to do so. Theo embarked for New York on the last day of December 1812, to be with her father, whom she had not seen since June of 1808. She and the pilot boat carrying her from South Carolina disappeared at sea, probably victim to a gale off Cape Hatteras. Rumors that the boat had been seized by pirates who sank it with all passengers on board could not have afforded Burr any comfort. Joseph Alston, less resilient than his father-in-law, never recovered from his double loss. On September 10, 1816, at the age of thirty-seven, he, too, was dead.

nine

ODD DESTINIES

Washington lived almost long enough to witness the election of Jefferson and Burr, two political figures he disliked heartily. Returning home drenched and cold from a horseback ride on a freezing December day in 1799, he contracted what may have been influenza or pneumonia. His condition was not helped by his doctors, who prescribed repeated purging and bleeding, in accordance with the prevailing medical lore, a procedure that killed many an ill person. He died on December 14, when he was not quite sixty-eight years old. One report attributed his death to his sitting too long in his wet clothes after hearing the disturbing news that some elections in Virginia had resulted in significant Republican victories.

He had little use for Jefferson since he had read a 1796 letter of his, not intended for publication, referring to persons "who were Sampsons in the field and Solomons in the council, but who have had their heads shorn by the harlot England."[1] Jefferson may or may not have had Washington in mind, but it was widely believed that he had intended the first President to be included in the company of shorn heads, and from that time he was not welcome at Mount Vernon. For Burr, Washington had never had any use since the early days of the Revolutionary War, and because the feeling was mutual, Burr did not attend the funeral ceremonies in Philadelphia, which, according to Troup, were also avoided by Jefferson.

Hamilton was present, but his reaction to the death of the man to whom he owed so much for opportunities to distinguish himself was remarkably restrained. Realizing that these opportunities were forever

gone, he wrote Washington's secretary, Tobias Lear: "Perhaps no man
. . . has equal cause with myself to deplore the loss . . . he was *an Aegis*
[i.e., protector or shield] *very essential to me.*" Striking a similar note in
a letter to Martha Washington, Hamilton reminded her, with what
Hendrickson characterizes as "singular infelicity," that he had long
enjoyed her husband's "numerous and distinguished marks of confidence and friendship of which you have yourself been a witness" and
that he could not "say in how many ways the continuance of that
friendship and confidence was necessary to me in future relations."[2] In
Washington's efforts to contain "the spirit of faction," he observed to
Rufus King, Washington had also been an "estimable man," whose
death "removes the control that was felt, and was very salutary."[3]
Washington in short, had been very useful to him and he had been
grateful for his friendship, but apparently Hamilton's attitude toward
his benefactor and protector had changed little since he wrote Schuyler
in February 1781 "that for three years past I have felt no friendship
for him and have professed none."[4]

Despite his cool response to Washington's demise, Hamilton's loss
of his "Aegis" may have been more deeply felt by him than his letters
reveal. Washington was not a father figure for all Americans in 1799,
but he was a commanding presence for many if not most, and he may
have been something more than this for Hamilton. Following his death,
Hamilton's political initiatives, all his biographers agree, were unprecedented in their recklessness and bad judgment, perhaps an indication
that Washington's "control" and steadying influence had been no less
"salutary" for him than they had been for the country. The first instance of Hamilton's grossly irresponsible behavior was his response
to the success of Burr and his fellow Republicans in capturing control
of the New York state legislature in early May 1800. Their victory,
for which almost everyone gave Burr credit, meant that New York
electoral votes in the forthcoming Presidential election would be cast
for the Republican candidates, thereby making their victory almost
certain. Profoundly disturbed by this development, Hamilton urged
Governor Jay to ask the legislature for a change in the law that would,
in effect, partially undo the election result by taking from the legislature its power to choose electors. Jay, appalled by the extremes to
which Hamilton would go in his determination to defeat Burr, whom
he termed in his letter to Jay "an atheist in religion and a fanatic in

politics," made no effort to comply with a request he may well have regarded as, in Bowers's words, "the blackest blot on Hamilton's record."[5] Henry Cabot Lodge, as usual more sparing of Hamilton, was still led to observe in 1882: "The proposition in this letter was one entirely unworthy of Hamilton."[6]

With respect to Maryland, where Hamilton feared that the ten electors chosen by popular vote would be more inclined to support Adams than Pinckney, he adopted a reverse course in urging a measure to insure that the state "vote by her Legislature," which was controlled by Federalists. "I am aware," he wrote Charles Carroll of Maryland on August 7, 1800, "of strong objections to the measure; but if it be true as I suppose that proponents are at Revolution and employ all means to secure success the contest must be very unequal if we not only refrain from unconstitutional and criminal measures, but even from such as may offend against the routine of strict decorum."[7] He did not indicate what he meant by "strict decorum," but clearly he had in mind a legislative action contrary to the spirit if not the letter of Maryland's law governing Presidential elections in that state.

In October, on the eve of the election, Hamilton abandoned all prudence in writing a pamphlet of fifty-four printed pages questioning the fitness for the Presidency of Adams, who was seeking a second term. The pamphlet, in the form of a letter, was designed to promote the candidacy of Charles Cotesworth Pinckney in place of Adams, but instead had the effect of dividing the Federalists, strengthening the election prospects of the Republicans, and significantly weakening if not undermining entirely Hamilton's position as the leading figure in the Federalist Party. Even his most faithful friends complained that his "character," as Troup put it, *is radically deficient in discretion* . . . Hence he is considered as an unfit head of the party."[8] If, as some historians maintain, Hamilton believed that by contributing to Adams's defeat he was preparing the way for his own Presidential nomination in 1804, his miscalculation was by far the worst of his entire political career.

Hamilton began the *Letter*, which was first published on October 24, 1800, by stating his conviction that Adams "does not possess the talents adapted to the *Administration of Government*, and that there are great and intrinsic defects in his character, which unfit him for the office of Chief Magistrate."[9] These defects encompassed opinions favoring "a blind and infatuated policy" during the war which had been "directly contrary" to Washington's recommendations "and which had nearly proved the ruin of our cause," a character "infected with some visionary notions," an "imagination sublimated and eccentric," and "a vanity without bounds, and a jealousy capable of discoloring every object." Related to these defects was "the disgusting egotism . . . and the ungovernable indiscretion of Mr. Adams's temper," besides which "in conversation, he repeatedly made excursions in the field of foreign politics, which alarmed the friends of the prevailing system." Although much inferior in all respects to Washington, Hamilton continued, Adams had been violently jealous of the first President and, Hamilton implied, of himself, so much so that he had "repeatedly indulged . . . in virulent and indecent abuse of me . . . denominated me a man destitute of every moral principle {and} has stigmatised me as the leader of a British faction." All this was far from the truth, Hamilton insisted, which was that his "private character," as judged by those familiar with it, entitled him "to declare, that in the cardinal points of public and private rectitude, above all, in pure and disinterested zeal for the interests and service of this country — I shrink not from a comparison with any arrogant pretender to superior and exclusive merit."

Three paragraphs near the end of the *Letter*, which in length, although not in malice, far exceeded anything he had written or was ever to write against Burr, Hamilton must have confused those who were still reading the pamphlet by declaring: "Yet with this opinion of Mr. Adams, I have finally resolved not to advise the withholding from him of a single vote." The following sentence could only have added to their bewilderment, stating that while the Federalists were not convinced that Adams was unfit to hold office, they would desert Adams and support Pinckney if, Hamilton implied, they had in their possession his own "knowledge of facts." Were they to do so, he rhetorically asked in another reference to "facts" disqualifying Adams for a second term, would they not be acting in accordance with "pure motives {and} cogent Reasons?"

Hamilton, as some of his friends maintained, may have intended his letter to circulate privately among a small number of Federalists, but if he thought that would be the case, he was even more naïve than he had been earlier when he imagined the Reynolds affair could be kept secret.

Burr may or may not have been the source of the copy that was

quickly published by Republican newspapers, as alleged by Matthew
Davis, but there can be no doubt that he was among those who recognized immediately that Hamilton had destabilized the Federalists
and undermined their confidence in his leadership. He also was aware,
as was Hamilton, but too late, that the *Letter* would work to increase
his own support in the Federalist Party, where some who were unhappy with Adams disliked Burr less than they disliked Jefferson.
While Adams did not lack defenders, one of whom, not surprisingly,
was his wife, Abigail, who referred to Hamilton as "the little General"
whose "weakness, vanity, and ambitious views" were comparable to
those of the sparrow in Sterne's *Sentimental Journey*,"[10] most of his
supporters focused more on Hamilton's defects than on Adams's virtues. But it was Federalist Noah Webster, whose surname and the
word "dictionary" are inseparable in the minds of many, who was
provoked enough to raise questions that others avoided discussing, at
least publicly, concerning Hamilton's mental state. In a letter to Hamilton accusing him of "extreme indiscretion," in connection with which
Webster also referred obliquely to the "private intrigues" that gave rise
to the Reynolds pamphlet, Webster wondered aloud whether Federalists as well as Anti-Federalists would believe henceforth that "your
ambition, pride, and overbearing temper have destined you to be the
evil genius of this country." In concluding his letter, he stated flatly:
"Your conduct on this occasion will be deemed little short of insanity."[11]

Ambition, vanity, pride, temper — all these and other character
flaws — were held responsible for Hamilton's costly blunder, and, in
addition, certain personal grievances. According to Troup, Hamilton
privately favored Jefferson for President in 1800 in any contest between Adams and the Virginian, which, if true, suggests that Adams
was almost another obsession of Hamilton in the months preceding the
election. His antagonism may have derived, at least in part, from Adams's opposition to his appointment in 1798 as Washington's second-
in-command. Nor was that Adams's only attempt to frustrate
Hamilton's military ambitions at a time when the relationship between
the United States and France was described by some as an undeclared
war. He infuriated Hamilton by refusing to make him Commander in
Chief after Washington's death, and in 1800, the war threat having
abated, he disbanded the Additional Army that had been organized

earlier in preparation for war. These actions, all of which drew angry protests from Hamilton, followed Adams's dispatch of peace commissioners to France, also opposed by Hamilton, who by now realized that in all probability he would never see active service in his recently acquired rank of major general.

While character defects and thwarted ambitions may suffice to explain Hamilton's animosity toward Adams, they hardly justify the *Letter*, which was viewed even before it was published as self-destructive and inimical to the Federalist cause by most of his friends who had seen it. They account even less for his urging Jay to call for an abrupt change in the method of choosing New York Presidential electors, which Jay, no less a Federalist than Hamilton, described as "Proposing a measure for party purposes which it would not become me to adopt."[12] This and other evidence of what Adair calls Hamilton's "dangerously irresponsible" behavior in 1800 has led even his most sympathetic biographers to speculate that he was manifesting some form of mental illness.[13]

Probably the first to suggest that he was suffering from "nervous instability" was his grandson, Allan McLane Hamilton, himself an alienist, or, in modern terms, a psychiatrist, who in 1911 described Hamilton's illness as ". . . alternating depression on the one hand and gayety on the other," or a form, in short, of manic depression, often referred to today as bipolar affective disorder.[14] Schachner, Mitchell, Flexner, and Hendrickson, among others, frequently refer to behavior they label "hysterical," "psychologically troubled," "deranged or paranoid," and "pathologically depressed." According to Hendrickson: "The question in Hamilton's case was, and is, whether in 1800 he was suffering from a paranoia . . . or only from a manic defense, which would prove to be a temporary response."[15] Frederick Scott Oliver, one of his most admiring biographers, avoids such terminology but nevertheless observes that Hamilton's "middle age instead of ripening his judgment, warped it," a statement not too dissimilar from Flexner's comment: "The great mind, so precocious at the start, never matured."[16]

However plausible some of these assessments may be, a clinical diagnosis almost two hundred years later that approximates those of modern medical science is not possible. But there is evidence of mood swings, particularly after 1800, that are characteristic of manic depression, the manic phase more or less describing his behavior as the

Presidential election approached, and the depressive phase more or less typical during the years that followed. The qualifying words are important: the two phases do not always exist in their extreme forms and frequently one or the other phase may initially be regarded as drug-related, or as having some connection with alcohol, stroke, or an organic brain disorder such as Alzheimer's disease. Still, in Hamilton's case at least, some clear signs of mania and depression appear to have been present at various times, but given the difficulties inherent in recognizing them at such a distance, the reader of these pages is invited to venture his own judgments.

In doing so, he should consider the fact that Hamilton never was in robust health, and that physical and mental conditions often interact with each other, although it is usually difficult to identify their precise relationship. Judging by the many references to his health in letters to and from relatives and friends, one may conclude that if he was not chronically ill, he often was ill enough to arouse concern. From 1777 to 1779 he suffered from frequent "fever and violent rheumatic pains," which, on one occasion, were sufficiently severe for his doctor to think "he could not survive."[17]

These illnesses may have been brought about or made worse by the bitter winter of 1777–78 at Valley Forge, and the even worse one of 1779–80 at Morristown, with six feet of snow and temperatures well below freezing, but there may have been other factors contributing to his poor physical condition.[18] In September 1778, he was advised by his friend and physician James McHenry, who later served as Secretary of War under Adams, "to get rid of your present accumulations," presumably a reference to Hamilton's experiencing prolonged constipation. McHenry prescribed in detail a diet for Hamilton that avoided fat, limited his intake of beef, mutton, and vegetables, the latter because "a load of vegetables is as hurtful as a load of any other food," and recommended water, "the most general solvent," and no more than three glasses of wine, "but by no means every day." Urging Hamilton to avoid pills unless "you should fall into a debauch," McHenry noted that Paracelsus, who took pills, died at thirty, whereas Lewis Cornare, who ate one egg a day, "lived to above ninety."[19] Perhaps Hamilton was not persuaded to modify his diet, or was suffering from a chronic digestive complaint not amenable to changes of food; Dr. David Hosack, who attended him after the duel, reported: "As his habit was delicate and had been lately rendered more feeble by ill health, particularly by a disorder of the stomach and bowels, I carefully avoided all those remedies which are usually indicated on such occasions."[20]

He was intermittently ill during and after the Revolutionary War, and following his marriage was frequently at the Pastures in Albany to recover from exhaustion. He may have suffered from a recurrent nephritis or kidney inflammation, but these ailments were less serious than the yellow fever which he and other family members contracted in August 1793.[21] Jefferson apparently believed that he was afflicted more by hypochondria than by acute infectious disease, yet Hamilton came very close to being one of the more than four thousand persons who died in the epidemic.[22] His recuperation at the Pastures that fall may have been helped along by news of Jefferson's retirement as Secretary of State, but it was some time before he fully recovered.

He was never entirely free from the symptoms of manic-depressive illness, whatever their cause or the extent to which they were affected by physical disease. In manic-depressive behavior, the depressive phase may precede one or more manic episodes, but the more common experience is the appearance first of a mood of excitability tending toward agitation, recklessness, grandiosity, and an exaggerated sense of one's superiority to others, and a tendency to embark on projects that are unwise and risky to oneself. The latter may include ill-advised sexual adventures, overindulgence in food or drink, and, increasingly in our time, shopping sprees. The depressive phase that follows mania can include loss of interest in life, feelings of hopelessness and despair, withdrawal from family and friends, sleeplessness, reduced appetite, and a variety of physical ailments, among which gastrointestinal problems are not uncommon. In extreme forms of manic-depressive illness, the manic phase of elated self-esteem too often is followed by an overpowering debilitating depression that ends in suicide; currently, an estimated one-fifth of manic depressives who do not receive treatment kill themselves.

Whether or not mania was an element in Hamilton's efforts in 1800 to deny New York Republicans their electoral-college victory and Adams his second term as President, the depressive mood that followed it is less open to question. The election of Jefferson, the man whom, Hamilton once wrote, he "ought to hate," and of Burr, the man he did hate, and his declining influence in the Federalist Party and with it the dwindling of his hopes of becoming President in later years, were only the beginning of a series of losses and defeats that added to the despondency which lasted until the end of his life. He wrote little in his letters about the deaths in the Schuyler family of forty-two-year-old Peggy Van Rensselaer in May 1801 and Catherine Van Rensselaer Schuyler, his mother-in-law, two years later, but something of his feeling for Peggy can be discerned in his confiding to Betsey on the occasion of her funeral: "All is as well as can be except the dreadful ceremonies which custom seems to have imposed as indispensable . . . and which at every instant open anew the closing wounds of bleeding hearts."[23]

By far the most grievous death of all was that of his son Philip, the oldest of his children, on November 23, 1801, mortally wounded in a duel. According to contemporary reports, Philip took umbrage at remarks made about his father by George Eacker, a Republican lawyer, at a July 4 celebration in 1801. Encountering Eacker at a New York theater a few months later, Philip and he exchanged insults that, in conformity with the dueling code of the day, resulted in Philip's issuing a challenge. At that point, certain similarities between the duel that killed Philip and the one that killed his father less than three years later almost inspire disbelief. Philip, in principle opposed to dueling, was said by his seconds and family members to have held his fire, thereby enabling Eacker to discharge the fatal shot. The pistol used by Philip, which according to some reports was the same one used later by Hamilton, then accidentally discharged into the air; Eacker's seconds claimed that Philip was aiming at Eacker when his gun fired. Unlike his father, Philip did not live long enough to provide his own version of what had transpired.

But if there is any uncertainty about the final moments of the affair that November day at Powles Hook, New Jersey, there is none whatever about Hamilton's response to the death of his son, who was "the brightest, as well as the ablest, hope of my family." Despair over the loss of Philip, only nineteen years old, which he referred to as "an event, beyond comparison, the most afflicting of my life,"[24] could only have deepened when it became clear that his oldest daughter, Angelica, who was close to her brother, had been deranged by his death and was likely to remain so for the remainder of her life.[25] Hamilton no doubt had her insanity and the deaths of Philip and Peggy in mind when he wrote Betsey a few days after her mother's death: "We live in a world full of evil. In the later period of life misfortunes seem to thicken around us." His urging her to "arm yourself with resignation" and "to meet disasters with Christian fortitude"[26] was advice he himself did not follow when he was confronted by political developments of which he disapproved. Nor could he free himself, the future was to show, from his obsession with Burr.

His mood of sorrow and depression is manifest in a letter of February 29, 1802, which, although it deals only with political disappointments, probably is reflective as well of his despair over Philip's death three months earlier. "Mine is an odd destiny," he wrote Gouverneur Morris. "Perhaps no man in the UStates has sacrificed or done more for the present Constitution than myself — and contrary to all my anticipations of its fate, as you know from the very beginning I am still laboring to prop the frail and worthless fabric. Yet I have the murmurs of its friends no less than the curses of its foes for my reward. What can I do better than withdraw from the Scene? Every day proves to me more and more that this American world was not made for me." Lest Morris imagine that it was made for him and that he might somehow fare better, Hamilton reminded his friend that while Morris was "by *birth* a native of this Country," he was "by *genius* an exotic," as he himself was, Hamilton seemed to be saying. Therefore, he instructed Morris: "You mistake if you fancy that you are more a favorite than myself or that you are in any sort of theatre s[uited] to you."[27]

Less than a week later, Hamilton wrote again to Morris, but this time he struck a much different note. Registering his support of the proposed Twelfth Amendment that required Presidential electors to cast separate or "distinct" ballots for "the person voted for as President, and . . . the person voted for as Vice-President," he went on to observe that "the present mode gives all possible scope to intrigue and is dangerous as we have seen to the public tranquility." He often linked the words "intrigue" and "dangerous" to his characterization of Burr's political behavior, and it was in this letter that he referred to Burr's attending the recent Washington's birthday dinner, a Federalist gathering, as the appearance of "a strange *apparition* which was taken for the V P" and which toasted " 'the union of all honest men.' " Should "the story be true," he commented, "tis a good thing if we use it well. As an *instrument* the person will be an auxiliary of *some* value, as a chief he will disgrace and destroy the party." His recommended strategy was that the episode be exploited for the purpose of drawing the Republicans' attention to his Federalist sympathies. As usual, he feared that the proneness to "folly" of most Federalists and Republicans would find expression in an outcome different from the one he was proposing, for, he concluded his letter, "What has wisdom to do with weak man?"[28] In April he was assured that "wisdom," after all, had prevailed, by a letter from another Federalist. The appearance and toast of the *"apparition"* at the Federalist banquet, James A. Bayard wrote on April 12, had indeed made an "impression" upon "a certain great personage," by whom he meant Jefferson, and had also been communicated "to the proud and aspiring Lords of the Ancient Dominion," a reference to Virginia, as well as Republicans elsewhere. Hamilton could be confident, Bayard continued, "that no eagerness to recover lost power will betray {Federalists} into any doctrines or compromises repugnant or dangerous to their former principles."[29]

But with Burr receiving a cordial welcome from some Federalists in the Carolinas and Georgia in the course of a trip South, ostensibly to visit Theo and her family, Hamilton could not be confident. He had long known of the negative "impression" Burr by that time had made on Jefferson—referring in a letter of June 3 to the relationship between them as "a most serious scism . . . a scism absolutely incurable." He also had no doubt, and of course no regret, that one of its effects was "a more bitter animosity between the partisans of the two men than ever existed between the Federalists and Antifederalists." Still, there was the danger that some of the leading Federalists would be drawn to Burr and "hope to soar with him to power," while many more would claim "to have no other object than to make use of him; while he knows that he is making use of them." As for himself, he declared, lest there be any doubt that he regarded Jefferson as equally unworthy, "in no event" would he be "directly or indirectly implicated in a responsibility for the elevation or support" of either Jefferson or Burr in 1804.[30]

Informed that, despite some support in both parties, Burr was regarded by many Federalists and Republicans as "not one of us," and aware of the near certainty that Burr would not be renominated in 1804 as the Republican candidate for Vice President, Hamilton should have been less haunted by the *"apparition"* than he had been earlier.[31]

But he was depressed in spirit and obsessed with Burr and could not be dissuaded from believing that the latter somehow, by some strategem or "intrigue," would come to power. Burr himself may have shared that conviction, although he knew by 1802 that Jefferson and his supporters in the Republic Party were no less opposed to him than were Hamilton and his Federalist allies. He also was aware that the Clintons, the Livingstons, and other New York Republicans, even including those who disliked Jefferson and resented Virginia's preeminent role in the nation's politics, were hostile. Finally, he could have no doubt that he was the principal target in a so-called Pamphlet War which was designed to destroy him politically, the successive publications of which in 1801–2 accused him of almost every variety of moral and ethical transgression. Apparently, these developments never convinced him that his political prospects were suffering from anything more than a temporary eclipse. Unlike Hamilton, Burr, who was rarely disheartened for long by any personal or political disappointment, tended to believe that, whatever the setbacks, his campaigns for office, like his courtships and speculations, would eventually be met with success.

With Jefferson, his relations were not always strained. Seven months after the 1796 election making him Vice President, Jefferson initiated a correspondence with Burr that continued at irregular intervals until Burr himself became Vice President in 1801. Perhaps he did so in the hope that his letters, "evidencing my esteem" for you, as the first one, on June 17, 1797, expressed it, would reassure Burr of his continuing friendship and confidence in him. Jefferson undoubtedly knew that Burr felt he had been "ill used" and "deceived" by Virginia the preceding November when, after being led to believe he would receive all twenty-one of the state's "second" electoral votes for Vice President, he received only one.[32] While it is probable that Burr was never fully persuaded that Jefferson held him in the "great & sincere esteem" he affirmed at the close of his letter, he clearly was pleased to hear from Jefferson, beginning his prompt answer: "I thank you my dear Sir, I thank you sincerely for your letter."[33] Certainly, Burr had reason to be grateful even if he suspected that Jefferson's only reason for writing was his awareness that in the Presidential elections of 1800 he would need the support of Burr and New York's electoral votes if he was to defeat Adams. Whatever its motives, the letter, which dealt with political issues facing the country, indicated that Jefferson, according to Dumas Malone, regarded Burr at that time "as a member of the inner band of leaders."[34]

In November 1798, Jefferson again signed himself "with sincere esteem Dear Sir your friend & ser{van}t.," and in a letter of February 1799 repeated those words. There were no further letters from Jefferson, or at least none recorded, for almost two years, toward the close of which he and Burr became the Republican nominees for President and Vice President. With the election apparently decided in their favor, Jefferson wrote Burr on December 15, 1800, congratulating him on the outcome of the election, which was, he assumed in the absence of an official vote count at that time, "that the two Republican candidates stand highest." He then commented that, while Burr "doubtless" was pleased with the result, he could only lament "the loss we sustain of your aid in our new administration," which "leaves a chasm in my arrangements, which cannot be adequately filled up." This letter, which ended "accept my respectful & affectionate salutations," clearly indicates that Jefferson believed that he had received more electoral votes than Burr and would be the President.[35] It may also suggest that he did not plan to remedy the "loss" of Burr by assigning him an important role in the "arrangements" he was about to make.

If Jefferson's intention was to inform Burr that he intended to govern without him, this message did not register with the future Vice President. "As to myself," he wrote Jefferson on December 23, "I will cheerfully abandon the office of V[ice]. P[resident]. if it shall be thought that I can be more useful in any Active Station. In short, my whole time and attention shall be unceasingly employed to render your administration grateful and honorable to our Country and to yourself." In a further effort to convince Jefferson of his loyalty, he added that in the event "the Votes should come out alike for us — My personal friends are perfectly informed of my Wishes on the subject and can never think of diverting a single Vote from you — On the Contrary, they will be found among your zealous adherents." He made similar statements to others, two of which were later cited by his enemies as evidence of his untrustworthiness and duplicity. Addressing the possibility that the election had resulted in a tied electoral vote for Jefferson and himself, and conscious of rumors that he was already soliciting support from the Federalist members of the House of Representatives, where, in the event of a tie, the election would be decided, he affirmed to Samuel Smith of Maryland, a Jefferson stalwart, that if the electoral votes were equal he "should utterly disdain all competition." Smith could be assured, he added in this letter of December 16, "that the Federal party can entertain no wish for such an exchange."[36]

Had Burr been certain by mid-December that he and Jefferson had each received seventy-three electoral votes, eight more than the sixty-five given to Adams, and that the tie therefore would be resolved by the House of Representatives, each state having one vote, he might have written a letter more like the one he sent Smith thirteen days later. His declaring in the earlier letter that he would "utterly disdain all competition" with Jefferson was understood by Smith and others, including many future historians, to mean that he would not accept election by a coalition of Federalist and Republican House members. That may be a misunderstanding of what he meant, as he made clear in his letter to Smith of December 29. He had been asked, he wrote, whether he would resign if chosen President, a question he regarded as "unnecessary, unreasonable, and impertinent." He had made no reply, he informed Smith, but if he had done so, "I should have said that as at present advised, I should not—What do you think of such a question? I was made a Candidate against my advice and against my Will; God knows, never contemplating or wishing the result which has appeared—and now I am insulted by those who used my Name for having suffered it to be used."[37]

Smith was disturbed by this letter, which appeared to him to contradict Burr's earlier one, but while we may doubt that Burr refrained from "contemplating or wishing" the Presidency for himself, we should also note that he did not, in any letter to anyone, declare that he would resign the office if he were offered it. Nor is there evidence, despite the many rumors to the contrary at that time and since, that he was making a determined effort to win over the Federalists, whose votes would be decisive when the House of Representatives balloted in February 1801. Although Jefferson recorded these rumors in his *Anas*, he absolved Burr from the charge of colluding with the Federalists; he wrote his daughter, Martha, on January 4: "The Federalists were confident at first that they could debauch Col. B . . . his conduct has been honorable and decisive, and greatly embarrasses them."[38]

Considering that in February the Presidency was within Burr's grasp, and almost certainly would have been his if he had given the Federalists the assurances they demanded, perhaps the word "honorable" was the least encomium Jefferson could bestow upon him. From today's perspective, it is difficult to imagine the degree to which Jefferson in 1801 was disliked and distrusted by Federalists, most of whom, despite Hamilton's vehement denunciations of Burr, probably would have gone over to Burr had he given them sufficient encouragement. Jefferson's reputation was such that Hamilton's friend, James McHenry, was led to observe that with him in office "we undoubtedly have to apprehend a change in some most essential points of our Government, and great national interests. If Mr. Burr succeeds, we may flatter ourselves that he will not suffer the Executive power to be frittered into insignificance."[39] Making the same point, Timothy Pickering, another Hamilton friend, also observed that "in case of war with any European power, there can be no doubt which of the two would conduct it with most ability and energy."[40] Replying to one of Hamilton's letters in support of Jefferson, John Marshall, another Federalist, who soon was to preside over the Supreme Court as Chief Justice of the United States, wrote that to Jefferson he "felt almost insuperable objections. His foreign prejudices seem to me totally to unfit him for the chief magistry of a nation which cannot indulge those prejudices without sustaining debt & permanent injury . . . By weakening the office of President he will increase his personal power."[41]

Looking back on the election in which he had favored Burr, Theodore Sedgwick in a letter to Rufus King on May 24, 1801, justified Federalist opposition to Jefferson on the grounds of their belief that he was "a sincere Democrat — hostile to the principles of our constitution . . . desirous of conforming in practice to the imbecile principles of the old confederation [which] would be directed by the arrogance of Virginia . . . It was believed that he had given evidence of an entire devotion to france under every form of her government {and} a rancorous hatred to G.B."[42] Burr, on the other hand, Sedgwick wrote his son, "is not a Democrat — He is not an enthusiastic theorist — He is not under the direction of Virginian Jacobins — He is not a declared *infidel* . . . He is not attached to any foreign nation, and his selfishness will prevent his ever being so — He is not an enemy to the navy, to commerce or national policy."[43] Even Abigail Adams thought it possible that "the bold, daring, and decisive Burr would serve the country better. At least he was no doctrinaire."[44]

It fell to Federalist Richard Peters of Pennsylvania to strike a note of humor, perhaps the only one, as the day approached for the balloting to begin in the House of Representatives. Noting that the Federalists in Congress were inclined to vote for Burr, Peters in a letter to King continued: "*Why*, I cannot tell unless it be on the principle of the man who had to choose a wife, either one or the other, of a tall or short woman; and he took the short one on the old adage, *of two evils choose the least*," Burr, of course, being a lesser evil than Jefferson by seven inches or more.[45]

Such humor was lost on Hamilton, who had never ceased to regard Burr as by far the greater evil, and never more so than when he was within one electoral vote of becoming the third President of the United States. From December 16, 1800, when Hamilton was certain of the electoral tie result, to January 30, 1801, twelve days before the House began balloting, he wrote at least fifteen letters, or an average of one every three days, in what gradually became a desperate or, in Schachner's phrasing, "hysterical" effort to convince Federalists inclining toward Burr that "Jefferson is to be preferred [as] not so dangerous a man and he has pretensions to character."[46] While he had no new charges to bring against Burr, he repeated all the old ones with renewed vehemence and, in a manner of speaking, brought them up to date. Burr, he wrote Oliver Wolcott, Jr., in December, could not be won over to the Federalist cause, or forced to abandon his "scheme of war with Great Britain as the instrument of {his} Power and Wealth . . . Adieu to the Federal Troy if they once introduce this Grecian Horse into their Citadel."[47] On December 23: "Burr loves nothing but himself." And a day later: "He is sanguine enough to hope everything — daring enough to attempt everything — wicked enough to scruple nothing."[48] On December 26, perhaps influenced by the Christmas spirit, he briefly interrupted his customary anti-Burr invective in confiding to Gouverneur Morris: "With *Burr* I have always been personally well. But the public good must be paramount to every private consideration."[49] Never before had he written to anyone that he was ever "personally well" with the man about whom he could find nothing good to say, and who the following day was depicted once again as "a voluptuary by system," without any "principle public or private."

While he had every right to retaliate against Jefferson for the latter's enmity toward him, Hamilton insisted, he would not indulge "personal considerations" when the nation's very survival was at stake. "For Heaven's sake," he pleaded with James A. Bayard on December 27, Bayard being a Delaware Federalist who was supporting Burr and who would cast his state's only vote in the House of Representatives, "exert yourself to the utmost to save our country from so great a calamity."[50]

The stream of letters, some of them exceeding five pages in length, did not cease until shortly before February 11, when the tied electoral vote became official and the House was forced to choose. By that time, Hamilton's friends had heard repeatedly that Burr was corrupt, profligate, "more cunning than wise," bankrupt, a Jacobin and admirer of Napoleon, a visionary who on occasion "has talked perfect Godwinism,"* and because he "has never appeared solicitous for fame," all the more dangerous as a man of "great ambition unchecked by principle, or the love of Glory."[51] But Hamilton was never able to change the perception of Sedgwick, which was shared by other Federalists, that Burr, unlike Jefferson, "holds to no pernicious principles, but is a mere matter-of-fact man."[52]

As expected, the first ballot did not decide the issue, and neither did the thirty-four that followed. Of the sixteen states, eight, or one short of the nine required, went to Jefferson: New York, New Jersey, Pennsylvania, Virginia, North Carolina, Kentucky, Georgia, and Tennessee. Burr received the votes of six states: Massachusetts, Rhode Island, Connecticut, New Hampshire, Delaware, and South Carolina. Maryland and Vermont, in what amounted to a two-state replay of the electoral-college result, were deadlocked by split delegations and therefore cast no votes. It is worth noting that had the voting been by individuals, not states, Jefferson would have been defeated on that first ballot. Of the total number of representatives who voted, Burr was supported by fifty-five, Jefferson by fifty-one. Also reflective of Burr's initial advantage were the divisions within the state delegations. In only two states, his own and Pennsylvania, was Jefferson's margin of vic-

---

* William Godwin (1756–1836) believed that man was rational enough to live in peace without government, laws, or institutions such as religion. In 1797 he married Mary Wollstonecraft, whose *Vindication of the Rights of Woman* was much admired by Burr and his wife, Theodosia.

tory greater than two, Virginia giving him fourteen votes to Burr's
five, and Pennsylvania nine votes to Burr's four. Burr's margins, on
the other hand, were eight in Masssachuetts, seven in Connecticut, six
in New Hampshire, and three in South Carolina. Jefferson won in
three of his eight states by only one vote: New Jersey, Georgia, and
Tennessee; of Burr's six states, Delaware with one representative was
the sole state he carried by only one vote.

Since the Federalists, not all of whom voted for Burr, constituted a
majority in the House, and most if not all the Republicans, including
the six from New York, probably voted solidly for Jefferson, the relatively close result in a number of states suggests that, had Burr exerted himself, he might well have been elected on the first ballot. But
he apparently refused to do so, notwithstanding the many allegations
at that time and continuing into the present that he sought to detach
some Republican votes from Jefferson, and actively solicited Federalist
support. Certainly, he was strongly urged by his Republican friends
to give the Federalists the assurances they sought, but he refused even
to leave Albany, where Theo was married on February 2, for Washington, where his appearance might have made a difference at any time
during the six days and thirty-six ballots that made Jefferson President. Still, some Federalists believed almost until the end that, as New
York Congressman William Cooper commented when the states' vote
was eight to six in Jefferson's favor, "Had Burr done anything for
himself, he would long ere this have been president." If a majority of
House members could decide the issue, he added, Burr "would have
it on every vote."[53] But by February 17 it was clear to Sedgwick and
other Federalists that, "without the cooperation of Burr," Jefferson
could not be defeated, and since Burr would not do "anything for
himself," Sedgwick informed his son: "The Gigg is, therefore up."[54]
On the second ballot that day, the Vermont Federalist representative
refrained from voting, thereby ending the division in the state's delegation and enabling the state's Republican congressman to cast its sole
remaining vote for Jefferson. With that action, Vermont became the
ninth state Jefferson needed for victory. By submitting a blank ballot,
Bayard of Delaware reduced Burr's total of states to five, and the four
Federalist congressmen from Maryland followed suit, giving that state
to Jefferson.

Few if any Federalists were pleased with the result, and some were angry at Burr because he refused to work with them to bring down Jefferson. In the final ballot, no Federalist changed his vote to Jefferson, but perhaps none was as bitter and unforgiving of Burr as Bayard. "The means existed of electing Burr," he wrote Hamilton, "but that required his cooperation. By deceiving one Man (a great blockhead) and tempting two others (not incorruptible) he might have secured a majority of the States. He will never have another chance of being President of the U. States and the little use he has made of the one that has occurred gives me but a humble opinion of the talents of an unprincipled man."[55] This, however, was not the opinion of every Federalist. Years later, when the election had passed into history, Judge John Woodworth, a New York Federalist elector in 1800, expressed some respect for Burr, pronouncing his "conduct in that affair entirely unexceptionable."[56]

Bayard may be right that only one stupid and two dishonest congressmen stood between Burr and the Presidency. There is no question that he was right, as the following years were to demonstrate, about Burr's prospects of ever becoming President. Hated by Hamilton no less in defeat than he had been in victory, having alienated those Federalists who had defied Hamilton by preferring him to Jefferson, and having incurred the displeasure of Republicans, who suspected him of attempting to steal the election from Jefferson, Burr, it was almost certain, would never have another opportunity to win any high elective office.

There also was some doubt, at that time and after, that Jefferson had refused to cooperate with the Federalists in an effort to get himself elected. At least twice prior to the first vote in the House, Hamilton urged Federalist friends "to obtain from Jefferson assurances on some cardinal points," as he expressed it in a December 1800 letter to Oliver Wolcott. The "points" were: "1 The preservation of the actual Fiscal System 2 Adherence to the Neutral plan 3 The preservation & gradual increase of the Navy 4 The continuance of our friends in the offices they fill except in the great departments in which they ought to be left free." On January 4, 1801, in a letter to McHenry, he again listed the four "assurances" they should seek from Jefferson "as the motive of our cooperation with him."[57]

Controversy attends the question, as it does so many questions related to the 1800 election, whether in fact Jefferson provided those "assurances." In 1805, when Burr had long since been discarded by Jefferson, he charged that Jefferson in 1801 had given such "assurances" to Samuel Smith, who in turn had relayed them to Bayard. Bayard had then, according to Burr's contention, which was supported by a deposition from Bayard, demanded more definite "assurances," which Smith provided the following day, informing Bayard "that he had seen Mr. Jefferson and had stated to him the points mentioned and was authorized by him to say they corresponded with his views." The principal question was, and is, whether, as Smith maintained, he had spoken to Jefferson in a general way about matters of policy "without his having the least idea of my object." Smith also denied ever telling Bayard "that I had any authority from Mr. Jefferson to communicate anything to him." Jefferson, in corroboration, insisted: "No proposition was ever made to me on that occasion by General Smith." He added that "very possibly" there was some discussion of the election, "as the general subject was the constant theme of conversation." But did Jefferson not have "the least idea" that Smith's interest in his views on the eve of the crucial vote in the House was politically motivated? He may or may not have given the Federalists the "assurances" they demanded, but, as Schachner observes, "Jefferson was too good a politician not to have realized why Smith had sought him out."[58]

Perhaps he was also too good a politician not to have possessed, in Joseph Ellis's characterization of him, "the internal ability to generate multiple versions of the truth,"[59] a talent shared, perhaps, by almost all Presidents and would-be Presidents since his time. As late as February 1, 1801, he still was ending his letters to Burr with expressions of "high respect and esteem," but not long after his inauguration, which Adams and many other Federalists did not attend, he began to give his Vice President ample reason to believe that "high respect and esteem" for him were not precisely what Jefferson was feeling. Most of Burr's patronage recommendations of Republicans as replacements for Federalists forced to vacate their posts were rejected, one of them being his close friend and later biographer Matthew Davis. In depriving Burr of influence in these appointments, Jefferson undoubtedly knew that he was further weakening his support in New York, where the Clinton forces, despite Burr's endorsement of George Clinton for the governorship in 1801, and other leading Republicans were already determined to deny him the Vice Presidential nomination in 1804. Jefferson's treatment of him suggests that by 1802, if not earlier, Jefferson, too, had made that decision, and it is probable that Burr suspected that was the case when, as Vice President, he took his seat on January 15, 1802, as presiding officer of the Senate.

He was soon called upon to resolve a tie vote on a measure to repeal the Judiciary Act of 1801, in accordance with which Adams was able to appoint Federalists to a number of circuit-court judgeships, the so-called midnight appointments, in the closing days of his Administration. Strongly favored by the Republicans, the repeal measure moved toward passage when the Senate approved it for a third or final reading on January 26, Burr voting with the Republicans. But when it was brought up the following day and there was again a tie vote, Burr supported a Federalist motion committing the bill for reconsideration to a select committee, where its ultimate passage was far from assured. Jefferson was not pleased, and he was no happier to learn in the following months that Burr was busy cultivating Federalists and Republicans in the South and elsewhere. By then, Burr no doubt had decided that, having little to hope for from Jefferson, and facing an uncertain future in his own state, he could move in no other direction if he were to sustain a viable political presence in the years ahead.

Burr's alleged efforts to take the Presidency from him in 1801 are often cited as the reasons for Jefferson's animosity. But this was not the explanation he himself later advanced. Nor did he attribute it to Burr's palpable, almost unimaginable insincerity in telling him, Jefferson confided to his *Anas*, in the course of a visit Burr made to Monticello on January 26, 1804, that his "acquiescence" in accepting the Vice Presidential nomination was "founded . . . in his desire of promoting my honor, the being with me whose company & convers{ation} had always been fascinating to him &c." Clearly, Burr, too, knew how "to generate multiple versions of the truth," but on this occasion, as on many others, without effect, Jefferson necessarily preferring his own variety of the truth to that favored by Burr. Perhaps forgetting that he had been friendly with Burr after becoming Vice President in 1796, he went on to write in his *Anas*, with a touch of acerbity: "I had never seen Colo. B. till he came as a member of the Senate [i.e., 1791]. His conduct very soon inspired me with distrust. I habitually cautioned Mr Madison against trusting him too much. I saw afterwards that under Genl. W's and Mr A's adm{inistratio}ns, whenever a great military app{oint}m{en}t or a diplomatic one was to be made, he came post{haste} to Philad{elphi}a to shew himself, & in fact that he was always at market [i.e., available]."[60] He did not mention that Adams had wished to make Burr a brigadier general, surely not a "great" military appointment, and that Adams was prevented from doing so by Washington, who, Adams suspected, had been persuaded by Hamilton that Burr's "talents at intrigue" rendered him unfit to serve as, in Adams's words, "a poor brigadier." Nor did Jefferson record that Burr had been recommended to Washington for a diplomatic appointment by, among others, James Madison, despite Madison's being "cautioned" by him not to trust Burr "too much."

Apparently, Burr also was unfit, in Jefferson's view, for any position in his Administration, or, even if he were to retire as Vice President "for the interest of the republican cause," deserving of "some mark of favor from me, which would declare to the world that he would retire with my confidence." Reminded by Burr of his letter three years earlier lamenting the "chasm" in his arrangements with regard to which Burr had offered his services, Jefferson offered an explanation of his failure to find a place for him in his Administration that was hardly superior in truthfulness to Burr's reasons, advanced earlier in their conversation, for agreeing to be nominated for Vice President. Making no reference to Burr's expressed willingness in his December 23, 1800, letter "to cheerfully abandon the office of V(ice) P(resident)" if he could be "more useful in any Active station," Jefferson informed him that he was only following precedents established by Washington and Adams. Adams as Vice President, he recalled, had desired a "foreign embassy," but President Washington, doubting that Adams "was a fit character for such an office," and convinced that it would not be proper to "send away the person who, in case of his death," would take his place, declined to make the appointment. Again, when Adams as President was contemplating "how desirable it would have been" to send Jefferson on a mission to France, he finally decided against it for "the same reasons Genl. Washington had done." When on December 15, 1800, Burr was being considered for appointment "to one of the great offices," Jefferson endeavored to make clear, the appointment was to be made only in the event that he was not elected Vice President. But "as soon as that election was known, I saw it could not be done," for the same reasons that had guided the thinking of Washington and Adams.[61]

Jefferson may genuinely have felt that he was bound by these decisions of the first two Presidents, but considering that Burr had offered to step down as Vice President, it is more likely that even before 1801 Jefferson had determined to do nothing that would improve Burr's chances of eventually succeeding him. Needing Burr to win New York and, with it, the election of 1800, he could not afford then to make him an enemy, but in January 1804, certain of reelection — he was to receive 162 electoral votes to Charles Cotesworth Pinckney's 14 — and anticipating, correctly, that in February George Clinton would be nominated for Vice President by the Republican congressional caucus, he could hardly afford to have Burr as a friend. When he learned that Burr had not received even one vote in the caucus, he knew that he would no longer have to pretend that he held him in "great and sincere esteem." If his *Anas* can be trusted, Jefferson's regard for Burr had never been more than pretense, and if Andrew Jackson can be believed, Jefferson was no less capable of pretense in his relationships with others. Jackson, who took his seat in the Senate in 1797, when Jefferson as Vice President became its presiding officer, soon decided that while "officially" Jefferson "was all that could be wished," in his "personal intercourse he always left upon you the impression of want of candor, sincerity, and fidelity."[62] Perhaps, however, Jackson's "impression" that Jefferson lacked "sincerity" was at least partly false. He was, as Brodie observes, "a good hater," and there was nothing insincere about his hatred of Hamilton and his dislike of Burr.

Early in their discussion on January 26, 1804, Burr drew Jefferson's attention to published "calumnies" in writings directed against himself, some of which he told Jefferson had originated with or been inspired by Hamilton. Burr was referring primarily to the efforts of James Cheetham, reflected in several publications that collectively comprised the Pamphlet War, to destroy his reputation and standing in the Republican Party and to promote doubts that he was a fit candidate for public office. Cheetham, who may have emigrated from England as late as 1798, began his career in America as a journalistic protégé of Burr, but, for unknown reasons, soon changed sides. Alert for opportunities to ingratiate himself with Jefferson and Republicans hostile to

Burr, he soon found one when Burr intervened to prevent the sale of a book titled *The History of the Administration of John Adams, Late President of the United States.* Although some important details are uncertain, Burr apparently intended to buy and destroy the entire printing of 1,250 copies, but in the end was unable to do so. In return for their cooperation, the author, John Wood, and his publishers, Manhattan booksellers William Barlass and Mathias Ward, had demanded a good deal of money, which Burr, on the verge of being forced to sell Richmond Hill, did not have.

Whatever Burr's reasons for attempting to suppress the book, they did not include an unfriendly portrait of himself. Thirty of its five hundred pages were given over to a "high eulogium on A.B.," he wrote Theo on March 8, 1802. He may have thought that the book's "low scurrility and illy-told private anecdotes" at the expense of Adams and other Federalists, and its claim "that some dozens of persons, by name, [were] being bribed by British gold," would, by inviting disbelief and charges of reckless irresponsibility, bring more discredit on himself and the Republicans than dishonor to Adams and the Federalists. But he also called to Theo's attention, and perhaps took into account, his discovery in perusing the book that "of all the Federal men, General Hamilton alone is treated with respect, even flattery." There was "a curious fact" as well, he reported to Theo: "Barlas[s,] a Scotchman, the publisher of the book, is private tutor to the children of General Hamilton."[63]

The Pamphlet War began in earnest on May 26, 1802, when the New York *Amer. Citizen*, of which Cheetham was co-publisher, advertised the appearance of Cheetham's *Narrative of the Supression by Col. Burr of the History of the Administration of John Adams . . .* In this pamphlet and the four which followed it, Cheetham attributed Burr's attempted suppression of Wood's *History* to his desire not to offend Federalists, whose support he would need if he were ever to be elected President. In a second pamphlet one month later, *A View of the Political Conduct of Aaron Burr, Esq., Vice-President of the United States*, Cheetham, in effect, back-dated his charge, stating: "The moment he [Burr] was nominated, he put into operation a most extensive, complicated, and wicked scheme of intrigue to place himself in the presidential chair. He spent at least one year's salary on *expresses* he sent hither and yon, and he seems to have carried on a *secret* correspondence with the federalists from the period of his nomination."[64]

Burr was not without defenders, some of whom were almost the equal of Cheetham in their employment of invective. But despite the efforts of Peter Irving, the brother of Washington Irving, both of them among his admirers, William Coleman, the editor of the Hamiltonian New York *Evening Post*, who to the surprise of many, probably including Hamilton, treated most of Cheetham's accusations with contempt, and William Van Ness, or, as he signed himself, "Aristides," the ablest polemicist of them all, they failed to put the lie to allegations that Burr was totally unprincipled and had connived with Federalists to deny Jefferson the Presidency. Two libel suits against Cheetham, two of the many he was to face during his career, one initiated by Burr and the other by some of his friends, neither of them conclusive, may have injured Burr more than Cheetham. In the first suit, Burr submitted Bayard's deposition that Jefferson had won the election by giving the Federalists certain "assurances," and it is probable that most Americans were as unwilling then as they are unwilling now to take Burr's and Bayard's word against that of Jefferson. Undoubtedly, today even more are unwilling to believe that Burr was innocent of "intrigue" in 1800–1 or, for that matter, at any time in his long life.

Burr, meanwhile, was continuing to serve as Vice President, a position he did not relinquish until March 2, 1805, two days before Jefferson and Clinton were sworn into office. Much of his final month as presiding officer of the Senate had been given over to the impeachment trial of Samuel Chase, Associate Justice of the Supreme Court, who had been indicted by the House of Representatives on charges that, as a Federalist, he had been biased against Republicans while on the Court.[65] According to some reports, Burr was propriety itself in his conduct of the trial, but others thought he had been less than decorous in his treatment of Chase. Chase, in any event, was found not guilty on all eight counts of the indictment, following which verdict Burr left the Senate chamber to draft the farewell speech he would deliver the next day.

There being no *Congressional Record* at that time, and hence no verbatim account of what he said, his address to the Senate survives only in a few brief summaries of his remarks found in letters, diaries, and, in one instance, a Federalist newspaper. As might be expected, these summaries, one of them a diary entry of John Quincy Adams, differ from each other in their emphases and in the statements they attribute to Burr. Adams, for example, has him calling the Senate's attention to the importance of "order and regularity," and adding: "There is scarce a departure from order but leads to or is indissolubly connected with a departure from *morality*." Burr may have intended these reflections to evoke in his listeners a memory of Hamilton, whose behavior, in his view, had been subversive of the political order and the rules of conduct governing it. But if this was his intention, he failed, since none of the Senators other than Adams mentioned his references to "order" and "morality," and if Adams, who liked Burr even less than his father, wondered what he had meant, he left no clue to that effect.

In describing the scene in the Senate when Burr concluded his farewell speech, Adams recorded: "Many of the members appeared deeply affected." Burr had spoken "with great dignity and firmness of manner," he added, and "was listened to with the most ernest and universal attention."[66] But perhaps not every senator was "deeply affected" in the same way. Adams noted that two senators, Robert Wright of Maryland and John Smith of New York, "were moved even to tears," and it was Smith who had introduced a bill in February "freeing from postage all letters and packets to and from Aaron Burr." After several readings, the bill was passed eighteen to thirteen, only to meet defeat in the House, where it was referred to a committee and "heard of no more." Among the thirteen senators who voted against the measure was Timothy Pickering, still grieving for his friend who had died at Burr's hands. "Who, Sir," he was quoted as saying on February 28 on the occasion of the final vote, "are dangerous men in this republic? Not those who have reached the summit of place and power, for their ambition is satisfied. I tell you, Sir, who are dangerous men. Those who have ascended to the last round *but one* on the political ladder, and whose vaulting ambition will never be satisfied until they have stood upon the topmost round. Sir, I vote against this bill."[67] The "Sir" he was addressing was, of course, the presiding officer of the Senate and the intended beneficiary of the measure, Aaron Burr.

The loss of the franking privilege was by far the least of the losses Burr was to experience during the years that followed. The future was to include his 1807 trial for treason in connection with the "Burr Conspiracy," an exile in Europe of almost four years, and the deaths within months of each other of the two people in the world he loved most. Surely these losses and dire events made for an odder destiny than the one Hamilton had claimed for himself in 1802. But Burr was never known to complain of fate or suggest that he deserved better of life. At no time during his eighty-year existence was he one of those "many men," among whom Hamilton perhaps should be included, that T. E. Lawrence wrote of as accepting "the death-sentence without a whimper to escape the life-sentence which fate carries in her other hand."

ten

THIRTEEN WEEKS TO WEEHAWKEN

By 1804 Hamilton had been engaged for some years in a ruthless and relentless effort to destroy Burr politically, and by late April of that year it appeared that he was on the verge of success. He was not Burr's only enemy or even the most prominent one; that honor, if honor it was, belonged to Jefferson. In New York, however, where Burr was making what turned out to be his last political stand as a gubernatorial candidate, Hamilton was Burr's most formidable opponent, and as such was responsible, to a significant extent, for his defeat. Burr's loss in that election, had there been no duel or later charge inspired by Jefferson of a "Burr Conspiracy," would not necessarily have terminated his career in politics, but his failure at the polls to gain decisive support from either of the two dominant political parties at the time, the Republicans and the Federalists, deprived him of a political base, at least in the short run. But the short run, had Hamilton lived as long as Jefferson, that is, until 1826, and not ceased to wage his campaign against Burr, might have been very long indeed.

Hamilton actively disliked a number of political figures, including Jefferson, John Adams, James Madison, James Monroe, and George Clinton, but his hatred of Burr, which was obsessive, was not entirely or even mainly a consequence of political rivalry. To describe it as "definitely pathologic," as biographer Nathan Schachner has done, is to hint at some of its deeper, hidden sources which predate the careers of both men.[1] To the extent that these sources can be identified, the duel can be said to have originated in their sharply contrasting personal histories and characters, and therefore to have been set in motion long before 1804. Had their two lives been differently constituted, Burr would not have felt the necessity to issue, and Hamilton the need to accept, the challenge that precipitated the duel. But by 1804 there was no turning away for either man from that fatal meeting on the dueling ground at Weehawken.

While the evidence is persuasive that Hamilton had disliked and distrusted Burr for a very long time, he apparently did not communicate these attitudes to paper until 1792, when Burr, although newly elected to the Senate, was contemplating a run for the New York governorship. Hamilton's published letters, which, as noted in the preface, are by no means the total number he wrote, do not calumniate Burr until September 21, 1792, when he confided to an unidentified correspondent that "{Burr} is unprincipled, both as a public and private man . . . He is determined, as I conceive, to make his way to the head of the popular party," by which he meant the Republican Party, "and to climb *per fas aut nefas** to the highest honors of the State, and as much higher as circumstances may permit. Embarrassed, as I understand, in his circumstances, with an extravagant family, bold, enterprising, and intriguing, I am mistaken if it be not his object to play the game of confusion, and I feel it to be a religious duty to oppose his career."[2] Less than a week later, on September 26, 1792, Hamilton, again castigating Burr in a letter to another unknown correspondent, wrote that Burr "as a public man . . . is one of the worst sort . . . secretly turning liberty into ridicule . . . In a word, if we have an embryo-Caesar in the United States, 't is Burr."[3]

During the following years, Burr was designated by Hamilton the "Catiline of America"[4] at least five times; a man of "an irregular ambition" and "prodigal cupidity"; "in his profession extortionate to a proverb"; "without doubt insolvent for a large deficit" and therefore capable of "a bargain and sale with some foreign power" perhaps leading to "a war"; a soldier who "gave indications of being a good officer, but without having had the opportunity of performing any distinguished action"; in addition to which "at a critical period of the war

---

* Also, as a variant, *per fas et nefas*, or, alternately, *by fair means or foul*. Hamilton was to employ this phrase in at least one other letter referring to Burr, and on April 10, 1804, the *Albany Register*, an anti-Burr paper, made use of it in reference to Burr's supporters in the forthcoming gubernatorial election.

[i.e., 1779] he resigned his commission assigning for cause ill health," although "he might without difficulty have obtained a furlough and was not obliged to resign"; "an opponent covertly and insidiously" of "the adoption of this Constitution"; a speaker "in all the jargon of Jacobinism . . . {who} thinks the present French constitution not a bad one." And as if all this were not enough, Burr "has in view nothing less than the establishment of Supreme Power in his own person."[5] Even Hamilton's grandson and biographer, Allan McLane Hamilton, more than one hundred years later acknowledged that Hamilton's "unremitting and bitter" attacks could not have led Hamilton to expect any "other ending than that which followed . . . [indeed] it is surprising that [Burr] did not force the duel upon some much earlier occasion."[6]

Burr perhaps did not challenge Hamilton earlier because he was unaware of Hamilton's implacable hostility until the election of 1800, when he and Jefferson were running together for President and Vice President. Even more remarkable is the testimony of contemporaries that Burr was never heard, at any time, to make a derogatory remark about Hamilton. If reports had earlier reached Burr of Hamilton's impeachment of his political principles and personal integrity, which is not impossible, inasmuch as Burr was usually well informed about doings in the Federalist camp, he either chose not to take them seriously — he was never someone whose self-esteem and sense of achievement depended upon political office — or dismissed them as the common and accepted coin of electoral politics.

The latter interpretation of Burr's seeming indifference to Hamilton's barrage of accusations is not improbable, considering their apparently amicable relationship in areas other than politics. As mentioned, they were not law partners but they sometimes collaborated in court proceedings, where, as co-counsel in both civil and criminal cases, they were, according to several accounts, a formidable combination. They met at social gatherings and dinner parties, and not infrequently were each other's guests at their respective homes, which were not far apart in the Wall Street area. While there is no evidence that the two wives, the doomed Theodosia Burr and Betsey Hamilton, were ever acquainted, Burr through his daughter, Theo, probably met Hamilton's daughter Angelica and other Hamilton children, and he undoubtedly was familiar with Church in connection with shared interests in the Manhattan Company and other enterprises.

This seemingly cordial and on the surface friendly relationship between Hamilton and Burr continued until the weeks before the 1804 New York gubernatorial election. But from the moment, if not before, that Burr was elected to the Senate in 1791 he was marked by Hamilton for political destruction, and his determination to thwart and frustrate Burr at every opportunity could well be characterized as a determination to destroy him *per fas aut nefas*. Burr's defeat of Schuyler that year, which Hamilton may have experienced as his own defeat at Burr's hands, resulted in an exacerbation of his animosity toward Burr, in keeping with which Hamilton urged his father-in-law "all through 1791," according to Hendrickson, "to take some kind of reprisal against Burr."[7] Schuyler, whose own political ambitions were as limited as his recovery from chronic hereditary gout and other ailments was uncertain, declined to follow his son-in-law's advice, writing him in January 1792: "As no good can possibly result from evincing any resentment to Mr. Burr for the part he took last winter, I have on every occasion behaved towards him as if he had never been the principal in the business."[8] Schuyler, like his son-in-law, strongly disliked and distrusted Burr, but his attitude lacked the obsessive quality that characterized Hamilton's view of Burr and as a consequence neither then nor later would Hamilton ever be convinced that "no good can possibly result from evincing any resentment."

While no one will ever know exactly what Hamilton said about Burr at the February 1804 gathering in Albany, it must have gone beyond an expression of "resentment" or remarks merely critical of Burr's politics. Ironically, it was a letter written by Schuyler that led to the publication of the statement responsible for the duel. Schuyler was replying to an earlier letter which, by design or otherwise, made its way onto a page of the *Albany Register*, a Republican newspaper. Written on April 12, 1804, by Dr. Charles D. Cooper of Albany to Andrew Brown of Bern (now Berne), a town fifteen miles west of Albany, the letter outlined a strategy by which undecided or wavering Federalist voters in the forthcoming gubernatorial election could be persuaded to cast their ballots for Morgan Lewis, the Republican candidate, rather than Burr, who was running as an independent. The "reflecting Federalists," Cooper wrote, would support Lewis, and to encourage further defections Cooper stressed that Hamilton "has come out decidely against Burr; indeed when he was here he spoke of him as a dangerous man, and who ought not to be trusted." Chancellor Kent, he also told Brown, "expressed the same sentiment," and while Van Rensselaer was "indifferent," Cooper was confident that Van Rensselaer would join the other "reflecting Federalists" after he talked with Church, in New York. Cooper gave Brown permission to show the letter "to some of {Van Rensselaer's} tenants," a reference to those who farmed or otherwise were employed on his property, which straddled three upstate counties. He no doubt did so in the belief that his letter would influence their votes.[9]

Cooper subsequently claimed that his letter to Brown, which had been entrusted for delivery to one Johan J. Deitz, also of Bern, had been "EMBEZZLED AND BROKEN OPEN,"[10] and his tone of anger and outrage suggests that his letter was not intended for publication. But Schuyler's letter in response, although not addressed to Cooper, and Cooper's second letter of April 23, probably were written for public consumption.

In his letter of April 21 to Dr. Samuel Stringer, chairman of the Albany Federal Republican Committee, Schuyler, contradicting Cooper, asserted that Hamilton had "declared to me that he would not interfere" in the coming election, and that the "decided opinion" of Van Rensselaer was "in favour of the election of Colonel Burr." Chancellor Kent, according to Schuyler, was also a Burr supporter, and as for himself, while it had been alleged that he and Van Rensselaer favored Morgan Lewis, he had the word of Judge John Tayler, Cooper's father-in-law, "that he had never heard that such a report was circulated." Schuyler, as is evident, neither affirmed nor denied the substance of the report as it pertained to him; in effect, he avoided taking any position.

Schuyler's letter to Stringer was circulated as part of an anonymous handbill before it appeared in the *Albany Register* on April 24.[11] Referring to the handbill as a "malignant attack" on his character inasmuch as it was based on "unfounded aspersions," Cooper again asserted that Hamilton and Kent regarded Burr as "a dangerous man," and "one who ought not to be trusted with the reins of government." Perhaps Cooper knew or suspected that Schuyler had been present on at least one occasion when Hamilton delivered, as Cooper phrased it, a "harangue" against Burr, for he added, "If, Sir, you attended a meeting of federalists at the city tavern where Gen. Hamilton made a speech on the impending election, I might appeal to you for the truth of so much of this assertion as relates to him." Kent's declaration, he added, had been witnessed by at least two Albany Federalists, whom he named, one a lawyer and the other a merchant, whose veracity could not be "impeached," and two other "federal gentlemen, high in office in this city" had declared for Lewis. Judge Nathaniel Pendleton of New York, still another prominent Federalist, who would be Hamilton's second in the duel with Burr, had announced for Lewis, and finally, Cooper insisted, he could not believe other than that Schuyler himself "entertained a bad opinion of Mr. Burr . . . presuming on the correctness of your mind, and the reputation you sustain of an upright and exemplary character, I could not suppose you would support a man who I had reason to believe, you held in the lowest estimation."

Had Cooper ended his letter at this point, in all likelihood there would have been no duel less than three months later, at least not then. But in a final effort to establish his credibility, Cooper assured Schuyler that it was "an invariable rule of my life, to be circumspect . . . and in this affair, I feel happy to think, that I have been unusually cautious — for really sir, I could detail to you a still more despicable opinion which General Hamilton has expressed of Mr. Burr."[12] Burr, perhaps, later knew or guessed to what Hamilton's "still more despicable opinion" referred, but neither then nor in almost two hundred years since has anyone come forward to repeat what Hamilton had said. Nevertheless, it is probable that had Cooper not added that last paragraph to his letter, the history of the United States in the early nineteenth century would have been very different.

Of the three letters, each contradictory of the other, all of them written in the days immediately preceding the 1804 New York gubernatorial election, Schuyler's raises the most difficult questions of veracity. To begin with, Schuyler, who was closer to Hamilton than he was to either of his two surviving sons, was, at the least, skirting the truth when he wrote that Hamilton had declared "he would not interfere." He may have been right about Van Rensselaer, however. While Van Rensselaer had little reason to support Burr, who in 1801 had favored his opponent, George Clinton, in the gubernatorial election he had lost, he may have preferred him to the Republican candidate, Morgan Phillips. Cooper's suggestion, on the other hand, that portions of his letter be shown "to some of {Van Rensselaer's} tenants" would seem to indicate he had little doubt of Van Rensselaer's political preference. Kent, as his published papers demonstrate, had made it clear to Lewis that he would not vote for him, but there is no evidence that he voted for his opponent. As a close friend and admirer of both Hamilton and Schuyler, it is extremely unlikely that he supported Burr, whom he had not favored against Schuyler in the Senate contest of 1791.

Schuyler's letter, in short, was hardly an accurate statement of the positions of Hamilton and Kent in the forthcoming election. In effect, he had gone to questionable lengths to assert that not all "reflecting Federalists" would cast their votes for Lewis, and that, in particular, these three prominent Federalists, two of them related to him, probably would not. But if he wished Burr defeated, as he undoubtedly did, why did he not choose to endorse the view presented in Cooper's first letter in support of Lewis, or at least remain silent?

An answer may begin to emerge with the publication in the *Albany Register* of Schuyler's letter to Stringer on April 24. Immediately preceding the letter and serving as a kind of preface was a statement headed "THE CAT OUT OF THE BAG or Burrism and Federalism united." Addressed to "REPUBLICAN ELECTORS," the statement began: "Read the following letter of General SCHUYLER to the Albany federal committee, and you will be convinced that Colonel BURR is the FEDERAL CANDIDATE. The LEADING federalists have pretended to be neutral, doubtless with a view to lull the republicans into a false security. But they now come out openly, and propose Colonel Burr as the candidate of their choice; they praise him in the most fulsome strain, and at the same time, with the malignity which has ever characterized their electioneering productions, they declare his opponents to be a pack of 'UNPRINCIPLED WRETCHES!' " Urging Republicans to "invigorate" their efforts on behalf of Lewis, the statement concluded that, by doing so, Republicans would prove they were not "the DUPES of an UNPRINCIPLED FACTION; and that you will not be SWINDLED out of your LIBERTIES by the DARK INTRIGUES of FEDERALISM and BURRISM UNITED." The letter was signed by the chairman of the "Republican Corresponding Committee," George Merchant.[13]

Read in conjunction with Cooper's two letters, the second of which, the reply to Schuyler, appeared in the same issue of the *Albany Register*, the letter served, as perhaps it was intended to serve, a purpose similar to the one Hamilton had earlier proposed when he referred to Burr's *"apparition"* at the Federalist celebration of Washington's birthday. Hamilton then had suggested that Burr's presence on that occasion be used to raise questions about his commitment to the Republican cause. By stressing, as Schuyler had done in his letter, which Hamilton may have inspired, that Burr had support from prominent Federalists, Merchant's letter, like Schuyler's, would tend to increase Republican misgivings and doubts about Burr, thereby offsetting Cooper's letters, which had the opposite tendency, namely, to increase Republican support for Burr by emphasizing that Lewis, the Republican candidate, was the choice of a number of "reflecting Federalists." In effect, Burr, who as an independent could not be elected without votes from both Republicans and Federalists, was condemned by Republicans not for what he said during the campaign, for he said very little and nothing he said was contrary to Republican principles, but because, it was alleged, he had the support of prominent Federalists. Lewis, on the other hand, who in fact was supported by them, was declared to be without such support by no less an authority than Schuyler. While Burr nominally was a Republican, Schuyler's letter undoubtedly contributed to the Republican vote for Lewis, although it may not have been a decisive factor, without adding any strength to the Federalist vote for Burr.

As a consequence, at least in part, Burr was defeated by almost nine thousand votes, a margin of loss larger than any previously recorded. If, as has been claimed, "for every Republican voting for Burr, a Federalist, influenced by Hamilton, voted for Lewis,"[14] the newly elected Republican governor may have owed his election, somewhat paradoxically, to two of the most prominent Federalists not merely in New York but in the nation. Certainly, Hamilton and his father-in-law were not responsible for all of those nine thousand votes; Burr had enemies who did not think the better of Hamilton and Schuyler, much less were influenced by them, because they opposed Burr. Many of these Republicans believed Burr had connived with Federalists in 1801 to defeat Jefferson for the Presidency when the election, because of their tie vote in the electoral college, was decided by the House of Representatives. But no one can doubt that the combination of Hamilton and Schuyler, both through letters and, in Hamilton's case, through "harangues," was a formidable one. Given Hamilton's efforts and those of Burr's other enemies, probably the election outcome would have been the same had Cooper's and Schuyler's letters not been published in the *Albany Register*, although Burr might well have lost by fewer votes. How these letters, none of which was addressed to the *Albany Register*, reached the newspaper is not known, but the relationships between the letter writers and those mentioned by them is a matter of record, and as such offers certain clues. To begin with, all of them were staunch Federalists, whereas the *Albany Register*, while not Federalist, was strongly anti-Burr. Cooper (1769–1831), trained as a physician, gradually abandoned medicine in favor of politics beginning with the 1804 election, and thereafter he held a number of minor political positions in New York. A land agent in Albany County and adjacent areas, as was his brother, William, for whose real estate transactions Hamilton served as attorney, and his father-in-law, John Tayler, Cooper was a fervent admirer of Hamilton.

John Tayler (1742–1829), at whose home on Albany's State Street Hamilton is supposed to have made his "despicable" reference to Burr, was the uncle and father by adoption of Cooper's wife, Margaret, who had been born out of wedlock. Tayler had served under Schuyler in the Revolutionary War and was an intimate friend of Hamilton and Schuyler. Andrew Brown, for whom Cooper's first letter was intended, had moved to Bern from Connecticut in 1789. We may infer from Cooper's letter that he was active in Federalist politics and that he may have had some connection with Van Rensselaer's tenants. Johan or Johannes Deitz, who was conveying the letter to Brown, was for several years an assemblyman in the state legislature. The connection between him and Cooper is not known.

Samuel Stringer (1734–1817), the Schuyler family physician, who also ministered to the Hamiltons when they were in Albany, had known Schuyler, under whom he had served in 1775–76, since 1755. A veteran of Ticonderoga and other campaigns, Stringer was defended by Schuyler when he was the subject of an inquiry in February 1777 concerning medicines he had purchased for the army. His relationship with Hamilton apparently was closer than that of physician, for on at least one occasion in 1791 Hamilton wrote Betsey, who was in Albany: "I wish you could prevail on Doctor Stringer to accompany you {to New York}. It would be a matter of course & pleasure to make him a handsome compensation. If you want money, you may either get it from your father or draw on Mr. Seton at New York for it."[15]

Clearly, the bond between the letter writers, including those mentioned by them, was not only politics. They were related to each other or knew each other well both personally and professionally. The most important among them were persons of prestige, wealth, and influence, had substantial land-holdings, and were the leaders in business and community affairs in the Albany area. Albany itself, with a population of about five thousand, insured a close interaction between its lawyers, doctors, newspaper editors, and political figures, and therefore it is highly improbable that the three letters made their way into print without the active cooperation of those concerned, if not at their instigation or following upon their initiative. Cooper's letter to Brown may well have been intercepted, as he suspected—Washington, Jefferson, Hamilton, and Burr all complained of mail being tampered with—but Schuyler's letter to Stringer and Cooper's second letter in response to it almost certainly would not have reached the *Albany Register*, much less been published, without Schuyler's consent. The link between the three letters written by Federalists and the Republican newspaper, and the motivation underlying both the writing and the publishing of the letters, could hardly have been any other than a shared opposition to the election of Aaron Burr.

Burr may have been familiar with Cooper's April 12 letter to Brown, which contained nothing personally offensive, but if he can be believed, he knew nothing of the later letter referring to Hamilton's "still more despicable opinion" until shortly before June 18, when he wrote Hamilton that Cooper's letter, "though apparently published some time ago, has but very recently come to my knowledge." Calling Hamilton's attention to the "still more despicable opinion" attributed to him by Cooper, Burr insisted on "the necessity of a prompt and unqualified acknowledgement or denial of the use of any expressions which could warrant the assertions of Dr. Cooper."[16]

But can we assume, as he said, that he did not know of Cooper's second letter until at least six weeks after it was written? Occasionally in Albany on legal business, Burr was no stranger there, and while evidence that he was in the Albany area between February and June has not come to light, he was not always in Washington presiding over the Senate or in New York during that period. Some years before, his daughter, Theo, had informed her stepbrother that she and her father did not receive Albany newspapers,[17] and while this still may have been true in 1804, it is unlikely his supporters there did not keep him informed about Federalist efforts and, in general, the progress of his campaign.

Another possible explanation is that Burr was familiar with Cooper's letter sometime before he wrote to Hamilton but, never one to be easily offended, did not attach special significance to Hamilton's remark. Perhaps he did not know until late May or early June, more than a month after the election, exactly what Hamilton had said about him, and, not knowing, attached no meaning other than a political one to Hamilton's remark. Unfortunately, Burr's correspondence during those months does not provide clues as to how or by whom he may have been informed of the remarks Hamilton had made meriting, in Cooper's opinion, the characterization of "still more despicable."

But what could Hamilton have said that justified Cooper's language? Biographers have largely refrained from speculating, but one recent biographer and several novelists have been willing to hazard conjectures. While their views of Hamilton and Burr differ widely, their imaginative guesses as to what Hamilton actually said have a common theme: women.

In his two-volume biography of Hamilton which appeared in 1976, Hendrickson suggests that Hamilton's remark related to his belief that his 1791–92 involvement with Maria Reynolds had been engineered by Burr as a sexual entrapment designed to discredit him. Hamilton himself, however, never made any known effort to connect Burr to his relationship with Maria Reynolds, although he must have known that Burr had handled her divorce suit. Burr, of course, may or may not have had an intimate connection with her before or after she met Hamilton, but there is no evidence that Hamilton referred to the Reynolds affair when he gave his "still more despicable opinion" of Burr.[18]

In her 1902 novel *The Conqueror*, which is a creative and not accurate celebration of Hamilton's life, Gertrude Atherton has cast Hamilton and Burr as lovers of Eliza Bowen Jumel, whom Burr much later, when he was near the end of his life, was to marry. Madame Jumel, who may have been a prostitute when she was a young woman, as some biographers have claimed, appears in Atherton's novel first as Mrs. Croix, having taken the name of her first husband, but by 1804 she is Madame Jumel. In love with Hamilton but angry at him for having broken off their affair, she visits Hamilton the night before the duel to tell him "that when you die, it will be by the hand of my deputy {Burr}. I tell you because I am determined that your last earthly thought shall be of me." Hamilton replies, with not much originality, "Cherchez la femme — toujours!" In a note Atherton writes "that {Madame Jumel} was at the bottom of the matter I should not have had the slightest doubt, even if it were not an accepted fact by both Hamilton's present family and hers." According to Hamilton's "present family," however, there was no affair between Hamilton and Madame Jumel.[19]

An earlier novel which received much less attention than *The Conqueror*, perhaps because it is partial to Burr, is *The Rivals: A Tale of the Times of Aaron Burr and Alexander Hamilton*.[20] Written by Jeremiah Clemens and published in 1860, *The Rivals* has Burr issuing the challenge because Hamilton had caused the insanity and death of one Adelaide Clifton, and destroyed the reputation of Margaret Moncrieffe, whom we have met earlier. But, again, as in the other stories linking Hamilton and Burr to various women, there is no evidence that either of them launched Moncrieffe on her career as a courtesan.

The speculations of earlier biographers and novelists as to the meaning of "more despicable" are timid indeed in comparison with that of one of America's most distinguished writers, Gore Vidal. In his historical novel *Burr*, which has gone through many printings since it was first published in 1973, Vidal's thesis is that the woman who came between Hamilton and Burr with fatal consequences was Burr's daughter, Theo. While Vidal is not the first, we noted earlier, to call attention to the extraordinary closeness of their relationship, which at times, and on both sides, verged on the seductive, no one else, through attribution or by any other literary device, has suggested Hamilton "said that Aaron Burr was the lover of his own daughter, Theodosia." This fictional statement is attributed to Samuel Swartwout, the real-life close friend of Burr, who in the novel follows it with: "Not until I was half-way home did I begin to wonder whether or not what Hamilton had said might, after all, be true." Swartwout then recalls Madame Jumel saying: *"He loved no one else!"*[21]

While Vidal, in his own words, "tried to keep to the known facts," and in this effort largely succeeded, the incest referred to and Hamil-

ton's alleged reference to it are not known facts. "The incest motif,"
Vidal explained in 1995, "is my invention. I couldn't think of anything
of a 'despicable' nature that would drive AB to so drastic an action." [22]
Vidal's "invention," in other words, is nothing more than that, but it
is, indeed, difficult to imagine any other remark of Hamilton's that
could have had a similar result. Nor can anyone be certain that the
relationship, whatever its nature, between Burr and his daughter was
not believed by Hamilton and others to be incestuous.

Hamilton himself hinted that this may have been his belief as early
as 1792 in a letter to Gouverneur Morris of June 22. Expressing a
willingness to meet Morris "in the field of mutual *confidential* communication," Hamilton proposed code names for Washington, five of his
cabinet officers, and nineteen senators and congressmen, including
Burr.[23] The President was to be Scavola, a first century B.C. Roman
tribune and consul; and Jefferson, Scipio, a reference to a patrician
Roman family of the second and third centuries B.C., the members of
which were known for their love of Greek culture and an addiction to
living well. For himself, Hamilton chose Paulus, the name of both a
prolific and a highly esteemed writer of the third century A.D. and a
successful general. But Burr was designated Savius, a Roman unknown to history except in ancient and obscure sources, and for good
reason. The Savius who is referred to was almost certainly Plautus
Saevius, a first century A.D. Roman who lived during the reign of
Tiberius and who was charged with seducing his son, an act said to
have scandalized even the most debauched Romans of his day. His
chronicler leaves no doubt that he would have been sentenced to death
had he not committed suicide before he was sentenced.[24]

Since Hamilton always chose carefully his own pseudonyms and the
code names or ciphers he devised for others, it is extremely unlikely
that Savius for Burr was a random selection. In other letters, he had
frequently styled Burr a "Catiline," and he could also have made use
of that designation. Nor were his other selections of Roman names as
obscure: Brutus for John Adams, Cato for Robert Morris, and Le-
onidas for Rufus King. But if it is difficult to believe that the choice
of Savius for Burr was an accident, it is much more difficult but not
impossible to imagine that Hamilton could have thought in 1792, when
Burr's daughter was nine years old, that she had been seduced by her
father. Certainly it is easier to believe that, in calling Burr Savius,

Hamilton intended only to indirectly remind Morris of Burr's success "in courting the *young* and the *profligate.*"

Vidal's "invention," however, could explain Hamilton's refusal to provide Burr with the "unqualified acknowledgment or denial of the use of any expressions" warranting Cooper's assertion, and it could also be the reason that neither Cooper nor Tayler nor Kent nor anyone else who had heard what he said left any record of his "more despicable opinion" of Burr. To repeat what he had said, assuming for the moment Vidal is close to the truth of the matter, would have deprived Hamilton of the opportunity to explain his remarks, since Burr then would have had no option other than to issue an immediate challenge. And not only Burr; Theo was a married woman in 1804 whose husband was a member of a distinguished South Carolina family, and given the concepts of family honor that were strong in the South, Hamilton might well have faced the pistols of her husband and her husband's proud and influential relatives. Had they repeated Hamilton's remarks, Cooper and the others might also have been at risk, although a lesser one, since in that era distinctions were not always made between the originator of a derogatory statement and those who repeated it. If Hamilton's defamation of Burr's character was less inflammatory than Vidal suggests, one has reason to wonder why no one present on the occasion interceded, or attempted to clarify the meaning of "still more despicable."

Whatever he said or meant, Hamilton may have had other reasons to refuse Burr's demands. Perhaps, as some biographers have proposed, he could not issue any denial without impugning his own credibility in the eyes of those who knew only too well what he thought of Burr as well as what he had said on that particular occasion. Perhaps he had too much pride to issue what would have been, in effect, an apology to a man whose political defeats he had been instrumental in bringing about, and whose political demise he could only welcome. Perhaps depression, both personal and political, was a contributing factor in the escalation of adversarial rhetoric that culminated in Weehawken. In addition to having lost his oldest and most cherished son, Philip, in a duel, he had seen his daughter Angelica become insane, and experienced the deaths of his mother-in-law and a favorite sister-in-law. While the Federalists continued to field candidates for office, the party's prospects and with them his political career, Hamilton knew, were at an end. Thomas Jefferson, another of his enemies, was assured of a second term as President and was likely to be followed by his Republican disciples and fellow Virginians Madison and Monroe. In a letter he wrote on the eve of the duel, Hamilton confessed that he might have been unfair to Burr, and this, too, could have played a role insofar as the duel served as penance. Finally, early in the correspondence with Burr leading to the duel, Hamilton may have somehow known that, whatever the outcome, the final confrontation would destroy Burr, whether or not it also destroyed him. In this expectation, he was not wrong.

Whatever doubts may attach to these possible reasons for Hamilton's refusing Burr the satisfaction of either an "affirmation or denial" of the "still more despicable opinion" of Burr attributed to him by Cooper, there can be no disagreement about the developments that followed Burr's initial letter of June 18. The letters that passed between Burr and Hamilton promote a feeling in the reader of a certain inevitability in the Weehawken confrontation, but they also reveal that, at various stages in the correspondence, compromises and a diffusion of mutual hostility were possible.

Hamilton's response to Burr's letter was both prompt and evasive. Writing Burr two days later, on June 20, Hamilton began, ominously, by stating his conviction that, having "maturely reflected on the subject," he could not, "without manifest impropriety, make the avowal or disavowal you seem to think necessary." Resorting to verbal tactics that remind us of his career as a distinguished trial lawyer, Hamilton insisted "that the phrase 'still more despicable' admits of infinite shades, from very light to very dark. How am I to judge of the degree intended?" Further questioning whether "Between Gentlemen" any exact discrimination was possible between the expressions "despicable" and "more despicable" in Cooper's letter, Hamilton doubted that Burr could be sure that even his "still more despicable" opinion "had exceeded the bounds which you would yourself deem admissible between political opponents." While he was willing to avow or disavow "explicitly any precise or definite opinion, which I may be charged with having declared of any Gentleman," he could not consent "to be interrogated as to the justness of the *inferences*, which may be drawn by *others*, from whatever I may have said of a political opponent in the course of a fifteen years competition." Invoking the word "delicacy," a favorite word of his that appears again and again in his letters, Hamilton insisted that to accede to Burr's demand would be to "expose my sincerity and delicacy to injurious imputations from every person, who may at any time have conceived the import of my expressions differently from what I may then have intended, or may afterwards recollect."[25] But if Burr could specify "any precise or definite opinion" Hamilton had presented, he stood ready to "avow or disavow" it explicitly. Beyond this, he could not go, and in effect throwing down his gauntlet, Hamilton expressed the hope that Burr would view the matter as he did, but if not, "I can only regret the circumstances, and must abide the consequences."

Burr could not or would not identify what Hamilton had said, and in his second letter, on June 21, the day following, he informed Hamilton that he found nothing in Hamilton's response of "that sincerity or delicacy which you profess to value." As to the meaning of "more disreputable," Burr added, with a touch of contempt for Hamilton's discussion of the phrase: "The Common sense of Mankind affixes to the epithet adopted by Dr Cooper the idea of dishonor . . . The question is not whether he has understood the meaning of the word or has used it according to Syntax and with grammatical accuracy, but whether you have authorized this application either directly or by uttering expressions or opinions derogatory to my honor." Hamilton's letter, in short, had given him "new reasons" for requiring "a definite reply."

At this point, perhaps the duel still could have been avoided. According to Van Ness, later Burr's second in the duel, who, alternating with Pendleton, subsequently Hamilton's second, carried these letters back and forth between Hamilton and Burr, Hamilton was informed by him that if, in the first letter, Hamilton had declared that "he could recollect the use of no terms that would justify the construction made by Dr Cooper it would in my opinion have opened the door for accommodation." Van Ness apparently believed after Burr's second letter that it was not too late to make the above declaration, but Hamilton, far from being amenable, insisted on June 22 that Burr withdraw his second letter in favor of one "which would admit of a different reply." Characterizing Burr's first letter as written "in a style too peremptory, {and making} a demand, in my opinion, unprecedented and unwarrantable," Hamilton informed Burr that he had no "definite reply" or "other answer to given than that which has already been given."

Had Burr withdrawn his second letter and written one "properly adapted," Hamilton, Pendleton wrote, "would be able to answer consistently with his Honor, and the truth, in substance That the conversation to which Doctr Cooper alluded turned wholly on political topics and did not attribute to Colo. Burr any instance of dishonorable conduct, nor relate to his private character." If Burr had in mind any other statement about him that Hamilton had made, Pendleton reiterated, he had only to specify it to obtain from Hamilton "an avowal or denial."

Pendleton may have tried to persuade Hamilton to issue the disclaimer whether or not Burr wrote a letter "properly adapted," but if he did so, he failed. The attitude of the principals if not the seconds was steadily becoming more intransigent, with Hamilton demanding citations of specific remarks on specific occasions, and Burr insisting on a broader denial to the effect that Hamilton had made no statements derogatory of Burr's honor at any time or place. Manifestly, this was a denial Hamilton could not provide without disavowing his anti-Burr letters and speeches dating back more than a dozen years. Burr, on his part, could not forget that the Cooper letter had been, in a sense, the culmination of Hamilton's long campaign against him, a campaign reflecting, as he observed to Van Ness, "a settled & implacable malevolence." Hamilton by June 26 had determined that in Burr's attitude toward him, according to Pendleton, he had discovered "nothing short of predetermined hostility." He did not mention that Burr by 1804 may have had reason for "hostility"; twice before they met at Weehawken, Burr later confided to a friend, Hamilton had averted a duel by apologizing to Burr for having gone too far in making remarks critical of his character.

Between charges of "implacable malevolence" and "predetermined hostility" there was little room for negotiation, and Pendleton and Van Ness became increasingly resigned to an event they both regarded with dread.

The hardening and broadening of Burr's demand that Hamilton issue a general retraction may reflect inquiries he had made proving beyond any doubt that Hamilton's "still more despicable opinion" at Tayler's in February, while it exceeded all previous efforts to charge him with gross immorality, was not the first such opinion Hamilton had offered since he had last apologized for "saying things," as Burr put it, "improper & offensive." Burr, as already mentioned, had long known of Hamilton's efforts to besmirch his political reputation, but he may have been unaware until 1804 of Hamilton's repeated declarations that he was flagrantly licentious and profligate in his personal life. While he knew that Hamilton had played a role in the publication of pamphlets and broadsides, during the Pamphlet War, accusing Burr of a variety of moral as well as political lapses, perhaps the extremes to which Hamilton had gone did not impress Burr until he read the Cooper letter. Burr may also have suspected that Schuyler's letter to Stringer and Cooper's response to it would not have appeared in the *Albany Register* had not Hamilton approved, a suspicion perhaps known to Hamilton that could explain Hamilton's seemingly gratuitous and irrelevant statement in his letter of June 20 that the "publication of Dr Cooper was never seen by me 'till after the receipt of your letter." Burr, knowing that Hamilton had a close family and friends in Albany, and that he and his father-in-law shared many confidences, probably did not believe him.

Thus the stage was set for Weehawken. Following further inconsequential exchanges between Pendleton and Van Ness, designed mainly to justify the positions of their principals, Van Ness on June 27 notified Pendleton that Burr, determined to vindicate his honor, "deems it useless to offer any proposition except the simple Message which I shall now have the honor to deliver." But even at that late date a compromise might have been attempted, apparently, had either side been willing to give ground. On June 28 Pendleton handed Van Ness a paper from Hamilton repeating his offer to avow or disavow specified remarks on specific occasions, and when Van Ness heard from Pendleton that it did not contain the "definite" proposition that Burr had demanded, "for an accommodation," acting on Burr's instructions he declined to accept it. There is no record of any further exchange between Hamilton and Burr; it remained for Pendleton and Van Ness to settle the time and place and other arrangements that were to follow upon the "simple message" or challenge.

Burr had no objection to Hamilton taking time to settle his legal and personal affairs, which he was able to do some days before the agreed date of July 11. What actually transpired during and immediately after the duel is to this day no less shrouded in uncertainty than other aspects of their relationship. Despite the attendance of Pendleton and Van Ness, the nearby presence of Dr. Hosack, Hamilton's friend and physician, and with him several boatmen who had transported the duelists across the Hudson, eyewitness accounts disagree on details both significant and minor.

Hamilton himself contributed to these uncertainties by writing Betsey on July 10 that he had decided to expose his own life rather than experience the "guilt of taking the life of {another}," and he apparently confided this intention to a few close friends, none of whom communicated it to Burr. But as Pendleton, the custodian of these papers, later observed, the relevant letters and other documents stating this intention would not have been delivered or made public had Hamilton not been killed. Had Burr been shot dead at first fire and Hamilton been alive at the conclusion of the duel, Pendleton still would have had a very good reason not to release them, for to do so would have exposed Hamilton to charges that he had lied about his intentions, with the aim of deceiving Burr. Such accusations, whether or not well founded, might even have had the effect of making the dead Burr a far more sympathetic figure than he had ever been when alive.

But did Hamilton honor his commitment to expose his own life? Pendleton and Van Ness, the two seconds, agreed that both Hamilton and Burr had fired, but they disagreed on the sequence and timing of the shots, and on much else. In their initial statement, a joint one six days after the duel, they were in accord that following the given word "present," "both of the parties took aim, & fired in succession, the Intervening time is not expressed as the seconds do not precisely agree on that point. The pistols were discharged within a few seconds of each other and the fire of Colo Burr took effect; Genl Hamilton almost instantly fell."

Two days later, on July 19, Pendleton presented his "confident opinion that General Hamilton did not fire first—and that he did not fire at all *at Col. Burr.*" Pendleton reminded readers of the *New-York Post*, where his statement appeared, that Hamilton had expressed "doubts whether he would not receive and not return Mr. Burr's first fire," doubts Pendleton had attempted to remove on the grounds that Hamilton's proposed inaction was "dangerous to himself and not necessary in the particular case." Subsequently, reported Pendleton, Hamilton announced that he had made up his mind "not to fire at Col. Burr the first time, but to receive his fire, and fire in the air." As proof of this determination, Pendleton continued, Hamilton declined to have the pistol's hair trigger set when he was handed the weapon, and had taken his position.

As further evidence that Hamilton had not fired at Burr, Pendleton recalled that when one of the boatmen, who was returning with the mortally wounded Hamilton to New York, prepared to replace the pistol in its case, Hamilton advised: "Take care of that pistol—it is cocked. It may go off and do mischief." In fact, the pistol had gone off. On the day following Hamilton's death, Pendleton and a friend he did not identify (Hamilton's brother-in-law John Barker Church), in a search of the dueling ground alleged that Hamilton's bullet had severed a tree limb "at an elevation of about twelve feet and a half—between thirteen and fourteen feet from the mark on which General Hamilton stood, and about four feet wide of the direct line between him and Colonel Burr." Pendleton accounted for Hamilton's remark to the boatman, and his being "not sensible of having fired at all," by suggesting that Hamilton, mortally wounded, had discharged his pistol involuntarily as the result of a muscle "exertion" brought on by his wound.

Representing Burr, Van Ness in his statement of July 21 and a later undated letter presented a version of the duel so different from Pendleton's as to make the reader believe that the two seconds had not witnessed the same event. According to the July 21 statement of Van Ness, Hamilton's preparations as he confronted Burr were careful and precise. First raising his pistol "as if to try the light," he observed that "the direction of the light" required him to use his spectacles, which he retrieved from a pocket and put on. "The word *present* was then given, on which both parties took aim. The pistol of General Hamilton was first discharged, and Col Burr fired immediately after, only five or six seconds of time intervening." In the interval, Van Ness first thought that Burr had been hurt, when, following Hamilton's shot, he perceived "a slight motion in his person," caused, Burr later told him, by a stone under his foot. Van Ness also recalled, as did Pendleton, that Burr took some steps toward the fallen Hamilton, perhaps as a sign of concern, but was urged to leave the area by Van Ness before

Hamilton's physician and the boatmen, hurrying to the scene, were able to identify him.

In a letter to Charles Biddle, a close friend of Burr, written at the latter's request, Van Ness went further in an effort to cast doubt on Pendleton's version of what had transpired. Hamilton, he began, had "levelled his pistol in several directions . . . and once, as appeared to me, at Mr. Burr." Insisting again that several seconds intervened between the first firing by Hamilton and Burr's fatal shot, Van Ness informed Biddle that Dr. Hosack, Hamilton's physician, would support this statement, "and it is also agree'd that Genl. H. fell *instantly* on Mr. B's firing, which contradicts the idea that Mr. B. fired first." Van Ness was making the point that Hamilton must have fired first since he "fell *instantly*," and because he did so, he would not have been able to fire after Burr discharged his pistol. Convinced that Hamilton was determined "to take, if possible, the life of his adversary," Van Ness assured Biddle that neither Burr nor he had ever heard of any intention on Hamilton's part to refrain from shooting. If Van Ness is correct in stating that Hamilton, testing the light, "levelled his pistol" once at Burr, Burr could hardly have believed that Hamilton had come to Weehawken, as Henry Adams later wrote, with the intention of inviting Burr to kill him.[26]

Hamilton may have fired involuntarily as a result of being struck by Burr's bullet, but careful studies of the pistol he used suggest other possibilities. The pistol, which today is owned by the Chase Manhattan Bank, was borrowed from his brother-in-law John Barker Church, and while it had been used by Church and by Hamilton's son Philip in earlier duels,* it had features not common to dueling pistols. Either Church or someone else had bronze fore ends, or weights, soldered onto the barrel, making the pistol, which was of English manufacture, heavier and therefore steadier and more accurate. It had adjustable front and rear sights, also adding to its accuracy, unlike other dueling pistols, which usually had one fixed front sight. Its bore was .544, as compared with the usual bore of .50 or less, a caliber greater than that of the United States heavy machine gun of World War II.

---

* Church apparently used the pistol in an earlier duel with Burr, in the course of which neither was wounded, though Burr had a button shot off his coat. Before the duel at Weehawken, Church is reported to have said to Hamilton, who owned a set of dueling pistols: "Why don't you use my pistols? I used them when I met Burr and made his button fly" (Chase Manhattan Bank, *The Church Pistols*). Philip Hamilton was holding the same pistol or its twin when he was killed.

Almost half an inch in diameter, the bullet, or round, if fired at close range would almost always inflict a fatal wound if it struck any vital part of the body. Finally, it had a single-set hair trigger that could be surreptitiously activated by the duelist, who, exerting a half pound instead of the customary ten- to twelve-pound pull on the trigger, could discharge the pistol quickly and with a minimum of effort. To set the trigger, he had only to push it slightly forward. In short, Church's pistol was designed less for dueling than for killing.[27]

But did Hamilton unobserved set the hair trigger? There can be no conclusive answer to that question, but the possibility is not easily dismissed. The belief that the hair trigger was not set and that a muscle "exertion," as Pendleton put it, followed his being shot, causing the pistol to discharge, assumes that the mortally wounded Hamilton was capable of a ten- to twelve-pound pull on the trigger. Further, if he did not intend to fire at Burr, why, according to Van Ness, did he conduct himself as if he had that intention, as was manifested in his wearing glasses, trying the light, and pointing his pistol at Burr? In dealing with these and other questions, biographers rarely if ever have attached importance to the simple but significant truth that the pistol did not go off by itself; whether he fired deliberately or involuntarily, Hamilton's finger must have been on the trigger.

If, on the other hand, the hair trigger was set, the pistol may have discharged when Hamilton touched the trigger too soon as he was lowering the pistol toward Burr from its initial position pointing upward, the usual procedure in dueling. As one arms expert has suggested, Hamilton may have "booby-trapped himself . . . [by] holding a little too tightly and accidentally fired before he had Burr in his sights."[28]

Despite evidence that Hamilton was not so innocent of intent to shoot Burr as he and most of his biographers have maintained, his pistol may have discharged by chance. If it did so, Hamilton must have gone to Weehawken knowing that he was not about to "expose" his life, as he had put it in his statement on the eve of the duel, but to forfeit it. This in turn implies that Hamilton knowingly embarked on a suicidal mission, but a mission that would also have suicidal consequences for Burr in the sense that he would suffer a self-imposed life sentence of political oblivion. Doubts may preclude a definitive answer to the question whether Hamilton intended to fire or not fire at Burr, but there can be no doubt of his long-standing intention to destroy him politically, an intention that would be fulfilled whether he killed Burr or was killed by him. Had he valued his own life more and hated Burr less, there probably would have been no fatal duel, but for the duel not to have happened would have required a history and a relationship between the two very different from the one described here.

eleven

A WORLD TOO SMALL?

O n the evening of July 10, 1804, less than twelve hours before he
and Hamilton were to confront each other on the ledge above
the Hudson River at Weehawken, Burr wrote a letter to his son-in-
law in which he discused the disposal of his property, including his
papers and letters, and his wish that Alston "take some notice" of
special friends by giving them mementos of himself or paying them
visits "if it should be my lot to fall." His most urgent concern in the
event of his death, he made clear, was not his debt-encumbered estate,
with the settlement of which Alston and his other executors would be
occupied for some time, but the continuing education of his daughter,
Theo, and his grandson. "Let me entreat you," he pleaded, "to stim-
ulate and aid Theodosia in the cultivation of her mind. It is indispensable to her happiness and essential to yours. It is also of the utmost
importance to your son. She would presently acquire a critical knowledge of Latin, English, and all branches of natural philosophy. All this
would be poured into your son. If you should differ with me as to the
importance of this measure, suffer me to ask it of you as a last favor."
As far as he could arrange matters, he would continue beyond the
grave, if that were to be the duel's outcome, to be a commanding
presence in his daughter's life.

Neither in this letter nor in the others Burr wrote on the eve of the
duel was there any apology for his having issued the challenge, or any
suggestion, as there was to be later in his life, that he might have dealt
differently with Hamilton. His only mention of him in his letter to
Alston was: "I have called out General Hamilton, and we meet tomorrow morning. Van Ness will give you the particulars."[1]

In one of several letters and statements he composed between June 28 and July 10, Hamilton struck a very different note. Declaring that his "religious and moral principles are strongly opposed" to dueling, and that his love for his wife and children together with his "sense of obligation" toward creditors was a further deterrent, Hamilton added that he was "conscious of no *ill-will* to Col. Burr, distinct from political opposition, which, as I trust, has proceeded from pure and upright motives." But he went on, in seeming contradiction of himself, to confess: "It is not to be denied, that . . . on different occasions, I, in common with many others, have made very unfavourable criticisms on particular instances of the private conduct of this Gentleman." Admitting that "it is probable" that these criticisms "were accompanied with some falsehoods," he added that he had "strong reasons for what I may have said, though it is possible that in some particulars, I may have been influenced by misconstruction or misinformation." Because of his possible error in having "injured" Burr, he continued, "I have resolved . . . to *reserve and throw away* my first fire, and I have thoughts even of *reserving* my second fire — and thus giving a double opportunity to Col. Burr to pause and reflect."

As if this admission were not enough that "in some particulars" he may have been misled about Burr, an admission which, if made earlier, might have resulted in the correspondence leading to the duel taking a different course, Hamilton added emphasis to it by expressing his "ardent wish that I may have been more mistaken than I think I have been, and that he by his future conduct may shew himself worthy of all confidence and esteem, and prove an ornament and blessing to the country."[2]

Hamilton may have thought that his "ardent wish" that Burr in the future prove himself to be a national "ornament and blessing" would be viewed as more sincere and gracious and less artificial and condescending than it was, but he could hardly have imagined, much less desired, that, in the event he was killed by Burr's pistol, his death would have so few adverse consequences for Burr that he would live to be recognized as "an ornament and blessing." Burr, however, may have been sanguine enough to genuinely believe that Hamilton's demise would not preclude his practicing law and continuing to pursue political interests. He knew that duels ending in fatalities, which were not uncommon events, usually did not bring to a close the political careers of the surviving duelists.[3] But if Burr assumed he could return from Weehawken and resume his normal life, he soon learned that Hamilton's death would not be seen in the same light as the deaths of other duelists, and that, while Hamilton had many enemies, few were willing, at least publicly, to come to his, Burr's, defense.

Four days after Hamilton's death in the early afternoon of July 12, his statement that he would *"reserve and throw away"* his first and perhaps even his second fire was published in the *New-York Evening Post*. By that time, rumors were already circulating that the confrontation at Weekawken had been not a duel but an execution which had been carefully planned in advance. Some of those who credited such rumors believed that Hamilton's declared intention not to fire first or perhaps at all had been communicated to Burr, which it had not, and that, as his second, Nathaniel Pendleton, reported, Hamilton had fulfilled his intention, his pistol accidentally discharging into the air only after he had been shot. Burr's avowed purpose, on the other hand, was to kill Hamilton as a consequence, the *Newport Mercury* insisted, of "a predetermined hostility and inveteracy of design, which no language could assuage . . . no honourable concession appease."[4]

Denying that Hamilton's death was the result "of a recent offense," presumably a reference to the remarks about Burr that Charles Cooper in his April 23 letter alleged Hamilton had made, the *New England Republican* held that Hamilton's death "had long been desired, and a pretext long sought for." A number of newspapers published poems and elegies submitted by their readers, some with the title "The Murder of General Hamilton," usually attributing Hamilton's death, in the words of the *Charleston Courier*, to "cold-blooded, deliberate malice," and the act, said the *Commercial Advertiser*, of "a desperate and relentless foe." No newspaper mentioned that Burr in a "a gesture of regret" had "attempted to go to his fallen antagonist" following the fatal shot, but had been prevented from doing so by his second, Peter Van Ness, out of concern that he would be seen by the approaching boatmen and others in Hamilton's party who might later be called as witnesses in legal proceedings. Nor did any newspaper recall that on the following day, before he knew Hamilton had died, Burr wrote Dr. Hosack inquiring as to "the present state of Genl. Hamilton and of the hopes which are entertained of his recovery."[5]

During the days and weeks that followed, in editorials, sermons, articles, and letters, Hamilton was compared favorably with, among others, Demosthenes, Curtius, Regulus, Alexander the Great, Cicero ("in eloquence"), Pericles, Aristides ("in justice"), Achilles ("in war"), Cato, Francis I, and Henry IV. He was also depicted as the "son of Washington," or the "martial son of Washington," and as second only to Washington in past times of war and peace. One of the more extravagant tributes argued that in Hamilton's life "we shall find more to praise and less to condemn that in almost any other person who has made so distinguished a figure . . . {Samuel} Johnson was rude, overbearing, and insufferable to all . . . {Isaac} Newton was absent, and enveloped from society in clouds of abstraction. {Jonathan} Swift was furious, sneering, harsh, and fastidious. The elder Pitt was, from excessive, capricious passion, at times the curse of his house. In short, if we examine the lives of almost all great men, we shall find them frail, feeble, and extravagant . . . Not so our illustrious warrior and statesman, Hamilton."[6]

Not everyone voiced these sentiments, but their voices were subdued. On July 20, John Randolph of Virginia observed to James Monroe that Hamilton's "violent death, at the hands of a man whom he persisted in discountenancing . . . which at first might be imputed to elevated principles, is I fear for the honor of human nature to be referred to personal pique against Mr. Burr, who is said to have injured him to a point which he, of all men in the world could least brook — his vanity."[7] Even more out of keeping with prevailing opinion, and unexpected considering their source, were the restrained comments Gouverneur Morris confided to his diary as he was preparing the oration he would deliver at his friend's funeral. He would "pass over" Hamilton's "illegitimate birth," he wrote, and while he could not avoid mentioning that he was "indiscreet, vain, and opinionated" if the "Character" presented in the address was not to be "incomplete," these qualities of Hamilton "must be told in such a manner as not to destroy the Interest. He was in Principle opposed to republican and attached to monarchical goverment" — this was not mentioned in his oration — "and also in Principle opposed to Dueling . . . I cannot thoroughly excuse him without incriminating Colo. Burr which would be wrong and might lead to Events which every good Citizen must deprecate . . . Colo. Burr ought to be considered in the same Light with any other Man who has killed another in a Duel."[8]

But as Morris observed of his audience shortly before he was to deliver his address, "their Indignation amounts almost to frenzy already." Burr was not to be treated as only another duelist who had dispatched his opponent in a fair contest. On July 21, Cheetham's newspaper, the *American Citizen*, informed its readers: "It has been for some time intimated by many of Mr. Burr's friends in language that could not be misunderstood by those who have calmly observed their conduct for two or three years back that General Hamilton must fall by the hand of Mr. Burr." Hamilton, according to Cheetham, was not the only one marked for destruction. "For some time previous to the late election, from twelve to fifteen of these bloody villains assembled together in the night, and under injunctions of secrecy and pledges of mutual support, planned the diabolical work and selected for destruction those who were viewed as the most formidable obstacles in the way of Mr. Burr's designs . . . Mr. Burr and his friends . . . some time ago determined that General Hamilton should at all events be *challenged* by Mr. Burr . . . Having determined on a challenge, it became necessary to seek for a cause." The "cause," Cheetham instructed his readers, was found "about six weeks ago" (or about a month before the duel) by "three of Mr. Burr's friends" in the files of the *Morning Chronicle*, the weekly newspaper edited by Peter Irving which had been founded by Burr as a counter to the *American Citizen*.

Two days later, Cheetham, in a further effort to support his charge that the duel had been carefully planned, alleged that Burr's "three friends" knew when and where the duel would take place before the final details were agreed upon by Pendleton and Van Ness on Monday, July 9. Two of these friends, Van Ness and Peter Irving, he added, visited the site on Sunday, July 8, the preceding day, and returned to it that evening. At ten in the morning of Wednesday, July 11, or three hours after the duel, Cheetham claimed, Matthew Davis "at the door of his auction room" stated that the cause of the duel was Cooper's letter of April 23 designating Burr's behavior in the version of it presented by Hamilton as "despicable" and "more despicable." From these "facts," among which Cheetham included his having been informed by Burr's partisans that he was "so good a shot, & so daily & uniformly in the *practice of shooting at a mark*" that they had no fear of the duel's outcome, Cheetham concluded that Davis and Irving had possessed a foreknowledge of the duel. One or the other of the two, he hinted, may also have been the individual who brought to Burr's attention Cooper's letter in the *Albany Register*, and both may have been among those of his friends whose "opinion," Van Ness reported, had encouraged Burr to write Hamilton his initial letter of June 18. Cheetham, in other words, was promoting the view that Hamilton's death had been the result of a conspiratorial effort involving a dozen or more of Burr's closest associates that had begun well before the April 1804 New York gubernatorial election.

When Cheetham levied this accusation on July 23, a coroner's inquest was already under way in New York, the first of three official inquiries, two of which were in New York and the third in New Jersey, called to determine, in the words of the coroner's inquest, "When, Where and by What Means the said, Alexander Hamilton, Came to his Death."[9] Cheetham was not one of the "Good and Lawful" men who constituted the coroner's jury, but he might well have been, the jury adhering closely to the spirit of his *American Citizen* editorials and even going beyond them in holding that on July 11 "Aaron Burr not having the fear of God before his eyes, but being moved and seduced by the Instigation of the devil . . . feloniously willfully and of his Malice aforethought . . . did then and there give . . . Alexander Hamilton . . . one mortal wound . . . of Which . . . [he] died." The inquest jury on August 2 also convicted Van Ness and Pendleton, the respective seconds, of having been accessories in "abetting aiding assisting Comforting and maintaining . . . Aaron Burr to kill and murder . . . Alexander Hamilton in manner aforesaid."[10]

Van Ness and Pendleton were the only ones charged with complicity, but they were not the only suspects. In a letter of July 26 Pendleton wrote that the inquest, which was still sitting, "have examined many witnesses," including, in addition to himself, Matthew Davis and a boatman, both of whom refused to testify and as a consequence were sent to jail. "Irvine," presumably Peter Irving, Pendleton reported, against whom there was a warrant, "has fled as I understand." The object of the inquest, he revealed, "was to ascertain the truth of a report that at a caucus of these and some others it was agreed that Burr should fight one or the other of five characters."[11] The inquest jurors, in short, were attempting to establish the "truth" of Cheetham's allegations.

On August 14, Burr, again with Van Ness and Pendleton named as accessories, was indicted in another New York proceeding, "The People v. Aaron Burr: *Indictment for fighting a duel &c.*" The italicized phrase apparently was a reference to the charge that Burr had violated a New York statute of 1803, "An Act to prevent dueling," which thereby disturbed "the peace of the people of the State of New York and their Dignity." On October 23, New Jersey followed suit with a murder indictment of Burr employing some of the same language as used in the New York coroner's inquest. But less than a month later the indictment was ruled invalid by a New Jersey court acting on a motion filed by the state's attorney general. Inasmuch as Hamilton had died in the city and state of New York, out of its jurisdiction, the court declared, a trial based on the indictment "would be totally ineffectual," since Burr could not be legally convicted. The New Jersey indictment did not mention Van Ness and Pendleton.

Burr's letters in the summer of 1804 suggest that he had not expected Hamilton's death to incite such public outrage and to lead to his condemnation as a murderer by Federalists and Republicans alike. The day after Hamilton's death, he wrote Alston: "The malignant federalists or tories, and the embittered Clintonians, unite in endeavouring to excite public sympathy in his favour and indignation against his antagonist."[12] On July 27 he mentioned for the first time, in another letter to Alston, that he was being driven "into a sort of exile" by the reaction to the duel that could "terminate in an actual and permanent ostracism."

He apparently was least prepared for the response of the Republicans. "All our intemperate and unprincipled Jacobins," he wrote Charles Biddle on July 18, "who have been for years reviling H. as a disgrace to the Country and a pest to Society are now the most vehement in his praise, and you will readily perceive that the Motive is, not respect to him but Malice to me." [13] But Biddle, who was to recall that in 1800 in the course of a visit to Burr and Theo he had encountered Hamilton as one of the dinner guests, and that Hamilton and Burr "appeared to be on good terms," was not entirely satisfied with the published accounts of events leading up to the duel. He asked for further details, which Burr supplied in a letter of July 18, beginning his account: "It is too well known that Genl. Hamilton had long indulged himself in illiberal freedom with my Character—He had a peculiar talent of saying things improper & offensive in such a Manner as could not well be taken hold of." Burr then revealed that in the past "on two separate occasions . . . having reason to apprehend that he had gone so far as to afford me fair occasion for {ca}lling on him [i.e., challenging him to a duel], he anticipated me by coming forward Voluntarily and making apologies and concessions — From delicacy to him and a sincere desire for peace, I have never mentioned these circumstances always hoping that the generosity of my Conduct would have had some influence on his — In this I have been constantly deceived . . . It is the opinion of all considerate Men here, that my only fault has been in bearing so much & so long."[14]

Within a short time, he was proven wrong, insofar as "considerate men" composed the juries that accused him of murder, and wrote the editorials condemning him to everlasting shame and disgrace. When their quite different "opinion" very soon became clear, he wrote Theo and her husband that, as he had no intention of allowing himself to be hung or shot, he was leaving New York for safer havens to the west and south. On the evening of July 21, a week after Hamilton's funeral, he departed from Richmond Hill in a boat that took him across the Hudson River to Perth Amboy, New Jersey, and by the twenty-fourth he had reached Philadelphia, where he stayed for a time with Biddle. There his characteristic sangfroid failed him when he became aware that at the request of Governor Morgan Lewis he might be extradited back to New York to face trial. Asking Theo in a letter of August 2 not to complain "if I omit to answer, or even to write," he made a rare request of her: "Don't let me have the idea you are dissatisfied with me a moment. I can't just now endure it."[15]

But his spirits improved as he made his way south to Virginia and Georgia, where he was warmly received by friends. He had least anticipated a cordial reception in Virginia, the "last state," he wrote Theo from Richmond on October 31, "I should have expected any open marks of hospitality and respect." Still, prudence dictated that he not write too much about these travels under duress. The "why and wherefore" of his journey to Richmond, he added, "must be reserved for 'The Travels of A. Gamp, Esq., A.M., LL. D., V.P.U.S.,' &c., &c., &c., which will appear in due time."[16] By November 5, he was again in Washington, presiding over the Senate, but judging it unwise to be seen in New York, he apparently made no effort to return there. He probably never imagined that he would not make a public appearance in New York for another eight years.

One of his staunchest Southern friends at that time was Andrew Jackson, at whose home in Nashville, known as the Hermitage, Burr was a guest in 1805 and 1806. Jackson was described by Burr in an 1805 letter to Theo as "a man of intelligence, and one of those prompt, frank, ardent souls whom I love to meet. The general has no children, but two lovely nieces [who] made a visit of some days, contributed greatly to my amusement, and have cured me of all the evils of my wilderness jaunt." Burr did not mention Jackson's dueling prowess or his telling her father, "Hamilton dead would prove a much more dangerous enemy to him than he ever could have been alive," but by that time Burr and his daughter could have had little doubt that Jackson was being proved right.[17]

Jackson's remark seemed to imply that Burr had been unwise to issue the challenge, whatever the provocation, but never one himself to decline an "interview," and, in the course of it, shoot to kill, he almost certainly did not believe, as did some others, that Hamilton for a variety of reasons had been under no obligation to accept. Biddle, who in his memoirs defended Burr against charges ranging from his having practiced target shooting before the duel to his having "intrigued to get appointed President," argued that Hamilton had confessed to maligning Burr, "who had a right to expect a different treatment from what he had experienced." He also recalled Burr's saying to him "a short time before the duel . . . that he was determined to call out the first man of any respectibility concerned in the infamous publications against him." Biddle could have had no doubt of Hamilton's "respectability," but he did not believe that Burr had "the idea then of having to call out General Hamilton." He was not aware that Burr, as noted earlier, had mentioned to Jefferson Hamilton's connection with the "infamous publications," in one of which Cheetham had accused him "of seduction and of dancing with a buxom wench at a 'nigger ball' given by one of his coloured servants at Richmond Hill."[18] When Biddle wrote his autobiography, first published in 1883, he maintained that Burr would have been elected New York governor in 1804 if he had not been opposed by Hamilton, who, he thought, would have apologized to Burr "had he fortunately been missed."[19]

While no friend of Hamilton shared Biddle's view that he had been in the wrong, at least a few believed that the duel could have been avoided had he been given different advice by those he consulted after receiving Burr's first letter. It is not known whether he discussed that letter and those that followed with Church, John Jay, Egbert Benson, and others, all of whom knew of the duel in advance, but he may well have done so and received some encouragement from Church, who had survived his 1799 duel with Burr, if not from Jay and Benson. Several of his friends were critical of Pendleton, who, they insisted, could have done more to promote a face-saving settlement similar to that which had ended other duels peaceably.

Most of the attention, however, focused on the role of Rufus King, who was the "very moderate and judicious friend" to whose advice Hamilton had referred prior to the duel in explaining his reasons for refusing the "disavowal required of me by Col. Burr." When the identity of King was revealed by Pendleton, and it was learned he had "confirmed" Hamilton's opinion that it would not have been "proper for me to be so questioned," King was blamed for not preventing the duel by, among others, Biddle, Federalist Josiah Quincy of Massachusetts, and a number of Hamilton's relatives, one of whom, perhaps the most outspoken of all, was Washington Morton, Hamilton's brother-in-law, who was married to Betsey's sister, Cornelia. King managed to make matters worse for himself by unexplainedly leaving for Boston a day or two before the fatal Wednesday, July 11. According to Pendleton, King did so because "the duel was inevitable" and "from political considerations, he might wish to be at a distance from the scene," or "to wash his hands of the affair," as a biographer later put it.[20] Whatever the reasons for his departure, he did not return to New York for several months.

If King himself can be believed, he was not fully aware that he had been charged with some responsibility for the duel until 1819, when, coincidentally, he was involved in the dispute with Hamilton's widow and her sons over possession of Hamilton's papers relating to Washington's Farewell Address. Informed of this accusation, he wrote his son, Charles King, that "so far from approving and promoting the duel, I disapproved of it and endeavoured to prevail on Genl. Hamilton not to meet Col. Burr." His father, Charles King added by way of elaboration, had advised Hamilton to affirm or deny only a "particular fact" specified by Burr, and, if this response was unacceptable to Burr, not under any circumstances to accept a challenge from him. But Hamilton's mind, Charles King added, "was made up on this subject, as also to throw away his fire, if they should meet, my father then endeavoured to prove to him, that if he, Mr. H., would persist in fighting, he owed to his family and the rights of self-defense to fire at his antagonist." Neither King addressed the question whether Hamilton should have been advised to affirm or deny that he "at any time or in any place expressed opinions unfavourable or derogatory to Col. Burr," the declaration Burr had asked for, and there was no suggestion by either that an apology by Hamilton should have been considered.

Nor was any question raised by the Kings or anyone else about the silence of others whose intervention might have helped in averting the duel. So far as is known, Charles Cooper never was asked and did not offer to explain what he had meant by "despicable" and "more despicable," and Philip Schuyler, if he was informed of the impending duel by Church or one of Hamilton's friends, made no effort to dissuade his son-in-law from the confrontation with Burr. Evidence is lacking, in fact, that during the more than three weeks between June 18, the date of Burr's first letter to Hamilton, and July 11, anyone other than King made even a limited effort to abort the meeting at Weehawken. Given Hamilton's obsession with Burr, his depression and sense of hopelessness, and his obstinate pride, probably no one could have urged him successfully even to offer Burr a token apology or an admission that, as he wrote in the statement Burr never saw until after the duel, some of his "animadversions" could have been mistaken. But the fact remains that no one on either side made a determined effort to resolve difficulties almost certain to produce a fatal result.

Whatever other outcome might have been possible, there can be little doubt that it was Hamilton's long-standing obsession with Burr, not his references to Burr which Cooper reported in his letter to Schuyler, or Hamilton's contribution to Burr's defeat in the 1804 gubernatorial election, both of which were among their consequences, that was the root cause of the duel which cost him his life. While many believed then, and some still believe, that Hamilton's role in the election was the significant factor, had that been the case the dueling grounds of New Jersey might have been littered with the bodies of other Burr enemies. Davis was not wrong to observe that "from the moment Aaron Burr was elected vice-president, his doom was unalterably decided, if the decision could be accomplished by a combination of wealth, of talent, of government patronage, of favouritism and proscription, inflamed by the worst passions, and nurtured by the hope of gratifying sordid ambition."[21] Davis's view could be dismissed as based on a prejudice in Burr's favor, if it had not been echoed many years later by Henry Adams, never suspected of friendliness toward Burr, who wrote in his history of the Jefferson Administration: "Never in the history of the United States did so powerful a combination of rival politicians unite to break down a single man as that which arrayed against Burr; for as the hostile circle gathered around him, he could plainly see not only Jefferson, Madison and the whole Virginia legion . . . not only DeWitt Clinton and his whole family interest, with Cheetham . . . by their side; but—strangest of companions—Alexander Hamilton himself joining hands with his own bitterest enemies to complete the ring."[22] Except for Cheetham, all of those whom Adams named were men of "respectability," and all had combined to defeat Burr, but only Hamilton received the "simple Message" summoning him to the fatal "Interview."

Had Hamilton not engaged for more than a dozen years in a determined campaign to destroy Burr politically through relentless defamation of his character, there would have been no reports of Hamilton's "illiberal freedom," in Burr's words, in making statements about his character that had culminated in the remarks at the Albany gathering to which Cooper had referred. But Hamilton may have begun actively to dislike Burr long before 1792, when his attitude toward Burr first found written expression. By that time, he had known him ten years or more, during which he had become aware that Burr possessed skills as a lawyer the equal of his own, and political talents and aspirations which, like his own, were not limited to winning elections in New York. Nor was it any secret from him that Burr enjoyed advantages he had been denied, of which insecure as he was, he must have been painfully aware. Whereas he had been illegimate, born of a mother accused of "whoring," after whose death he had had to support himself, and an improvident father of whose identity as his biological father he may not have been absolutely certain, Burr was the son of a mother and father of impeccable reputation and comfortable means, and the grandson of one of the most eminent clergymen in eighteenth-century America.

Rejected by the College of New Jersey in Princeton, which had been chosen for him by Hugh Knox, his mentor in St. Croix, and by those who had befriended him in Elizabethtown, Hamilton had further cause for envy in Burr's admission to the college, of which his father and grandfather had been president. Repeatedly denied the opportunity to win glory on the battlefield in the war he had wished for in his 1769 letter to Ned Stevens, in lieu of which he did not regard as adequate compensation his service as Washington's aide-de-camp, he could not have been happy to hear then or later of Burr's exploits at Quebec and elsewhere, the latter including his leading the retreat north from lower Manhattan in 1776, which he himself may have witnessed. Perhaps it seemed to him, well before 1792, that, because of accidents of parentage and happenstance, Burr was able to achieve almost effortlessly what he could achieve only by overcoming obstacles with an expenditure of physical and nervous energy that often left him drained and exhausted.

Biographers and some of his contemporaries who have rejected the view that Hamilton's enmity toward Burr was entirely occasioned by political rivalry have suggested, as was mentioned earlier, that the competition between them extended to women, and again Hamilton had cause for jealousy and resentment. The reference to "personal pique" resulting from Hamilton's "vanity" as the cause of the duel, the remark of John Randolph of Virginia that was quoted earlier, has been generally understood to mean that, in Randolph's view, Hamilton was angry at Burr for appropriating the affections and sexual favors of one or more women in whom they both were interested. Of these women, perhaps Maria Reynolds has the most serious claim to consideration, presuming that she and Burr knew each other some time before he represented her when she sued for divorce in 1793. Some may think that possibility strengthened by the short interval between the commencement of Hamilton's affair with Maria in the summer of 1791, which continued until at least August 1792, and the date of Hamilton's first known letter, of September 21, 1792, referring to Burr as "unprincipled, both as a public and private man."[23] But there is no evidence whatever that if Burr was involved with Maria, Hamilton was aware of it, or that Burr was connected in any way with Hamilton's affair with Maria.

But even if, as some biographers hint, Hamilton knew or suspected that Maria was more taken with his rival for her attentions than she was with him, Hamilton would not have required still more reasons to augment his bitter dislike of Burr. Had he needed one, however, he easily would have found it in Burr's being preferred to his father-in-law in 1791 for a seat in the United States Senate. Aware that many in New York saw Schuyler as the suppliant "tool" of his son-in-law and therefore voted for his opponent, Hamilton may have experienced Burr's victory as his own defeat. Although there can be no more certainty that he did so than there can be about the alleged existence of a troika involving Maria and her two alternating bedtime companions, it may be significant that all through 1791 Hamilton urged Schuyler to retaliate against Burr.

Neither Maria nor any other female Hamilton and Burr may have competed for accounts adequately for the intensity and duration of Hamilton's obsession, an obsession which far surpassed in strength and depth his hatred of Jefferson, Adams, and others he viewed as his enemies. While the deeper roots of this obsession are beyond the reach of any inquiry distant in time, they can be glimpsed, however tentatively, in the similarities of character, personality, behavior, and even physical characteristics of Hamilton and Burr, similarities of which Hamilton's obsession with Burr suggest he was to some extent conscious, and by which he felt threatened. The perceptive question first raised by Douglass Adair in 1955 points in this direction by asking whether Hamilton's attitude toward Burr was based on projection, defined by Adair as "the process by which a man identifies in an antagonist his own secret desires. To what extent is Hamilton's analysis of Burr in 1801 a mirror of his own heart and personality? From a very superficial knowledge of Burr, I would say that he and Hamilton were much more alike both as men and as politicians than either was like Adams, or Jefferson, or Washington."[24]

But if Hamilton and Burr were mirror images of each other, as Adair suspects, the images were distorted in a mirror that was missing large pieces and was cracked. Through the process of projection, Hamilton was enabled to see in Burr those illicit and inappropriate fantasies, desires, and impulses of his own which he did not wish to confront and which, by relentless opposition to Burr, who represented his "bad" self, he could strive to bring under control and render harmless. At the same time, he could not permit himself to see in Burr, because they also put him at risk though in a different way, those qualities that others, including some of his own admirers and Burr's critics, were able to discern in Burr and admire. Thus it was not Hamilton who was driven by unlimited ambition, but Burr; not he who lusted for power and admired Caesar and Napoleon, but Burr; not he who secretly consulted with a foreign power, but Burr; not he who was "bold, enterprising, and intriguing," but Burr; not he who was ambivalent about the Constitution, but Burr; not he who in the war was without "opportunity of performing any distinguished action," but Burr; not he who engaged in unethical practices, but Burr; not he who was "profligate" and a "voluptuary," but Burr; not he who valued the ability to "[be at all] times supple — {and} often dissemble," but Burr.

Nowhere reflected in Hamilton's image of Burr were those qualities noted by Hamilton's admiring biographer, Frederick Scott Oliver, such as "dignity unruffled by misfortune or success. He was never arrogant and never abased . . . deferred hopes and private sorrows, the neglect and contumely of his fellow-countrymen found him still the same — smiling, courteous, considerate for the feelings of those whom he met. He also had an extraordinary courage, daring to undertake, persistent in the carrying out, and patience under failure and adversity. His charm made him a conqueror in all societies, nor was it a thing cultivated merely for his own advantage (though, doubtless, he must have known its utility), but sprang spontaneously from a sympathetic and affectionate nature, from an eager and ever youthful interest in thought and in men. He was wanting in enthusiasm in public life" — one of Burr's faults, according to Hamilton, was that he "never appeared solicitous for fame" — "but he was equally wanting in misanthropy. His enemies prevailed, he suffered great misfortunes; but he never appears, like the good men Jefferson and Monroe, malicious and revengeful. He could lead men of all ranks — not, like Hamilton, only leaders. He was tolerant of foibles, was not impatient of interested motives." Lauding Burr's generosity, although he "gave away upon an impulse what was already hypothecated to others," Oliver added that "at least he did not spend upon himself . . . He gave because he could not resist appeals, because he could not help giving . . . His charity was of the heart."[25] Oliver did not mention, perhaps because he was unaware, that, "unlike Hamilton, he was even tender with his servants. It is quite impossible to conceive of Hamilton writing friendly letters to his men and women domestics and slaves."[26] Hamilton's grandson, Allan McLane Hamilton, quoting some of Oliver's passages, appended his observation that "few historians have been found who were willing to accord to Burr a single virtue; yet, in spite of certain grave defects of character, there is, after all, much that appeals to the just and fair-minded critic."[27] But not to his grandfather, who, if he saw any of the qualities in Burr that were perceived by Oliver and his own grandson, left no record to that effect.

There was another aspect of the mirror image Hamilton never alluded to, so far as is known, but of which he could hardly have been unaware. Not only were he and Burr almost the same age and about the same height, but, as Bowers reports, there "were probably no other two men in the America of their day who were so much alike. Physically both were small, compactly built, of militant carriage, with penetrating eyes of different colors, and of persuasive voices. Both were dandies in their dress . . . courtly, Chesterfieldian, and dashing . . . In conversation one was scarcely more scintillating than the other, and both were fond of badinage, and adept in compliments to the ladies. Both were gallants, attractive to, and attracted by, women of wit and beauty. Neither was above the intrigues of love, with ideas of morality that would have been appreciated in the London of the Restoration."[28]

If, it seems permissible to speculate, Hamilton was conscious of these resemblances and of other qualities in Burr which mirrored himself, he may have made a positive identification with Burr which, because of unwelcome feelings associated with it, was also illicit and inappropriate. He could concede, as he had to Rufus King, that he was "personally well" with Burr, but he could not admit even to himself that he was in any way drawn to him because he and Burr in certain respects were very much alike. In all such identifications of one man with another, especially those rooted in affection or, as may have been the case with Hamilton, a consciousness of similarities, there are underlying homoerotic elements and, in the case of some men, a concommitant and compelling need to defend against an attraction that is experienced as unacceptable in terms of prevailing social and introjected models of masculinity. The language of Hamilton's earlier letters to Laurens and to Betsey about André—his comparing himself, for example, in writing Laurens, to a "jealous lover, when I thought you had slighted my caresses"—features elements that, had Laurens lived to enjoy a longer relationship with Hamilton, might have proved sufficiently disturbing to provoke in Hamilton a negative response. But assuming Hamilton would have had less need to attach to Laurens, through the mechanism of projection, an image of himself which he could not accept and which, by means of projection, he could deny existed, his response to Laurens would not have been as hostile.

Had it not been that for Hamilton unacceptable negative and positive self-images were fused in the person of Burr, and that both, had he given them uninhibited expression, would have threatened to obliterate the image of himself he had created and presented to the world, probably there would have been no obsession leading to the duel resulting in his death. The obsession, in essence, permitted Hamilton to cast off those aspects of himself which were denied full admission to consciousness and which, had he been unable to rid himself of them, might have destroyed him from within long before Burr's pistol destroyed him from without.[29] But as his reckless behavior before, during, and after the 1800 election demonstrated, to the consternation of his friends, not to mention the provocations that led to the duel, the obsession did not always serve to protect Hamilton from the demons lurking at the threshold of his awareness. While his proneness to jealousy of Burr, whether with respect to political rivalry, to Burr's more fortunate beginnings, or, as some believe, to women for whose favors they competed, was a contributing factor, it was not responsible for the obsession.

Lending support to the view that Hamilton's death was a suicide is his reported serenity on the eve of the duel, a phenomenon often seen in those who have decided to take their own lives. Depressed and made despondent by the death of his son and the insanity of his daughter, and realizing that he and the Federalists were a spent force, he may have gone to Weehawken with the intention of forfeiting his life, as Henry Adams later thought possible, but not without dealing one last and lasting defeat to Burr by making it appear that there would have been no blood shed had Burr not been bent on revenge. He had not given Burr, he knew, any reason to reserve his own fire, or to fire and miss, as earlier he had not tried to persuade him that, in Albany and elsewhere, his remarks about Burr's conduct and character had been misunderstood. But whether he did or did not allow himself to be fatally shot, he made it certain, ironically, that Burr would not disappear from memory even if he had not been charged later with conspiracy to commit treason. Had it not been for the fatal duel, Burr would have been as obscure in history as most of our other Vice Presidents.

Hamilton's fame, of course, was assured, but there also is irony in

Burr's unintentionally adding to it by making him a fallen hero more appreciated in death than he ever was in life. Had he realized he was doing so, and that Hamilton, as Jackson foresaw, would be far more costly to him dead than alive, he still would have been unable to persuade himself that Hamilton's "animadversions" were no worse than Cheetham's, which, he had assured his son-in-law in 1802, "would do no harm to me personally."[30] Between this letter to Alston of July 3, 1802, and the duel on July 11, 1804, he had witnessed the erosion of his influence with both Republicans and Federalists, and with it his hopes of winning either national or state office, the demise of which, in New York, owed much to Hamilton. Burr was not, as Oliver observed, "revengeful," but he believed, as he remarked to someone who was condemning the evils of war, that "slander has slain more than the sword," and he had been slandered repeatedly.[31]

While he was less ambitious than Hamilton, and sometimes affected an indifference to his political fortunes, as in his comment to Theo, "Tante mieux" (So much the better), following his defeat in the 1804 election, he placed a high value on the rewards of office, if not always the office itself, and enjoyed the honor and recognition that accompanied it. A "mere matter-of-fact man," as Sedgwick called him, he was a pragmatist rather than an ideologue, and more able than Hamilton to detach himself emotionally from the political warfare of his time. He was also by nature sanguine, perhaps excessively so, Andrew Jackson suggested, relying "too much on what people said, and did not sufficiently watch what they were doing at the same time." Perhaps he was naïve as well, as Jackson hinted in commenting, "Burr is as far from a fool as I ever saw, and yet he is as easily fooled as any man I ever knew."[32]

His disposition to view life and death, success and failure, acceptance and rejection, with an equanimity bordering on nonchalance sometimes made him appear unfeeling and even cold. "Mrs. Brockholst Livingston dead," he informed Theo on November 3, 1801, "Mrs. Van Ness has this day a son. Thus, you see, the rotation is preserved, and the balance kept up."[33] "Frank Van Berkel," he wrote Monroe on September 6, 1796, "lately shot himself—which many think the most rational thing he ever did."[34] On August 11, 1804, when he was still in Philadelphia and Celeste again was on the scene, he wrote Theo: "If any male friend of yours should be dying of ennui, recommend to him to engage in a duel and a courtship at the same time."[35] These remarks, which approach flippancy, suggest that Burr had to limit his affectual response to the cruelties of human existence, and that one of his means of doing so was to treat them as of no more consequence than any other outcome in life. His need to minimize the pain that accompanied loss no doubt derived from the deaths, when he was still very young, of his parents and grandparents. In the future he would also experience the deaths of his daughter and only grandchild, but we have no testimony from any of his friends that he ever spoke of these deaths, and they are never mentioned in his letters that have come down to us.

His stoicism was another defense against the large and small adversities of life, as was his quick wit and his sense of humor, which, apparently, never deserted him. Certain anecdotes may be more invented than not, but they accord with what we know of his character, as reflected in his usual retort when it was alleged, sometimes with impressive evidence, that he had fathered an illegimate child: "When a woman does me the honor to name me as the father of her child, I trust I shall always be too gallant to show myself ungrateful for the honor."[36] A story related in the Kent family has Burr and the Chancellor walking on opposite sides of Nassau Street years after the duel, and the Chancellor seeing Burr across the way. Rushing over to confront him, Kent "exclaimed, with a voice choked with passion, 'You are a scoundrel, Sir! — a scoundrel!' Burr flushed at the epithet, and was about to make a hasty answer . . . checking himself, as he paused to consider the age and dignity of his adversary, he contented himself with raising his hat, and making a sweeping bow, exclaimed, 'The opinions of the learned Chancellor are always entitled to the highest consideration.' " Kent, according to his family, was left "somewhat surprised and mortified."[37]

Kent's judgment of Burr, inasmuch as he was a friend and admirer of Hamilton, can be more easily understood than that of several modern historians who have gone much further than Kent in condemnation of Burr. Fawn Brodie, Jefferson's biographer, has been the most extreme, stating: "In the end, it was Hamilton's telling the truth about Burr that cost him his life." The "truth," Brodie argues, included his being "a cool and diabolical liar," and "where there is so much grandiose lying there must be delusion and madness." Referring to the "pathology of Aaron Burr," she adds that he was "a fairly unambiguous case of paranoia" whose "life before 1805 had already shown patterns of betrayal and conspiracy." Among those betrayed were Burr's wife, Theodosia, with regard to whom Brodie does not supply details, and Jefferson in their electoral contest of 1801, whom, she asserts, Burr was planning to assassinate later. Because of these patterns of betrayal that she attributes to Burr, she is able to surmise that "he must have pondered with special curiosity" the treachery of Benedict Arnold.[38]

George Dangerfield's more restrained view is that "Aaron Burr was an adventurer and nothing more . . . a human upas tree, under whose shade all reputations, not the least his own, were apt to sicken. No man was more sincerely anxious to write dishonesty into the Decalogue."[39] In his biography of Jefferson, Joseph Ellis makes a parenthetical comment that "any gathering that included Burr possessed the potential to look like a conspiracy." Observing that there were resemblances in ambition, "style," and temperament between Hamilton and Burr, Ellis contends that Burr's "singular advantage over Hamilton, and indeed all competitors, was a total disregard for any moral or political principle that obstructed his path to power."[40]

Hamilton has fared far better in the treatment accorded him by biographers and historians, whose general tendency, as is manifest in the biographies by Henry Cabot Lodge and Broadus Mitchell, is to emphasize his admittedly great gifts and treat his political and moral lapses as contrary, or "not becoming," to his character; Burr's lapses, on the other hand, are seen as altogether in keeping with his character and as typical of the behavior to which he was addicted.[41] But no modern admirer since the historians John Fiske and Nicholas Murray Butler has been as extravagant as Kent, who wrote Betsey that he had "very little doubt that if General Hamilton had lived twenty years longer, he would have rivalled Socrates, or Bacon, or any other of the sages of ancient or modern times, in researches after truth and in benevolence to mankind."[42] Fiske came close to emulating Kent in expressing his certainty in 1902 that, as a political philospher, Hamilton was "worthy to rank with Montesquieu and Locke."[43] Lord Bryce in his *The American Commonwealth* of 1888 did not question that Washington was "a more perfect character" and that Hamilton was "of a virtue not so flawless," but, reminding us of Talleyrand's earlier appraisal, he was confident that only Hamilton among Americans was "in the front rank of a generation which included Burke and Fox and Pitt . . . Wellington and Napoleon."[44]

His words "not so flawless" would have been judged a gross understatement by the Adamses, John and his son John Quincy, especially the elder Adams, who wrote a year after Hamilton's death that his "Vice, Folly, and Villany are not to be forgotten, because the guilty Wretch repented, in his dying Moments. Although David repented, we are nowhere commanded to forget the affair of Uriah: though the Magdalene reformed, we are not obliged to forget her former Vocation: though the Thief on the cross was converted, his Felony is still upon Record. The Prodigal Son repented and was forgiven, yet his Harlots and riotous living . . . cannot be forgotten. Nor am I obliged by any Principle or Morality or Religion . . . {because} he died a Penitent . . . {to} conceal his former Character at the Expense of so much injustice to my own . . . this Scottish Creolian Bolingbroke in the days of his disappointed Ambition and unbridled Malice and revenge . . . Born on a speck more obscure than Corsica, from an Original not only contemptible but infamous, with infinitely less courage and Capacity than Bonaparte . . . would, in my Opinion, if I had not controlled the fury of his Vanity . . . have involved {the United States} in all the Bloodshed and distractions of foreign and civil War at once."[45]

John Quincy Adams, who had much less reason than his father for hostility to Hamilton, credited him with "talents . . . of the highest order," but also described his "ambition {as} transcendent, and his disposition to intrigue irrepressible. His consciousness of talent was greater than its reality . . . he was of that class of characters which cannot bear a rival—haughty, overbearing, jealous, bitter and violent in his personal enmities, and little scrupulous of the means he used against those who stood in the way" of his ambition.[46]

Enmities of the kind referred to by John Quincy Adams were not among Burr's faults. He seems never to have been critical of Jefferson during the years they both aspired to the Republican leadership, and to have had a high regard for John Adams, as earlier he had had for Hamilton, according to several of Hamilton's friends. "Colonel Burr . . . in his visit to my family last spring," Benjamin Rush wrote Adams on August 14, 1805, "spoke of your character to me with respect and affection. Your integrity was mentioned by him in the highest terms of commendation."[47] While Burr had much more reason than Adams

to detest and resent Hamilton, until the end of his long life, for cease-
lessly maligning his character and provoking the duel, he is not known
to have ever accused Hamilton of "Vice, Folly, and Villany," in Adams's words, or to have spoken contemptuously of his origins, or to
have compared him to Napoleon Bonaparte. He instead made a comment that Hamilton hardly deserved, and one which perhaps reveals
more about Aaron Burr's character than any other single statement
attributed to him. "If I had read Sterne more, and Voltaire less," he
remarked in his later years, referring to Uncle Toby in *Tristram Shandy*,
"I should have known that the world was wide enough for Hamilton
and me."[48]

It is difficult to believe that Hamilton, had he survived the duel and
had Burr been killed, would have been capable of a similar admission.

EPILOGUE

The obsequies on the occasion of Hamilton's funeral in New York City on Saturday, July 14, 1804, were not inferior, in the opinion of some who were present at both, to those observed when George Washington was laid to rest in 1799. The funeral procession, which began in front of the Churches' house on Robinson Street (now Park Place) and ended at Trinity Church, probably evoked more memories of Hamilton's military career than of his far more significant contributions to the nation's political and financial stability. The procession along Pearl and Beekman streets to Broadway was led by a band of uniformed soldiers playing "melancholy music," followed by companies of artillery, infantry, and militia, the Society of the Cincinnati, and "clergy of all denominations." On "top of the coffin was the General's hat and sword, his boots and spurs reversed across the horse . . . {which was} dressed in mourning {and} led by two black servants dressed in white, and {wearing} white turbans trimmed with black." Next were the family and relatives, military officers, civil dignitaries, representatives of foreign governments, Columbia College officials, professors, and students, and "various officers of the respective Banks, Chamber of Commerce and Merchants."

While the procession was moving toward Trinity Church, the guns of British and French frigates in the harbor were fired at intervals of a minute for "forty-eight minutes," as was the artillery at the Battery.[1] The personnel of the *Cybelle* and the *Didon*, the two French frigates, must have been aware that July 14 marked the fifteenth anniversary of the 1789 storming of the Bastille in Paris, the event celebrated in

France as the beginning of the French Revolution which was so vehemently condemned by Hamilton, but neither Gouverneur Morris in his funeral address nor any other American publicly took note of the coincidence.

Not long after his burial, Hamilton's family and friends discovered that, despite an annual income estimated to have been at least $12,000 to $14,000 ($144,000 to $168,000) during the last years of his life, he apparently owed as much as $60,000 ($720,000) when he died.[2] According to Morris, the property Hamilton owned and the money his clients owed him would not suffice to pay off this debt. While the property, Morris estimated, might eventually be worth $70,000 or $80,000 ($840,000 or $960,000) if sold at auction, it "would not, in all probability, fetch forty" ($480,000).[3] Some part of Hamilton's indebtedness was the construction expense of his country home, the Grange, but it was a small part; the cost of the Grange "plus that of the land on which it stood could not have been over $10,000" ($120,000).[4] Undoubtedly, a substantial portion of his debt was traceable to his living beyond his means; his expenditures over a period of only six months, from January to July 1804, were an estimated $11,840 ($142,080).

The largest part of the debt derived, however, from his speculations in "wild lands," mainly in upstate New York, which began shortly after the Revolution. Although most of Hamilton's friends, including John Jay, thought it wiser to purchase land in New York City and its suburbs and became rich as a result, Hamilton persisted in buying land in Oswego County and elsewhere. In 1795 be acquired 75,000 acres in Oswego, which by 1804 had not appreciated in value.[5]

Apparently, the considerable property Betsey inherited from her father when he died in November 1804, four months after her husband, was not used to pay Hamilton's debts but instead, according to her grandson, was devoted to charitable purposes. Her inheritance included "not only large tracts of land in Saratoga and at Oswego but houses and lots in New York as well," and, in addition, "property down in the heart of the city below Canal Street" which she received in exchange for the Grange.[6] Since "all of this was sold or given away in alms . . . had she not ultimately been awarded her husband's back pay in the Army, which amounted to about $10,000 ($120,000), she would have been penniless."[7]

Why Betsey would have been "penniless" is far from clear, considering that Gouverneur Morris and other friends of Hamilton raised sufficient funds for her and the seven children to retain possession of the Grange for "some thirty years" and to provide the family with an income. Hamilton's grandson, Allan McLane Hamilton, and some biographers since have assumed that their efforts to make the family financially secure were unsuccessful, but that was not the case. The Hamilton Fund, as it came to be called, was a trust fund established by Morris, King, and others, subscriptions to which were in the form of four hundred shares worth $200 each, or a total of $80,000 ($960,000) if all shares were bought. By April 1805, the fund had on deposit at the Bank of New York $39,700 ($476,400). While it is not known if the fund was fully subscribed, and if so by when, the undated list of share subscribers in the possession of the Bank of New York indicates that at least 367 shares worth $73,000 ($880,000) were purchased by 126 individuals in amounts ranging from one to ten shares. Among those holding ten shares, apparently the maximum number each purchaser was allowed, were Church and Stephen Van Rensselaer; Nathaniel Pendleton, Robert Benson, and Robert Troup were each purchasers of one share. The names of Morris and King do not appear on the list, presumably because they held some of the thirty-three shares whose ownership is not recorded by the Bank of New York.[8]

Whatever the true state of the Hamilton family's finances following his death, Betsey in 1806 helped found New York's first orphan asylum, and she later became the second head, or director, of the city's Orphan Asylum Society. She also devoted herself to finding a biographer for her late husband among his various friends, but it was not until 1834 that the first volume of Hamilton's earliest biography, that written by her son, John C. Hamilton, was published. Recommending the book, to which she must have contributed much, she wrote her friend Anne Grant in Edinburgh that the book showed "the moral and intellectual development of a mind always exerted to promote the honor of his country and the happiness of his fellow-creatures, but of a character perhaps too frank and independent for a Democratic people."[9] In her reply, Mrs. Grant observed: "I hardly suppose the Fathers of the Revolution contemplated anything like equality such as seems the object of general aspiration with you, and in which our lower class begin very fast to emulate yours. Such certainly were not the views of Generals Washington and Hamilton."[10]

Betsey, who sometimes was referred to as "Mrs. General Hamilton," would not tolerate any criticism of her husband, or any suggestion that his public and private life had been less than exemplary, and she had a long memory when it came to those who, she believed, had treated him unfairly. A family reminiscence has her being paid a social visit by former President James Monroe when she and he were very old, and she soon made it clear that she had never forgiven him for his role in the exposure of the Reynolds affair. " 'Mr. Monroe,' " she addressed him without sitting down or offering him a chair, " 'if you have come to tell me that you repent, that you are very, *very*, sorry for the misrepresentations and slanders, and the stories you circulated against my dear husband, if you have come to say this, I understand it. But, otherwise, no lapse of time, no nearness to the grave, makes any difference.' " When she stopped speaking, Monroe "took up his hat and left the room."[11]

An early rumor still believed by a few historians and biographers despite a lack of evidence is that Betsey and Burr met on a steamboat en route to Albany. There may be some truth in the report that her son, William Stephen Hamilton, seven years old when his father died, sometime later encountered Burr in St. Louis and challenged him to a duel. Burr, declining the "invitation," is said to have told William: "I don't fight children."[12]

When Betsey died in Washington on November 9, 1854, at the age of ninety-seven, she was the last survivor in her generation of the Schuyler family except for her younger sister, Catherine, or Kitty, whose death came three years later. She had lived through the administrations of eleven Presidents, from Washington to Franklin Pierce, the twelfth President, who in 1854 had been in office two years. While she was proud of having known Washington, it is highly unlikely that he or any other American stood as high in her estimation as the husband she had mourned for more than half a century. All during her married life and her widowhood, seventy-five years in all, she carried with her in a small pouch hanging from her neck a love poem Hamilton had written when he had courted her at Morristown. It began

> *Before no mortal ever knew*
> *A love like mine so tender-true . . .* [13]

The poem was buried with her when she joined her husband, and her sister Angelica, whose grave was nearby, in Trinity churchyard.

Hamilton's widow did not record her thoughts when she first heard of the "Burr Conspiracy" and his indictment for treason, but she may have reflected that since a conviction could carry with it a death sentence, Aaron Burr finally was to receive the punishment he deserved. Since the "Conspiracy," which has been the subject of two books and has been dealt with at length by Burr's biographers, and the more than three decades that passed between the beginning of the "Conspiracy" and his death in 1836 are beyond the scope of this book, they will be discussed here only briefly. Readers who wish to know more about the "Conspiracy" are referred to Walter F. McCaleb's *The Aaron Burr Conspiracy* (New York, 1903), which exonerates Burr of the charge of treason; and Thomas P. Abernathy's *The Burr Conspiracy* (New York, 1954), which contends that Burr did have treasonable intentions. Readers should also bear in mind that the summary account of the "Conspiracy" presented here does not claim to resolve the question of Burr's guilt or innocence, on which scholars have been unable to agree for almost two hundred years. The truth has been elusive, and because it is likely to remain so, the "Conspiracy" probably will continue to be the most controversial and disputed episode of Burr's life.

The "Conspiracy" may be dated to August 6, 1804, less than a month after Hamilton's death, when Anthony Merry, the British Minister to the United States, informed Lord Harrowby, the British Foreign Secretary in London, of "an offer from Mr. Burr . . . to lend his assistance to His Majesty's Government in any manner in which they think fit to employ him, particularly in endeavouring to effect a Separation of the Western Part of the United States from that which lies between the Atlantick and the Mountains, in its whole extent."[14]

A later letter from Merry to Harrowby, dated March 29, 1805, not quite four weeks after Burr addressed the Senate for the last time, added further details: "Mr. Burr . . . told me that the Inhabitants of Louisiana notwithstanding that they are almost all of French or Spanish Origins, as well as those in the Western Part of the United States, would, for many obvious Reasons, prefer having the Protection and Assistance of Great Britain to the Support of France, but that if His Majesty's Government should not think {it} proper to listen to this overture, Applications will be made to that of France who will, he had reason to know, be eager to attend to it in the most effectual manner." Despite "the known Profligacy of Mr. Burr's Character," Merry assured his superior in London that "if a strict Confidence could be placed in him, he certainly possesses perhaps in a much greater degree than any other Individual in this Country all the Talents Energy, Intrepidity and Firmness which are requisite for such an enterprise."[15] Clearly, if Burr really meant what Merry reported him to have said, he was contemplating a treasonable act against the United States.

Between the March 1805 date of Merry's second letter and Burr's treason trial in March–April 1807, Burr persuaded a number of persons to join him in or lend financial support to an expedition whose goal, he told some of them, was, in the event of a war between Spain and the United States, to liberate Spanish-held territory in the south and west of the country, including portions of what is now Florida, Alabama, and Mississippi, and go on to free Mexico from Spanish rule. Apparently, many of those who volunteered to join him were promised a share of the 300,000 acres Burr had purchased along the banks of the Washita River in Louisiana, an area known as the Bastrop land.

Not long after Burr began to plan his expedition, Jefferson heard reports that Burr and James Wilkinson, by then the ranking army general, were engaged in recruiting several thousand armed men, who, in a flotilla, would proceed down the Mississippi River to New Orleans and from there to territory in the south and west, their goal being the establishment of a new country, with Burr at its head. At that time, despite a history of disputes with Spain about the boundaries of Florida, the Spanish claiming more land than the United States was willing to concede, the two nations were at peace.

But Jefferson was aware of substantial public support for an effort to eject the Spanish from Florida and elsewhere in North America, and that many would welcome a war for that purpose. For a time he hesitated to take any action, thereby lending support to rumors, later said by Burr to be true, that he initially favored the expedition. Whether he did or did not do so, Jefferson, convinced by November 27, 1806, that Burr's ultimate objective was Mexico City, signed a proclamation warning the country that "sundry persons . . . are conspiring . . . to . . . set on foot . . . a military expedition against the dominions of Spain." He urged that all civic officials and military officers give their full attention to "searching out & bringing to condign punishment all persons engaged or concerned in such enterprise."[16] On January 22, 1807, two months later, he identified Burr by name, in a message to Congress, as the principal organizer of the "unlawful enterprise."[17]

Jefferson's proclamation and message owed much to information supplied by Wilkinson, who had turned informer. Perhaps the most important piece of evidence attesting to the "Conspiracy" was the so-called Cipher Letter of July 22–29, 1806, that Wilkinson alleged he had received from Burr, a copy of which he sent to Jefferson. "I have at length OBTAINED FUNDS, and have ACTUALLY COM-MENCED," the letter began, "The EASTERN DETACHMENTS ... will RENDEZVOUS ON *Ohio* ON 1 NOVEMBER." The letter, written in cipher, with revisions and additions supplied by Wilkinson — which is now believed to have originated with someone other than Burr — went on to state that Burr, his daughter and grandson, followed later by Alston, would "PROCEED WESTWARD 1 AUGUST — never to RETURN." Accompanied by five hundred or a thousand men in boats, Burr would move rapidly downriver to Natchez, and from there proceed, with the support of British and American naval units, to "SEIZE OR TO PASS BY" Baton Rouge. The "PEOPLE OF THE COUNTRY TO WHICH WE ARE GOING ARE PRE-PARE(D) to RECEIVE US — THEIR AGENTS, NOW with ME, SAY THAT IF WE will PROTECT THEIR RELIGION and will not SUBJECT THEM TO A FOREIGN POWER, THAT IN THREE WEEKS ALL will be SETTLED."[18]

But even before Congress received Jefferson's message of January 22 and a copy of the Cipher Letter, Acting Governor Cowles Mead of the Mississippi Territory, in accordance with Jefferson's earlier proclamation, had ordered Burr to appear before a special session of the Mississippi Supreme Court in early February 1807. When Burr notified Mead of his willingness to do so, he and his expedition were camped on the western side of the Mississippi River across from Natchez. And there, at an embankment on the river called Cole's Creek, Mead's men sought to assure themselves that Burr's plans "are not directed against the United States or its territories."[19] The militia detachment of some thirty men carefully searched the camp and the nearby river to determine if Burr was concealing men, boats, weapons, and supplies. They had reason to be suspicious: search as they might, they found only between sixty and a hundred men, with an arsenal of "three muskets, six fusees {rockets or flares}, eleven rifles—two blunderbusses, thirteen brace of pistols five swords and three or four pounds of powder."[20]

In the course of the next few months, Burr was the defendant in seven trials or other judicial proceedings, all of which ended with a judgment that he was not guilty or that there was insufficient evidence for a conviction. The culmination of these court appearances was his trial for treason, which began in Richmond on August 3, 1807. The presiding judge was Chief Justice John Marshall. Despite the testimony of Wilkinson and others, the attorneys for the government were unable to prove that Burr had committed an overt act of treason in assembling his expedition and moving it down the Mississippi. On September 1, 1807, after only twenty-five minutes of deliberation, the jury rendered a verdict "that Aaron Burr is not proved to be guilty under this indictment by any evidence submitted to us. We therefore find him not guilty."[21] This was less than the simple and unqualified "not guilty" declaration Burr wanted, but Marshall upheld the decision, and although Burr was ordered to appear in Ohio on misdemeanor charges and required to post bail of $3,000 pending his trial there, Burr for all intents and purposes was acquitted of the most serious offense known in American law and the only crime specifically defined in the Constitution.

But what were his intentions when he and his expedition set out from Blennerhassett Island on the Ohio River, the home of Harman Blennerhassett, an Irishman who had built a mansion there that he was to lose as a consequence of supporting Burr and lending him a large amount of money? Historians who believe that Burr was planning to establish an empire in the south and west outnumber the biographers who maintain that Burr never contemplated a "Separation" of the western states and territories from the rest of the United States, or an invasion of Spanish Florida and Mexico, except in the event of a war with Spain, in the absence of which he had nothing more in mind than settlement of the Bastrop tract. Others, however, basing themselves on maps in the possession of Burr and Wilkinson, insist that the expedition from the first had as its aim the independence of Mexico, and that Burr planned to make Mexico and adjoining American territory his base for the resumption of a political career. According to Lomask and other biographers friendly to Burr, in his discussions with Merry and later with Don Carlos Martinez de Yrujo, the Spanish Minister in the United States, Burr assumed that the governments they represented, neither of which much liked Jefferson's America, might welcome a "Separation" that would reduce the threat to their own interests, territorial and otherwise. Burr therefore told them, Lomask maintains, only what they wanted to hear, in the hope that their governments would finance all or part of his expedition.

Another minority view, advanced by some who are unable to take seriously a "Conspiracy" undertaken by so few with such limited means, is that Burr was either unbelievably naïve or, worse, deranged at the time, having inherited the tendency toward mental instability that reportedly characterized one or more ancestors on his mother's side. There also are those who hold that the "Conspiracy" was designed as an act of vengeance against Jefferson, who, by refusing to appoint Burr to any office in his Administration or offer him even minimal political support, had convinced Burr that his hostility was almost as unrelenting as that which had been manifested by Hamilton. Finally, and inevitably, more than a few historians and Hamilton biographers view the "Conspiracy" as convincing evidence that on those occasions when Hamilton had designated Burr "a dangerous man" he was, if anything, understating the truth.

Whatever his motivations and goals between 1805 and 1807, and despite the fact that he was believed by Andrew Jackson, after some initial uncertainty, to be innocent of any treasonable intent, an opinion shared by Washington Irving, who attended the Richmond trial, Burr's reputation never recovered. The reputations of others also suffered damage.[22] Wilkinson, the key witness against Burr, failed to convince anyone that he had joined Burr only to gather information about the "Conspiracy" for delivery to the government. Forced to concede that he had altered the Cipher Letter to conceal his own early involvement, and had made other changes adverse to Burr, he came within two votes of himself being indicted on charges related to treason when he finished his testimony. An enduring if minor mystery of early American history is why Wilkinson, regarded by many as untrustworthy and unscrupulous, who also was widely rumored, correctly, to be secretly a paid agent of Spain, was trusted by Hamilton, who had recommended him for promotion; Jefferson and Madison, who did not block his further advancement in the army after the trial; and for a time Burr.

Questions also have been raised about Jefferson's eagerness to see

Burr indicted and convicted. John Adams complained to Benjamin Rush in February 1807 that "Mr. Jefferson has been too hasty in his message in which he has denounced {Burr} by name and pronounced him guilty. But if his guilt is as clear as the noonday sun, the first magistrate {Jefferson} ought not to have pronounced it so before a jury had tried him."[23] Andrew Jackson was, as usual, more blunt. "It looked to me," he observed of Burr's arrest, "as if Jefferson had brought over here some of those *lettres de cachet* they used in the French Revolution when they wanted to cut a man's head off because he didn't agree with them."[24]

Little is known of Burr's movements following his acquittal until, traveling under the name "G. H. Edwards," he took a packet boat from New York to Falmouth, England, on June 9, 1808. For some weeks or months prior to his departure, he secretly was given hospitality by Rebecca Blodget, formerly a married woman of Philadelphia, described as "a notable beauty and wit," whose relationship with Burr had begun in 1794 and who in 1809 unsuccessfully petitioned James and Dolley Madison to "drop the prosecution against him."[25]

By that time, he had been abroad almost a year, mainly in England and Scotland, and in the next three years he was to travel in Sweden, Germany, France, and other countries. Everywhere, his journal recorded in some detail, but almost always without naming names, there was an abundance of opportunities for "muse," his term for sexual intercourse, and interesting sights to be seen, but he had not come to Europe for "muse" or tourism. Far from having abandoned those intentions which gave rise to the "Conspiracy," intentions referred to in his correspondence with Theo as "X," he again sought support for them from the British, French, and Spanish governments, and once more he may have told their representatives what they wanted to hear. Some of them listened politely, some ignored him, and some treated him as an undesirable alien, possibly a secret agent for one or the other of the warring European powers. While he was often threatened with imprisonment or deportation, and shunned by all but a few Americans whether in their official capacities or as ordinary citizens, Burr was befriended by Jeremy Bentham, William Cobbett, William Godwin, and other notables. Cobbett and an unidentified friend who may have been James Mill, the utilitarian philosopher and father of John Stuart Mill, only months after Burr's arrival in London discussed the desirability of his becoming a member of Parliament.[26] Some of these admirers occasionally lent him money and otherwise provided for him, but he was often without funds, and was forced to pawn the few possessions he had, some of them bought as gifts for his daughter and grandson, or go to bed hungry and, when he could not afford fuel for his fire, cold.

By March 28, 1812, when he left England for Boston on his way to New York, this time under the name "Mr. Arnot," he had abandoned "X" for good. The future was to show that he had also left behind any hopes or dreams he may have had for another chance to redeem himself on the political center stage. Resuming his legal career, which continued until shortly before his death, he tried to find surrogates for those he had loved and lost by turning to his wife's relatives and to children, some of them reportedly his natural children, who were his wards or whom he adopted. He lent his support, such as it was, to Jackson in the Presidential campaigns of 1824, 1828, and 1832, but there is no evidence that the two met again after his return from Europe.

Burr permitted none of these interests to interfere with "muse," the availability and frequency of which apparently were little affected as the years passed, but it was not "muse" which led him to become a husband for the second time, on July 1, 1833, when he was seventy-seven years old. His bride, who was fifty-eight and married at least twice before, was none other than Eliza Bowen Jumel, to whom we were introduced earlier by Gertrude Atherton as the alleged mistress of Hamilton and Burr, a woman whose wealth by 1833 was as impressive as was, perhaps, her amatory experience. However scarlet Eliza's past, if certain accounts of it can be believed, she was long a member of the New York Society Library, a patroness of the arts, and the owner of a sumptuous home on New York's Harlem Heights, not far from the East River. In the brief time she and Burr were married, her husband, whose finances had improved little since he had had to borrow money for his passage back to America, appropriated or otherwise acquired from her a large sum of money, she later claimed. She also accused him of having committed adultery with "one Jane McManus . . . and other females."[27] On July 12, 1834, she sued Burr for divorce, in response to which action he accused her of adultery with several men. Her absolute divorce granted, they shared court costs, and Burr by agreement was not awarded any alimony.

In a little more than two years he was dead, having suffered a minor stroke in 1830 and a more serious one in 1834 after his divorce. But he was still alive, although confined to his bed, when Sam Houston defeated the Mexicans at the Battle of San Jacinto in April 1836 and Texas declared its independence. *"There!"* he is reported to have exclaimed. "You see? I was right! I was only thirty years too soon! What was treason in me thirty years ago, is patriotism now!"[28] At his death on Staten Island on September 14, 1836, he was living in a hotel at Port Richmond, a name which may have evoked memories of happier days at Richmond Hill in the dying man. His funeral in Princeton on September 16 attracted little notice.

Burr's reputation was such that for twenty years no marker identified his grave, which was near those of his father and his grandfather in the Princeton cemetery. There is an inscribed bronze plaque on his grave now, placed there in 1995 by the two hundred members of the Aaron Burr Association as a replacement for an older, worn one, but Burr's reputation has not gained any luster with time. While the reputations of other Americans of the past rise and fall, reflecting new information or changed attitudes toward them and the eras in which they lived, Burr's reputation remains more or less what it was during the last thirty years of his life. It is as if a great many Americans who have heard of Burr assume that there was, in fact, a "Burr Conspiracy," and do not know or may not care that he was acquitted of the charge of treason. Perhaps this is in keeping with the eagerness of many Americans, as Richard Hofstadter observed in 1965, to believe in conspiracy theories of history.

Certainly, Burr has suffered by comparison with the man he killed, for there can be no question of Hamilton's nation-building achievements and Burr's relative unimportance in those early years, but the comparisons are not entirely in Hamilton's favor. Whatever may be said about Burr's behavior in political office, he was never threatened with impeachment, as Hamilton was in 1792–93, and none of Burr's affairs with women, unlike Hamilton's involvement with Maria Reynolds, ended in scandal. Nor did Burr have a sister-in-law whose relationship with him was comparable to that which existed between Angelica Schuyler Church and her sister's husband which aroused so much adverse comment.

But Hamilton gains from other comparisons, not least the belief that his life, unlike Burr's, replicated the Horatio Alger myth which holds that character and hard work can carry almost anyone from humble beginnings attended by poverty to wealth and a respectable position in society. Hamilton's life rightly is seen and celebrated as one of the great American success stories; Burr's life, which was so advantaged at the start, is generally viewed as almost a total waste and failure.

Much that was forgiven Hamilton, who was out of favor with Federalists and held in contempt by Republicans when he died, would not, if he had survived the duel, been so easily forgiven or so quickly forgotten. The manner of his death, as his obituaries demonstrate, evoked the type of emotional response that today we associate with assassinations of public figures, especially those who die young, and Hamilton was not yet fifty when he died. Whatever the basis of this response, which transcends even the most bitter differences of politics and race — as, in our time, it did following the assassinations of President John F. Kennedy, his brother Robert, and Martin Luther King, Jr. — the response to Hamilton's death obliterated the shadows that had darkened his reputation, and conferred on him a kind of martyrdom. Burr, who was not martyred, lived on, surviving Hamilton by more than thirty years, an accomplishment in longevity some of those who revere Hamilton may regard as yet another insult to Hamilton's memory.

Burr, finally, is seen by many historians and ordinary Americans as a defiant rather than a repentant sinner who had no use for conventional morality and standards of behavior. In our national psyche, perhaps he represents the repressed primitive underside of human nature, the side of uninhibited lust and greed, which many Americans, reflecting the nation's Puritan roots, deny exists in their innermost selves. Unlike other political figures of his time who today are esteemed, Burr was not secretive about his pursuit of women, and he did not pretend that he kept his private interests wholly separate from the public policies he favored. He was not tense, controlled, or acquisitive, all characteristics carried to excess by Jefferson, according to Fawn Brodie, and Burr was not, like Hamilton, insecure, restless, and driven; apparently, many Americans find these qualities of Jefferson and Hamilton more acceptable in leaders, although not eminently desirable, than they find those associated with Burr. He did not affect to occupy the high moral ground in or out of office, and he rejected absolutes in politics, whether of good or evil, and in law certainties of right or wrong. Perhaps this relativism, which makes him more typically American in this respect than Hamilton and even, to some extent, Jefferson, would receive greater recognition and appreciation if he had made it a rule to defend himself against repeated charges of depravity and corruption that were levied against him. No matter what he was accused of, Burr rarely bothered to explain, and he never complained. Hamilton did a good deal of both.

One of Burr's sins, in short, may have been a surfeit of hubris, which some have viewed as arrogance. If he had shown himself to be less proud and more vulnerable, he might evoke more sympathetic treatment from historians and biographers today. Burr, however, did not live his life in accordance with the precepts that Americans regard as truisms, one of the most favored of which is that "pride goeth before a fall." Few public figures in our history have fallen from grace as fast and as far as he did, but Aaron Burr retained his pride until the end.

NOTES

The publications listed in the notes that follow are cited in three principal ways: 1. If an author and publication are mentioned only once in the text, the note will list the author's full name, the title of the book, article, or pamphlet, the volume number if there are volumes, the publisher and place and date of publication, and the page or pages quoted. For example Ronald Tree, *History of Barbados* (New York: Random House, 1972), 50. 2. If a publication is cited frequently, it will be referred to by the author's name, volume number if there are volumes, and page or pages quoted. For example, Lomask, II, 123. 3. If several works by one author are cited, those will be listed by the author's name, a short title, volume number if there are volumes, and page or pages quoted. For example, Schachner, *Hamilton*, 234. In cases where the author has condensed two volumes or more of biography into a later, one-volume edition, the multivolume edition is referred to by author, volume and page number(s), and the condensed edition by author, short title, and page number(s). For example, Mitchell, II, 127; and Mitchell, *Concise Biography*, 89. Publications that fall into categories (2) and (3) and all other publications not fully identified in the notes are listed in the bibliography.

The following abbreviated titles are used for published collections of letters, papers, and other documents:

HS   Harold C. Syrett et al., *The Papers of Alexander Hamilton*, 27 vols. (New York: Columbia University Press, 1961–80).

HL   Henry Cabot Lodge, ed., *The Works of Alexander Hamilton*, 12 vols. (New York: Putnam, 1904).

PAB   Mary-Jo Kline et al., eds., *Political Correspondence and Public Papers of Aaron Burr*, 2 vols. (Princeton: Princeton University Press, 1983).

PTJ   Julian Boyd et al., eds., *The Papers of Thomas Jefferson*, 27 vols. (Princeton University Press, 1950–97).

PJM   William T. Hutchinson and William M. E. Rachal, eds., *The Papers of
          James Madison*, 6 vols. (Chicago: University of Chicago Press, 1960–
          72).

PWW   Arthur Link et al., eds., *The Papers of Woodrow Wilson*, 69 vols. (Prince-
          ton University Press, 1966–93).

one
BASTARDY AND LEGITIMACY

1. Letter to Benjamin Rush, Jan. 25, 1806. Schutz and Adair, 48. Adams was
   less knowledgeable about other aspects of Hamilton's early life, writing on
   one occasion that Hamilton had never "perfectly acquired a national character" because he was in the West Indies "till he went to Scotland for education, where he spent his time in a seminary of learning till seventeen
   years of age." Quoted in Cantor, 97. Hamilton never went to Scotland or
   anywhere outside continental North America before or after his arrival from
   the West Indies.

2. Quoted in Parton, I, 235.

3. Quoted in Warshow, 3.

4. The earlier date of 1755 is favored by Mitchell, Miller, the *Columbia Encyclopedia*, the *Dictionary of American Biography*, the *Oxford Companion to American
   Literature*, and other sources; 1757 is supported by the Hamilton family, Flexner, Atherton, Hendrickson, Daniels, Schachner, Loth, and others. In his
   autobiography published in 1915, Allan McLane Hamilton, his grandson, who
   in an earlier biography of his grandfather had endorsed the family's belief
   that 1757 was the correct birth date, changed it to 1756. A moment of for-
   getfulness, no doubt. *Recollections*, 16.

5. Atherton and Schachner regard Hamilton as the older brother; Hendrickson,
   as the younger. Flexner—to confuse matters further—in statements thirteen
   pages apart has Hamilton both younger and older than his brother. *Hamilton*,
   18, 31.

6. Letter to Alexander Hamilton, his father's brother, May 2, 1797, in A. M.
   Hamilton, *Intimate Life*, 14. In HS, the addressee's name is given as "William
   Hamilton [who] was H's uncle and laird of Grange, Ayrshire, Scotland." XXI,
   79.

7. A copy of the first three verses of the poem, which is among the Hamilton
   papers in the Library of Congress, has the notation (following the third verse):
   "Written by A. H. when 18 years old." This copy apparently was made by
   Hamilton's grandson, Alexander Hamilton, the son of James A. Hamilton,
   who was the third of Hamilton's sons. HS, I, 39.

8. Lodge, troubled by the difficulty of reconciling Hamilton's age and the dates

of his role as witness, nevertheless remained convinced that Hamilton was born in 1757. While "it is certainly not a little remarkable that a child of that tender age could have been accepted a competent witness . . . it is not in the least impossible." 284.

9. Dismissing Pickering's suspicions, Lodge blamed the Hamilton family, especially John Church Hamilton, for indirectly encouraging the supposition by failing to provide reliable evidence pertaining to Hamilton's origins. "It can be said that Colonel Pickering's memoranda are mere gossip," he asserted. "Such they are on their face, and nothing would be more distasteful to me than to print them, if they could thus be put aside. They could be condemned in this way if we had a clear, authentic, and well-proved account of Hamilton's origin . . . this is not the case." 291, 294.

10. Flexner, *Hamilton*, 19. Flexner refers to Atherton's *Adventures of a Novelist* as his source for this statement. In her earlier book, *The Conqueror*, Atherton does not indicate any such belief. In *Adventures* she notes that Washington's and Hamilton's "enemies spread the story they were father and son. What foundation they thought they had for this particular bit of scandal is unrecorded. Levine specifically states that Rachel was on Barbados in 1756. Interesting if true." 353.

11. John Adams was not alone in lamenting the deification of Washington that began almost immediately after his death on December 14, 1799. The eulogy in the Senate delivered by its president pro tem, Samuel Livermore, Adams felt, was excessive in its declaration that "Our country mourns her father . . . our greatest benefactor and ornament . . . Favored of heaven, he departed without exhibiting the weakness of humanity . . . Magnanimous in death, the darkness of the grave could not obscure his brightness . . . Washington yet lives on earth in his spotless example, his spirit is in heaven. Let his countrymen consecrate the memory of the heroic general, the patriotic statesman, and the virtuous sage." Quoted in Smith, II, 1021.

12. Ronald Tree, *History of Barbados* (New York: Random House, 1972), 50. Washington's visit to Barbados in 1751 was his only trip outside continental North America. Flexner, among others, suggests that Washington's childlessness "presents a very strong presumption that Washington was, although not impotent, sterile. Martha [Washington] had had four children in quick succession by a previous husband but she had none by Washington." "Postscript to History," *American Heritage*, 41/4 (Feb. 1990), 107. Some urologists familiar with Washington's medical history hypothesize that he may have suffered from urethritis or, according to one urologist, genitourinary tuberculosis. M. J. V. Smith, M.D., *Boston Globe*, May 26, 1974.

13. JCH, II, 2.
14. AMH, *Intimate Life*, 1–13.
15. Hendrickson, I, 10–11.

16. Flexner, 23; Hendrickson, I, 11.

17. According to Hendrickson, James was apprenticed as a carpenter before or after his mother's death. I, 22.

18. Hamilton's biographers differ about the timing of these events, and some question whether they even occurred. A few suggest that Rachel abandoned James, and Schachner and Mitchell, among others, assign different dates to the separation. Schachner also gives her age as thirty-two; she was thirty-nine when she died.

19. AMH, *Intimate Life*, 29.

20. Ibid., 7.

21. HS, III, 617. These letters are also included in AMH, *Intimate Life*, and Atherton, *Some Letters*.

22. AMH, *Intimate Life*, 3; Hendrickson, I, 7.

23. HS, XVIII, 505. The true significance of these remarks apparently was lost on Hamilton's grandson, who cited them only as evidence that Hamilton "really was the son of James Hamilton and was aware of the fact." *Intimate Life*, 4.

24. HS, III, 617; AMH, *Intimate Life*, 6. In the same letter Hamilton mentions that a letter of May 31, 1785, and "one other are the only letters I have received from you in many years."

25. HS, XX, 161–62. In Aug. 1803, Stevens wrote Hamilton that he had been to St. Croix and had inquired there about the existence of a will left by Hamilton's father. It was never found.

26. AMH, *Intimate Life*, 13; HS, XXI, 77.

27. JCH, I, 2–3.

28. *Intimate Life*, 9.

29. *Alexander Hamilton*, An Address Delivered at the Hamilton Club of Brooklyn, N.Y., Jan. 11, 1913. Today there is a Hamilton Hall on the Columbia campus, and the medal Columbia awards to its most distinguished alumnus is called the Hamilton Medal.

30. An exception is Cooke, who comments that if Rachel encouraged Hamilton's precocity, "Alexander either forgot or spurned acknowledgement of the debt . . . Hamilton's reticence about his childhood and family suggests memories more painful than that of illegitimacy alone . . . he said little about his mother's relatives on St. Croix . . . Was his evasiveness the result of his awareness of Rachel's unsavory repute . . . ? Hamilton's silence about his mother was matched by the empty formality of his infrequent references to his father." 3.

31. Mitchell, I, 373.

32. Not long after Peter Levine's death, Hamilton wrote his wife: "You know the circumstances that abate my distress, yet my heart acknowledges the rights of a brother. He dies rich, but has disposed of his fortune to strangers. I am told he has left me a legacy. I did not inquire how much." But inquire he

NOTES

did, enclosing a letter to Levine's executor in one to General Nathaniel Greene, who was commander in the South, asking Greene to forward the letter to the executor, a Mr. Kane. As in the case of his father's death some years later, there apparently was no legacy. Still another inquiry in 1786 concerned the estate of one John Hallwood, described by Hamilton as "a relative of mine" on his mother's side. Hamilton believed that he had been left one-fourth of the estate, but again, there is no record of any inheritance. Schachner, *Hamilton*, 17–18.

33. HS, XX, 456. For whatever reasons, it does not appear that Hamilton began to repay her until July 1796, by which time she and her daughter had lived in Burlington, New Jersey, four years, "where we have suffered and still suffer every hardship incident to poverty." These payments may have begun earlier, but the first mention of them in Hamilton's Cash Book, in which he recorded financial transactions, is July 11, 1796. In the letter he wrote his wife just before the duel, he stated: "Mrs Mitchell is the person in the world to whom as a friend I am under the greatest obligation. I have [not] hitherto done my [duty] to her." Ibid.

34. HS, III, 474–75, 573–74.

35. Ibid., 574.

36. HS, I, 4. The last sentence is omitted in Fish.

37. Ibid., 6–7.

38. *Concise Biography*, 16. On September 6, 1772, Knox submitted to the *Royal Danish American Gazette* an article Hamilton had written about a hurricane the preceding August. The article, in the form of a letter to his father, who was living on St. Kitts at the time and probably never saw it, was published, and attracted much attention with its graphic if somewhat overly dramatic description of "the most dreadful Hurricane" in memory. Hamilton may have written other poems for the *Gazette* in late 1772, but his authorship is not established. HS, I, 34–39.

39. When he heard that Burr had attended a Federalist banquet on Washington's birthday, February 22, 1802, Hamilton referred to Burr as an "apparition."

40. Diary of the Reverend Ezra Stiles of Yale. Stiles was reacting to reports of the senior Burr's death. Quoted in Schachner, *Burr*, 17.

41. Quoted in Wandell, I, 10; Schachner, *Burr*, 11.

42. Wandell, I, 10.

43. Quoted in Wandell, I, 7–8. She added: "I always said I would never be married in ye Fall nor Winter, and I did as I said, and am glad on 't." Wandell, I, 7–8.

44. Quoted in Wandell, I, 11.

45. Quoted in Lomask, I, 17.

46. Quoted in Schachner, *Burr*, 42.

47. Large families were fairly common in the late eighteenth century, partly be-

cause of the high mortality rate of infants and children. The birth of many children gave some guarantee that the father, especially if he was a farmer or shopkeeper, would have sons to share the work with him and take his place when he was gone. Birth control was not unknown in the eighteenth century and earlier, but the methods employed were primitive and far from reliable.

48. Davis, I, 25–26; Parton, I, 51–53; Lomask, I, 22.

49. Parton, I, 53.

50. Ibid.; Parkes, 28.

51. This version has not gone unchallenged. According to one biographer of Jonathan Edwards, his grandmother, Elizabeth Tuttle Edwards, who "was not of sound mind," gave birth to a child whose father was not Richard Edwards, her husband. Until they were divorced twenty-four years after their marriage, in the course of which they had six children, there were "periodic episodes of infidelity . . . of perversity . . . even threats of physical violence." In the same account, "one sister of Elizabeth is said to have killed her own son, and a brother to have killed another sister with an axe." Winslow, 18–19. Elizabeth, in another account, "proved . . . to be of unsound mind." Perry Miller, 15. Daniels, Parmet and Hecht, and others share this view, but there is no mention of Elizabeth's instability in Tracy or the DAB. Daniels quotes Charles Burr Todd, "historian of the Burr family," as the confirming source, but in Todd's *The True Aaron Burr* Jonathan Edwards is referred to only as the grandson of "Richard Edwards, who in 1667 married Elizabeth, daughter of that William Tuthill who in 1635 removed from Old England to New England and became one of the founders of the city of New Haven, Conn." Daniels, 43; Parmet and Hecht, 6; Todd, 1.

52. Davis, I, 27. Parton and other biographers have discounted this report, which may have originated with Burr himself, on the grounds that Princeton in those days was too small and unsettled to provide much opportunity for "dissipation." Perhaps so, but a village with buildings of various sorts, one of which was a tavern, does not in and of itself make the case. A point sometimes overlooked is that Princeton was on the main road from New York to Philadelphia, and coaches traveling from one to the other, a distance of about one hundred miles, often stopped there for the night, or to rest the horses. At the tavern, which may not have been the only one in the village, gambling at billiards was permitted, and there may well have been other diversions. Burr also visited his Edwards relatives in Elizabethtown, a small but prosperous community of several hundred inhabitants, which offered amenities not available in Princeton.

53. Quoted in Parton, I, 55–57.

54. Much later, when both Burr and Paterson were long dead, one of the latter's grandsons claimed that all of Burr's essays in college were written by his grandfather. Corroborative evidence is lacking, but Burr may have received

some assistance from Paterson, a 1763 graduate, who was serving as "a sort of unofficial dean of alumni." Hendrickson, I, 28.

55. As is so often the case, biographers differ on the facts. Mitchell, Hendrickson, and others assert that he disembarked in Boston; Flexner and others that he arrived in New York. The disagreement is hardly important.

two
THE CANNON'S MOUTH

1. J. C. Hamilton, the source of this report, does not make clear what led Rachel to send her son to what apparently was a Hebrew school when he was "so small that he was placed standing by [the teacher's] side on a table." According to A. M. Hamilton, the assertion that Hamilton could read the Decalogue in Hebrew is a "misstatement upon the part of an enthusiastic biographer." He probably was referring to his uncle or to Atherton, although he does not mention either by name. But neither he nor Atherton was able to clarify the circumstances which resulted in Hamilton's being "sent to a small school that happened to be kept by a Jewess," in Atherton's words. One can only speculate that the experience may have had some connection with Rachel's marriage to Levine, assuming that he was Jewish, or that Rachel herself may have had some interest in Jews or in the Jewish religion. AMH, *Intimate Life*, 21; Atherton, *The Conqueror*, 58.

2. HS, I, 126; Atherton, *The Conqueror*, 121.

3. Douglass Adair, *William and Mary Quarterly*, 3rd series, II, 197–98.

4. The complete title: *A Full Vindication of the Measures of the Congress, from the Calumnies of their Enemies; In Answer to a Letter, Under the Signature of A. W. Farmer, Whereby His Sophistry is exposed, His Cavils confuted, His Artifices detected, and his Wit ridiculed; in a General Address to the Farmers of the Province of New-York. Veritas magna est & proevalebit. Truth is powerful, and will prevail* (New York: Printed by James Rivington, 1774). HS, I, 45–79. Almost all of Hamilton's biographers, beginning with J. C. Hamilton, credit him with delivering a "Speech in the Fields" in New York on July 6, 1774, defending the rights of the colonists. No copy of it has been found, and the editors of his *Papers* note: "There is no contemporary evidence, newspaper or other, that H made such a speech or even attended the meeting." HS, I, 43.

5. The full title: *The Farmer Refuted: or A More impartial and comprehensive View of the Dispute between Great-Britain and the Colonies, Intended as a Further Vindication of the Congress: in Answer to a Letter From A. W. Farmer, Intitled A View of the Controversy Between Great-Britain and Her Colonies: Including a Mode of determining*

the present Disputes: Finally and Effectually, etc. (New York: Printed by James Rivington, 1775). HS, I, 81–165.

6. HS, I, 94–95. Hamilton was quoting from Hume's Essay VIII, "Of the Independency of Parliament," *Essays and Treatises on Several Subjects* (1753).

7. According to Jefferson, Hamilton, on a visit to his quarters, stared at portraits on the wall of Francis Bacon, Isaac Newton, and John Locke, the three greatest men in history, in Jefferson's view. Hamilton's reaction was: "The greatest man that ever lived was Julius Caesar." Quoted in Brodie, 267, from Paul L. Ford, ed., *The Writings of Thomas Jefferson*, IX, 296. Brodie, an admiring biographer of Jefferson, also reported that his jealousy of Hamilton extended to his telling Washington "stories of his attacks on the Constitution and republican government."

8. HS, I, 159.

9. Ibid., 176–78.

10. Hamilton was inclined to see a serious "crisis," or menace to law and order, develop well before others became aware of it. He urged that Philadelphia, which was threatened by the British in September 1777, be evacuated before, according to Adams, it was necessary, and again, in 1783, he recommended evacuation of the city when there was a danger that some units of the army might mutiny. On several occasions, notably the Shays' and Whisky Rebellions, he strongly favored calling out army or militia detachments to deal with the disaffected citizenry, and in February 1799 he desired "to use military force against the Virginians . . . {convinced} that the Virginia and Kentucky Resolutions provided ample justification." Douglass Adair, *William and Mary Quarterly*, 3rd series, II, 296. Following Hamilton's death, Adams commented: "Mr. Hamilton's imagination was always haunted by that hideous monster or phantom, so often called a *crisis*, and which so often produced imprudent measures." Quoted in ibid., 297.

11. Quoted in Parton, I, 368.

12. Another, less credible story is that Burr reached Montgomery en route to Quebec disguised as a priest, "making use of his French and Latin . . . Passing from one pious family to another." Brown, 226. Brown may have based this tale on Davis, who treats it as true. Davis, however, does not mention Burr's alleged effort to retrieve Montgomery's body.

13. The eyewitnesses, as reported by Wandell, were a Lieutenant Jennings and a Private Wakeman. 63–64. Flexner, among other biographers, doubts that Hamilton was involved in the retreat with Burr. Arguing that Hamilton and his men made their own way northward after abandoning their guns, Flexner maintains that if Hamilton had followed Burr, Burr "would not have missed a chance to state that he had nobly saved Hamilton's life." Flexner, *Young Hamilton*, 112. Mitchell's version is that shortly after Knox found he was cut off, Burr "came by and told that the way was open to the Bloomingdale Road.

In a march of eight miles in rain, dragging the guns, all escaped to Harlem Heights by nightfall." *Concise Biography*, 34. Davis does not mention Hamilton in his account of the retreat.

14. Quoted from Francis Hopkinson, "The Battle of the Kegs," in Tharp, 425.

15. Quoted in Lomask, I, 109.

16. James Wilkinson, a habitual liar, stated in his *Memoirs* that he was in Princeton when "there was but one gun fired at the college, and this from a six-pounder, by an officer who was not advised the enemy had abandoned it; the wall recoiled, and very nearly killed my horse as I passed in the rear of the building." Assuming that Wilkinson, for once, was telling the truth, we still do not know that Hamilton was the officer to whom he referred. I, 144–45.

17. Quoted in Padover, 35.

18. Schutz and Adair, 45–46, 111.

19. Quoted in Lomask, I, 52.

20. HS, I, 255.

21. Ibid., 243.

22. Ibid., 307; II, 408–9.

23. Lomask, I, 55–56.

24. Quoted in Parton, I, 84.

25. Quoted in Davis, I, 135. According to Davis, Burr also was a supporter of Gates.

26. Palmer, 2, 5. As Palmer expresses it, "The actual captain remained in Europe and disappeared from history. The fictitious lieutenant general came to America and became a world figure." 4.

27. Davis, I, 136–37.

28. Parton, I, 131. According to Todd, Burr spent that time "in recruiting [recovering] his shattered health." 10. In a February 1791 letter to Theodore Sedgwick, Burr recalled that in July 1779 "he was so low as to be unable to walk fifty yds . . . was wavering between life & Death until the Summer of 81 when I began to recruit but Continued for some years feeble." Seeking a pension "for Depreciation of my pay and for other Compensations for Military Service," Burr added as a postscript: "Dont let my Name appear in the Papers as a Petitioner if to be avoided." PAB, I, 69–70.

29. HS, II, 600–1.

30. Ibid., 601–2.

31. Ibid., 637.

32. Ibid., 667–69.

33. Brodie, 139.

34. Ibid., 146.

35. Ibid.

36. Quoted in Buell, 208.

37. Mitchell, I, 256–61; Cooke, 29; Hendrickson, I, 327–34; Henry S. Carrington, *Battles of the American Revolution* (New York, 1876), 638–39. Accounts of the Battle of Yorktown and Hamilton's role in it differ considerably from one another. The editors of his *Papers* regard Carrington as the "best brief account."

38. HS, II, 18.

39. Quoted in Brodie, 25.

40. When a bill was introduced in Congress authorizing the President to open American ports to black Haitian commerce, a form of limited recognition, Jefferson, greatly alarmed, wrote: "We may expect therefore black crews & supercargoes & missionaries thence into the southern states; & when the leven begins to work, I would gladly compound with a great part of our northern country, if they would honestly stand neuter. If this combustion can be introduced among us under any veil whatever, we have to fear it." Quoted in Schachner *Jefferson*, II, 622. Expanding on this theme, J. C. Miller adds that Jefferson, "the avowed champion of the rights of man, drew the color line in human freedom to a much greater degree than Hamilton . . . he could not welcome the prospect of a black republic in the Caribbean. And so Jefferson reversed the policy of Adams and Hamilton . . . He gladly abetted Napoleon's efforts to coerce and starve the blacks into subjection . . . That the French failed to reconquer San Domingo was not owing to any lack of effort on President Jefferson's part." *Paradox*, 559–60.

   While almost all of Jefferson's biographers deal with his racist attitudes, they do not agree on whether he was more prejudiced than many of his contemporaries or, for that matter, more prejudiced than many Americans today. Perhaps his best-known defenders are the historians Dumas Malone, Julian Boyd, Merrill Peterson, Willard Sterne Randall, and Fawn Brodie. Brodie's controversial thesis is that he fathered at least five children with Sally Hemings, one of his mulatto slaves. Jefferson fares less well with historians Eric McKitrick, Leonard Levy, Gordon Wood, Paul Finkelman, Peter Onuf, and Garry Wills. Joseph J. Ellis and others have attempted to strike a balance between these opposing views. See, in particular, Ellis's *American Sphinx: The Character of Thomas Jefferson* (New York: Alfred A. Knopf, 1997).

41. HS, II, 18.

42. HS, II, 441–42. See also Mitchell, I, 216; Randall, 513–96, and his "Why Benedict Arnold?," *American Heritage*, Sept./Oct. 1990, 60–73.

43. Mitchell, I, 216.

three
HUSBANDS, WIVES, LOVERS

1. J. C. Hamilton's "unsatisfactory and inexact statements" are related to his "mistake of not publishing the letters of his father in their entirety, for what reason it does not appear." A. M. Hamilton, *Intimate Life*, 3.
2. Davis, I, 91, 181–82.
3. Ibid., v–vi.
4. Walter Hart Blumenthal, *Women Camp Followers of the American Revolution* (Philadelphia: George S. MacManus Company, 1952), 68; Randall, *Arnold*, 151. The existence of Jacataqua is not established, but there is evidence, according to Blumenthal, that camp followers on both sides were a problem during the Revolutionary War. Washington, he reports, issued at least twenty-five field orders regarding women; the British forces in New York and its outposts, numbering 23,489 men, had attached to them 3,615 women.
5. *Memoirs of Mrs. Coghlan, Daughter of the Late Major Moncrieffe, Written by Herself* (New York: T. H. Morell, privately printed, 1864), 42. "Had it been my lot," she added in her *Memoirs*, which were first published in London in 1794, "to have been united in wedlock with *the man of my affections*, my soul and body might now have been all purity . . . let my example serve as a salutary caution to other brothers — to other fathers — how they attempt to influence the choice . . . of inexperienced female youth." Ibid.
6. Davis, I, 86–92. Parton was the first to dispute Davis's account by quoting the *Memoirs* at length. I, 88–96.
7. Parmet and Hecht, 34.
8. Daniels, 48.
9. Hendrickson, I, 250–51. He implies that both Cornelia and Polly were Hamilton's "mistresses."
10. McDonald, 15.
11. Quoted in Humphreys, 173.
12. J. C. Hamilton and H. C. Lodge give the date of the letter as December 1779, but on the basis of its contents, the editors of Hamilton's *Papers* establish the date as eight months earlier. HS, II, 34.
13. Ibid., 37.
14. Ibid., 34.
15. Mitchell, I, 200.
16. Hendrickson, I, 241–42.
17. McDonald, 16.
18. HS, II, 270. Hamilton's grandson mistakenly identifies the letter's recipient as Peggy's older sister, Angelica, by that time married almost three years to John Barker Church.
19. Quoted in Hendrickson, I, 251.

20. HS, II, 348.
21. Quoted in Miller, *Paradox*, 65.
22. Gerlach, *Schuyler and Revolution*, 17–19.
23. In a monograph published by the American Antiquarian Society, Professor McCusker established approximate 1991 values for pounds and dollars in the period 1782–96, as follows:

	1782–96 dollars	*1991 dollars*
New York £100	*$333.33*	*$3,298.02*
Virginia £100	*$333.33*	*$4,397.32*

The above table takes into account a Consumer Price Index with a base of 100 in 1770 rising to 1,629 in 1991. It should be noted that the depreciation of paper money circulating during the Continental Congress, commemorated by the expression "not worth a Continental," led Congress in March 1780 to declare paper money no longer recognized as legal tender. But some paper money continued to circulate. By December 1778, 600 Pennsylvania silver dollars or 681 Continental paper dollars were worth 100 silver dollars.

For the estimate of equivalent values in 1997, I am indebted to Professor McCusker, who took the trouble of sending me this later calculation from Cambridge, England, where he was on leave of absence from Trinity University. The table of 1991 values excerpted above is from his *How Much Is That in Real Money? A Historical Price Index for Use as Deflator of Money Values in the Economy of the United States* (Worcester, Mass.: American Antiquarian Society, 1992. See especially pp. 325, 333, 352–53).

24. East, *Business Enterprise*, 103–7.
25. Daniels, 38.
26. *The Journal of William Maclay* (New York: A. & C. Boni, 1927), 228. It should be noted that Maclay, a senator from Pennsylvania, had little use for Schuyler or his son-in-law.
27. Miller, *Paradox*, 65.
28. Ibid.; Brodie, 265.
29. HS, II, 542–43.
30. Ibid.
31. Mitchell, I, 202.
32. Gerlach, *Schuyler and Revolution*, 17–18.
33. Mitchell, I, 208.
34. HS, III, 603. Hamilton's restraint is all the more difficult to understand if at the time he was benefiting from "the almost surreptitious aid of his father-in-law," which, according to Schachner, he was receiving when he served as Secretary of the Treasury. *Hamilton*, 341. Most letters that passed between Hamilton and Schuyler were destroyed, and there are few references in the surviving correspondence, or in other papers, to their financial transactions at any time in their relationship.

35. Hendrickson mistakenly gives the date as July 23, 1779, by which time the Churches were parents. I, 254.

36. Quoted in Schachner, *Hamilton*, 391–92; Hecht, 374.

37. The portrait by Ralph Earle in the Museum of the City of New York was painted in 1787.

38. A. M. Hamilton, *Intimate Life*, 96.

39. "Mrs. Hamilton to Mrs. Grant," June 13, 1834, in Grant, 259.

40. For several hundred years, dating back at least as far as the time of Archbishop Thomas Cranmer (1489–1556), British law had prohibited marriage between a man and his dead wife's sister or half sister. The bill to repeal the ban, one of the most controversial measures to come before Parliament in the nineteenth century, was finally passed in 1907, but only after it was introduced forty-seven times and debated in sixty-five sessions. Not until 1960 in Britain was a law approved that allowed marriage of a man to his former wife's sister, aunt, or niece, whether the wife was living or not. Jefferson, of course, did not marry after his wife, Martha, died in 1782, but if, as alleged by Fawn Brodie and others, Sally Hemings was his mistress, and assuming, as do Brodie, Jonathan Daniels, and Eric McKittrick, that she was fathered by John Wayles, Martha Jefferson's father, he was involved with a woman who was his deceased wife's half sister.

41. Dangerfield, 203; HS, IV, 293–94; XVI, 609; Mitchell, II, 757.

42. Quoted in a letter to Alice C. Coffin from Henrietta C. Church, Trumbull's granddaughter, date unknown. Trumbull painted portraits of Hamilton, Schuyler, and, in 1784, Angelica and her son, Philip, born April 14, 1778. Informing his wife of Philip's birth, Trumbull wrote: "The *Old Lady* {Catherine} not to be behind her daughter is in a promising way to make the General the father of another what think you of this?" Warren H. Smith Library, Hobart College. Catherine's baby, born May 15, died young.

43. Quoted in Gerlach, *Schuyler and Revolution*, 307.

44. Humphreys, 225.

45. History of Parliament Trust, *The House of Commons 1790–1820, 441–43.* On October 24, 1783, Jeremiah Wadsworth, Church's business partner, who was in London, wrote Peter Colt, a Hartford, Connecticut, merchant who knew Church: "Mr. Carter has found all his friends and relatives well and a most cordial reconciliation has taken place between them . . . He therefore assumes his real name John Barker Church. The firm of the House will in Future be Wadsworth and Church." Conn. Historical Society: J. Wadsworth Papers, Box 135, Folder L. According to an undated letter written by one of his grandsons, who quotes Church's brother, "Uncle Richard," Church's father "not approving of his wish to go into the army or the bar, placed him with some great London merchant . . . but for some reason or other did not succeed in it . . . the circumstances that induced him to go to America are unknown to me." The grandson, who did not sign his letters, added: "I remember Father

saying . . . that Grandpa ran away . . . to avoid marrying a heiress." Church family scrapbook, Hobart College.

46. HS, III, 515; East, 80–94; Dangerfield, 97; Mitchell, I, 346–47.
47. HS, III, 129.
48. Humphreys, 215.
49. Letter to Laurens, May 22, 1779, in HS, II, 53.
50. HS, XX, 334.
51. Quoted in Phelan, 8.
52. Quoted in Swiggett, 178.
53. HS, IV, 279.
54. The later date is cited by the editors of the *Papers* with no month or day attached. Christoph, however, gives Catherine's birth date as November 4, 1779.
55. HS, IV, 374–76.
56. A. M. Hamilton, *Intimate Life,* 56.
57. HS, III, 55–60.
58. Church Folder, New-York Historical Society. She mistakenly dated the letter 1779, in January of which, one is tempted to speculate, she may have met Hamilton or heard something of him.
59. Hendrickson, I, 555.
60. HS, V, 342.
61. Ibid., 339–40. The editors suggest that "this abominable business" was "probably . . . a case at some country court, for the Supreme Court met only in January, April, July, and October." 343.
62. HS, V, 497.
63. Ibid., 501–2.
64. Hendrickson speculates that the "unexpected step" may relate to Angelica's parents' disapproval of the "absent hours" she spent with Hamilton, a disapproval they "perhaps . . . would soften in their letters he now was forwarding to her." He does not explain, if this was the case, why their "disapproval" did not extend to their son-in-law as well. I, 554–59. In citing this letter, Hendrickson omits any reference to Betsey and the lengthy footnote to Angelica which she added. In another letter to her, written by Hamilton on October 2, 1791, he informed Angelica that "Betsey consents to everything except that I should love you as well as herself and this you are too reasonable to expect." Hendrickson's version, which omits "except," is: "Betsey consents 'that I should love you as well as herself and this you are too reasonable to accept.' " II, 130.
65. So far as is known, Steuben's letter to Angelica has not been published before.
66. HS, VI, 50.
67. A. M. Hamilton, *Intimate Life,* 57–94.
68. Church Folder, New-York Historical Society.

69. HS, VI, 280.
70. A. M. Hamilton, *Intimate Life*, 57, 294.
71. Ibid., 259.
72. Church Folder, New-York Historical Society; A. M. Hamilton, *Intimate Life*, 108. Also omitted is a paragraph informing Betsey that in the event her husband "resigns there will then be no reason for my not going immediately to New York and be under his and your care until Mr. Church can leave this country."
73. A. M. Hamilton, *Intimate Life*, 232.
74. HS, XX, 56.
75. Ibid., 233. The editors observe that this letter could have been written in the summer of 1795.
76. HS, XX, 235–36.
77. Quoted in Schachner, *Hamilton*, 390; Hecht, 373. "Ciominie" may be a misreading of "Cicisbeo," the "name formerly given in Italy to the recognized gallant of a married woman." *The Oxford Companion to English Literature*, 4th ed. (June 1967).
78. Schachner, *Hamilton*, 390.
79. Van Doren, 127, 155. Burr in his letters to Theo made several references to "Catherine C.," one of them on November 7, 1803, reading "Catherine C. la la." But there can be no certainty this was the Churches' oldest daughter.
80. Letter to Benjamin Rush, Sept. 1807, in Schutz and Adair, 93.

four

ENDINGS AND BEGINNINGS

1. HS, II, 254.
2. Ibid., 270.
3. Ibid., 255.
4. Ibid., 34–35. Words in parentheses, the editors note, were taken from J. C. Hamilton, ed., *The Works of Alexander Hamilton* (New York, 1851).
5. AMH, *Intimate Life*, 46. In a reminiscence of Hamilton, G. W. P. Custis, presumably a relative of Martha Custis Washington, referred to him as "this symetrical, almost girlish engine of thought, intercourse, and public science." Quoted in Baxter, 220.
6. According to Hendrickson, the "friendship" between them was "of the most intense and instantaneous kind." I, 285.
7. Not all biographers and historians agree that this letter, written in a disguised hand, originated with Hamilton. Clinton's own notes, however, indicate that Hamilton was the author, and the argument of his letter, in the opinion of

Carl Van Doren, a strong proponent of the view that he was the author, is similar to that used in the letter to Laurens. In a letter to Betsey, Hamilton denied that he had suggested an exchange. HS, II, 446, quoting Van Doren's *Secret History of the American Revolution*, 366.

8. HS, II, 449.

9. Ibid., 467.

10. Ibid., 448.

11. Quoted in Davis, I, 82.

12. Quoted in Hendrickson, I, 372.

13. Letter to Major James McHenry, Feb. 18, 1781, in HS, II, 569.

14. Ibid., XXVI, 407. Hamilton was advising Laurens, who had been appointed to a diplomatic post in France, to substitute the qualities mentioned for "the honest warmth of your temper."

15. AMH, *Intimate Life*, 261. He suggests that some of this "bad taste" was due "to the fact that he had been more or less flattered and his head for the time turned."

16. HS, II, 569. The editors note that the material in brackets was taken from Steiner, *James McHenry*, 35.

17. Ibid., 563–64. In one manuscript copy of the letter, the word "half" is crossed out.

18. Ibid. The editors comment that three versions of this letter exist, no two of which are in complete agreement. In the copy they publish, based on the manscript, many words are crossed out with and without substitutions, suggesting that Hamilton, assuming it was he who made the changes, had difficulty composing the letter. In the version published by J. C. Hamilton, the sentences quoted above beginning "the more extraordinary" and ending "an inviolable silence" are omitted.

19. HS, II, 575–76.

20. Ibid., 244–46.

21. Ibid., 635.

22. "A.B." and "Publius" were only two of the names Hamilton used in some of his letters and articles. Others were "Anti-Defamer," "Candor," "T.L.," "New Yorker," "Federal Republican," "An American," "Civis," "Fact," "Camillus," "Metellus," "Plain Honest Man," and perhaps "Detector" and "Americus." It is highly probable but not certain that he wrote under the last two names. New-York Historical Society *Quarterly*, XXXII (Oct. 1948), 291.

23. The six "Continentalist" articles are in HS, II and III.

24. Eric Homberger, *The Historical Atlas of New York City* (New York: Henry Holt, 1994); Henry Collins Brown, *The Story of Old New York* (New York: E. P. Dutton, 1934); *The Columbia Encyclopedia*, 3rd ed.

25. HS, III, 86–90; Hendrickson, I, 365–66.

26. HS, III, 93–94.

27. Quoted in Mitchell, I, 279.

28. HS, III, 253.

29. Hamilton had requested that he be allowed to retain his service rank in retirement. In making the appointment, citing advice from Hamilton's "particular friends," Washington informed him that he could not make an exception to the rule requiring officers who were retiring to relinquish their rank.

30. However much the Burrs read books, one doubts that they or most other book readers ever went so far as to emulate an acquaintance of Chesterfield "who was so good a manager of his time, that he would not even lose that small portion of it which the calls of nature obliged him to pass in the necessary-house, but gradually went through all the Latin poets in those moments. He bought, for example, a common edition of Horace, of which he tore off gradually a couple of pages, carried them with him to that necessary place, read them first, and then sent them down as a sacrifice to Cloacina." Letter of Dec. 11, 1747.

31. Quoted in Davis, I, 308. It has not been possible to identify Macbeau or Beloe. Apparently Burr, if not also Theodosia, had some interest in science, to judge by his contributing to a fund for the purchase of "scientific equipment" established by the College of New Jersey. In 1796 he and other alumni, including Madison, subscribed $122 ($1,464) for the purchase of "instruments and materials most necessary to exhibit the leading experiments in chemistry." Quoted in Wertenbaker, 109.

32. Quoted in Davis, I, 301. Burr was a founder of the New York Society Library, and in 1789 both he and Hamilton were members of the Library — which is thriving still in New York City — with the right to withdraw books. The Library records show that in 1789 Burr withdrew *Revolutions of Geneva in the Eighteenth Century*, which he kept for nine days, and a book by Swift, which he returned in two days. His Library borrowing in 1790 included Gibbon (presumably the *Decline and Fall*), nine volumes of Voltaire, and forty-four volumes of *Universal History from the Earliest Account of Time*, described by the Library as "a compilation by several authors and published 1747–66 . . . Volumes 22–65 are labeled Modern and those are the volumes that Mr. Burr read, all of them straight through, in chronological order. He kept at it solidly and steadily, finishing the forty-fourth volume a year and a half later, December 28, 1791. Then he took out Mrs. Montagu's Dialogues." During the same period of time, only two titles were taken out in Hamilton's name by "Mr. Rensselaer," one book titled *Edward Mortimer* and another titled *Eleonora*. The Library's "ledger doesn't reveal" whether these books were read by Hamilton or his brother-in-law.

33. Quoted in Davis, I, 224–26; Schachner, *Burr*, 75.

34. Quoted in Davis, ibid. See also Parton, I, 132; Schachner, *Burr*, 74–75; Lomask, I, 69.

35. Parton, I, 63.
36. Quoted in R. K. Root, "Introduction" to the Everyman's Edition of *Letters* (London: Dent, 1986; first published 1929), xi. Root characterizes Samuel Johnson's much quoted comment that the *Letters* "teach the morals of a whore and the manners of a dancing-master" as "grossly untrue." Johnson may have been retaliating for Chesterfield's neglect of his *Dictionary* when it was first published in 1755. Although Chesterfield praised the work not long after, Johnson wrote him bitterly: "Had [your notice] been early, [it would have been] kind; but it has been delayed till I am indifferent, and cannot enjoy it; till I am solitary and cannot impart it; till I am known, and do not want it." Johnson had addressed the "Plan" of the *Dictionary* to Chesterfield. *Oxford Companion to English Literature*, 4th ed. (1967), 162.
37. HS, I, 259.
38. Quoted in Davis, I, 363.
39. Quoted in ibid., 361–62.
40. Ibid., 373–374. His insistence that words be used correctly may have related to a similar interest of his father, assuming that Aaron Burr, Sr., was one of the authors of *The American Grammar: Or, A Complete Introduction to the English and Latin Languages*. The book, compiled by Robert Ross (1726–99), was re-issued in 1782, "with revisions by Aaron Burr and Samuel Finley." There were, of course, other Burrs not related to Burr's father, one of whom may also have been named Aaron.
41. Brodie, 447–48. According to a publication of the University of Virginia, Jefferson believed that "women needed to know how to read and write, but that was all the formal education they should have . . . Changing (the) University to include women took almost 150 years." While a few women were admitted to the university in the 1890s, not until 1970 did its "doors open fully." University of Virginia News Service, *University Journal*, Feb. 17, 1993. Jefferson was the first but by no means the last President whose name is associated with democratic values to insist that women, blacks, and other minorities were inferior to white males. Woodrow Wilson, also a Virginian by birth, as president of Princeton University declined to open the university to black enrollment, and no black students were admitted until they arrived in the navy's V-12 program during World War II. His two terms as President of the United States (1913–21) saw "the spread of segregation within the government departments," with black employees almost entirely confined to the lower ranks of the civil service. August Heckscher, *Woodrow Wilson* (New York: Charles Scribner's Sons, 1991), 292.
42. Quoted in Davis, I, 294.
43. Quoted in Wandell, I, 110–11.
44. PAB, I, 182.
45. Quoted in Wandell, I, 113.

46. Quoted in Davis, I, 256.
47. Davis begins Theo's side of the correspondence with her letter of March 17, 1802; Van Doren dates the same letter, the earliest in his volume, March 17, 1803. In Davis, the only earlier letter of Theo's was to her future husband, Joseph Alston, dated January 13, 1801. Davis, I, 423; II, 220; Van Doren, 104.
48. Mitchell, I, 353. This version of the legislative proceedings related to the slavery issue differs substantially from that in Hendrickson, I, 119–20. See also Schachner, *Burr*, 85.
49. Quoted in Lomask, I, xi, from John Quincy Adams, *Memoirs of John Quincy Adams*, IX, 429.
50. Mitchell, I, 387.
51. Brodie, 456.
52. Today a marble plaque, incised with gilded letters and attached to the front of a modest building at 56, rue Jacob, on Paris's Left Bank, reads:

En ce bâtiment
Jadis Hôtel D'York
Le 3 Septembre 1783
DAVID HARTLEY,
Au Nom Du Roi D'Angleterre,
BENJAMIN FRANKLIN,
JOHN JAY, JOHN ADAMS
Au Nom Des Etats-Unis D'Amérique
Ont Signé Le Traité Définitiv De Paix
Reconnaissant L'Independance
Des Etats-Unis.

It was not until January 14, 1784, however, that Congress ratified the treaty. That date marks the formal end of the war.
53. Mitchell, I, 333.
54. Phocion (*c.* 402–318 B.C.) was an Athenian general who "was a leader of the peace party and urged conciliation with the Macedonians." This was an appropriate name, in the context, for Hamilton to use. *Columbia Encyclopedia*, 3rd ed.
55. Mitchell, I, 343–44.
56. Kent, *Memoirs*, 31.
57. Davis, II, 22.
58. Kent, *Memoirs*, 31.
59. Schachner, *Burr*, 90.
60. Lomask, I, 87. In his correspondence, Holmes often expressed a personal philosophy not unlike Burr's in disdaining absolutes and any belief in eternal

verities. He once wrote the British socialist theoretician Harold J. Laski, a frequent correspondent, that "when I say that a thing is true I only mean that I can't help believing it — but I have no grounds for assuming that my can't helps are cosmic can't helps — and some reason for thinking otherwise. I therefore define the truth as the system of my intellectual limitations." Mark DeWolfe Howe, ed., *Holmes–Laski Letters: The Correspondence of Mr. Justice Holmes and Harold J. Laski, 1916–1935* (Cambridge: Harvard University Press, 1953), II, 1124. See also Novick, 158 passim.

61. Hendrickson, I, 561–73. Lomask, I, 113; Schachner, *Burr*, 87–90.

62. Hendrickson, I, 569. Hendrickson adds, apparently as an explanation for Gouverneur's letter, that he "probably was not aware Hamilton's own mother's name had been Levine."

63. HS, XXV, 340.

64. Jonathan D. Sarna, Benny Kraut, and Samuel K. Joseph, eds., *Jews and the Founding of the Republic* (New York: Markus Wiener Publishing, 1985), 85.

f i v e

FROM CINCINNATI TO PHILADELPHIA

1. William S. Thomas, M. D., *The Society of the Cincinnati* (New York: G. P. Putnam's Sons, 1935). In 1996 the membership of the Cincinnati was about three thousand American and French descendants of Revolutionary War officers. There was also a Society of Daughters of the Cincinnati, which was established in 1894.

2. Unlike the Cincinnati, the American Legion was open to all ranks when it began in Paris in 1919 as Pershing Post #1. Given the frequency of wars in which Americans have participated, the membership of the American Legion and other veterans' organizations has been regularly replenished.

3. PAB, II, 775–76. Some biographers have mistakenly named Burr as an early member of the Society of the Cincinnati. See, for example, Hendrickson, I, 426.

4. The Bank of New York, with twenty branches in New York City alone, is justifiably proud of its connection with the nation's first Secretary of the Treasury. At its headquarters is a miniature portrait of Hamilton, in back of which is a lock of his hair, and a two-hundred-year-old gold pendulum clock, known as the Hamilton Clock, which was given to Hamilton in 1800 by a client.

5. Quoted in Mitchell, I, 346.

6. Mitchell, I, 347. The history of the Bank of New York, commissioned by it for its two hundredth anniversary in 1984, does not mention the voting change engineered by Hamilton, and makes no reference to Church. Contradicting

other sources, this publication states that Hamilton owned one and a half shares, Burr three. Herbert S. Parmet, *200 Years of Looking Ahead*, published for the Bank of New York, 1984.

7. Parmet, 22.

8. John C. Miller, quoted in Parmet.

9. Mitchell, I, 333.

10. Warshow, 177.

11. Quoted in Daniels, 73.

12. Quoted in Farrand, *Framing*, 7.

13. Benson (1746–1833), in the course of his long life, was a lawyer, judge, member of Congress, and New York's first attorney general. He was a founder of the New-York Historical Society.

14. Commager, ed., *Documents*, I, 132–34.

15. The so-called Rebellion was the event that led Jefferson to make his celebrated remark: "The tree of liberty must be refreshed from time to time with the blood of tyrants. It is its natural manure." At the time, he was attempting to allay the fears of John and Abigail Adams, both of whom believed that Shays' Rebellion was a forerunner of anarchy. Brodie, 241.

16. Letter of Robert Yates and John Lansing to the Governor of New York, 1787, in Commager, ed., *Documents*, 149–50.

17. Parton, I, 171.

18. Quoted in Farrand, *Framing*, 39.

19. A story that may or may not be true is that Gouverneur Morris, who was as tall as Washington, walked up to the somewhat stiff and formal Washington — acting on a wager with Hamilton — patted him on the shoulder, and said, "My dear General, how happy I am to see you look so well." Washington, as reported, "fixed his eye on Morris for several minutes with an angry frown, until the latter retreated abashed, and sought refuge in the crowd." Hamilton, having lost the bet, had to give a dinner party for Morris and twelve friends, at which Morris is supposed to have said, "I have won the bet, but dearly paid for it, and nothing could induce me to repeat it." Quoted from Parton's *Life of Thomas Jefferson* in Michael Kernan, "In 1789, a farmer went to New York to become President," *Smithsonian* (20, June 1989), 94–96. A slightly different version is in Farrand, *Framing*, 22.

20. The accounts of Madison and Yates were published in Max Farrand, ed., *The Records of the Federal Convention of 1787* (New Haven: Yale University Press, 1911), 3 vols. Madison's notes were first published in 1840; Yates's in 1821. References to Yates's notes in the following pages are to the second edition (1839) of his *Secret Proceedings and Debates of the Convention Assembled at Philadelphia, in the Year 1787, For the Purpose of Forming the Constitution of the United States of America. From Notes Taken by the Late Robert Yates, Esquire, Chief Justice of New York, and Copied by John Lansing, Jun., Esquire, Late Chancellor of that*

State, Members of That Convention (Albany, 1821). This edition will be cited here as *Secret Debates.*

21. Quoted in A. M. Hamilton, *Intimate Life,* 51. Morris continued: "General Hamilton hated Republican Government because he confounded it with Democratic government, and he detested the latter because he believed it must end in despotism and be, in the meantime, destructive of public morals."

22. James Franklin Beard, ed., *The Letters and Journals of James Fenimore Cooper* (Cambridge: Harvard University Press, 1960), 32.

23. Quoted from a letter to Timothy Pickering, Sept. 16, 1803, in A. M. Hamilton, *Intimate Life,* 51–52.

24. Hamilton's notes appear in Farrand, *Notes,* I, 304–11. According to Henry Adams, Hamilton "at a New York dinner, replied to some democratic sentiment by striking his hand sharply on the table and saying, 'Your people, sir, — your people is a great *beast!*' " Unfortunately, Adams does not identify the date or place of this declaration, which, whether or not these exact words were spoken, is consistent with Hamilton's view of what someone with similar views called "the great unwashed." Adams, *History,* I, 85.

25. Differences in the two accounts are discussed, especially with reference to Madison's and Yates's reporting of Madison's own remarks, in Arnold A. Rogow, "The Federal Convention: Madison and Yates," *The American Historical Review* (LX, Jan. 2, 1955), 323–35. When Madison edited his *Notes,* he was allied with Jefferson and therefore had good reason to appear in the *Notes* as less a supporter of national supremacy and more in favor of democratic principles and states' rights than he was in 1787, when he was closer to Hamilton in his views than to Jefferson. There can be little question that in editing his papers he took notice of the changed climate of opinion in the early nineteenth century. Yates, an opponent of Hamilton, was inclined to stress Hamilton's anti-Republican sentiments, but it is undeniable that Hamilton's own notes for his speech are more in keeping with Yates than with Madison.

26. His influence and reputation were not helped by perceptions of him as haughty and vain. "His manners are tinctured with stiffness," wrote William Pierce of Georgia, a fellow delegate, "and sometimes with a degree of vanity that is Highly disagreeable." Quoted in Mitchell, I, 381. Two French observers of America in the 1780s described Hamilton as an "homme d'esprit, d'une médiocre probité" (a spirited man of mediocre integrity), having "un peu trop de pretensions et trop peu de prudence" (too much pretension and too little prudence). Quoted from Farrand, *Records of Federal Convention* 3, 234, in Mitchell, I, 619.

27. Quoted in Yates, 147.

28. Quoted in Farrand, *Framing,* 207.

29. The most important differences between them included a bicameral legislature

elected, respectively, for six years (Senate) and two years (House of Representatives), a president elected for four years whose veto power was not absolute, and governors elected by the states, in addition to other provisions of the Constitution for which Hamilton in his plan did not propose alternatives. There also was nothing in his plan concerning the amending process and the powers of the lower house of the legislature.

30. Hendrickson, I, 495.

31. Quoted in Schachner, *Hamilton*, 206; Mitchell, I, 412.

32. Mitchell, I, 383.

33. Beard, *Economic Interpretation*, 149.

34. Robert A. Brown, *Charles Beard and the Constitution* (Princeton: Princeton University Press, 1956), 200.

35. Beard, *Economic Interpretation*, 151.

36. Quoted in Brodie, 267.

37. Quoted in Schachner, *Hamilton*, 207.

38. Assuming that Burr had little interest and participated even less in many of the great political events of the 1780s, he presumably would not have entirely agreed with Justice Holmes's observation a hundred years later that "as life is action and passion, it is required of a man that he should share the passion and action of his time at peril of being judged not to have lived." Novick, *Honorable Justice*, 176. But it should be noted that Holmes, who was wounded three times in the Civil War, made these remarks in a Memorial Day speech. Holmes was paying tribute to Civil War veterans on both sides who had died. Given that context, we should also remind ourselves, in fairness to Burr, that he cannot be faulted for any lack of "action and passion" when he served in the Revolutionary War.

39. Davis, I, 286. Quoted in Parton, 171–72. Parton does not indicate to whom Burr addressed these words.

40. These remarks attributed to Burr are taken from a reminiscence of Robert Troup, Hamilton's friend. Troup's account continues: "Hamilton had replied that he could not effect a *coup d'état* if he wanted to, and that he was 'too much troubled with that thing called morality to make the attempt.' To which Burr had replied in French, 'General, all things are moral to great souls.' " Brodie, 387, quoting from "Narrative of Col. Robert Troup," in N. Schachner, "Alexander Hamilton as Viewed by His Friends," *William and Mary Quarterly*, 3rd series, IV (April 1947), 216–17.

41. Of the many editions of *The Federalist*, the one mainly relied upon here is that edited by Jacob E. Cooke. *The Federalist* (Middletown, Conn.: Wesleyan University Press, 1961).

42. A Hamilton family legend is that Hamilton wrote some of the papers on sloops carrying him to and from Albany.

43. See chap. 4, note 14.

44. The articles quoted, #11 published Jan. 31, and #15 published March 20, 1788, are reprinted in Edward S. Corwin, *Court Over Constitution* (Princeton: Princeton University Press, 1938), Appendix, 231–62.

45. In *The Social Contract* (1762), Rousseau distinguished between the will of the people as reflected in elections and statutes and what he called the general will ("volunté generale"), by which he meant the enduring wisdom of the people that is and should be beyond the reach of legislatures and may even be in conflict with them. Whether or not he derived his view of the Constitution from Rousseau, Hamilton clearly believed that it embodied the general will of the American people, which it would be the function of the courts to enforce.

46. The broadside is included among Hamilton's published papers and may be found in HS, IV, 645–46.

six

SEIZING THE DAY

1. PAB, I, 33. Burr was unaware that New York had ratified the Constitution three days earlier, making it the eleventh state to do so.

2. Mitchell, I, 463–64.

3. HS, V, 225–26.

4. PAB, I, 72–77.

5. N.Y. Laws, 14th Sess., Chap. 42, in PAB, I, 77–78.

6. In August and September 1792, Hamilton and Schuyler were unable to acquire in behalf of Church a tract of 45,000 acres adjoining the Macomb purchase, the acres having been sold to Dutch speculators. According to a letter of September 24 from William Henderson, Hamilton's agent in the matter, to Hamilton, William Constable was in England endeavoring to sell, either on his own account or for the benefit of Macomb, a million acres for "as low as a *shilling* Sterling per acre; if this information be true, Mr. Church may make a better purchase from him, than he can from any person here; and of such quantity as he likes. I expect to sail for England at the first Week in the next month, and if you think I can serve him in the Negociation, I will do so with utmost pleasure." HS, XII, 421–22.

7. HS, III, 171–77.

8. Quoted in Mitchell, II, 163, 608.

9. Ibid., 163. "It may be," Mitchell comments, "that Hamilton, in the intimacy of his own home, disclosed too much to a friend who had a pressing ulterior motive."

10. Ibid., 167; PTJ, 18, 654.

11. Philip Livingston used the expression "Jew Brokers" in a letter to Duer explaining why he was unable to come to his assistance. "I sent out to Jew Brokers," he wrote Duer, for loans on his securities, but was unsuccessful in obtaining them. Mitchell, II, 175.

12. Quoted in ibid., 83.

13. Bowers, 67.

14. Yale University Library, *Papers of Alexander Hamilton*, Vol. 17, 340.

15. "Tully," or Marcus Tullius Cicero (106–43 B.C.?), was the great Roman orator, philosopher and political figure, the enemy of Cataline.

16. HS, I, 56.

17. Tench Cox, Letter Two in *Letters from America to a Friend in England* (1794).

18. Parrington, Book III, Part I, 295.

19. PAB, I, 68.

20. Miller, *Paradox*, 355.

21. Pennsylvania Senator Willim Maclay, quoted in Lomask, I, 142. This opinion of Schuyler was shared by Chancellor Livingston, who, although professing esteem for both Hamilton and Schuyler, wrote to Morgan Lewis: "There is one view in which the State will certainly be the gainer by [Burr's election]. Schuyler . . . is supposed to be led by the Treasury [i.e., Hamilton]. This idea has not been very honourable to the State and they begin to think it has not been very productive of their interests." Quoted in Dangerfield, 249.

22. Quoted in Taylor, 156–59. Abraham Yates, another "middling" man, who had risen from cobbler to chairman of the committee that had drafted the 1777 New York State constitution, was held in contempt by both Hamilton and his father-in-law. Schuyler referred to him scathingly as "one of the Senate of this State . . . Recorder of the City of Albany—and Postmaster General, late Cobbler of Laws and Old Shoes." Quoted in Saul Cornell, "Politics of the Middling Sort," in Gilje and Pencak, 154.

23. PAB, I, 65.

24. Quoted in Mitchell, II, 136; Hendrickson, II, 107. In his *Lives*, Plutarch reported that Marcus Cato's "hatred and fear of Carthage were so intense that he ended every speech, every letter, every vote, and every conversation with the words 'Ceterum censo, Carthaginem esse delendum' [In my opinion, Carthage must be destroyed], usually given as 'Delenda est Carthago.'" *The Macmillan Book of Proverbs, Maxims, and Famous Phrases* (1948 and 1976).

25. Kent, *Memoirs*, 39–40.

26. HS, XI, 2.

27. Ibid., 6–7.

28. Ibid., 37–38, where the date of Jay's selection by New York City Federalists is given as February 9. In PAB, I, 105, the date is given as February 16.

29. Quoted from Chilton Williamson, *American Suffrage: From Property to Democracy*

1760–1860 (Princeton: Princeton University Press, 1960), 70–93; 188–203, in Ernst, 175.

30. The disputed 1792 gubernatorial election in New York is dealt with extensively in PAB, I, 106–22. See also HS, XI, 378–79, 588–91; HS, XII, 99–100; Ernst, 173–80; Schachner, *Burr*, 110–14; Lomask, I, 168–73.

31. HS, XI, 588–89.

32. HS, XII, 99–100.

33. Quoted in AMH, *Intimate Life*, 58. Hamilton, as mentioned, never traveled to London or anywhere outside the United States. The reunion with the Hamiltons about which Angelica was so ecstatic did not occur until the Churches returned to America in 1797.

34. Boyd, xiv. See also Samuel Flagg Bemis, *Jay's Treaty: A Study in Commerce and Diplomacy*, rev. ed. (New Haven: Yale University Press, 1962); Boyd, 32–33. Boyd is certain that Washington "was wholly unaware" of Hamilton's "covert consultations," which, together with other efforts of his, were responsible for "the worst fate that could befall the Chief Executive in his conduct of public affairs—that of deliberate misrepresentation on the part of a trusted member of his cabinet." 20, 25.

35. According to Boyd, "[Samuel Flagg] Bemis demonstrated beyond question that the principal architect of the Treaty of 1794 was not John Jay who negotiated it, but Alexander Hamilton, who laid the foundation for it by his indefatigable efforts to bend American foreign policy toward a closer connection with Great Britain." ix.

36. PAB, I, 215.

37. Ibid.

38. That Burr probably was without ulterior motives is suggested by his withdrawing from the New York Society Library in 1789, as earlier mentioned, a book titled *Revolutions of Geneva in the Eighteenth Century*. Perhaps his interest in this history of revolutions is evidence that he was, in fact, planning to write a book of his own on the American Revolution.

39. Davis, I, 408.

40. PAB, I, 181.

41. Letter to an unidentified correspondent, Sept. 21, 1792, in HS, XII, 408.

42. Quoted in Wandell, I, 122.

43. S. E. Burr, *The Influence of His Wife and Daughter on the Life and Career of Col. Aaron Burr* (Linden: Virginia: Burr Publications, 1975).

seven

LES LIAISONS DANGEREUSES

1. Quoted in Miller, *Paradox*, 523; Brodie, 318; from John Adams, *Works*, IX, 277.

2. Hamilton's pamphlet was titled *Observations on Certain Documents Contained in No. V & VI of the "History of the United States for the Year 1796," in which the Charge of Speculation Against Alexander Hamilton Late Secretary of the Treasury, is Fully Refuted. Written by Himself.*

3. Hamilton's letters to Betsey, who was in Albany, indicate that she arrived there sometime before July 27 and did not rejoin him until September 4, at the earliest. He may have begun his affair with Maria Reynolds sometime before August 9, when, citing his concern for Betsey's health, he wrote to her in Albany: "I cannot be happy without you. Yet I must not advise you to urge your return." One day later, on August 10, he requested her again "not to precipitate your return," and followed this on August 21 with a letter stating: "You said that you would not stay longer at Albany than twenty days which would bring it to the first of September . . . my extreme anxiety for the restoration of your health will reconcile me to your staying longer." On September 4, he wrote Betsey, apparently by that time about to set out for Elizabethtown, that he was suffering from a "kidney complaint" and, since he was unable to meet her there, was sending in his place a Treasury Department clerk. HS, IX, 6–7, 24, 26, 87.

4. The most complete account of the Reynolds affair is in HS, XXI, 121–85. No biography of Hamilton neglects the affair, but the most balanced treatment of it is in Mitchell, II, 399–422.

5. Callender spared no one, not even Washington, whom he called "the grand lama of Federal adoration, the immaculate divinity of Mt. Vernon." As for Adams, he was "that strange compound of ignorance and ferocity, of deceit and weakness . . . a hideous hermaphroditical character." Quoted in Brodie, 321. He was often drunk and was found dead in the James River in July 1803, apparently having drowned in three feet of water. He was buried the same day. Since he had many enemies, it is possible he was murdered.

6. PAB, I, 312.

7. Ibid., 318.

8. In the eighteenth century, "Badger baiting . . . was the cruel sport of setting on dogs to draw out a badger from its hole . . . Then it was the strongest possible term for irritating, persecuting, and injuring a man in every way." Hendrickson, II, 122.

9. HS, XXI, 238. Hamilton's tendency to see himself and the country as endangered by "Jacobins" and other enemies within conforms to Hofstadter's conception of the "paranoid style," which he defines as "the feeling of persecution

... systemized in grandiose theroies of conspiracy ... the spokesman of the paranoid style finds it directed against a nation, a culture, a way of life whose fate affects not himself alone but millions of others ... His sense that his political passions are unselfish and patriotic ... goes far to intensify his feeling of righteousness and his moral indignation." *Paranoid Style*, 4.

10. Boyd, PTJ, vol. 18, 653.

11. According to the editors of HS, Maria and Clingman were living in Virginia in 1798 and moved to England at a later time. In 1803, Reynolds "stated that he was forty-four years old and a laborer in Harlem." HS, XXI, 141.

12. See in particular HS, XVI, 26–27, 129, 160, 219, 492. The connection between Hamilton, Church, and Seton is not mentioned by most of Hamilton's biographers.

13. HS, XII, 572–76.

14. PTJ, vol. 24, 355.

15. HS, XII, 348.

16. HS, XI, 426–45.

17. Ibid., 429, 432.

18. Ibid., 439.

19. Hofstadter, *American Political Tradition*, 22–23.

20. Quoted in Schachner, *Jefferson*, I, 20, from P. L. Ford, ed., *The Works of Thomas Jefferson*, II, 5. The Sterne allusion is to *Tristram Shandy*.

21. Quoted in Brodie, 182, 282.

22. The Adams quote is in Brodie, 263. The Jackson quote is in Buell, I, 172.

23. Quoted in Mitchell, 356. "Thus, although Hamilton never realized it," Miller comments, "President Jefferson's real 'crime' against the Federalists consisted in stealing their political principles. By the end of his second term as President, he had left them little more than their fear of democracy, their penchant for suppressing dissent and their fondness for settling the dispute with France by force." Miller, *Paradox*, 539.

24. In 1797, the United States and France were close to an armed conflict as a consequence of the Jay Treaty, regarded by the French as forging an alliance with Great Britain. The French demonstrated their displeasure by harassing American shipping and, among other hostile acts, refusing to accept the credentials of Pinckney as American Minister to France.

25. Quoted in Ticknor, II, 113; I, 261. Ticknor (1791–1871), an American who lived in Paris many years, was reporting a conversation with Baron Pichon, who had served under Talleyrand in the French Foreign Ministry and also as Secretary of Legation in the United States.

26. Ticknor, II, 113. Napoleon, for his part, had no illusions about his Foreign Minister, who, he later said, "était toujours en état de trahison" [was given to betrayal]. He was "so prescient and so faithless," writes one historian, "he

NOTES 315

resembled a delicate political barometer. His fidelity to any regime was an assuarnce of its stability; when he showed a disposition to betray it, that was a sign that its existence was in danger." Dangerfield, 313. Totally amoral, opportunistic, and unscrupulous, Talleyrand had no difficulty lending his services to "the *ancien regime*, the Revolution, Napoleon, the Restoration, and the July monarchy." *Columbia Encyclopedia*, 3rd ed. But he was not without wit and a certain perverse charm, nor, despite lameness and an unprepossessing physical appearance, was he unattractive to women. One of several illegitimate children he fathered is believed in France to have been the painter Delacroix.

27. In a letter to Hamilton on August 6, 1798, Schuyler reported a rumor that "Tallerain [Talleyrand] is dismissed [as Minister of Foreign Affairs] and that we shall have no war. I hope the latter is unfounded for I feel that war with all its calamities, would be less Injurious to my country, than a peace which might be followed, and probably would be with the reintroduction of the pernicious and destructive principles which prevail in France." HS, XXII, 57. The rumor was premature. Talleyrand did not resign until June 1799.

28. Schachner, *Burr*, 280.

29. Brodie, 308.

30. The most complete account of Miranda's career is William Spence Robertson, "Francisco de Miranda and the Revolutionizing of Spanish America," *Annual Report of the American Historical Association for the Year 1907* (Washington, D.C.: Government Printing Office, 1908), 189–537. According to Robertson, Hamilton and Knox "may have assured Miranda that they would, under certain circumstances, aid him in his self-imposed task . . . [their] interest declined when the magnetism of Miranda was withdrawn and when political circumstances changed." 252.

31. Robertson, 363.

32. Quoted in Smith, II, 973. See also HS, XXII, 6.

33. HS, XXII, 69.

34. Ibid., 82, 86.

35. Ibid., 5.

36. Quoted in Lomask, I, 215.

37. HS, XXII, 477.

38. Ibid., 42.

39. HS, XX, 376–77.

40. Ibid., 375, 418, 445.

41. Quoted in Smith, II, 908; Hecht, 322–23.

42. HS, XX, 574–75. On another occasion, McHenry "simply recopied Hamilton's letter in his own hand, added a few paragraphs, and handed it to Adams as his own program." Hendrickson, II, 392–93. See also Miller, *Paradox*, 477–78.

43. PAB, I, 269. Gallatin was informed of Burr's complaint by James Nicholson in a letter of May 7, 1800. The reference to Virginia's "party leadership" is from Kurtz, *Presidency of John Adams*, quoted in PAB, I, 269.

44. Microfilm of Burr Papers, New-York Historical Society.

45. PAB, I, 339.

46. The preceding and following discussion of the Holland Land Co. and alien-land legislation is based on PAB, I, 338–40. See also Lomask, I, 218–21; Hendrickson, II, 576–77.

47. Church, who shared Hamilton's view of Burr, was challenged by him to a duel as a consequence of remarks he had made about the loan. In the first exchange of shots, on September 2, 1799, the only casualty was a button shot off Burr's coat. When Church made amends before a second round, the duel came to an end.

48. J. A. Hamilton, 4.

49. Parmet and Hecht, 119.

50. PAB, I, 295. According to Lomask, Lamb had lent Burr "at least forty thousand dollars [$480,000] and was endorsing his notes with abandon . . . Lamb never saw a cent of the . . . $3,500" Burr was able to raise. Lomask does not mention Lamb's difficulties in connection with the embezzlement. Lomask, I, 114.

51. Thomas P. Abernathy, *The South in the New Nation* (Baton Rouge, 1961), 149, quoted in PAB, I, 289.

52. HS, XXV, 296.

53. Quoted in Parmet and Hecht, 113–14. They concede, however, that "Burr's precise role in this affair may never be known . . . his precise motives may never be determined . . . If Burr's land ventures had become involved in international intrigue, the scheme could only be deduced, and even then in a superficial way." Ibid., 117–18.

54. Quoted in ibid., 118, from a letter to John Rutledge. See also his letter to Gouverneur Morris, Dec. 24, 1800, in Padover, 442.

eight
FAREWELLS TO ALL THAT

1. Schachner, *Hamilton*, 355. Douglass Adair's "The Disputed Federalist Papers," first published in 1944, is regarded by most historians as the definitive work on the authorship. See Adair, *Fame*, 27–74.

2. HS, XX, 170.

3. Schachner, *Hamilton*, 354.

4. HS, XX, 175.

5. Ibid.

6. Schachner, *Hamilton*, 355. Hendrickson echoes this statement by writing that "although most of the general ideas were Washington's, the organization, elaboration, and phrasing of the text were Hamilton's." II, 368.

7. Brant, *Madison*, 441.

8. Quoted in ibid., 442.

9. King, VI, 618–19.

10. Adams to Benjamin Rush, Feb. 25, 1808, in Schutz and Adair, 105. Adams summarized this view of Washington and Hamilton on at least two other occasions, when he observed to Rush that the Federalists had regarded Hamilton as "everything and Washington but a name" and Hamilton as "the soul and Washington the body." Ibid., 35, 105.

11. Madison's "Memorandum on a Discussion of the President's Retirement, 5 May (1792)," and his draft of the farewell speech which he sent to Washington the following month, may be found in PJM, 14, 299–304, 319–24. Hamilton's drafts and related letters to and from Washington are in HS, XX, 169–83, 264–88.

12. Quoted in HS, XX, 172–73. Neither Mitchell nor Miller refer to these recollections of Betsey Hamilton. According to Mitchell, when "she was nearly ninety years old and living in Washington, happening to be in the Capitol, she called on the Librarian of Congress and told him how Hamilton, in preference to revising Madison's draft, undertook 'to prepare a different one.' She reiterated that this was 'a secret, about my husband, and you must not tell it until I am gone.' " Mitchell, *Concise Biography*, 326. Mitchell does not explain how this "secret" relates to her earlier wish to have it known that Hamilton was the author of the Farewell Address.

13. *Documents of American History*, 174–78.

14. PAB, I, 366–76. When Burr referred to Benedict Arnold and William Blount to demonstrate that American nationality did not necessarily preclude treachery, he could not imagine that in 1807 he himself would face conspiracy charges similar in certain respects to those that led to Blount's impeachment in 1798. A Tennessee senator, Blount was accused of organizing a military expedition with British assistance to seize portions of Louisiana and Florida from Spain, the consequence of which would be to open the entire length of the Mississippi River to free navigation. Expelled from the Senate, which, however, did not act on the impeachment charges enacted by the House of Representatives, Blount was elected to the Tennessee legislature and died in 1800 while serving in it.

15. *Documents of American History*, 178–85.

16. HS, XXI, 495.

17. Ibid.

18. Miller, *Paradox*, 483. Mitchell is more sparing of Hamilton. In his 1957 two-

volume biography, he writes that Hamilton "accepted the laws directed against supposed subversion, and took precautions . . . that army officers were loyal, but he never showed enthusiasm for a punitive policy." II, 426. But in the later, one-volume biography, Mitchell added: "Still, the degree to which he accepted the laws against supposed subversion was not to his credit." *Concise Biography*, 333.

19. Microfilm of Burr Papers, New-York Historical Society.

20. Schachner, *Hamilton*, 202. This story, which is probably apocryphal, was first recounted by a friend of Hamilton almost forty years after he supposedly made the statement.

21. Quoted in Mitchell, *Concise Biography*, 373. Mitchell adds: "(Hamilton's return to religion—he had been pious as a youth—is also known from other sources.)"

22. Quoted in Parton, 2, 330. Burr's visitor was the Reverend Dr. J. Vanpelt of the Dutch Reformed Church, who later wrote: "I did not administer the holy sacrament to him, nor did he suggest or request me to do it." Ibid., 329.

23. PAB, II, 748. The year of the letter is known to have been 1802, but not the month in which Hopkins, who died in 1803, wrote it.

24. Microfilm of Burr Papers, New-York Historical Society.

25. The most complete accounts of the roles of Burr and Hamilton in organizing the Manhattan Company and its bank are Beatrice G. Reubens, "Burr, Hamilton and the Manhattan Company, Part I: Gaining the Charter," *Political Science Quarterly*, LXXII (Dec. 1957), 578–607; and "Burr, Hamilton and the Manhattan Company, Part II: Launching a Bank," *Political Science Quarterly*, LXIII (March 1958), 100–25. See also HS, XXII, 446–51; PAB, I, 399–403; Dangerfield, 289–93.

26. HS, XXII, 449.

27. The value of the Manhattan Company charter has hardly diminished in almost two hundred years, as a financial service reported in 1956, when it praised the Chase Manhattan Bank as an institution that "could . . . acquire insurance companies, savings and loan associations, real estate companies, and even industrial concerns. Chase-Manhattan is already to a certain degree a real estate holding company . . . This is a fabulous charter . . . This is principally what makes the shares attractive . . . in relation to other leading bank situations." Quoted in Reubens, II, 115. Since these lines were written, the Chase Manhattan Bank has expanded into investment banking, and in 1996, when it merged with Chemical Bank of New York, it became the largest bank in the United States in terms of assets.

28. A typical view is that "Banking being more profitable than water, the Manhattan Company wasted little effort on providing a safe or adequate water system." Geology Professor Julian Kane, in a letter to *The New York Times*, May 5, 1995.

29. The Tenth Legion was the crack Roman army that spearheaded the conquest of Jerusalem in A.D. 70. Made up of veterans who had fought in wars throughout the Roman Empire, the Tenth Legion was permanently stationed in Jerusalem after the city's fall, and in A.D. 73 it laid seige to Masada, the last Jewish stronghold, on the shore of the Dead Sea. Theo, who had probably read Caesar's account of the Gallic Wars, must have had in mind the Roman soldiers' reputation for fearlessness and invulnerability, qualities which had made the Tenth Legion famous. Burr's allies were sometimes also known as the "Little Band," but this designation clearly had less to recommend it. Hamilton's favored name for the Burrites was "myrmidons," the Greek word for ants, but as used by Hamilton it referred to a legend that Zeus, after a devastating plague, had turned ants into men who were ferocious warriors, following their leaders with blind devotion.

30. Van Doren, 419–20.

31. D. S. Alexander, I, 144. Burr's allegedly innumerable affairs with women of all types, the subject of so much adverse comment by both his contemporaries and his modern critics, were in keeping with his belief that one's happiness could not be complete unless it included enjoyment of the senses, among which sexual pleasure was uppermost. In this respect, he resembled Jeremy Bentham (1748–1832), the founder of utilitarianism, who wrote that sex "was the 'highest enjoyment' that nature had bestowed upon man." Certainly, Burr would not have disagreed with Bentham's holding in 1821 with reference to "the sexual act . . . [that] Unless and until effects not only noxious but noxious in a preponderant degree can be shewn to flow from it, the operation can not but be acknowledged to be not simply innoxious but positively beneficial; for unless attended with pleasure it never is performed." Not surprisingly, when Burr arrived in London in 1808, he was eager to meet the English philosopher, and not long after he did so and heard him expound his philosophy, which included the doctrine that happiness should be the sole object of legislation, he confessed that he was in awe of him. Dinwiddy, *Bentham* (Oxford: Oxford University Press, 1989), 41.

32. Van Doren, 46–47.

33. Ibid., 306.

34. Ibid., 48.

35. Ibid., 69.

36. Ibid., 21.

37. Ibid., 3.

38. Ibid., 5.

39. Ibid., 47.

40. Ibid., 51.

41. Letter of Dec. 16–18, 1793, Microfilm of Burr Papers, New-York Historical Society. The letter as it appears in Van Doren has a word deleted. 8.

42. Van Doren, 75.

43. Quoted in Brodie, 175–76.

44. D. S. Alexander, 145.

45. Bradford, *Wives*.

46. Vidal, 271–72.

47. Letter to John Rutledge, Jr., Jan. 4, 1801, in HS, XXV, 297.

48. Quoted in Brant, *Madison*, 47.

49. Parton, 2, 302.

50. Quoted in Bradford, *Damaged Souls*, 92.

51. Letter of April 21, 1797. Microfilm of Burr Papers, New-York Historical Society.

52. Letter of Dec. 18, 1794. Microfilm of Burr Papers, New-York Historical Society.

53. Quoted in Dorothy Valentine Smith, "An Intercourse of the Heart: Some Little-Known Letters of Theodosia Burr," *New-York Historical Society Quarterly* 37, No. 1 (Jan. 1953), 43. Theo's letter as published by Smith does not include her poem. The date of her birth is given as 1782, the year her parents were married, which does not correspond to the date given by Parton and Lomask.

54. Van Doren, 431.

55. King, III, 459. Troup described "Allston" as "ordinary—his manner pedantic—his temper not very soft—his politics violent on the democratic side." Burr's insistence early in Theo's life that she be educated differently from her female contemporaries probably was responsible for Troup's having no kinder words for Theo, whose "reading," he had heard, "has been wholly masculine . . . she is an utter stranger to the use of the needle, and quite unskilled in the different branches of domestic economy."

56. Quoted in Anthony, 158.

57. Microfilm of Burr Papers, New-York Historical Society.

58. PAB, I, 442.

59. Microfilm of Burr Papers, New-York Historical Society.

60. PAB, I, 445.

61. Microfilm of Burr Papers, New-York Historical Society.

62. Letter to Samuel Smith, April 21, 1801, in PAB, I, 569.

63. Van Doren, 84, 87.

64. Ibid., 92. Lady Mary Wortley Montagu (1689–1762) wrote the letters when she lived in Constantinople, where her husband served as British Ambassador.

65. Ibid., 442.

66. Ibid., 224.

67. Ibid., 338.

68. Ibid., 336.

69. It is not certain when Burr learned of his death, on June 30, 1812, not long after his tenth birthday.

nine

ODD DESTINIES

1. Letter to Philip Mazzei, April 24, 1796, quoted in Brodie, 285; Daniels, 161.
2. HS, XXIV, 184.
3. Letter of Jan. 5, 1800, in King, III, 173.
4. HS, II, 566.
5. Bowers, 454.
6. Quoted in Adair, *Fame*, 152.
7. Quoted in Wandell, I, 199.
8. Quoted in HS, XXV, 170.
9. The full title was *Letter from Alexander Hamilton, Concerning the Public Conduct and Character of John Adams, Esq. President of the United States*. It is reprinted in HS, XXV, 169–234, and it is this text which is quoted here.
10. Quoted in Smith, II, 1048.
11. Quoted from Harry Warfel, ed., *Letters of Noah Webster* (1953), in Smith, II, 1045. See also Cantor, 106–8.
12. Quoted in Wandell, II, 196. Hamilton's confidential letter to Jay, like the later one excoriating Adams, also found a publisher.
13. Adair, *Fame*, 152.
14. AMH, *Intimate Life*, 43. He further described the illness as one "common to many active public men characterized by varying moods."
15. Hendrickson, II, 498. Hendrickson does not define what he means by "manic defense," to which subject he devotes an entire chapter. See also Schachner, *Hamilton*, 194–95; Flexner, 3–7; Hendrickson, II, 226–41, 307, 406, 458, 498–505.
16. Oliver quoted in Bowers, 37; Flexner, 3.
17. Quoted in Mitchell, I, 140.
18. Hamilton in a letter to Washington mentioned that he often fell ill during the summer months.
19. HS, I, 550–51. The editors identify Cornare as a Venetian nobleman who, after an illness when he was forty, ate only one egg each day, and was ninety-eight years old when he died in 1566. McHenry assured Hamilton that if he adhered to the dietary prescription he would become his own "councellor in diet, for the man who has had ten years experience in eating and its consequences is a fool if he does not know how to choose his dishes better than his doctor."

20. HS, XXVI, 346.

21. In August 1791, Tench Coxe in a letter mentioned Hamilton's "old nephritic complaint." HS, VI, 827.

22. "Hamilton is ill of the fever," Jefferson wrote Madison. "He has had two physicians out at his house the night before last. His family think him in danger, & he puts himself so by his excessive alarm. He had been miserable several days before, from a firm persuasion he should catch it. A man so timid as he is on the water, as timid on horseback, as timid in sickness, would be a phenomenon if the courage of which he has the reputation in military matters were genuine. His friends suspect it is only an autumnal fever he has." Quoted in Desmond, 178.

23. Letter of March, 16, 1801, in HS, XXV, 348–49.

24. Quoted in Miller, *Paradox*, 549. Several biographers of Hamilton mistakenly give Weehawken as the site of the duel.

25. Angelica never fully recovered from Philip's death. Until she died at age seventy-three, she spoke of her brother as if he were still alive.

26. Letter of March 16–17, 1803, in HS, XXVI, 94–95.

27. HS, XXV, 544–45.

28. Letter of March 4, 1802, in HS, XXV, 558–59.

29. Ibid., 600.

30. Letter to King, in HS, XXVI, 13–14.

31. On April 9, 1802, Troup wrote King: "Burr will doubtless be dropped at another election, if they can do it without endangering Jefferson." King, IV, 103–4.

32. He did not record in writing that he had "no confidence in the Virginians," and did not want to "be trifled with" as he had been in 1796, until 1800, when he again was being urged to seek the Vice Presidency. It is likely, however, that he had expressed this view earlier to close friends in the South as well as elsewhere. See PAB, I, 269, 433, 451.

33. Ibid., 301.

34. Malone, 323.

35. PAB, I, 358, 390, 469–70.

36. Ibid., 471–74. "As to my friends," he continued in his letter to Smith, "they would dishonor my Views and insult my feelings by harbouring a suspicion that I could submit to be instrumental in counteracting the Wishes & expectations of the U.S."

37. Ibid., 479.

38. Quoted from Paul Leicester Ford, ed., *Works* (New York, 1896), VII, 478. Jefferson earlier had praised Burr in a letter to Pierce Butler of August 11, 1800, where he commented: "He has certainly greatly merited of his country and the Republicans in particular, to whose efforts his have given a chance of success." Quoted in Smith, II, 1057.

39. Letter to King, Jan. 2, 1801, in King, III, 362.

40. Letter to King, Jan. 5, 1801, in ibid., 366.

41. Letter of Jan. 1, 1801, in HS, XXV, 290. In a letter of December 28, 1800, Marshall wrote Edward Carrington that he considered the election "a choice of evils & I really am uncertain which would be the greatest." Ibid., 291.

42. Letter to King, May 24, 1801, in King, III, 455.

43. Letter of Jan. 11, 1801, quoted in PAB, I, 482.

44. Quoted in Smith, II, 1061.

45. Letter of Jan. 18, 1801, in King, III, 371.

46. Letter of Dec. 16, 1800, to Oliver Wolcott, Jr., in HS, XXV, 257. See also Schachner, *Burr*, 193.

47. HS, XXV, 286–87.

48. Letters to Harrison Gray Otis and Gouverneur Morris, in ibid., 271–72.

49. It was in this letter that Hamilton stated: "[If t]here be [a man] in the world I ought to hate it is Jefferson." Ibid., 275.

50. Ibid., 276–77.

51. Ibid., 315, 321–23.

52. Ibid., 311.

53. Quoted in Schachner, *Burr*, 206.

54. Quoted in PAB, I, 486.

55. HS, XXV, 345.

56. Quoted in Schachner, *Burr*, 206.

57. HS, XXV, 288, 292–93.

58. Quoted in Schachner, *Burr*, 208.

59. Ellis, *American Sphinx*, 302.

60. Quoted in PAB, II, 821–22.

61. Ibid.

62. Quoted in Buell, 207.

63. Davis, 2, 182–83.

64. Quoted in Lomask, I, 317.

65. Not to be confused with Salmon P. Chase, Chief Justice from 1864 to 1873, who earlier had been Lincoln's Secretary of the Treasury. The Chase National Bank, which opened in September 1877, was named for him, and it continued in business until 1955, when it was acquired by the Burr-founded Bank of the Manhattan Company, becoming the Chase Manhattan Bank.

66. Quoted in PAB, II, 914.

67. Quoted in Upham, IV, 67–68.

1. Schachner, *Burr*, p. 117. In his later biography of Hamilton, Schachner took issue with efforts to view Hamilton's life and character as "in effect the products of a pathological compensation for the irregularities of his birth. This thesis owes its origin to the current trend toward psychoanalytical interpretations of historical figures. Whatever may be the value of psychoanalysis in the hands of competent practitioners with patients under immediate observation and control, it is obviously a dangerous instrument in the hands of lay biographers." *Hamilton*, 2.
2. HS, XII, 480–81; Padover, 440.
3. HS, *passim*.
4. Catiline (*c.* 108–52 B.C.) was a Roman politician who was accused by Cicero, probably falsely, of conspiring to replace him, the incumbent consul, with himself. Catiline may well have plotted murder and committed treason, but both Julius Caesar and Cato the Younger testified in his favor, a fact apparently overlooked by or unknown to Hamilton. *Columbia Encyclopedia*, 3rd ed.
5. HS, XII, 408; Padover, 440–42.
6. AMH, *Intimate Life*, 348.
7. Hendrickson, II, 109.
8. Ibid.
9. HS, XXVI, 244.
10. Ibid., 243.
11. Ibid., 245.
12. Ibid., 245–46.
13. Microfilm of the *Albany Register*, April 17–May 4, 1804. American Antiquarian Society.
14. DeAlva Stanwood Alexander, 138. Alexander based this statement on a comparison of the voting returns with those for state senators in 1803.
15. HS, XXVI, 619. The biographical data for Cooper, Tayler, Brown, Deitz, and Stringer are taken from Joel Munsell, *The Annals of Albany* (Albany: Munsell & Rowland, 1858 and 1871), Vols. 1, 3, 4, 9; Cooper Family Papers; Office of General Services, *Governors of the State of New York* (Albany: after 1966); *Dictionary of American Biography; American Biographical Archive* (New York State Library).
16. HS, XXVI, 242–43. Except where noted, all references to letters and other documents related to the duel are based on HS, XXVI, 235–349.
17. In 1797 or 1798, Theo, Burr's daughter, wrote her half brother John Bartow Prevost, who, with Burr, had been elected to the New York State Assembly: "We do not take Albany papers but if when you make a speech you will write

to me on what day that great event took place I will go to the office for a newspaper." Quoted in Parmet and Hecht, 128. By "office," she may have meant her father's law office, where, as opposed to their residence, Albany newspapers were available.

18. Hendrickson, I, 611–47.

19. Atherton, 509, 535. The biographies of Hamilton written by his descendants do not confirm Atherton's statement. According to his grandson, Allan McLane Hamilton, whose book was published nine years after Atherton's but the index of which does not refer to her work, Hamilton's "name has been quite unjustifiably connected with that of Madame Jumel . . . Certainly it is absurd to say that Hamilton had an amour with her, as has been suggested, and this gossip may, with other contemporary scandal, be disregarded. *Intimate Life*, 55–56.

20. Clemens (1814–65), characterized in the *Dictionary of American Biography* as a "soldier, novelist, senator" who, though a Southerner, was a Unionist and a supporter of Lincoln in 1864, declared Burr to have been "unsurpassed as a soldier, unrivaled as a lawyer, pure, upright, and untarnished as a statesman," thus promoting a view of Burr that could fairly be described as also "unrivaled." Hamilton, however, was no less "unrivaled" in that "the world never presented such a combination of greatness and meanness, of daring courage and vile malignity, of high aspirings and of low hypocrisy. Shrewd, artful, and unscrupulous . . . no tool too base to be used (by him) when its services were needed. Loose in his own morals."

21. Vidal, 272–73.

22. Personal communication.

23. HS, XI, 545–46.

24. Hieronymus, *The Chronicles*, Section 172, 23–24. Hieronymus, an early Church father (third or fifth century A.D.), was also known as Eusebius Sophronius. See also A. Pauly and others, *Real Encyclopadie d. Classiken Altertumwissenschaft*. According to Lomask, "Saevius's claim to fame was that he was ordered by a court to take his own life after being convicted of corrupting his son." I, 160.

25. Hamilton and his contemporaries attached great value to "delicacy" and used the word in a variety of contexts. In Hamilton's correspondence, it appears frequently, usually as a reference to character traits or as descriptive of behavior he admired, such as discretion, refinement, pride, sensitivity, regard for the feelings of others, awareness of what was proper and dignified, and, as used above, integrity and reputation.

26. Adams, *History*, II, 189.

27. The characteristics of the pistol that have been mentioned are based on X-ray and other studies of it commissioned by the U.S. Bicentennial Society with the cooperation of the Chase Manhattan Bank. The results of these

studies are discussed in the bank's publication *The Church Pistols*; James R. Webb, "The Fateful Encounter," *American Heritage* 26/5 (Aug. 1975), 45–93; Merrill Lindsay, "Pistols Shed Light on Famed Duel," *Smithsonian*, 7/8 (Nov. 1976), 94–98.

28. Lindsay, 96. Lindsay adds: "I have booby-trapped myself many times shooting target guns with single- or double-set triggers, and my only excuse was the tension of a competitive match. Even though no one was pointing a loaded pistol at me, I squeezed too hard too soon and blew my hopes by throwing away a shot, high in the sky."

eleven

A WORLD TOO SMALL?

1. Davis, II, 326.
2. HS, XXVI, 280.
3. Andrew Jackson, a veteran of several duels, who killed an opponent in 1806, went on to become the two-term seventh President (1829–1837).
4. The source of these quotations and those that follow from newspapers, unless otherwise indicated, is *A Collection of the Facts and Documents Relative to the Death of Major-General Alexander Hamilton: With Comments: Together With the Various Orations, Sermons, and Eulogies . . . By the Editor of the Evening Post* (William Coleman). First published in 1804 and reissued in 1972 by Shoal Creek Publishers, Austin, Texas.
5. Mitchell, 372; PAB, II, 330.
6. *A Collection*, 170. The "elder Pitt" is a reference to William Pitt, 1st Earl of Chatham (1708–78), known in British history as the "Great Commoner." A holder of various offices during the reigns of George II and George III, he favored an accommodation with the American colonies, although not their independence, and electoral reform.
7. Quoted in Wandell, 2, 325–26.
8. HS, XXVI, 324–29. Morris was in demand as an orator at funerals. He delivered the eulogy over the coffins of Washington and George Clinton. Perhaps he was better chosen for Hamilton's funeral than for that of Washington, at which his words, according to Robert Troup, "had the effect of a cold historical narrative, not that of a warm and impassioned address." He had left the church, he wrote Rufus King, "a most mortified and wounded man! Not a tear was compelled to roll! Hardly was a sigh excited." Letter of Jan. 1, 1800, in King, III, 170.
9. HS, XXVI, 319.
10. Ibid., 320.

11. Ibid., 318–19.
12. PAB, II, 883; Davis, II, 327.
13. PAB, II, 887.
14. Ibid.
15. Van Doren, 472.
16. Davis, II, 348.
17. Ibid., 372.
18. Quoted in Alexander, *Political History*, 137.
19. Biddle, *Autobiography*, 303.
20. Quoted in King, IV, 392; Ernst, 283.
21. Davis, II, 99.
22. Quoted in Daniels, 290.
23. HS, XII, 480–81. Lomask gives both 1793 and 1795 as the date of Maria's divorce.
24. Adair, *Fame*, 153.
25. Oliver, 413, 417–18; Hamilton is quoted in PAB, I, lxx.
26. Bowers, 450.
27. AMH, *Intimate Life*, 428.
28. Bowers, 449.
29. The literature dealing with the phenomena of projection, identification, and projective identification as conceptualized in clinical psychiatry and psychoanalysis is extensive. Melanie Klein in 1946 was the first to use the term "projective identification," but because there has been no agreement on its meaning, the concept "remains one of the most loosely defined and incompletely understood of psychoanalytic conceptualizations." Still, projection and identification as dealt with here are viewed as having some connection and overlap, but not an explicit linkage. The statement quoted above is from Thomas H. Ogden, "On Projective Identification," *International Journal of Psychoanalysis* (1979), 60, 357.
30. Davis, II, 205.
31. Quoted in Parton, II, 276.
32. Quoted in Buell, I, 173.
33. Van Doren, 69.
34. Microfilm of Burr Papers, New-York Historical Society.
35. Van Doren, 174.
36. Quoted in Parton, II, 302; Wandell, II, 322. Adams could be equally "gallant" and good-humored, as he demonstrated when as President he was charged with having "sent General Pinckney to England in a United States frigate to procure four pretty girls as mistresses, two for the General and two for himself. 'I do declare upon my honor,' Adams wrote William Tudor, 'if this be true General Pinckney has kept them all for himself and cheated me out of my two.' " Quoted in Smith, II, 1034.

37. Kent, *Memoirs*, 36.
38. Brodie, 387–405.
39. Dangerfield, 299. The upas tree of Java secretes a poisonous sap.
40. Ellis, 174.
41. In the July/August 1988 issue, *American Heritage* magazine published the results of its survey of fifty historians, including all members of the Society of American Historians, and journalists and politicians, who were asked to rate the "most overrated and underrated Americans," living or dead. Judged "most overrated," with six votes each, were John F. Kennedy and Ronald Reagan. Woodrow Wilson and Harry S Truman received three votes each, and Thomas Jefferson two. Alexander Hamilton and Aaron Burr were given one vote each (Hamilton was nominated by Joan Peterson Kerr, then editor of *American Heritage*, and Burr by Henry Steele Commager). The "most underrated," with two votes each, were John Quincy Adams (who also received one vote as "perhaps" overrated), Ulysses S. Grant, and James K. Polk. Franklin D. Roosevelt and Lyndon B. Johnson were not included in either category.
42. Kent, *Memoirs*, 328.
43. Fiske, *Essays Historical and Literary* (1902), I, 187.
44. Bryce, II, 8. Woodrow Wilson has been quoted by Vernon L. Parrington and others as saying of Hamilton that he "was a great man, but not a great American." Parrington, I, 306. According to Professor John M. Murron of Princeton University, however—to whom I am grateful for the information—no such statement has been found in Wilson's writings. Personal communication, Dec. 30, 1995. The statement may have originated as a paraphrase of Wilson's observation in 1904 that Hamilton was "a transplanted European in his way of thinking . . ." He had earlier (1893) described Hamilton as "one of the greatest figures in our history . . . American historians, though compelled always to admire him, often in spite of themselves, have been inclined, like the mass of men in his own day, to look at him askance. They hint, when they do not plainly say, that he was not 'American.' He rejected, if he did not despise democratic principles." Wilson, PWW, 8, 369; 15, 214. There also is no evidence that Wilson ever characterized Burr as "so maligned, so misunderstood," as claimed by Lomask. In an address of October 1896, he included a reference to "Aaron Burr, with genius enough to have made him immortal and unschooled passion enough to have made him infamous." PWW, 10, 18.
45. Quoted in L. H. Butterfield, ed., *The Adams Papers: Diary and Autobiography of John Adams* (Cambridge: Harvard University Press, 1961), 3, 434–35. "Corsica" presumably was a reference to the birthplace of Napoleon, with whom Adams was comparing Hamilton, and the term "Creolian" probably intended by Adams to suggest that Hamilton was of mixed ancestry. Bolingbroke, or Henry St. John, Viscount Bolingbroke (1678–1751), was an English statesman of conservative or Tory persuasion who was regarded as untrustworthy,

corrupt, irresponsible, and profligate. Accused of acting against British interests in negotiations with France in 1713 and other intrigues which contradicted official policy, he was impeached. He escaped to France before his trial
and was pronounced guilty by Parliament, as a consequence of which he was
excluded from the House of Lords when he returned to England.
46. Quoted in Padover, 2.
47. Quoted in Schutz and Adair, 33.
48. "My uncle Toby," says the narrator in *Tristram Shandy*, "had scarce a heart
to retaliate upon a fly . . . an over-grown one which had buzz'd about his nose,
and tormented him cruelly all dinner-time . . . he had caught at last, as it flew
by him; — I'll not hurt thee, says my uncle Toby, rising from his chair, and
going a-cross the room, with the fly in his hand, — I'll not hurt a hair of thy
head: Go, says he, lifting up the sash, and opening his hand as he spoke, to
let it escape; — go poor devil, get thee gone, why should I hurt thee? — This
world surely is wide enough to hold both thee and me." Lawrence Sterne,
The Life and Opinions of Tristram Shandy, Gentleman (New York: Odyssey Press,
1940; first published 1759–1767), II, 113.

EPILOGUE

1. *New-York Evening Post*, July 17, 1804, in HS, XXVI, 322–29.
2. AMH, *Intimate Life*, 414; Mitchell, II, 548. Although he was buried as a hero
and a martyr, his funeral expenses were treated no differently from those of
lesser mortals. They included the costs of the coroner's inquest ($5,25), his
mahogany coffin ($25.00), "pay to Sundry persons" ($700.41), "tolling of
three Bells" ($9.00), and Dr. Hosack's bill "To attendance &c during his last
illness" ($50.00), for a total of $789.66 ($9,500). HS XXVI, 317, 321, 329.
3. Letter of Gouverneur Morris to Robert Morris in King, IV, 410.
4. Mayer and East, 379.
5. JAH, 8.
6. AMH, *Alienist*, 29.
7. Ibid. In his *Reminiscences*, James A. Hamilton wrote that his father "was so
poor at his death that his property was not sufficient to pay his debts." 8.
8. Mayer and East, 383–85. James A. Hamilton notes only: "Several of his
friends advanced money." Ibid.
9. Grant, 259.
10. Ibid., 263. Anne Grant, who was of Tory persuasion, may have had in mind
the Reform Act of 1832, the first major effort in Britain since the reign of
Elizabeth I to significantly enlarge the suffrage.
11. AMH, *Intimate Life*, 116–17.

12. Ibid.

13. Desmond, 264.

14. PAB, II, 891.

15. Ibid., 926–29.

16. Quoted from Ford, ed., *Writings of Jefferson*, 8, 481–82, in ibid., 979–80.

17. Ibid., 982.

18. Careful research by Mary-Jo Kline and her colleagues, the editors of Burr's *Political Correspondence and Public Papers*, supports the hypothesis that the letter was written by Jonathan Dayton, "former Federalist senator from New Jersey, longtime associate of AB and Wilkinson, and enthusiastic partner in schemes for speculation in the West." The letter is reprinted and the research reported in Ibid., 973–90.

19. Ibid., 1010.

20. Ibid., 1016.

21. Ibid., 1040.

22. Irving, a Federalist who had admired Hamilton, was not impressed by certain local customs as well as judicial proceedings in Richmond, where, at one point, the grand jury which was awaiting the late arrival of Wilkinson was dismissed for "five or six days, that they might go home, see their wives, get their clothes washed, and flog their negroes." He noted in a letter that ladies especially were sympathetic to Burr, and went on to express his view: "I am very much mistaken, if the most underhand and ungenerous measures have not been observed toward him. He, however, retains his serenity and self-possession unshaken." But two weeks later, after visiting Burr in the "Penitentiary, a kind of State prison," he found less "cheerfulness," Burr having been deprived "from all intercourse with society," and although "a man against whom no certainty of crime" has been proven, "confined by bolts, and bars, and massy walls in a criminal prison." Quoted in Paul M. Angle, *The American Reader* (New York: Rand McNally, 1958), 145–46. See also Warner, 55–56.

23. Schutz and Adair, 76.

24. Quoted in Buell, I, 202–3. Burr's reputation has fared better in parts of the South and West where Hamilton was never popular and Burr was, and to some extent still is, identified with early efforts to expel the Spanish from areas now part of the United States. In recent years, Burr has been accorded sympathetic treatment by Gore Vidal, who has some family roots in the South, in his novel *Burr*, and by Eudora Welty, a lifelong resident of Jackson, Mississippi (in Burr's time, LeFleur's Bluff), whose short story *First Love* deals with an imaginary meeting in a Natchez tavern between Burr and a man who may have been fashioned after Harmon Blennerhassett. In 1985, an account of the Natchez Trace, the historic road from Natchez to Nashville over which Burr traveled under guard to his trial in Richmond, and on which Meriwether Lewis was murdered or committed suicide in 1809, notes that Burr was "a

very popular figure until a smear campaign by Jefferson cast doubts about his patriotism . . . Recent evidence," writes the author, a specialist on Tennessee history, "has suggested that Burr might have been framed." James A. Crutchfield, *The Natchez Trace: A Pictorial History* (Nashville, Tenn.: Rutledge Hill Press, 1985), 113.

25. Blodget, who apparently was in love with Burr most of her life and saw him intermittently after his return to New York, wrote Madison that "what ever is valuable in myself" she owed to Burr. She may not have done Burr a favor, however, by giving as her reason for not having requested a pardon for him from Jefferson: "Heaven forbid that I shou'd ever place myself in the light of an inferior to Thomas Jefferson, a *thing* whose principles religious, moral & political, are alike weak & wicked. A shifting, shuffling Visionary, An old woman in her dotage! A wretch without nerve! Pardon me, Sir." *Papers of James Madison. Presidential Series* (Charlottesville, Va.: University of Virginia Press, 1984), 33–34. A letter to Dolley Madison from Theo in June 1809, asking her to intervene with her husband in Burr's behalf, makes no mention of Jefferson, but Theo was no more successful than Rebecca in obtaining a pardon for her father. Their letters did not elicit any known response from either Madison.

26. PAB, II, 1071. Burr himself made an unsuccessful effort in London to acquire British citizenship on the grounds that he had been born in a British colony in 1756, well before American independence.

27. Quoted in Lomask, II, 401.

28. Quoted in Parton, II, 319.

SELECTED BIBLIOGRAPHY

(Adair, Douglass). Trevor Colbourn, ed. *Fame and the Founding Fathers: Essays by Douglass Adair*. New York: W. W. Norton, 1974.

(Adair, Douglass). "A Note on Certain of Hamilton's Pseudonyms," *William and Mary Quarterly*, 3rd Series, XII, 2 (April 1955), 282–97.

Adams, Henry. *History of the United States During the First Administration of Thomas Jefferson*, 2 vols. New York: Charles Scribner's Sons, 1932; first published 1889.

Alexander, DeAlva Stanwood. *A Political History of the State of New York*. Vol. I, 1774–1832. New York: Henry Holt, 1906.

Alexander, Holmes. *Aaron Burr: The Proud Pretender*. New York: Harper & Brothers, 1937.

Anthony, Katherine. *Dolley Madison: Her Life and Times*. New York: Doubleday, 1949.

Atherton, Gertrude. *The Conqueror: A Dramatized Biography of Alexander Hamilton*. New York: Frederick A. Stokes, 1902.

― ― ―. *A Few of Hamilton's Letters*. New York: Macmillan, 1903.

― ― ―. *Adventures of a Novelist*. New York: Liveright, 1932.

Bass, Robert D. *Gamecock: The Life and Campaigns of General Thomas Sumter*. New York: Holt, Rinehart and Winston, 1961.

Baxter, Katherine Schuyler. *A Godchild of Washington*. New York: F. Tennyson Neely, 1897.

Beard, Charles A. *An Economic Interpretation of the Constitution of the United States*. New York: Macmillan, 1957; first published 1913.

Bemis, Samuel Flagg. *Jay's Treaty: A Study in Commerce and Diplomacy*, rev. ed. New Haven: Yale University Press, 1962.

Bowers, Claude G. *Jefferson and Hamilton: The Struggle for Democracy in America*. Boston: Houghton Mifflin, 1925; reprinted 1972.

Boyd, Julian P. *Number 7: Alexander Hamilton's Secret Attempts to Control American Foreign Policy*. Princeton: Princeton University Press, 1964.

Bradford, Gamaliel. *Damaged Souls.* Boston: Houghton Mifflin, 1922.

———. *Wives.* New York: Harper & Brothers, 1925.

Brant, Irving. *James Madison: Father of the Constitution, 1787–1800.* Indianapolis: Bobbs-Merrill, 1950.

Brodie, Fawn. *Thomas Jefferson: An Intimate History.* New York: W. W. Norton, 1974.

Brown, Robert E. *Charles Beard and the Constitution: A Critical Analysis of "An Economic Interpretation of the Constitution."* Princeton: Princeton University Press, 1956.

Bryce, James. *The American Commonwealth,* 2 vols. New York: Macmillan, 1919; first published 1893.

Buell, Augustus C. *History of Andrew Jackson,* 2 vols. New York: Charles Scribner's Sons, 1904.

Burdett, Charles. *Margaret Moncrieffe: The First Love of Aaron Burr.* New York: Derby and Jackson, 1860.

Cantor, Milton, ed. *Hamilton.* Englewood Cliffs, N.J.: Prentice-Hall, 1971.

Christoph, Florence A. *The Schuyler Families in America Prior to 1900.* Albany: The Friends of the Schuyler Mansion, 1992.

Clemens, Jeremiah. *A Tale of the Life and Times of Aaron Burr and Alexander Hamilton.* 1860.

Commager, Henry Steele, ed. *Documents of American History,* 6th ed. New York: Appleton-Century-Crofts, 1958.

Cooke, Jacob E. *Alexander Hamilton.* Charles Scribner's Sons, 1982.

Cooper, Thomas. *Some Information Reflecting America Collected by Thomas Cooper.* London, 1794.

Cornell, Saul. "Politics of the Middling Sort." In Paul A. Gilje and William Pencak, eds., *New York in the Age of the Constitution.* A New-York Historical Society Book. Rutherford, N.J.: Fairleigh Dickinson University Press, 1992.

Dangerfield, George. *Chancellor Robert R. Livingston of New York 1746–1813.* New York: Harcourt, Brace, 1966.

Daniels, Jonathan. *Ordeal of Ambition: Jefferson, Hamilton, Burr.* New York: Doubleday, 1970.

Davis, Matthew, L., ed. *Memoirs of Aaron Burr,* 2 vols. New York: Harper & Brothers, 1836 and 1837.

Desmond, Alice Curtis. *Glamorous Dolly Madison.* New York: Dodd, Mead, 1946.

———. *Alexander Hamilton's Wife: A Romance of the Hudson.* New York: Dodd, Mead, 1952.

Didier, Eugene L. "Aaron Burr as a Lawyer," *The Green Bag* XIV, 10 (Oct. 1902), 451–59.

Dinwiddy, John. *Bentham.* Oxford: Oxford University Press, 1989.

Draper, Theodore. *A Struggle for Power: The American Revolution.* New York: Times Books/Random House, 1996.

Ellis, Joseph J. *American Sphinx: The Character of Thomas Jefferson.* New York: Alfred A. Knopf, 1997.

Emery, Noemie. *Alexander Hamilton: An Intimate Portrait.* New York: G. P. Putnam's Sons, 1982.

Ernst, Robert. *Rufus King: American Federalist.* Chapel Hill: University of North Carolina Press, 1968.

Farrand, Max, ed. *The Records of the Federal Conmvention of 1787,* 3 vols. New Haven: Yale University Press, 1911.

– – –. *The Framing of the Constitution of the United States.* New Haven: Yale University Press, 1913.

Fish, Hamilton. *New York State: The Battleground of the Revolutionary War.* New York: Vantage Press, 1976.

Flexner, James Thomas. *The Young Hamilton: A Biography.* Boston: Little, Brown, 1978.

– – –. *Maverick's Progress.* New York: Fordham University Press, 1996.

Gerlach, Don R. *Philip Schuyler and the American Revolution in New York 1733–1777.* Lincoln, Neb.: University of Nebraska Press, 1964.

– – –. "Philip Schuyler and the New York Frontier in 1781." *Narrative of the Revolution in New York.* A New-York Historical Society Book, 1975.

Gordon, John Steele. *Hamilton's Blessing: The Extraordinary Life and Times of the National Debt.* New York: Walker, 1996.

Gordon-Reed, Annette. *Thomas Jefferson and Sally Hemings: An American Controversy.* Charlottesville: University Press of Virginia, 1997.

Grant, Anne. *Memoirs of an American Lady.* New York: Dodd, Mead, 1903.

Hamilton, Allan McLane. *The Intimate Life of Alexander Hamilton.* New York: Charles Scribner's Sons, 1911.

– – –. *Recollections of an Alienist Personal and Professional.* New York: Doran, 1915.

Hamilton, James A. *Reminiscences of James A. Hamilton.* New York: Scribner, 1869.

Hamilton, John C. *Life of Alexander Hamilton,* 2 vols. New York: Halsted & Voorhies (Vol. 1), 1834; Appleton (Vol. 2), 1840.

– – –. *A History of the Republic of the United States . . . as Traced in the Writings of Alexander Hamilton and of His Contemporaries,* 7 vols. New York: Appleton, 1857–1864.

Hecht, Marie B. and Herbert S. Parmet. "New Light on Burr's Later Life." *New-York Historical Society Quarterly* 47, 4 (Oct. 1963), 399–419.

Hecht, Marie B. *Odd Destiny: The Life of Alexander Hamilton.* New York: Macmillan, 1982.

Hendrickson, Robert. *Hamilton,* 2 vols. New York: Mason/Charter, 1976.

History of the State of New York. New York: Columbia University Press, 1932.

Hofstadter, Richard. *The American Political Tradition and the Men Who Made It.* New York: Random House/Vintage Books, 1974; first published 1948.

– – –. *The Paranoid Style in American Politics.* New York: Alfred A. Knopf, 1965.

Humphreys, Mary Gay. *Catherine Schuyler*. New York: Charles Scribner's Sons. New York Heritage Series: Women of Colonial and Revolutionary Times, No. 4, 1897 (reprinted Spartenburg, S.C.: The Reprint Co., 1968).

James, Marquis. *Andrew Jackson: The Border Captain*. Indianapolis: Bobbs-Merrill, 1933.

Jenkinson, Isaac. *Aaron Burr: His Personal and Political Relations with Thomas Jefferson and Alexander Hamilton*. Richmond, Ind.: M. Collston, 1902.

Kammen, Michael. *Mystic Chords of Memory: The Transformation of Tradition in American Culture*. New York: Alfred A. Knopf, 1991.

(Kent, Chancellor). Kent, William, ed. *Memoirs and Letters of James Kent, Ll.D*. Boston: Little, Brown, 1898.

(King, Rufus). King, Charles R., ed. *The Life and Correspondence of Rufus King*, 6 vols. New York: G. P. Putnam's Sons, 1896.

(King, Rufus). Ernst, Robert. *Rufus King: American Federalist*. Chapel Hill: University of North Carolina Press, 1968.

Knapp, Samuel Lorenzo. *The Life of Aaron Burr*. New York: Wiley & Long, 1835.

Lodge, Henry Cabot. *Alexander Hamilton*. Boston: Houghton Mifflin/American Statesmen Series, 1882 and 1898.

Lomask, Milton. *Aaron Burr*, 2 vols. New York: Farrar, Straus and Giroux, 1979 and 1982.

Loth, David. *Alexander Hamilton: Portrait of a Prodigy*. New York: Carrick & Evans, 1939.

McDonald, Forrest. *Alexander Hamilton*. New York: W. W. Norton, 1979.

Malone, Dumas. *Jefferson and the Ordeal of Liberty*. Boston: Little, Brown, 1962.

Mayer, Josephine, and Robert A. East. "The Settlement of Alexander Hamilton's Debts: A Footnote to History." *New York History* 18 (1937), 378–85.

Miller, John C. *Alexander Hamilton: Portrait in Paradox*. New York: Harper & Brothers, 1959.

Mitchell, Broadus. *Alexander Hamilton*, 2 vols. New York: Macmillan, 1957 and 1962.

———. *Alexander Hamilton: A Concise Biography*. New York: Oxford University Press, 1976.

(Morris, Gouverneur). Davenport, Beatrix Cary, ed. *A Diary of the French Revolution by Gouverneur Morris 1752–1816*, 2 vols. Boston: Houghton Mifflin, 1939.

Novick, Sheldon M. *Honorable Justice: The Life of Oliver Wendell Holmes*. Boston: Little, Brown, 1989.

Oliver, Frederick Scott. *Alexander Hamilton: An Essay on American Union*, new ed. New York: G. P. Putnam's Sons, 1927.

Padover, Saul. *The Mind of Alexander Hamilton*. New York: Harper & Brothers, 1958.

Palmer, John McAuley. *General von Steuben*. New Haven: Yale University Press, 1937.

Parkes, Henry Bamford. *Jonathan Edwards: The Fiery Puritan*. New York: Minton, Balch, 1930.

Parmet, Herbert S., and Marie B. Hecht. *Aaron Burr: Portrait of an Ambitious Man*. New York: Macmillan, 1967.

Parrington, Vernon L. *Main Currents in American Thought*. New York: Harcourt, Brace, 1927.

Parton, James. *The Life and Times of Aaron Burr*, enlarged ed., 2 vols. Boston: James R. Osgood, 1877; first published 1857.

Perkins, James Breck. *France in the American Revolution*. Boston: Houghton Mifflin, 1911.

Phelan, Helene C. *The Man Who Owned the Pistol*. Privately Printed. Almond, New York, 1981.

Pidgin, Charles Felton. *Theodosia: The First Gentlewoman of Her Time*. Boston: C. M. Clark, 1907.

Randall, Willard Sterne. *Benedict Arnold: Patriot and Traitor*. New York: Morrow, 1990.

Rogow, Arnold A. "The Federal Convention: Madison and Yates." *The American Historical Review* LX, 2 (January 1955), 323–35.

Schachner, Nathan. *Aaron Burr: A Biography*. New York: Frederick M. Stokes, 1937.

— — —. *Alexander Hamilton*. New York: Appleton-Century, 1946.

— — —. *Thomas Jefferson: A Biography*, 2 vols. New York: Appleton-Century-Crofts, 1951.

Schutz, John A., and Douglass Adair, eds. *The Spur of Fame: Dialogues of John Adams and Benjamin Rush, 1805–1813*. San Marino, Calif.: Huntington Library, 1966.

Seton, Anya. *My Theodosia*. Boston: Houghton Mifflin, 1941.

Shephard, Jack. *The Adams Chronicles. Four Generations of Greatness*. Boston: Little, Brown, 1975.

Shneidman, J. Lee, and Conalee Levine-Shneidman. "Suicide or Murder? The Burr–Hamilton Duel." *Journal of Psychohistory* 8 (1980–81), 159–81.

Shreve, Royal Ornan. *The Finished Scoundrel: General James Wilkinson, sometime Commander-in-Chief of the Army of the United States, who made intrigue a trade and treason a profession*. Indianapolis: Bobbs-Merrill, 1933.

Smertenko, Johan J. *Alexander Hamilton*. New York: Greenberg, 1932.

Smith, Page. *John Adams*, 2 vols. New York: Doubleday, 1963.

— — —. *Jefferson: A Revealing Biography*. New York: American Heritage, 1976.

Stephanson, Anders. *Manifest Destiny: American Expansion and the Empire of Right*. New York: Hill and Wang, 1995.

Swiggett, Howard. *The Extraordinary Mr. Morris*. New York: Doubleday, 1952.

Syrett, Harold C., and Jean G. Cooke, eds. *Interview at Weehawken*. Middletown, Conn.: Wesleyan University Press, 1960.

Taylor, Alan. *William Cooper's Town: Power and Persuasion on the Frontier of the Early American Republic.* New York: Alfred A. Knopf, 1995.

Thane, Elswyth. *Dolley Madison: Her Life and Times.* New York: Macmillan, 1970.

Tharp, Louise Hall. *The Baroness and the General.* Boston: Little, Brown, 1962.

Ticknor, George. *Life, Letters, and Journals of George Ticknor,* 2 vols. Johnson Reprints, 1968; first published 1876.

Todd, Charles Burr. *The True Aaron Burr.* New York: A. S. Barnes, 1902.

— — —. *A General History of the Burr Family in America.* New York: E. Wells Sackett. 1878.

Tuckerman, Bayard. *Life of General Philip Schuyler 1733–1804.* New York: Dodd, Mead, 1903.

Upham, Charles W. *The Life of Timothy Pickering,* 4 vols. Boston: Little, Brown, 1873.

Van Doren, Mark, ed. *Correspondence of Aaron Burr and His Daughter Theodosia.* New York: Covici-Friede, 1929.

Vidal, Gore. *Burr.* New York: Random House, 1973.

Wandell, Samuel M., and Meade Minnigerode. *Aaron Burr,* 2 vols. New York: Putnam, 1925.

Warner, Charles Dudley. *Washington Irving.* Boston: Houghton Mifflin, 1881. American Men of Letters Series.

Warshow, Robert Irving. *Alexander Hamilton: First American Businessman.* New York: Greenberg, 1931.

Wertenbaker, Thomas Jefferson. *Princeton 1746–1896.* Princeton: Princeton University Press, 1946.

Williams, Stanley T. *The Life of Washington Irving,* Vol. I. New York: Oxford University Press, 1935.

Winslow, Ola Elizabeth. *Jonathan Edwards 1703–1758.* New York: Macmillan, 1940.

INDEX

Aaron Burr Conspiracy, The (McCaleb), 277

Aaron Burr v. John Julius Angerstein (1802), 172

Abernathy, Thomas P., 277

Adair, Douglass, 183, 206, 264

Adams, Abigail, 147, 165, 205, 215–16, 307*n15*

Adams, Henry, 248, 262, 267, 308*n24*

Adams, John, 40, 43, 76, 105, 108, 114, 115, 117, 220, 223, 228, 264, 271, 288*n1*, 289*n11*, 294*n10*, 313*n5*, 317*n10*, 328*n45*; in election of 1800, 212, 214; Hamilton's code name for, 240; and illegitimacy question, 4; and Jefferson's Presidency, 159, 222, 282; Presidency of, 119, 160–66, 180, 183, 203–7, 222, 296*n40*, 327*n36*; Reynolds affair denounced by, 150; and Shays' rebellion, 307*n15*; Society of Cincinnati criticized by, 103; suppression of book on, 224; as Vice President, 61, 126–27, 142, 147

Adams, John Quincy, 96, 225–26, 271, 328*n41*

Adams, Samuel, 26, 115

Albany Federal Republican Committee, 232

Albany Register, 180, 183, 229*n*, 231, 232, 234–37, 245, 256

Alien and Sedition Acts (1798), 179–83

Allen, Ethan, 30, 52, 172

Alston, Aaron Burr, 194, 199–200, 251, 269

Alston, Joseph, 194–96, 199, 200, 251, 257, 268, 320*n55*

Alston, Theodosia Burr, 75, 88, 91–95, 103, 148, 188–200, 211, 218, 224, 230, 238–40, 251, 258, 259, 268, 269, 319*n29*, 320*n55*, 324–25*n17*, 331*n25*

Alston, William, 194

American Citizen, 104, 105, 224, 255, 256

American Commonwealth, The (Bryce), 270

American Legion, 104, 306*n2*

André, Maj. John, 79, 266

Angerstein, John Julius, 172

Annapolis Convention, 97, 108, 110, 111

Anti-Federalists, 114, 117, 122, 123, 127, 135–37, 195, 205, 211

Arnold, Benedict, 32, 35, 36, 52, 79, 180, 192, 270, 317*n14*

Arnold, Margaret (Peggy) Shippen, 52–53

Articles of Confederation, 82, 84, 86, 97–98, 102, 105, 108, 110, 111, 113, 118, 126

Astor, John Jacob, 148

Atherton, Gertrude, 7, 12, 16, 27, 238–39, 283, 288*n5*, 289*n10*, 293*n1*, 325*n19*

Bancroft, George, 6

Bank of New York, 67, 106–7, 130, 139, 156, 186, 187, 275, 306*n4*, *n6*

Bank of North America, 106

Bank of the United States, 82–83, 133–36, 186, 187

Barber, Francis, 26–27

Barlass, William, 224

Bayard, James A., 211, 217–20, 225

Beard, Charles A., 120–21

Beckley, John, 152

Beckwith, George, 144–45

Bellamy, Joseph, 34

Bemis, Samuel Flagg, 312*n25*

Benson, Egbert, 110, 260, 307*n13*

Benson, Robert, 275

Bentham, Jeremy, 282, 319*n29*

Biddle, Charles, 248, 257, 259, 260

Bill of Rights, 125

Blaine, James G., 192

Blennerhassett, Harmon, 280, 330*n24*

Blodget, Rebecca, 282, 331*n25*

Blount, William, 180, 317*n14*

Board of War, 43

Bolingbroke, Henry St. John, Viscount, 328–29*n45*

Boston Tea Party, 26

Boudinot, Elias, 27–29

Bowers, Claude, 133, 266

Boyd, Julian, 131, 154–55, 296*n40*, 312*n34*

Brant, Chief Joseph, 172, 190

Brant, Irving, 176

British Constitution, 116, 117

British Foreign Office, 172

Brodie, Fawn, 192, 223, 269, 270, 285, 294*n7*, 296*n40*, 299*n40*

Brown, Andrew, 231, 232, 236, 237, 294*n12*

Bryce, Lord, 270

Bulluck, Catherine, 55

Bunker Hill, Battle of, 32, 35, 111

Burgoyne, Gen. John, 38, 60

Burr, Aaron: affairs of, 54–56; and Alien and Sedition Acts, 180–81; attitude towards women of 90, 91; birth of, 17, 19; birth of children of, 103; business dealings of, 96, 168–74, 185–87; Chesterfield and, 89–90; childhood and adolescence of, 5, 19–22; Church and, 75; and Constitution, 121–22, 125–26; death of, 283–84; debts of, 96; Dolley Madison and, 167–68; in duel, 3, 198, 245–53; education of, 22–24, 26, 28, 114; in election of 1796, 164–67, 179; in election of 1800, 201, 202, 204–5, 213–20; European exile of, 226, 282–83; and events leading to duel, 231–38, 241–45, 259–62; excoriation by Hamilton of, 145–47, 150, 172, 204, 228–30; family background of, 4, 17–19, 24–25; Hamilton's envy of, 24–25, 148, 262–67; historians' views on, 269–70; Jefferson and, 211–15; law practice of, 84, 95–96, 98–102; and male friends, 79–80; marriage of, 47, 53, 88–89; military promotion denied to, 161–63; on national bank, 135–36; New York homes of, 85; in

New York politics, 95, 127–29, 136, 139–43, 166–67, 180, 187–88, 202, 231; novels about, 238–41; and Pamphlet War, 212, 223–25; and reaction to Hamilton's death, 253–59, 267–68; relationship with daughter, 91–92, 94–95, 188–200; religious views of, 183–85; during Revolutionary War, 29, 34–37, 39–42, 44–47; and Reynolds affair, 153–54; Richmond Hill estate of, 147–49; in Senate, 102, 136–39, 143–45; and Society of the Cincinnati, 103–5; stoicism of, 268–69; treason charges against, 226, 277–82; Vice Presidency of, 220–23, 225–26; and wife's death, 93–94

Burr, Aaron Sr., 17–20
Burr, Daniel, 17
Burr, Elizabeth Pinckney, 17
Burr, Esther Edwards (mother), 17–20, 53
Burr, Sarah (Sally; sister), *see* Reeve, Sally Burr
Burr, Theodosia (daughter), *see* Alston, Theodosia Burr
Burr, Theodosia Prevost, 47, 53, 56, 88–89, 91–94, 105, 114, 148, 217*n*, 230, 270, 303*n31*
Burr Conspiracy, The (Abernathy), 277
Butler, Nicholas Murray, 12, 13, 270
Butler, Pierce, 322*n38*

Callender, James T., 152–53, 313*n5*
Calvinism, 17
Carrington, Edward, 158
Carroll, Charles, 203
Catherine the Great, Empress of Russia, 89
Catiline, 324*n4*
Cazenove, Theophile, 169, 170

Champlin, Christopher G., 65
Charleston Courier, 253
Chase, Salmon P., 323*n65*
Chase, Samuel, 225
Chase Manhattan Bank, 172, 186, 248, 318*n27*, 323*n65*, 325*n27*
Cheetham, James, 223–25, 255, 256, 259, 262, 268
Chesterfield, Philip Dormer Stanhope, Earl of, 89–91, 303*n30*, 304*n36*
Church, Angelica Schuyler, 13, 46, 54, 59–60, 62–67, 69–76, 84, 91, 129, 134, 151, 159, 277, 284, 299*n42*, 300*n64*, 312*n33*
Church, Elizabeth, 75
Church, John Barker, 13, 64, 66–69, 75, 84, 101, 144, 153, 247–49, 299*n45*, 301*n72*; business dealings of, 67–68, 106–7, 120, 128, 130–31, 136, 156, 158, 173, 186, 187, 230, 275, 306*n6*, 310*n6*; death of, 76; and duels, 260, 316*n47*; in Society of the Cincinnati, 104
Church, Philip, 75, 299*n42*
Civil War, 309*n38*
Clemens, Jeremiah, 239, 325*n20*
Clifton, Adelaide, 239
Clingman, Jacob, 151, 155, 314*n11*
Clinton, DeWitt, 262
Clinton, Gen. Henry, 44, 79
Clinton, George, 112, 125, 127, 136–43, 163, 166–67, 212, 220, 223, 225, 228, 233, 301*n7*, 326*n8*
Cliosophic Society, 23, 24
Cobbett, William, 282
"Coelia" (Hamilton), 16
Coghlan, Mrs., 55, 297*n5*
Coleman, William, 225
Colt, Peter, 299*n45*
Columbia University, 5*n*, 12, 120, 273, 290*n29*
Commercial Advertiser, 253

Committee of Correspondence, 26
Concord, Battle of, 30, 32, 34
Congress, U.S., 92, 96, 143–44, 161,
    166, 180, 181, 195, 216, 279,
    296n40; Alien and Sedition Acts
    passed by, 179; Constitution ratified
    by, 84; and establishment of
    national bank, 133, 135;
    impeachment motions against
    Hamilton in, 156; power to overrule
    Presidential vetoes by, 119; Report
    on Manufactures to, 134, 151;
    Reports on the Public Credit to,
    129, 133; Supreme Court and, 124
Connecticut Wits, 142
Conqueror, The (Atherton), 238–39
Constable, William, 130, 310n6
Constitution, U.S., 83, 84, 102, 114,
    118–23, 129, 143, 181, 210, 230,
    265, 280; ratification of, 108, 112,
    120, 121, 125–26, 131; Supremacy
    Clause, 98; Tenth Amendment, 133;
    Twelfth Amendment, 210
Constitutional Convention, 24, 30, 31,
    97, 98, 108, 110, 112–22, 183
Continental Congress, 33, 34, 38, 42,
    43, 51, 77, 86–87, 98, 105–6, 111,
    113, 176, 298n23
Conway Cabal, 43
Cooke, Jacob E., 290n30
Cooper, Charles D., 231–34, 236–38,
    241–45, 253, 256, 261
Cooper, James Fenimore, 117
Cooper, Margaret, 236
Cooper, Myles, 29
Cooper, William, 117, 140–41, 218,
    236
Cornare, Lewis, 207, 321n19
Cornwallis, Lord, 38, 48–50, 83
Cox, Trench, 135
Cranmer, Thomas, 299n40
Cruger, Catherine Church, 69, 75

Cruger, Nicholas, 14, 126
Custis, G.W.P., 301n5

Dangerfield, George, 270
Daniels, Jonathan, 299n40
Davis, Jefferson, 192
Davis, Matthew, 54–56, 96, 99, 121,
    146, 205, 220, 255, 256, 261–62,
    294n12
Dayton, Jonathan, 330n18
Declaration of Independence, 31, 34,
    180
Deitz, Johan J., 232, 236
Delacroix, Eugène, 315n26
Delage, Nathalie, 147, 196–99
Desmond, Alice Curtis, 167
Duane, James, 43, 136
Duer, William, 130, 137, 151, 311n11
Dutch Reformed Church, 184

Eacker, George, 209
Economic Interpretation of the Constitution
    of the United States, An (Beard), 120
Edinburgh, University of, 15
Edwards, Elizabeth Tuttle, 292n51
Edwards, Jonathan, 17, 18, 20–23, 34,
    185, 292n51
Edwards, Pierpont, 22, 94, 142
Edwards, Rhoda Ogden, 21, 22
Edwards, Richard, 292n51
Edwards, Sarah Pierpont, 17, 20
Edwards, Timothy, 21–22, 28, 94
Elizabethtown Academy, 27
Ellis, Joseph J., 220, 270, 296n40
Episcopal Church, 184
Eustache, Maj. John S., 45
Eustis, William, 195–98

Farmer Refuted, The (Hamilton), 31, 32,
    104

Fawcett, John, 9
Fawcett, Mary, 9
Federalist, The, 3, 24, 28, 66, 115, 122–25, 158, 175, 179
Federalists, 95, 114, 136–38, 143, 144, 146, 147, 208, 211, 212, 221, 228, 230, 231, 268, 317*n10*, 330*n22*; and Adams Presidency, 164–65; Alien and Sedition Acts enacted by, 179; anti-Semitism of, 100; in election of 1800, 203–6, 213–20; and France, 160, 163, 177; and Hamilton's death, 257, 260, 267; and Manhattan Company, 173, 186–88; in New York State politics, 113, 127, 139–41, 167, 233–38; and Pamphlet War, 224–25; and Reynolds scandal, 150; in Society of the Cincinnati, 105; Washington's birthday celebrated by, 120, 235
Finkelman, Paul, 296*n40*
Fiske, John, 270
Flexner, James Thomas, 206, 288*n5*, 289*n10*, *n12*
Floyd, William, 167
Fox, Charles James, 69, 144, 159
Franklin, Benjamin, 114, 183
Frederick the Great, King of Prussia, 45
French and Indian War, 60
French Revolution, 40, 147, 158, 177, 179, 182, 196, 273–74
Fries, John, 183
Full Vindication of the Measures of Congress (Hamilton), 30, 31

Gallatin, Albert, 143, 166, 194
Gates, Gen. Horatio, 42, 43, 52, 163
Gay, Peter, 51
Gazette of the United States, 100
George III, King of England, 31

George IV, King of England, 69
Gerry, Elbridge, 114
Giles, William Branch, 156
Godwin, William, 217*n*, 282
Grant, Anne, 275, 329*n10*
Grant, Ulysses S., 328*n41*
Great Awakening, 17
Greene, Gen. Nathanael, 38, 291*n32*
Greenleaf, James, 171
Green Mountain Boys, 30

Hamilton, A. M., 10, 12
Hamilton, Alexander: Adams and, 126–27, 164–66, 204–6; adolescence of, 5, 14–17; affairs of, 54, 56, 64–66, 68–76, 150–56, 192–93, 284; and Alien and Sedition Acts, 181–83; Anglophilia of, 29–30; at Annapolis Convention, 108, 110–11; attitude toward blacks of, 50–52; attitude toward women of, 90–92; birth of, 4–6, 8; birth of children of, 87, 103; and Burr's election to Senate, 137, 143; business dealings of, 96, 106–8, 156–57, 173–74, 186, 187; as commissioner of New York taxes, 85–86; in Continental Congress, 86, 87, 105–6; death of, 3, 253–59, 267–68, 273–75; debts of, 96; in duel, 3, 198, 245–53; education of, 14, 26–29; and election of 1800, 202–5, 215–17, 219; envy of Burr, 24–25, 148, 262–67; and events leading to duel, 231–38, 241–45, 259–62; excoriation of Burr by, 145–47, 150, 172, 204, 223, 228–30; family background of, 4, 6–9; *Federalist* essays by, 115, 122–25, 175, 179; and foreign policy, 144–45, 157–61; and framing of Constitution, 112–21, 126; historians' views of, 270–71; law

Hamilton, Alexander (*cont.*)
practice of, 84, 97–102, 169, 171;
and male friends, 77–79; manic
depressive illness of, 206–10;
marriage of, 57–64, 77, 88; national
bank advocated by, 82–83, 133, 135;
New York homes of, 85; and New
York politics, 127, 139–43, 231;
novels about, 238–41; and Pamphlet
War, 223, 224; relationship with
daughter, 191; relationship with
parents and brother, 9–14; religious
views of, 184; revolutionary
polemics of, 30–32; during
Revolutionary War, 29, 32–34, 37–
46, 48–50, 52–53, 79–82; as second-
ranking general in army, 161–64; as
Secretary of Treasury, 102, 107,
109, 129–35, 139; in Society of the
Cincinnati, 103–5; Twelfth Amendment supported by, 210–11; and
Washington's death, 201; and Washington's Farewell Address, 175–79
Hamilton, Alexander Jr. (son), 13,
103
Hamilton, Allan McLane (grandson),
8, 54, 58, 61, 206, 230, 265, 275,
288*n4*, 290*n23*, 293*n1*, 325*n19*
Hamilton, Angelica (daughter), 13, 92,
103, 148, 191, 192, 209, 230, 241,
322*n25*
Hamilton, Elizabeth Schuyler (Betsey;
wife), 10, 13, 61, 79, 91, 93, 100,
104, 130, 230, 260, 266, 270, 274–
76, 301*n72*, 302*n7*, 317*n12*; in
Albany, 148, 236, 313*n3*; courtship
of, 58–60, 62; death of, 65, 276–77;
domestic interests of, 88; and duel,
246; and husband's affairs, 64–66,
69–74, 151, 155, 300*n64*, 313*n3*;
marriage of, 59, 63; and mother's
death, 209, 210; during

Revolutionary War, 48–49; and
Washington's Farewell Address, 177–
78; in yellow fever epidemic, 144
Hamilton, Emma, 69
Hamilton, James (brother), 5, 9, 10,
290*n17*, *n18*
Hamilton, James Sr. (father), 4–10,
28
Hamilton, James Alexander (son), 11,
13, 170, 178, 329*n7*
Hamilton, John Church (son), 5, 7,
11–13, 27, 29, 37, 40, 54, 58, 139,
275, 289*n9*, 293*n1*, *n4*, 297*n1*,
302*n18*
Hamilton, Philip (son), 13, 62, 71, 87,
209, 210, 241, 248, 322*n25*
Hamilton, Rachel (mother), 5–9, 11–
14, 16, 28, 52–53, 100–1, 289*n10*,
290*n18*, *n30*, 293*n1*
Hamilton, William, 69
Hamilton, William Leslie, 7
Hamilton, William Stephen (son), 276
Hamilton Fund, 275
Harison, Richard, 171
Harlem Heights, Battle of, 37
Harrowby, Lord, 277
Harvard University, 195
Hemings, Sally, 152, 296*n40*, 299*n40*
Henderson, William, 310*n6*
Hendrickson, Robert, 8, 10, 153, 202,
206, 238, 288*n5*, 290*n17*, 300*n64*,
301*n6*, 317*n6*, 321*n15*
Henry, Patrick, 50, 115
Hessians, 34, 37
Hieronymus, 325*n24*
*History of the Administration of John
Adams, Late President of the United
States, The* (Wood), 224
*History of the United States for the Year
1796* (Callender), 153
Hofstadter, Richard, 158, 284, 313–
14*n9*

Holland Land Company, 168–70
Holmes, Oliver Wendell Jr., 99, 306–
    7n60, 309n38
Hopkins, Samuel, 185
Hosack, David, 207–8, 246, 253,
    329n2
House of Representatives, U.S., 112,
    131, 132, 152, 213–14, 216–20, 225,
    226, 235
Houston, Sam, 284
Howe, Adm. Richard, 36
Howe, Gen. William, 36, 37, 44, 60
Hume, David, 31–32, 136

Irving, Peter, 225, 255, 256
Irving, Washington, 225, 281, 330n22

Jacataqua, 55, 297n4
Jackson, Andrew, 50, 148, 159, 223,
    259, 268, 281–83, 326n3
Jacobinism, 179, 182, 215, 217, 230,
    313n9
Jay, John, 33, 50–51, 66, 103, 122,
    140, 141, 144–46, 163, 167, 173,
    175, 202–3, 206, 260, 274,
    312n35
Jay, Sarah Livingston, 58
Jefferson, Martha (Patsy), 192, 214
Jefferson, Martha Wayles, 58
Jefferson, Thomas, 32, 54, 98, 108,
    147, 222, 237, 259, 264, 265, 269–
    71, 285, 286, 294n7, 307n15, 308n25,
    322n22, n38; agrarianism of, 134,
    188; and Alien and Sedition Acts,
    181, 182; alleged affairs of, 150, 156;
    and assumption plan, 132–33; and
    Bill of Rights, 125; in Committee of
    Correspondence, 26; daughters'
    relationship with, 191–92; debts of,
    96; on education of women, 92–93,

304n41; elected President, 196, 201,
    211–15, 218–20, 225, 228, 230, 235;
    in election of 1796, 164–66; and
    framing of Constitution, 114, 115,
    117, 119, 121, 123; Hamilton's code
    name for, 240; Livingston and, 24;
    marriage of, 58, 299n40; and
    Miranda, 161; and New York
    politics, 138–40; in Paris, 66;
    Presidency of, 3, 180, 221, 242, 262;
    racism of, 51, 296n40; during
    Revolutionary War, 49–50; and
    Reynolds affair, 153, 154; as
    Secretary of State, 131, 144–46, 157–
    59, 208; Society of Cincinnati
    criticized by, 103; tampering with
    mail of, 237; and treason charges
    against Burr, 278–79, 281–82,
    331n25
Jews, 100, 132
Johnson, Lyndon B., 328n41
Johnson, Samuel, 254, 304n36
Jumel, Eliza Bowen, 16, 238–39, 283,
    325n19

Kane, Julian, 318n28
Kennedy, John F., 328n41
Kennedy, Robert, 285
Kent, Chancellor, 66, 98–100, 138,
    232–34, 241, 270
Kentucky Resolutions, 181
King, Charles, 260–61
King, John F., 285
King, Martin Luther Jr., 285
King, Rufus, 74–75, 109n, 114, 136,
    141–45, 166, 177, 178, 194, 202,
    215, 216, 240, 260–61, 266, 275,
    322n31, 326n8
King's College, 5n, 29, 30, 32, 34
Klein, Melanie, 327n29
Kline, Mary-Jo, 330n18

Knox, Gen. Henry, 37, 111, 161–63, 294*n13*
Knox, Hugh, 14–15, 17, 26, 28, 33, 262, 291*n38*, 315*n30*

Lafayette, Marquis de, 50, 60, 81, 86
Lake George, Battle of, 63
Lamb, John, 170–71, 316*n50*
Lansing, John, 112–14
Laski, Harold J., 306*n60*
Laurens, John, 45, 50, 52, 57, 59, 64, 77–80, 90, 117, 123, 266, 267, 302*n7, n14*
Lawrence, T. E., 227
Lear, Tobias, 202
Ledyard, Isaac, 139, 140
Lee, Gen. Charles, 44–46
Lee, Gen. Henry (Light-Horse Harry), 24, 50, 134
Lee, Robert E., 24
Le Guen v. Gouverneur & Kemble, 99–101
Letters to His Son and Others (Chesterfield), 89, 90
Levine, John Michael, 6–9, 12, 28, 100–1, 290–91*n32*
Levine, Peter, 8, 9, 11, 14, 101
Levy, Leonard, 296*n40*
Lewis, Meriwether, 330*n24*
Lewis, Morgan, 231–35, 258, 311*n21*
Lexington, Battle of, 30, 32, 34
Lincoln, Abraham, 192, 323*n65*, 325*n20*
Lincoln, Gen. Benjamin, 163
Lindsay, Merrill, 326*n28*
Liston, Robert, 172
Livermore, Samuel, 289*n11*
Livingston, Brockholst, 24
Livingston, Mrs. Brockholst, 268
Livingston, Catherine (Kitty) Schuyler, 27–28, 90–91, 114, 276

Livingston, Chancellor, 106, 136, 138, 146, 311*n21*
Livingston, Philip, 311*n11*
Livingston, Robert R., 42
Livingston, William, 26–28, 42, 114
Lodge, Henry Cabot, 6, 8, 16, 193, 203, 270, 288*n8*, 289*n9*
Lomask, Milton, 280–81, 325*n24*
Lott, Cornelia, 56, 59
Loyalists, 30

McCaleb, Walter F., 277
McCulloch v. Maryland (1819), 133
McCusker, John J., 60*n*
McHenry, James, 9, 66, 67, 80, 81, 119, 161, 163, 165, 166, 207, 215, 219, 315*n42*, 321*n19*
McKitrick, Eric, 296*n40*, 299*n40*
Maclay, William, 61, 311*n21*
McManus, Jane, 283
Macomb, Alexander, 128, 171, 310*n6*
Madison, Dolley, 24, 167–68, 282, 331*n25*
Madison, James, 40, 105, 138, 146, 157–58, 166, 192, 221–22, 228, 262, 281, 282, 308*n25*, 322*n22*; at Annapolis Convention, 108–10; and assumption plan, 131–33; and Bill of Rights, 125; at College of New Jersey, 24, 28, 303*n31*; at Constitutional Convention, 114–19; *Federalist* writings by, 122, 175; marriage of, 167–68; Presidency of, 199, 242; and Reynolds affair, 155, 156; and treason charges against Burr, 282, 331*n25*; Virginia Resolutions drafted by, 181; and Washington's Farewell Address, 175–79
Malcolm, Col. William, 41
Malcolm's Regiment, 41–42, 46

Malone, Dumas, 213, 296n40
Manhattan Company, 172, 173, 186–
  88, 230, 318n27, 323n65
Marshall, John, 124, 133, 215, 280
Martinez de Yrujo, Don Carlos, 281
Mason, George, 114
Mason, John, 184
Massachusetts Amendment
  Resolutions, 180–81
Mather, Cotton, 17
Mather, Increase, 17
Mead, Cowles, 279
Mercer, John F., 157
Merchant, George, 234, 235
Merry, Anthony, 277, 278, 281
Mifflin, Gen. Thomas, 55–56
Mill, James, 282
Mill, John Stuart, 282
Miller, John C., 182, 296n40, 314n23
Miranda, Gen. Francisco de, 40, 160–
  61, 315n30
Mississippi Supreme Court, 279
Mitchell, Ann Lytton, 14, 52
Mitchell, Broadus, 52, 63, 131, 206,
  270, 290n18, 294n13, 317n12
Moncrieffe, Margaret, 55–56, 239
Monmouth, Battle of, 44–45, 162
Monroe, James, 105, 146, 150–54,
  228, 242, 254, 265, 268, 276
Montague, Mary Wortley, 198,
  320n64
Montgomery, Gen. Richard, 32, 35–
  36, 52
Moore, Benjamin, 184
Morning Chronicle, 255
Morris, Gouverneur, 42, 68, 114, 117,
  146, 156, 210, 216, 254–55, 274,
  275, 307n19, 308n21, 326n8
Morris, Robert, 61, 68, 82, 85–86,
  110, 114, 119, 129, 130, 144, 168,
  240–41
Morris, Mrs. Robert, 170

Morton, Cornelia Schuyler, 260
Morton, Washington, 260
Muhlenberg, Frederick A.C., 151–
  53

Napoleon, Emperor of France, 159–
  60, 217, 272, 314n26, 328n45
Narrative of the Suppression by Col. Burr
  of the History of the Administration of
  John Adams (Cheetham), 224
Native Americans, 128
Nelson, Lord, 69
New England Republican, 253
New Jersey, College of, 14, 15n, 17,
  18, 22–24, 26–29, 262, 303n31
New Jersey Plan for Government,
  114, 118
New Orleans, Battle of, 50
Newport Mercury, 253
Newton, Isaac, 243
New York, College of, 5
New York Assembly, 33, 95, 112,
  169, 172, 180, 181, 183, 186
New York Common Council, 186
New York Council of Revision, 13
New York Land Office Commission,
  128–29
New-York Post, 246, 253
New York Society Library, 283,
  303n32, 312n38
Nicholson, John, 185
Nicholson, Maria, 194
Notes on the State of Virginia
  (Jefferson), 51, 188

Ogden, Matthias (Matt), 22, 28, 29,
  34, 41, 80
Oliver, Frederick Scott, 206, 265, 266,
  268
Onuf, Peter, 296n40

Orphan Asylum Society, 275
Otis, Harrison, 65

Pamphlet War, 212, 223–25, 245
Paracelsus, 207
Paris, Treaty of, 66, 106
Parrington, Vernon L., 135
Parton, James, 21, 23, 45, 47, 81, 89,
    121, 193, 292n52
Paterson, William, 24, 47, 114, 292–
    93n54
Pendleton, Nathaniel, 177, 233, 243–
    47, 249, 253, 255–57, 260, 275
Peters, Richard, 216
Peterson, Merrill, 296n40
Phillips, Morgan, 233
Pichon, Baron, 314n25
Pickering, Timothy, 6, 8, 165, 166,
    181, 215, 226, 289n9
Pierce, Franklin, 276
Pierce, William, 308n26
Pierrepont, Evelyn, 97
Pinckney, Charles Cotesworth, 104,
    114, 161, 203, 204, 223, 314n24,
    327n36
Pinckney, Thomas, 164, 166
Pitt, William, 243, 326n6
Plutarch, 311n24
Polk, James K., 328n41
Practical Proceeding in the Supreme Court
    of the State of New York (Hamilton),
    86
Prevost, Augustine James Frederick,
    88
Prevost, Frances, 196
Prevost, John Bartow, 88, 94, 193–94,
    324–25n17
Princeton, Battle of, 39
Princeton University, 17, 24, 55,
    304n41
Putnam, Gen. Israel, 36, 55, 56

Quebec campaign, 32, 35–36, 46, 52,
    55, 170
Quincy, Josiah, 260

Randall, Willard Sterne, 296n40
Randolph, Edmund, 114, 142
Randolph, John, 254, 263
Reagan, Ronald, 328n41
Reed, Joseph, 35
Reeve, Sally Burr, 19–21, 47, 88
Reeve, Tapping, 34
Report on Manufactures (Hamilton), 31
Republicans, 95, 98, 146, 147, 159,
    168, 182, 201, 205, 209, 212, 224,
    225, 228, 229, 242, 268, 271; in
    election of 1796, 164; in election of
    1800, 196, 203, 208, 213, 214, 218,
    219; in election of 1804, 223; and
    Hamilton's death, 257, 285; Jews
    as, 100; and Judiciary Act, 221;
    and Manhattan Company, 186–88;
    in New York politics, 113, 167, 180–
    81, 202, 220, 231, 234, 235, 237;
    and Reynolds affair, 150, 152–54;
    and Washington's Farewell Address,
    177, 179
Revolutionary War, 29–50, 52, 59–61,
    66, 103, 111, 129, 139, 145, 146,
    181, 198, 201, 208, 236, 297n4,
    306n1, 309n38
Reynolds, James, 150–52, 154–55
Reynolds, Maria, 16, 52, 53, 54, 61–
    62, 66, 73, 150–56, 204, 205, 238,
    263, 264, 276, 313n3, 314n11
Rivals, The (Clemens), 239
Rivington, James, 33
Rochambeau, Comte de, 50
Roosevelt, Franklin D., 328n41
Ross, Robert, 304n40
Rousseau, Jean-Jacques, 89, 310n45
Royal Danish American Gazette, 16

Rush, Benjamin, 40, 93, 271, 282, 317n10
Rutgers, Elizabeth, 98
Rutgers v. Waddington (1784), 97–98

San Jacinto, Battle of, 284
Saratoga, Battle of, 38, 52, 111
Schachner, Nathan, 206, 216, 220, 228, 288n5, 290n18, 298n34, 324n1
Schuyler, Catherine Van Rensselaer, 13, 59–60, 62, 63, 67, 148, 151, 209, 241, 299n42
Schuyler, Gen. Philip, 13, 59–64, 71, 81–82, 129, 148, 151, 202, 209, 261, 299n42, 311n21, n22, 315n27; British sympathies of, 144–45, 160; business dealings of, 60–61, 107, 120, 130, 131, 136, 168–70, 298n34, 310n6; Church and, 66–67; in New York State politics, 112, 127, 137–39, 141, 166, 168, 231–37, 245, 264; during Revolutionary War, 42–43, 48, 60–62
Schuyler, Philip Jr., 71
Schuyler, Sarah Rutsen, 71
Seabury, Samuel, 31
Sedgwick, Theodore, 127, 135, 137, 142, 146, 215, 217, 218, 268, 295n28
Sedition Act (1798), 179–83
Senat, Madame, 196–97
Senate, U.S., 102, 136–39, 143, 145, 163, 165, 167, 169, 181, 221, 223, 225–26, 229, 231, 234, 258, 264, 277, 289n11
Seton, William, 156
Shays, Daniel, 111–12
Shays' Rebellion, 33, 97, 110–12, 182, 294n10, 307n15
Smith, Adam, 129

Smith, John, 226
Smith, Page, 159
Smith, Samuel, 220
Smith, William Stephens, 171
Society for American Historians, 328n41
Society of the Cincinnati, 103–5, 306n1
Society for Establishing Useful Manufactures, 108, 130
Spring, Samuel, 35
State Department, U.S., 139, 145
Sterne, Laurence, 272, 329n48
Steuben, Baron von, 45–46, 50, 57, 60, 71, 72, 103
Stevens, Edward (Ned), 10, 11, 15, 17, 30, 33, 50, 162, 263, 290n25
Stevens, Thomas, 6
Stiles, Ezra, 18
Stony Point, Battle of, 111
Stringer, Samuel, 232, 234, 236, 237, 245
Sumter, Thomas Jr., 198, 199
Supreme Court, U.S., 24, 99, 118, 124, 133, 181, 215
Swartwout, Samuel, 239
Swift, Jonathan, 243

Talleyrand-Perigord, Charles Maurice de, 69, 156, 159–60, 270, 314n25, 315n26, n27
Tayler, John, 232, 236, 241
"Tenth Legion," 188, 194, 319n29
Ticonderoga, Fort, 30, 42, 52, 111, 236
Todd, Charles Burr, 292n51, 295n28
Toussaint L'Ouverture, 51
Treasury, U.S., 107, 129–31, 135, 154, 156
Trespass Act, 97–98
Tristram Shandy (Sterne), 272, 329n48

Troup, Robert, 10, 75, 100, 101, 127, 137, 138, 143, 153, 163, 186, 187, 194, 201, 203, 205, 275, 309*n40*, 320*n55*, 322*n31*, 326*n8*
Truman, Harry S., 328*n41*
Trumbull, John, 67, 142, 299*n42*
Tudor, William, 327*n36*

U.S. Bicentennial Society, 325*n27*

Van Berkel, Frank, 268
Van Buren, Martin, 56
Vanderlyn, John, 196
Van Doren, Carl, 302*n7*
Van Ness, Peter, 253, 255–57
Van Ness, William, 225, 243–49, 251
Van Ness, William Peter, 196
Van Rensselaer, John, 67
Van Rensselaer, Margarita (Peggy) Schuyler, 58, 65, 77, 209, 241
Van Rensselaer, Stephen, 104, 140, 167, 186, 231–34, 236, 275
Venable, Abraham B., 152
Vidal, Gore, 192, 239–41, 330*n24*
View of the Political Conduct of Aaron Burr, Esq., Vice-President of the United States, A (Cheetham), 224
Vindication of the Rights of Woman (Wollstonecraft), 91, 217*n*
Virginia, University of, 92, 304*n41*
Virginia Bill of Rights, 114
Virginia Plan of Government, 114, 118
Virginia Resolutions, 181, 182
Voltaire, 272

Waddington, Joshua, 97
Wadsworth, Jeremiah, 64, 68, 106, 164, 299*n45*
Walker, Betsey, 153
Ward, Mathias, 224

War of 1812, 50
Washington, George, 17, 63–64, 87, 88, 147, 160, 165, 222, 223, 254, 263, 264, 276, 294*n7*, 307*n19*, 313*n5*, 317*n10*; appointment of second-in-command to, 161–64, 205; attribution of Hamilton's paternity to, 7, 289*n10*, *n12*; death of, 201–2, 273, 289*n11*, 326*n8*; Farewell Address of, 40, 175–79, 260, 317*n11*; Federalist celebrations of birthday of, 210, 235, 291*n39*; Hamilton's code name for, 240; marital infidelity charges against, 156; Presidency of, 3, 102, 126–27, 133, 134, 142–46, 157, 159; rebellions put down by, 33; in Revolutionary War, 30, 35–48, 50, 54, 57, 62, 77–82, 204, 297*n4*; in Society of the Cincinnati, 103–5; tampering with mail of, 37
Washington, Martha Custis, 7, 57, 58, 202, 289*n12*, 301*n5*
Watson, James, 139–40
Wayles, John, 299*n40*
Wayne, Gen. Anthony, 87
Wealth of Nations, The (Smith), 129
Webb, Col., 59
Webster, Noah, 205
Welty, Eudora, 330*n24*
Western Inland Lock Navigation Company, 169, 170
Whiskey Rebellion, 33, 134, 182, 294*n10*
Wilkinson, Col. James, 43, 278–81, 295*n16*, 330*n18*, *n22*
Wills, Garry, 296*n40*
Wilson, James, 114
Wilson, Woodrow, 304*n41*, 328*n41*, *n44*
Witherspoon, John, 28
Wolcott, Oliver Jr., 165, 166, 184, 216, 219
Wollstonecraft, Mary, 91, 217*n*

Wood, Gordon, 296*n40*

Wood, John, 224

Woodworth, John, 219

World War I, 104

Wright, Robert, 226

Yale University, 17, 18, 47

Yates, Abraham, 311*n22*

Yates, Robert, 112–18, 123, 124, 127, 167, 308*n25*

Yorktown, Battle of, 40, 50, 162